A Case Study of a
Soviet Republic

Other Titles in This Series

Hungary: An Economic Geography, György Enyedi

The Future of Agriculture in the Soviet Union and Eastern Europe: The 1976-1980 Five-Year Plans, edited by Roy D. Laird, Joseph Hajda, and Betty A. Laird.

Population and Migration Trends in Eastern Europe, edited by Huey Louis Kostanick

The German Democratic Republic: A Developed Socialist Society, edited by Lyman H. Legters

Yugoslavia After Tito: Scenarios and Implications, Gavriel D. Ra'anan

The Liberated Female: Life, Work, and Sex in Socialist Hungary, Ivan Volgyes and Nancy Volgyes

The Soviet Agrarian Debate: A Controversy in Social Science, 1923-1929, Susan Gross Solomon

Perspectives for Change in Communist Societies, edited by Teresa Rakowska-Harmstone

Westview Special Studies on the Soviet Union and Eastern Europe

A Case Study of a Soviet Republic:
The Estonian SSR
edited by Tönu Parming and Elmar Järvesoo

The Estonian SSR is the most industrially advanced and urbanized of the Soviet republics and also, perhaps logically, has the most Western life style and the highest standard of living. This in-depth study of the Estonian SSR not only describes the current Estonian scene, but also analyzes the postwar Soviet years, concentrating on the factors that have led Estonia to its present status. All chapters were written especially for this volume by subject specialists fluent in Estonian. In sum, it is the most detailed and comprehensive study of a Soviet republic available in English, and it supports the editors' argument that analysts' traditional preoccupation with events and decisions at the political center of the Soviet Union has been unsatisfactory for a thorough understanding of the country: much more attention must be given to the individual union republics.

Tönu Parming holds a doctorate in sociology from Yale University and is now assistant professor of sociology at the University of Maryland. Elmar Järvesoo obtained his doctorate in agrarian economics from the Friedrich Wilhelm University in Berlin. He is currently professor of agrarian marketing at the University of Massachusetts.

Published with the cooperation of the Estonian Learned Society in America.

A Case Study of a Soviet Republic

The Estonian SSR

edited by
Tönu Parming and Elmar Järvesoo

Foreword by Edward Allworth

Westview Press • Boulder, Colorado

*Westview Special Studies on the Soviet Union
and Eastern Europe*

Published in 1978 in the United States of America by
  Westview Press, Inc.
  5500 Central Avenue
  Boulder, Colorado 80301
  Frederick A. Praeger, Publisher and Editorial Director

Library of Congress Cataloging in Publication Data
Main entry under title:
A Case Study of a Soviet Republic: The Estonian S. S. R.
  (Westview special studies on the Soviet Union and Eastern Europe)
  1. Estonia. I. Parming, Tönu. II. Järvesoo, Elmar. III. Series.
DK511.E5E7777   947'.41   77-671
ISBN 0-89158-247-9

Printed and bound in the United States of America

Contents

PART 4. HIGHER EDUCATION, RESEARCH, AND SCIENCE

Foreword

Edward Allworth

A delicate but portentous kind of group tension grows in the multiethnic Soviet Union today. It is marked by imperfect interaction and partial disconnection between various eponymous nationalities and the Soviet socialist republics (SSRs) named for them. With each passing decade, it becomes increasingly obvious that territorial and demographic discrepancies set off nationality from SSR in almost every case. This trend may signal the end of the formative stage and the start of a degenerative stage in the development of the SSRs. Those horizontal, spatial imperfections that reveal the misalignment between the body of an eponymous ethnic group and the SSR "garment" designed for it are accentuated by additional gaps.

Neither constitutional nor other statutory guarantees ensure that any Soviet nationality will be provided with an SSR of its own or an appropriate lesser unit. (Consider the homeless Soviet Germans, Jews, and Poles, each of whom numbered far more than a million persons in 1970.) Should such new administrative units be created, they would not necessarily bear ethnic names. Several Soviet subunits, in addition to the ordinary krais, oblasts, and raions, in fact already carry ethnically neutral designations. Yet the Daghistan Autonomous SSR, the Gorno-Badakhshan Autonomous Oblast, and the like are populated densely by one or more long-defined nationalities speaking distinct languages.

These arrangements insulate a nationality from precise contact or identification with the pertinent territorial-administrative structure of the state. This hiatus significantly differentiates the group further from the people of a true nation state. More pointed still are the deprivations related to the absence of a nationality-oriented government or an ethnic political party at any level. Formally, local administration in the USSR—organized as it is around the subunits mentioned—becomes SSR government, ASSR administration, and on down the unit hierarchy, but never government of and for an ethnic group. Rather than representing some single nationality, the branches of the dominant Soviet political force, the Communist party, always refer to geographical areas, not to SSRs or nationality groups.

Because such distancing affects every nationality-oriented SSR, to what extent can it be said that studying one Soviet socialist republic is the equivalent of scrutinizing them all? The matter of comparability among the fourteen nationality SSRs (excluding the Russian SFSR) is raised by implication in conjunction with any serious investigation of the developments in a single SSR. That question, in turn, inevitably poses a further basic problem: To what extent can the examination of any SSR be regarded as an inquiry into the life of its eponymous nationality?

The detailed account offered in this volume presents, in parallel sections, the evolution of the artistic, cultural, economic, social, and political life of the Estonian SSR. In examining the degree to which the coincidence between SSR and nationality holds true for Soviet Estonia in the 1970s, this book lays a foundation upon which an answer may be worked out to this vital question.

Recent statistical compilations (*Narodnoe khoziaistvo*, 1974; Katz et al., 1975:441-465) have ranked the ESSR high among SSRs in certain economic and social-cultural indicators but below the majority in political vitality and demographic factors other than concentration and urbanization. Thus, while the impressive material and other external achievements of the ESSR are shared by few other republics in the Soviet Union (compare Latvia, Lithuania, Georgia, and Armenia), if these latter two distinguishing features were disregarded, the considerable accomplishments of the ESSR might elicit only passing curiosity from observers of Soviet affairs. Attention would then be predictably focused upon the superior performance of this administrative unit as providing further confirmation of the noticeably uneven development of the various regions of the Soviet Union as late as the mid-1970s.

However, if the material and cultural gains made by a given union republic prove to be inseparable from that republic's principal identifying characteristic as the homeland for a certain nationality, links between achievements and specific ethnicity will have been established.

The fact that its population constitutes a very small part (0.56 percent) of the Soviet total (*Itogi 1973*: 9, 15) further tests the basis of scholarly focus upon the ESSR. To merit special research treatment, an area and its people must ordinarily represent something more than a minute, albeit highly productive, fraction of an ostensibly homogeneous country. While certain segments of ESSR society are beset by the social ills seen in modern, urbanized countries almost everywhere, the tensions now significantly affecting the ESSR as a whole emanate almost entirely from existing ethnic differences and rivalries related to these differences. Such tensions are persistently underscored by the potential for intergroup conflict or nationality disintegration. In some measure, too, foreign academic interest is often attracted to this region because of the brevity of the period that has elapsed since Soviet military forces seized Estonia for the USSR.

Primarily for these reasons—ethnic distinctiveness and the short duration of Soviet control—analysis of a selected constituent Soviet republic offers intellectual rewards. This is especially true at a time when the viability of the structure of union republics in the USSR is subject to some debate. It has been hinted that SSR demarcation may disappear with the promulgation of the new, long-awaited Soviet constitution (*Program*, 1963:115; Semenov, 1961:25; Hazard, 1975:227-229). This eventuality is prefigured in aspects of the Soviet system which have worked persistently for unification. Strong forces push for conformity in cultural expression, economy, politics, social organization, language use, communications, and the like. Yet the union republics markedly differ from each other, not only economically and politically but also in qualities crucial to the issue of ethnic group identity.

Sufficient physical concentration of a nationality's population plus vigorous self-assertion seem to constitute the irreducible requirement for affirmative ethnic group vitality. Moreover, the maintenance of a nationality's corporate health may be greatly enhanced if it can, while moving into an era of accelerating development, preempt many significant new positions and occupations as they open up in the society and economy. Otherwise, these positions may be filled (as they often are in rapidly changing, less developed administrative units of the USSR) by specialists from outside the constituent republic and its eponymous nationality.

The strength of the ethnic attachments of Estonians who accept such new responsibilities is problematical. In politics, many of them are known to have a cosmopolitan or even Moscow orientation (Allworth, 1977, ch. 5). "Sufficient" physical concentration of a nationality's population depends both upon intangible retentive traits and self-assertiveness. Assuming a reasonably balanced cross section of society, considerably less than the entire aggregate of an ethnic group, so long as it is well concentrated and in communication, may be adequate for sustaining group identity and vigor. This is particularly noticeable when detached members of the group settle in nearby administrative units or countries. For example, only 62 percent of all Soviet Armenians lived in the Armenian SSR in 1970, up from 55.7 percent in 1959 (*Itogi 1959*, 1962:210; *Itogi 1970*, 1973:253, 263, 305, 320, 324). Yet in those years Armenians constituted more than 88 percent of the population in their SSR, more than 9.6 percent of the population in neighboring Georgia, and 9.4 percent of the total in the adjacent Azerbaidzhan Republic. Armenians made up more than 95 percent of the population inhabiting their union republic's capital, Yerevan, in 1970.

In this regard, Soviet Estonians—91.9 percent of whom live inside their SSR boundaries—rank high among most eponymous SSR nationalities but somewhat below their fellows in the Soviet Baltic region as well as the USSR's Georgians and Turkmens (Katz et al., 1975:445). In 1970, 55.7 percent of Tallinn's population was Estonian—the largest concentration of urban Estonians in the union republic. Those 200,000 people may constitute "sufficient" strength for ethnic maintenance in the city, if the needed close contacts and retentive traits prevail among the group. That is particularly likely to be true in view of the ESSR's substantial general urbanization, encompassing all ethnic groups (see figure 2, ch. 1), which reached 65 percent in 1970. Although only 54.7 percent of the Estonians in the ESSR had by that year settled in its towns and cities, that percentage was higher than those for all other SSR namesake nationalities, within their appropriate union republics, except for the Armenian Republic. The nonrural percentage among eponyms in nationality SSRs ranged from 14.4 percent for Kirgizia to 62.6 percent for Armenia (*Itogi 1970*, 1973:152-318).

Concentration in urban centers plays an important role in preparing ethnic groups for further steps in modernization. Moreover, urban concentration of the eponymous population may help ensure that vital decision making and planning—which, in the nationality areas of the USSR, customarily involve outsiders and their interests and are carried on in the cities—will be influenced by ethnic Estonians. Thus, whether or not Soviet authorities eventually act to erase or drastically alter SSR boundaries, the presence of a large Estonian urban concentration is important—perhaps crucial—to the future of this highly Westernized region and nationality. The current urbanizing trend among Estonians, therefore, indicates a demographic tendency favorable to the nationality's well-being.

All indications point to a diminishing of the rural population in the ESSR. Low population densities recorded in 1965 for the islands (12.5 persons per square kilometer), western regions (15 persons), and southwestern regions (18.5 persons), as well as for the central and southeastern parts of the union republic, suggest this possibility (Laas, 1967:236). These figures contrast strikingly with the high densities prevalent in the northern (61.7 persons) and northwestern (42.2 persons) reaches of the ESSR in the same year. The average density for the ESSR as a whole in 1975—31.6 persons per square kilometer—obscures these differences, along with the fact that the ongoing concentration of population in the northern regions was accompanied by an actual reduction in numbers on the islands and in the west, while the demographic situation in the south remained stable (Aarna et al., 1975:42-43). Less than 12 percent of the rural populace in the ESSR in 1970 was made up of outsiders. Presumably, the decline in the rural population largely reflects the departure of Estonians from the land (*Itogi 1970*, 1973:319). As the bulk of the Estonian indigenous population gradually moves from rural districts into the cities, vacant places may begin to appear on the ethnic map of the ESSR. The distribution and density patterns of ethnic Estonians thus may prove to be influential factors, insofar as they stimulate further immigration of outsiders, in determining the destiny of either the ESSR or the Estonian nationality.

The ESSR has few competing nationality groups of note-worthy size inside its borders. The four groups numbering more than 5,000 persons in 1970—Ukrainians, Byelorussians, Finns, and Jews—are mainly city people. Their combined total (70,643) constitutes only 5.2 percent of the ESSR's population (*Itogi 1970*, 1973:317). Russians, who in 1970 made up 24.6 percent of the total population, for the most part were concentrated (89.2 percent) in a few compact urban districts. Unlike other constituent republics, the ESSR suffers relatively little loss of territory to the resident Russian population. The main Russian settlement areas in the ESSR are found, as might be expected, along the union republic's periphery. One narrow (fifty-kilometer) strip follows the west bank of Lake Peipus around Kallaste; another, some sixty-five by twenty-five kilometers, runs westward from Narva along the gulf. The capital, Tallinn, and its contiguous metropolitan area on or near the Gulf of Finland, houses most of the remaining resident Russians (*Narody*, 1964:17). Russian military forces have virtually converted Estonia's two largest offshore islands in the Gulf of Finland, Hiiumaa and Saaremaa, into garrison preserves. Considerable numbers of Russians are located there, as well (*Atlas SSSR*, 1969:98). According to tourists, the movement of Estonians to and from these islands is restricted.

So long as the SSRs exist under present conditions, they will experience tensions—mainly because the eponymous nationality territory in each union republic does not closely coincide with the assigned SSR boundary. The lack of exact geographic correspondence between an SSR and its eponym leads to ethnic ambiguities. Such ambiguities become troublesome for the namesake group when vacuums within the SSR attract outsiders to the area, especially to its inner spaces. Ethnic peace and stability depend on population distribution as well as on concentration and urbanization of nationalities.

An adequate demographic base is another essential element in maintaining ethnic group vitality, especially if it is combined with vigorous self-assertion. The more a population base varies from the ideal (great concentration, strong urbanization, wide and deep distribution, and isolation or assimilation of outsiders), the more forcefully and visibly ethnic group feeling must assert itself. However, a good demographic foundation does not preclude the need for active group expression through words and deeds (Allworth, 1974:325-326, 333).

The ESSR's pattern so far in the 1970s—combining favorable demography with group assertiveness— augurs well for the eponymous nationality in years ahead. Ethnic Estonian leadership in a great range of endeavors is active and progressive. Not only at the political center of the union republic but also in its secondary cities and regions, native energy and talent have been applied. That kind of consistent, effective guidance at all levels of society and administration cannot help but be a unifying force. Solidarity within a modern eponymous group results to a large extent from intellectual and artistic leadership, and the Estonian elite is providing this in abundance. At both the lower and middle levels and the highest levels within the ESSR, Estonians fill most positions of major responsibility. Only two of the twenty-three ministerial positions in the union republic government were held by Slavic outsiders in 1975 (*Directory*, 1975:71-72; *Eesti Nôukogude Entsüklopeedia*, 1968-1976). That pattern has accompanied a relative stability in adminstration, owing in large part to the long tenure enjoyed by many ministerial appointees (Hodnett and Ogareff, 1973:93-119). Similar longevity is the norm among Communist party secretaries and key subordinates.

Representatives of the eponymous nationality have a special obligation to their ethnic group in an SSR's nonpolitical framework as well. This obligation often entails subtly protecting the nationality's interests in an ethnically demoralizing climate and in a hostile political-social organization. The willingness and capacity of native ethnic leaders in an SSR to play this crucial, if unofficial, role in large part determines the wellbeing of the eponymous national group. To date, Estonian leaders in many fields have proved equal to that challenge.

Thus, evidence for the extensive deployment of an Estonian infrastructure appears abundant in recent studies. Analyses of the roles played by academic and popular historians, cultural leaders, economic managers, professional politicians, and religious figures in the Soviet Baltic region in the 1970s have shown how effective these opinion makers, always important, have recently become in sustaining their nationality groups under Soviet conditions (Allworth, 1977, chs. 2-7). The diversity of fields in which Estonian personnel are solidly established in depth is demonstrated in this book.

The dichotomy between an SSR and its eponym becomes

obvious in this Estonian case study. The chapters about astronomy, computerization, demography, economy, ethnography, higher education, and scientific research for the most part treat the union republic as their subject. The authors examining the church, the Communist party elite and nationalism, drama, and literature predictably focus their attention mainly upon the ESSR's eponymous nationality. How could it be otherwise? If the peculiar rules of the Soviet game plan—which deny the oneness of an SSR and its nationality group—were abrogated, particularly in the arena of nationality affairs, all these chapters would doubtless emphasize a nationality and state inextricable from one another.

In this regard, how different is the situation of the ESSR from that of comparable SSRs? Third smallest in land area and least populous of those fourteen SSRs, the Estonian SSR nevertheless benefits from advantages denied to most of the others. The existence, from 1918 to 1940, of the independent Republic of Estonia left the ESSR with an invaluable legacy of practical statecraft. Moreover, the ESSR did not come under Soviet rule until a generation later than most other republics. The discrepancy between nationality homeland and territorial boundaries which mars the development and contentment of many other SSR eponyms is insignificant in Estonia. Although some loss of Estonian areas occurred in 1945 around Narva (including part of the city itself), and the arbitrary transfer of Petseri and adjacent lands from the ESSR to the Russian SFSR temporarily detached some thousands of Estonians from the ESSR's population, the union republic today geographically matches the preannexation republic.

All in all, an exceptionally harmonious common identification characterizes the Estonian nationality and territory and the ESSR. In this sense, the ESSR is unique among the Soviet republics. Thus, it probably will be less affected by the kinds of tensions apparent in other SSRs and less vulnerable to the vicissitudes in the fortunes of the SSRs as a group.

References

Aarna, A., et al., eds.

1975   *Nôukogude Eesti: Entsüklopeediline teatmeteos* [Soviet Estonia: An Encyclopedic Reference Work]. Tallinn: Valgus.

Allworth, Edward

1974   "Detente, Human Rights and Nationality Group Rights in the Soviet Union." Testimony presented in hearings before the Subcommittee on Foreign Affairs. U.S. House of Representatives, Ninety-third Congress, Second Session. Washington: U.S. Government Printing Office.

Allworth, Edward, ed.

1977   *Nationality Group Survival in Multi-Ethnic States: Shifting Support Patterns in the Soviet Baltic Region.* New York: Praeger Publishers.

Atlas SSSR

1969   Second ed. Moscow: Glavnoe Upravlenie Geodezii i Kartografii pri Sovete Ministrov SSSR.

Directory of Soviet Officials

1975   Vol. 3, *Union Republics.* N.p.: Central Intelligence Agency.

Eesti Nôukogude Entsüklopeedia

1968-   [The Estonian Soviet Encyclopedia]. Eight vols.
1976   Tallinn: Valgus.

Hazard, John N.

1975   "The Status of the Ukrainian Republic under the Soviet Federation," in *Ukraine in the Seventies*, ed. Peter J. Potichnyi. Oakville, Ont.: Mosaic Press.

Hodnett, Grey, and Val Ogareff

1973   *Leaders of the Soviet Republics, 1955-1972.* Canberra: Department of Political Science Research,

School of Social Sciences, Australian National University.

Itogi vsesoiuznoi perepisi naseleniia 1959 goda: SSSR (svodnyi tom)

1962   Moscow: Gosstatizdat. TsSU SSSR.

Itogi vsesoiuznoi perepisi naseleniia 1970 goda

1973   Vol. 4, *Natsional'nyi sostav naseleniia SSSR, soiuznykh i avtonomnykh republik, kraev, oblastei i natsional'nykh okrugov.* Moscow: Statistika.

Katz, Zev, Rosemarie Rogers, and Frederic Harned, eds.

1975   *Handbook of Major Soviet Nationalities.* New York: The Free Press.

Laas, K.

1967   "Eesti NSV rahvastik möödunud seitseaastakul" [The Population of the Estonian SSR during the Past Seven Years]. In *Majandusteadus ja Rahvamajandus: Aastaraamat 1966* [Economics and the National Economy: Yearbook for 1966]. Tallinn: Eesti Raamat.

Narodnoe khoziaistvo SSSR v 1974 g. Statisticheskii ezhegodnik

1975   Moscow: Statistika.

Narody evropeiskoi chasti SSSR

1964   Vol. 2. Moscow: Nauka.

Program of the Communist Party of the Soviet Union

1963   New York: International Publishers.

Semenov, P. G.

1961   "Programma KPSS o razvitii sovetskikh natsional 'nogosudarstvennykh otnoshenii." *Sovetskoe gosudarstvo i pravo*, vol. 12: 15-25.

Acknowledgments

We wish to acknowledge with gratitude the cooperation of our colleagues in preparing and revising manuscripts for the substantive chapters in the present volume, and the contribution of Reet Värnik for translating the manuscript for chapter 5 into English.

Tönu Parming
Elmar Järvesoo

The Contributors

EDWARD ALLWORTH, who holds a Ph.D. from Columbia University (1959), is Director of Columbia's Program on Soviet Nationality Problems. Among his many works are, as editor and coauthor: *Soviet Nationality Problems* (1971), *The Nationality Question in Soviet Central Asia* (1973), and *Nationality Group Survival in Multi-Ethnic States* (1977).

ELMAR JÄRVESOO was born in Pati, Estonia, in 1909. His academic credits include a B.S. in agricultural sciences from the University of Tartu in 1934 and a Ph.D. in agrarian economics from Friedrich Wilhelm University, Berlin, in 1939. He is professor of agricultural marketing at the University of Massachusetts at Amherst. Dr. Järvesoo has been Fulbright visiting professor at the Helsingin Kauppakorkeakoulu (Finland) and the Svenska Handelshögskola (Sweden) in economic growth theory, 1966, and visiting professor in agrarian economics at the University of Freiburg (West Germany), 1972. He is the author of numerous articles on Estonian economics.

GEORGE KURMAN was born in Tallinn, Estonia, in 1942. He holds a B.A. in liberal arts from Cornell University (1962) and a Ph.D. in comparative literature from Indiana University (1969). Presently associate professor of English at Western Illinois University, he was visiting professor of comparative literature at Carleton University in the summer of 1972. He is the author of *Literatures in Contact: Finland and Estonia, Development of Written Estonian,* and several articles on Estonian literature.

TEODOR KÜNNAPAS, born in Pärnumaa, Estonia, in 1902, was awarded a B.A. from the University of Tartu and a Ph.D. in psychology from the University of Stockholm in 1959. Presently docent of psychology at the University of Stockholm, he is the author of several articles on Estonian higher education and the book *Suured mõtlejad.*

xxi

REET NURMBERG-HOWELL was born in Angelholm, Sweden, in 1945. She has a B.A. in physical education from the University of Toronto (1967) and a Ph.D. in education and physical education from the University of California at Berkeley (1972). Presently associate professor of physical education at San Diego State University in California, she is the author of several articles on sports and physical education in Estonia and the Soviet Union.

VALDAR OINAS, born in Tartu, Estonia, in 1942, was awarded a B.S. in astronomy from Indiana University and a Ph.D. in astronomy from the California Institute of Technology in 1971. He is assistant professor of astronomy at Queensboro Community College, New York.

TÖNU PARMING was born in Pärnu, Estonia, in 1941. He has a B.A. in sociology from Princeton University (1964) and a Ph.D. in sociology from Yale University (1976). Presently assistant professor of sociology at the University of Maryland, he is the author of *The Collapse of Liberal Democracy and the Rise of Authoritarianism in Estonia* and several papers on Estonian and Baltic demography and nationalism.

JAAN PENNAR was born in Tallinn in 1924. His B.A. in economics was awarded by Bates College in 1947 and his Ph.D. in political science by Princeton University in 1953. He is presently director of the Estonian Service for Radio Liberty. Formerly counselor at the New York office of the Institute for the Study of the USSR and a senior fellow at the Research Institute on Communist Affairs, Columbia University, he is coauthor of *Modernization and Diversity in Soviet Education* and of several articles on nationalism and political trends in postwar Estonia.

GUSTAV RÄNK, born in Saaremaa, Estonia, in 1902, holds a B.A. in ethnography from the University of Tartu (1925) and a Ph.D. in ethnography (University of Tartu, 1938). Presently docent of ethnography at the University of Stockholm, he formerly was professor of ethnography at the University of Tartu and visiting professor at the universities of Helsinki, Turku, and Oslo. The author of numerous articles and monographs on Estonian ethnographic topics, he is considered to be the leading authority on Estonian ethnography.

VELLO SALO was born in Pôltsamaa, Estonia, in 1925. His degrees include a Lic. phil. in philosophy from Pontificia Universitas Gregoriana (1951) and a Ph.D. in biblical sciences from the Pontificium Institutum Biblicum in Rome (1976). He is now a lecturer at St. Augustine's Seminary, Toronto. Formerly professor of biblical studies at St. John's Seminary, Mossul, Iraq, he is editor of the series *Maarjamaa* and the author of a book and several articles on religion in postwar Estonia.

HEINO SUSI was born in Tallinn in 1925. He has a B.S. in chemistry from the Technische Hochschule, Aachen, Germany (1950) and a Ph.D. in chemistry from Purdue University (1955). He is presently a supervisory research chemist for the Agricultural Research Service and assistant professor of chemistry at Drexel Institute of Technology.

REIN TAAGEPERA, born in Tartu in 1933, holds a B.S. in engineering physics (University of Toronto, 1959), a Ph.D. in physics (University of Delaware, 1965), and an M.A. in international relations (University of Delaware, 1969). In addition to serving as associate professor of political science at the University of California at Irvine, he has been editor of *Estonian Events* (later *Baltic Events*), a newsletter on Soviet Estonian and Baltic events, and coeditor of *Problems of Mininations: Baltic Perspectives*. He has written many articles on political processes and trends in Soviet Estonia.

REIN TURN was born in Tartu in 1931. His degrees include a B.S. in engineering (1957) and a Ph.D. in engineering (1963) from the University of California at Los Angeles. Presently a senior systems analyst for the Rand Corporation, he is the author of *Computers in the 1980s* and a creator of computer terminology in Estonian.

MARDI VALGEMÄE was born in Viljandi, Estonia, in 1935. Valgemäe, who holds a B.A. in English from Rutgers University (1957) and a Ph.D. in English from the University of California at Los Angeles (1964), is professor of English at Lehman College, City University of New York, and the author of *Accelerated Grimace: Expressionism in the American Drama of the 1920s* and several articles on Estonian drama and theater trends.

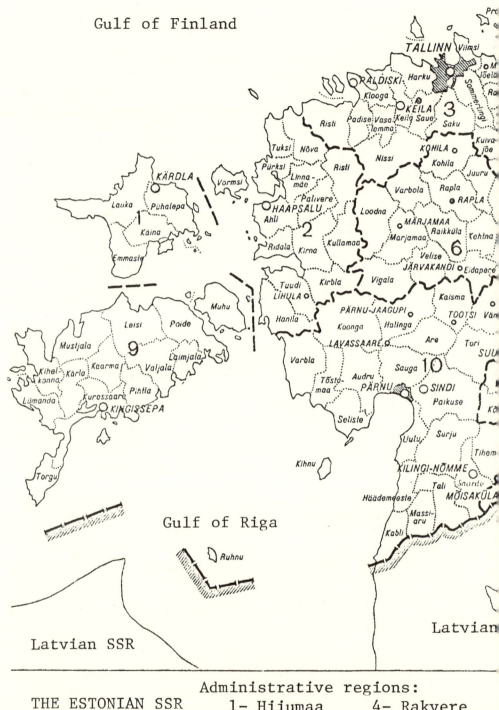

Gulf of Finland

Gulf of Riga

Latvian SSR

Latvian

THE ESTONIAN SSR

Administrative regions:

1- Hiiumaa   4- Rakvere
2- Haapsalu   5- Kohtla-Jär
3- Harju   6- Rapla

- Paide
- Jõgeva
- Kingissepa
10- Pärnu
11- Viljandi
12- Tartu
13- Valga
14- Põlva
15- Võru

Introduction

Tönu Parming and Elmar Järvesoo

For a prolonged time, and even into the present, "Soviet studies" in the United States in actuality has meant "Russian studies." Thus, Russian history has been taught as Soviet history, Russian culture as Soviet culture. American students have been routinely promised summer study tours of the Soviet Union, only to visit Moscow and Leningrad. Indeed, the perception of the Soviet Union as merely a Russian state has permeated both scholarship and public opinion in the English-speaking West to an appreciably greater degree than within the Soviet Union itself. A second traditionally dominant characteristic of American Soviet studies has been the tendency to examine that vast country by focusing on the political and other decision-making processes in Moscow, and to analyze societal processes per se by focusing on the Communist party and its ideology. Early specialists paid little attention to the union republics and to the significance they might have in the political, economic, cultural, and scientific life of the Soviet Union as a whole. Perhaps an exception here might be the study of "Soviet nationality issues," which has gained prominence in recent years.

A major impetus for change in American Soviet studies came with the cold war and the simultaneous influx of scholars who had fled from Soviet control in Eastern Europe. The cold war focused the interest of Washington on Soviet affairs to a degree that had not existed earlier, and thus stimulated greater financing for academic programs. A simultaneous increase in public interest in the Soviet Union, especially in its non-

1

Russian aspects, resulted from the political activism of the various emigré groups, whose scholars also provided an instant cadre of specialists with a fluency in non-Russian Soviet languages. As a result, American scholarship has begun slowly to look at the Soviet Union within a more encompassing framework, focusing on republic-level as well as on union-level processes and issues and on Russian as well as non-Russian aspects of the society and its affairs. Since the early 1970s, major momentum to such studies has been provided by Columbia University's Program on Soviet Nationality Problems. Not only has this program stimulated interdisciplinary contacts within the context of an ongoing seminar, it has also provided academic training for a new generation of American specialists.

This book is largely the result of the editors' conviction that Soviet studies and sovietologists must pay greater attention to the union republics. The completed manuscript, we feel, proves our point. The work was intended primarily to provide a scrutiny—a study in depth—of one Soviet republic, the Estonian SSR.

At the outset, it was our intent to cover all important aspects of Soviet Estonian society. In this regard, what was "important" was determined on the basis of earlier scholarship and conversations with colleagues. Unfortunately, we were not fully successful in meeting this goal, either because we could not locate qualified scholars in some areas or because we could not solicit cooperation. Three topics which we were not able to adequately cover are (1) the nature and extent of native resistance to Soviet rule before the end of Stalinism, (2) cultural developments, other than in literature or the theater, and (3) the impact of the exile Estonian community on developments within Soviet Estonia. (It might be noted that, to date, these topics have been inadequately covered even in Estonian-language sources in the West.)

As chapter manuscripts arrived, we discovered several other areas which merit much greater attention. Among these are (1) pre-Soviet history as a force determining the character of a given republic and of differences between republics, (2) the role of the local party elite in determining the local course of events, and (3) the roles of such noneconomic factors as native scholarship and science in advancing native identity and societal uniqueness. It is clear that knowledge of these areas is important to a full understanding not only of the total society—the Soviet Union—but also of specific republics.

We had initially hoped to shed light on various exchanges between Soviet Estonia and the non-Estonian Soviet Union, but we discovered through our network of contributors that this was an overly ambitious goal. Some of the restrictions here were due to the unavailability or inadequacy of pertinent data or sources and others to the fact that an inadequate amount of related information is available on the other union republics and areas of the Soviet Union. Further research into all of the union republics will be necessary, especially on specific, narrow topics, in order to ascertain the nature of interrepublic exchange.

Factors Shaping the Contemporary Nature of Soviet Estonia

A recurring question asked by observers of the Soviet Union in recent years is, what makes the Estonian SSR so different from the other republics? Why is its culture so Western—by Soviet standards, even avant-garde? Why is its level of industrialization so high and its industry and agriculture, by Soviet standards, so efficient? In part on the basis of the chapters in this volume, it is possible to identify eight important and interactive explanatory factors.[1]

1. The first and foremost factor is Estonia's pre-Soviet history.[2] When it was absorbed by the Soviet Union in 1940, Estonia was no longer an emergent nation nor an underdeveloped society. Rather, its populace was fully literate and its educational level among the highest in the world. Its agricultural base had been radically altered through land reform, and an appreciable number of steps had been taken to modernize (or create) the supportive infrastructure and agricultural research base. Also, the Estonian economy during the second half of the 1930s was rapidly industrializing. Hence, during the Soviet period it was possible to build upon an existing educational, scientific, and economic-technical base.

Furthermore, a major accomplishment of the two-decade interwar republic was the development of a strong national cultural identity which had extensive roots in and ties with Western Europe. Indeed, Estonia's cultural links with the West predate not only the Soviet period but also both the republic of

1918-1940 and czarist Estonia (1721-1918). A major element in this link as well as in the development of a strong national identity was the University of Tartu, founded in 1632. The university has a long and distinguished tradition in the sciences and the humanities. Among other early distinctions, it offered the first graduate program in medicine in czarist Russia and the first university-based program in agricultural studies. During the period of the independent republic, the university also established a solid foundation in those studies necessary for the development of a strong national identity rooted in culture: native history, ethnography, language, and literature.

An important aspect of the historical link to non-Russian Europe was its multichannel nature. For example, the Estonians are a Finno-Ugric people, and by absorbing Estonia the Soviet Union acquired one of the leading centers of Finno-Ugric studies in Europe. This move provided Soviet Estonia with the potential for contacts with two other such centers, Hungary and Finland. Indeed, the fact that periodic Finno-Ugric conferences were held on a rotating basis in Tallinn, Helsinki, and Budapest during the preceding two decades is evidence that such contacts reached beyond the Soviet Union's borders. Finno-Ugric studies within the Estonian SSR employ a sizable number of scholars who, as a side benefit, must devote much study to the native language, ethnography, and other aspects of the collective past.

Another tie of a similar nature exists with Poland and East Germany. Poland ruled southern Estonia briefly several centuries ago, and relations between Poland and Estonia during the interwar decades were in some respects better than those among the three Baltic republics themselves. Furthermore, many Baltic Germans resettled in what is now East Germany either in 1939-1940 or after World War II. The contemporary ties between Estonia and these two countries are evidenced by the frequent use of the latters' archives by Estonian scholars and by Polish and East German participation in Estonian scholarly symposia. Relations between Soviet Estonia and East European countries with which the former had insignificant or nonexistent ties before the war—Bulgaria, Rumania, and Czechoslovakia—have remained appreciably weaker during the postwar years. Poland, Hungary, and East Germany, in turn, have maintained better and more encompassing contacts with Western Europe during the postwar period than have most East European countries or the Soviet society as a whole.[3] In any case, Estonia's historical links to the West along this channel appear more favorable than those of any other Soviet republic, including Latvia and Lithuania.

2. Soviet Estonia has had a very special link to the West through the country of its ethnic kinfolk to the north, Finland. Not only have cultural and scholarly relations been traditionally strong, but Finland lately has enjoyed a "special relationship" with Moscow which facilitates the use of this channel of contact. Estonians not only can and do watch Finnish television, they can also, to a great degree, readily understand the closely related language. Finnish Communist publications are at times available legally within Soviet Estonia. While the Finnish Communist newspaper *Kansan uutiset* may not be a fully impartial source of information, it clearly outrates either *Pravda* or the Estonian party's own *Rahva Hääl*.

Additionally, there has been a considerable amount of personal contact between the Finns and Estonians, especially after Stalin's death. A direct tourist boat line links Helsinki and Tallinn, and it is used by thousands of Finns every year. While the number of Estonians visiting Finland is quite a bit smaller, it is nevertheless sizable for a Soviet people. Soviet Estonian scholars, especially language instructors, have been on the faculties of Finnish universities for a decade, the study of Estonian being mandatory for many Finnish students. In any case, no other Soviet people or republic has such a direct and extensive link to either the West or to non-Russian Europe.

3. Estonia retained from the pre-Soviet period an excellent scientific base, which has been further expanded during the postwar period. Within Estonia's small territory is concentrated an extraordinary amount of native scientific talent. Not only has this talent facilitated achieving preeminence in certain areas of Soviet science, it has also contributed directly to the postwar industrial expansion within Estonia. Furthermore, science has long been an important conduit in contacts with the West. During the pre-republic period, the predominantly German and Baltic German faculty of the University of Tartu had excellent ties with major German intellectual centers. During the 1920s, a number of foreign scholars taught at the university while a native cadre was being prepared. The latter, in turn, received a great deal of advanced specialized education outside of Estonia. Perhaps equally important was the ex-

change of publications between the University of Tartu and other European and even North American universities. The impact of all these ties with non-Russian Europe was carried over into the Soviet period.

4. In terms of its effects on Estonian society, the brutality of the years of World War II and Stalinism was not totally negative. Indirectly, there were several positive long-range consequences. Because their emerging prewar industrial base was destroyed by either direct war activity or German/Russian requisitioning and equipment/plant evacuations, the Estonians had an extraordinary opportunity to apply existing technical and managerial expertise to the development of a fully modern industrial base, at least by Soviet standards. In this respect their situation resembled that of postwar Germany. Similarly, although Stalinist brutality led to the eradication or westward flight of the prewar middle class and many cultural and scientific leaders, the resulting vacuum allowed a massive upward movement of new and fresh talent. After Stalinism these people could, within the general confines of Soviet policies, innovate in industrial reconstruction and culture. Perhaps a similar situation existed in regard to industrialization and science in Soviet Latvia. Other areas of the Soviet Union lacked either a prewar industrial base or a strong prewar scientific-technical tradition; hence they had neither technical experience nor personnel after World War II.

5. A large share of Estonia's surviving cultural and intellectual elite fled westward in 1944 to escape the Soviet reoccupation of Estonia. This group established a competing culture and in many areas a competing scholarship as well—a fact which at times has been embarrassing to Soviet authorities. There is evidence that the literary achievements of the emigré community, which quantitatively as well as qualitatively outproduced Soviet Estonia into the 1960s in spite of its small population base, directly contributed to the literary thaw within Soviet Estonia. Furthermore, some observers have noted the influence of exiled writers on Soviet Estonia's younger writers. Younger-generation exiled scholars and cultural figures have made direct contacts with their colleagues in Soviet Estonia from the moment that this became possible. Some such contact has occurred through Finland, where a number of exiled scholars and activists have studied, especially since the mid-1960s.

Soviet reactions to the exile community's political activism have perhaps also indirectly intensified cultural contacts. Some Soviet Estonian cultural figures have been sent to the West, apparently with the aim of undermining the solidarity of the exile community. This practice inevitably exposes the traveler to both exile and Western culture and society. Also, Soviet Estonian cultural ensembles have made tours in Western Europe in response to tours by equivalent groups from the exile community. The prevalence of Soviet Estonian language instructors at Finnish universities since the late 1960s may very well represent a similar kind of response, since Soviet authorities had found it irritating that such positions were previously held by emigré scholars. The emigré community has also, of course, exerted political pressure on the Soviet authorities, especially by mobilizing Western public opinion, in addition to providing a number of informed observers of the Soviet Estonian scene.

The extent of the influence of the emigré community on processes within Soviet Estonia is extraordinarily difficult to assess. Its activities have included cultural competition, political activism directed against Soviet rule, and even economic contributions. From the late 1950s through the 1960s, emigrés sent a large quantity of consumer goods to relatives in Soviet Estonia—a practice which, given that state's small population and territory, made an unexplored but potentially important contribution to Estonia's relative consumer prosperity after the war.

While other Soviet peoples have exile populations, the Estonian case might be unique for several reasons. One unique factor is the mediating role played by Finland. Second, the largest Estonian emigré grouping is in nearby Sweden, where the Latvian population is of very small size and Lithuanians and Ukrainians are practically nonexistent. Sweden has been the traditional center of Estonian exile culture, scholarship, and political activity. Finally, Estonian emigré influence transcends the ethnic Estonian group. After Estonia in 1939-1940 saw the departure of its Baltic German minority, that group became prominent in West Germany and, to a lesser degree, in East Germany. While Latvia also lost its Baltic Germans, Estonia's prewar relations with its Baltic German population had been appreciably more friendly than those of Latvia. Estonia also saw the resettlement of its Swedish population to Sweden, and this group has remained active there. Some influence might even be present in Israel, where an association of Estonian and Latvian Jews exists in Tel Aviv and where a number of scientific works from Soviet Estonia have been translated into English. Estonia's prewar relations with its Jewish group were probably better than such relations anywhere else in the territory of the contemporary Soviet Union. Estonia's University of Tartu had what at that time was one of the few university chairs of Jewish studies in the world, and in 1927 the country received a special certificate from the Jewish National Fund in Palestine for its friendly treatment of Jews.

6. The attitudes of native Estonians, inside as well as outside the Communist party, merit attention. These attitudes reflect the effects of the strong cultural identity developed during the interwar years. Thus, Estonian youth have chosen to maintain their identity, the new generation of scientists has chosen to remain in Soviet Estonia in spite of greener scientific pastures elsewhere in the Soviet Union, and the new generation of cultural leaders has chosen to modernize the language rather than abandon it. Most children of intermarried parents in Estonia formally choose an Estonian ethnic identity upon reaching adulthood.

Estonia also preserved from the interwar years a pragmatic attitude toward politics, wherein cultural nationalism appears to be stronger than political nationalism. It must be kept in mind that the founders of the republic were not steering a deliberate course toward political sovereignty in 1918; the early preference was for autonomy within a federated, democratic Russian state. The option of full sovereignty was exercised only when Russia, with the advent of its Soviet order, regressed into societal chaos. The Estonian peasant in 1918 had been politically mobilized to fight for statehood, not on the basis of a lofty ideology of political nationalism, but by a more pragmatic consideration—namely, the need for an effective resolution of the pressing land issue by the leaders of the newly proclaimed republic. Although there have been demands for the reinstatement of political sovereignty in Soviet Estonia, most political resistance during the postwar period appears to have been primarily a response to the early Stalinist repression, the general cultural and political repression of the Soviet system, and the ever-present threat of Russification. It has been noted by some observers that, if Moscow were more true to its own federal constitution and to Leninism in supporting cultural pluralism, and if Russian immigration and chauvinism were kept in check, Estonia might not be especially disloyal to the central political authority. Indeed, complaints noted by visiting Western journalists are usually directed at cultural and political repression and Russification rather than at socialism as a basis for societal organization.

Also applicable to this factor is the nature of the Communist party and its elite. As might be expected in any large political movement or organization, party ideology and practice span both hard-line Stalinism and moderatism. It appears, however, that the party elite in Soviet Estonia is concentrated at the end of moderatism. While fully devoted to the ideological and theoretical principles of the party, it is not imbued with Stalinist or hard-line tendencies of the kind that have been identified in Soviet Latvia, for example, by some observers. The Estonian party elite, which is composed in large degree of the progeny of earlier Estonian emigrants to Russia, appears well suited to act as a mediator between the central authorities in Moscow and the local population.

7. Industrialization must be judged an independent variable in some respects. The level of industrialization in Estonia reflects its prewar economic heritage; its inherited and expanded scientific, technical, and managerial expertise; the decision of Moscow to invest sizable amounts of capital and resources in the Estonian SSR; and, to some extent, the ability of the local party elite to modify centralized goals, policies, and programs to the republic's advantage. The high standard of living and the extent of urbanization obviously go hand in hand with the advanced level of economic development.

Many contemporary societal problems in Soviet Estonia probably reflect more the level of urbanization and industrialization than the fact of Soviet rule. These problems include industrial pollution, worker and youth alienation (leading in Estonia to alcoholism instead of drugs), high divorce rates, and family stresses related to the high rate of education and employment among women. All of these problems are also manifest in Western societies at a commensurate level of industrialization. Industrialization has also been closely associated with the immigration of Russians to Estonia, a matter of great native resentment and a factor which has spurred both native nationalism and anti-Russian attitudes.

8. An important variable in postwar Soviet Estonian developments has been Soviet state policy as such; that is, major decisions made in Moscow. The traditional approach in the West has been to look only at the negative aspects of such decisions, at the repressive side of Moscow's policies. Yet Estonia's rapid industrialization has been possible in part because of the allocation of large quantities of capital and raw materials and the availability of markets. In any case, prewar Estonia had been dependent for all three on foreign states. While the uninterrupted development of the prewar economy would probably have led to a higher standard of living than currently exists and to a less repressive political and cultural framework, the recovery of the war-destroyed economy probably would not have been faster without Soviet rule. Estonia's rapid recovery reflects a conscious Moscow decision, regardless of what motivated that decision. Industrialization has had positive as well as negative consequences for Soviet Estonian society.

Moscow is seemingly tolerant of Soviet Estonia's uniqueness. While the high level of Soviet Estonian economic and cultural development can be explained partly on the basis of the state's pre-Soviet heritage, it is important to bear in mind that its ties to the West—so important to cultural and scientific life and, in some respects, to economic development as well—exist largely at the pleasure of the central authorities in Moscow. The reasons for Moscow's tolerant attitude remain unexplored. To some degree, after the end of Stalinism, historical momentum might have been the deciding factor. Yet identifiable and concrete benefits have resulted from Moscow's tolerance of Estonian uniqueness.[4] First, Estonia's relatively advanced educational, scientific, and economic prewar base has made possible excellent returns from a relatively small investment of Soviet resources. Second, Estonia's uniqueness, regardless of how it was achieved, is advantageous for Soviet propaganda purposes. While Estonians both in Soviet Estonia and in the West routinely insist that achievements were made in spite of Soviet rule, for Moscow's purposes it is only important that they were made within the framework of Soviet socialism. Soviet Estonia provides living proof that it is possible to achieve an advanced industrial-urban society within the Soviet system. Furthermore, especially because of the Finnish-

Estonian boat connection, Soviet Estonia is a major tourist attraction that brings in a great deal of foreign currency.

Because of several characteristics, Soviet Estonia provides a superb setting for experimentation—as, for example, in the application of computers to various aspects of management. From a cultural standpoint, Soviet authorities may safely allow the introduction of Western ideas, literature, and plays to Estonia in order to appraise what their consequences would be for Soviet society in general. After all, except for 1 million Estonians, no one in the Soviet Union understands Estonian, and the ethnic Estonians have not indicated a willingness to migrate; hence, social and cultural experiments can be confined to a small territory and population.

Another reason for Moscow's tolerance is the realization that eradication of Estonia's strong cultural identity would be very costly. A policy of tolerance eases exile political pressures and fosters economic productivity and pride in scientific-educational achievements. Finally, Soviet Estonia provides the union with cultural figures, scientists, and athletes of international stature. All these are benefits which undue repression would clearly restrict. Perhaps Soviet central authorities have failed to comprehend that local-level political resistance is motivated largely by their own repressive and confining policies and by threats of Russification, rather than by principle. In any case, it appears that it is to Moscow's advantage to tolerate certain Estonian idiosyncrasies, so long as performance levels remain high and political or ideological deviance remains low.

These eight factors are the major variables explaining Estonia's uniqueness within the Soviet system. While some of them apply to other republics and Soviet peoples as well, it is clear that Soviet Estonia enjoys a relative advantage among union republics. These eight variables are neither fully independent nor dependent, according to the traditional methodological notions of causality. Rather, they have a number of important component elements which are interrelated in a complex manner. It may be virtually impossible to define all these elements empirically, and thus quantitatively unravel the interrelationships.

It should be further noted that Soviet Estonia during the postwar years experienced three major periods of development. First there were the dark years of Stalinism, characterized not only by political repression but also by slow economic progress and cultural stagnation. An attempt was made during this time to forge Estonia fully to the Soviet mold. Toward the end of the 1950s there was a slow but nevertheless important burst of change, an obvious reflection of Khrushchev's early attempt at de-Stalinizing Soviet society. After a decade of steady but slow progress, another period of abrupt change in the direction of improvement occurred during the late 1960s and early 1970s, perhaps reflecting the consolidation of power by Brezhnev. However, these three periods reflect more than internal Soviet political shifts. Progressive change may also be noted during the periods in regard to the aforenoted major variable clusters. Additionally, the Estonian experience reflects the time required for a new generation of cultural leaders and scientists to be trained and then to apply itself. Clearly, further study of all these factors and their interrelationships is in order, not only for Estonia, but for the other Soviet republics as well.

A Brief Commentary on Sources

In the present volume we have attempted to minimize the utilization of source notes. Most references to sources appear in the text according to the contemporary American social-science notation system. The author's name, the year of the referenced publication, and, if applicable, page numbers are provided in parentheses, usually at the end of a sentence. The lists of references that follow each chapter are purposely thorough, giving special attention to important sources published in the major Western languages, especially English.

When applicable, transliteration of names from Russian usually follows the Modern Language Association system. There are two important exceptions: First, ethnic Estonian names, which originally are always in the Latin alphabet, retain their original spelling. At times Western scholars transliterate such names by way of Russian sources, a practice that leads to peculiarities in spelling; e.g., this book refers to the Estonian Communist party leader as "Käbin," not "Kebin," a form sometimes used in the West. Second, Russian names which have been transliterated into Estonian in published sources in Soviet Estonia are spelled here just as they occur in such sources.

Few books about Soviet Estonia have been published in the West. There are three important exceptions, all written from the exile viewpoint and largely the work of nonscholars. The ten-volume *Eesti riik ja rahvas Teises Maailmasôjas* [The Estonian State and People during the Second World War], edited by Richard Maasing et al. (Stockholm: Kirjastus EMP [Eesti Majandus ühisus Produkt], 1954-1962), covers the first year of Soviet rule (1940-1941) and the subsequent German occupation (1941-1944) in great detail. The early postwar period is covered by eight brief booklets in English issued as a series, East and West, by Boreas in London between 1947 and 1956. More recent years are partially covered in volumes 5 and 6 of the multivolume *Eesti saatusaastad 1945-1960* [Estonia's Years of Fate, 1945-1960], edited by Richard Maasing et al. and published, respectively, in 1968 and 1972 in Stockholm by EMP.

A more contemporary accounting has been presented by Andres Küng, a Swedish-born journalist and free-lance writer of Estonian ancestry who visited Soviet Estonia in a professional and official capacity in the second half of the 1960s. Küng has published books on Soviet Estonia and the Soviet Baltic in several languages. Of his works, the most accessible to Western scholars is *Estland zum Beispiel,* published in Stuttgart by Seewald in 1973.[5] The forte of Küng's work is the presentation of information on what Estonians themselves think of Soviet rule, as reflected in their opinions on the best and worst of Soviet Estonian society. His reports are based on actual interviews, with officials as well as with ordinary people. Most Western journalists, unfortunately, lack Küng's competency in Estonian, a limitation that prevents them from conducting spontaneous interviews.

An extensive list of English-language periodicals, bibliographies, books, and pamphlets on Estonian subjects, compiled by Marju Rink Parming and Tönu Parming, was published by the Estonian Learned Society in America in 1974: *A Bibliography of English-Language Sources on Estonia* (nearly 700 entries). Bibliographies of German-language materials on Estonia, of the work of exiled Estonian scholars in various fields since 1940, and of Soviet Estonian materials are also available. A guide to bibliographical resources compiled recently by Marju Rink Parming appeared in the *Journal of Baltic Studies* 7, no. 3 (1976).

Several periodicals in English have dealt exclusively or extensively with Estonian or Baltic subjects. *Baltic Review* appeared in Sweden from 1946 through 1949 in two volumes, and a journal with an identical title was published in New York City from 1953 through 1971 (numbered 1 through 38). The Lithuanian quarterly *Lituanus* has appeared in the United States since 1954. The *Journal of Baltic Studies* (published in the United States by the Association for the Advancement of Baltic Studies) has existed since 1970, at first under the name *Bulletin of Baltic Studies*. Two important newsletters providing current information are *Newsletter from behind the Iron Curtain*, published in Sweden since 1952, and *Estonian Events* (later *Baltic Events*), published between 1967 and 1975, mostly by Dr. Rein Taagepera of the University of California at Irvine. In the area of literature, the University of Oklahoma's *Books Abroad* has included many articles and reviews on Estonian and Baltic topics.

Specialized periodicals are also available in German. *Acta Baltica*, the yearbook of the Institutum Balticum in Königstein, has been published since 1960-1961, and *Commentationes Balticae*, a series of brief monographic works issued by the Baltisches Forschungsinstitut at Bonn University, appeared in 1954 (the latter series is now defunct). Publications in other Western languages (that is, other than in English, German, or the three Baltic languages) are rare. However, the point is slowly being reached at which scholars not fluent in Estonian can follow Soviet Estonian events through English- and German-language secondary sources on most topics of significance, and bibliographical reference works will soon meet most scholarly needs.

Most existing sources on Soviet Estonia are in Estonian, written either in the West or in Soviet Estonia. There is, however, no guide to the former, especially to articles and newspapers. The opposite is the case with Soviet Estonian publications, the bibliographical guides to which are excellent. However, such guides are not readily available in Western libraries. Furthermore, neither exile nor Soviet Estonian sources are readily available in Western libraries.

Both traditional emigré and Soviet Estonian sources have been imbued with and even defined by political-ideological considerations. In the case of the exiles, this bias has been evidenced by utopian conceptualizations of prewar Estonia and by emphasis on the negative aspects of postwar Soviet rule in Estonia. Indeed, a great deal of exile writing has dealt directly with political issues at the expense of culture and social change.[6] In the case of Soviet Estonian sources, the problem derives from party control over publication. Thus, Soviet Estonian sources present a utopian conceptualization of *postwar* Estonia and emphasize the negative aspects of the *prewar* republican period. The party's rules, furthermore, have proscribed what issues may be covered by scholars. Consequently, certain topics appear to be off limits: the negative effects of Soviet economic policy (industrial pollution, persevering housing problems), social problems per se (crime, alcoholism), and the massive immigration of Russians (the perceived or real threat of Russification).

Finally, it should be noted that several types of important sources on Soviet Estonia are very difficult to obtain in the West or for the Western scholar: literature in manuscript form or which is printed in less than fifty copies in a nonpublic publication sector; scholarship in manuscript form or unpublished dissertations and theses; and local newspapers, which often are critical of social issues but which cannot be legally sent to the West. Yet both exile and Soviet sources are indispensable to a scholar dealing with Soviet Estonia. Exile newspapers published in Sweden and North America are often the first Western sources to report data, trends, and change. Often they are good guides to non-Estonian journalistic accounts as well, because the exile press reprints or digests many Western newspaper pieces dealing with Estonian topics. Soviet Estonian sources are important not only for data; in many areas, descriptive as well as analytical work of high quality exists in published form. Unfortunately, not all Soviet Estonian assertions and data can be verified through cross-checks; but many can, and others can be subjectively verified by Western newsmen or tourists. In many areas, checks can be made as to the reliability and validity of data—a necessary step, given the number of cases for which different Soviet Estonian sources report different quantitative data about a given item (for example, economic production, vital rates).

A special recurring difficulty in assessing Soviet Estonian trends quantitatively has been the official tendency to report changes over time by using a base index of 100—usually assigned to 1940—in lieu of absolute figures. The use of 1940 as a base year is deceptive for two reasons: First, at times less than one-half of the calendar year appears to be used in affixing the index base (Estonia became a Soviet republic in mid-1940). Second, even if 1940 is used as a full year, it is important to note that most indicators of economic and other societal activities declined abruptly from 1938 and 1939 because of the impact of war. While we have emphasized that knowledge of Estonia's prewar history is crucial to understanding the present nature of the Estonian SSR, there is no inherent value in comparing things of today with those of yesterday in every field of observation. This often needless but incessant comparison inflicts a political taint on both traditional exile and Soviet Estonian publications in that it defines the issues inevitably in terms of what should be or could be, instead of what is and why.

In the case of Western scholarship a noticeable trend away from the exile bias began in the study of the Soviet Baltic in 1968 with the formation in the United States of the Association for the Advancement of Baltic Studies, which among other things provides an outlet for younger scholars of Baltic ancestry who are fluent in their native languages, politically less committed to the past, and educated largely in the West. The association's biennial conferences have also attracted a large number of scholars not of Baltic ancestry. (A similar development has occurred in Sweden during the past few years.)

The contributors to the present effort are subject specialists in the areas on which they have written chapters, and all have earlier publications to their credit on their particular topics. All of the chapters were written specifically for this book; there are no reprints, although several of the chapters consolidate and update earlier articles. Furthermore, all of the chapter authors are competent in Estonian. With a few exceptions, they received their higher education in North America, and most are presently on the faculties of American universities.

We hope we have succeeded in our attempt to eliminate politically imbued scholarship through our choice of contributors and by setting guidelines which required authors to focus, not on how things could or should be, but on how they are and why. Yet it might be appropriate to comment here that a particular political framework is not the only factor that influences scholarship dealing with the Soviet Union. Neither political nor ideological orientations are the only factors which influence, temper, or bias scholarship.

Notes

1. These factors find lengthier treatment in Tönu Parming, "Developments in Nationalism in Estonia since 1965," in George Simmonds, ed., *Nationalism in Eastern Europe and the USSR during Brezhnev and Kosygin* (Detroit: University of Detroit Press, 1977); also see Tönu Parming, "The Historical Roots of Nationality Differences in the Soviet Baltic," in Edward Allworth, ed., *Nationality Group Survival in Multi-Ethnic States* (New York: Praeger, 1977).

2. An extensive listing of English-language sources on the Estonian past is available in Marju R. Parming and Tönu Parming, comps., *A Bibliography of English-Language Sources on Estonia* (New York: Estonian Learned Society in America, 1974). Many articles in English during the 1918-1940 period are listed in Tönu Parming, *The Collapse of Liberal Democracy and the Rise of Authoritarianism in Estonia* (London: Sage, 1975).

3. For a recent study of some of the pertinent aspects of such contacts, see Roman Szporluk, ed., *The Influence of East Europe and the Soviet West on the USSR* (New York: Praeger, 1975).

4. Many relevant issues are covered by V. Stanley Vardys in "The Role of the Baltic Republics in Soviet Society," in Roman Szporluk, ed., *The Influence of East Europe and the Soviet West on the USSR* (New York: Praeger, 1975).

5. Küng's works have appeared also in Swedish and Estonian, and reportedly in Hebrew and Icelandic. The Swedish-language works are *Estland en studie i Imperialism* (Stockholm: Bonners, 1971) and *Vad händer i Baltikum* (Stockholm: Aldous, 1973). The referenced German-language work is a translation of the former. In Estonian the updated version was entitled *Saatusi ja saavutusi* (Lund: Eesti Kirjanike Kooperatiiv, 1973).

6. The reference here is to writing on Soviet Estonia, which in the West has appeared most often in the framework of political organizations and which largely represents the work of nonscholars. The many older-generation exiled Estonian scholars have continued to publish prolifically in many fields, primarily on historical and pre-Soviet topics and times. The critical appraisal here is not applicable to them.

Part 1
Population and Political Processes

1

Population Changes and Processes

Tönu Parming

As in many other aspects of its society, so also demographically, Soviet Estonia has a tendency to be different from most other Soviet republics. For example, it is the Soviet Union's most urbanized republic; it has the lowest rate of natural increase and the lowest rate of marriage, as well as one of the highest divorce rates. Many trends presently observable in Soviet Estonia have their roots in earlier history. This applies to demographic trends as well, although population changes are also directly linked to Soviet activities and policies. This chapter surveys major changes since 1940.

Any student of Soviet Estonian population processes must be willing to pursue bits and pieces of data in all types of publications and to collate these to understand what has been and is transpiring. Unfortunately, many of the necessary publications are not readily available even in the major research libraries of Western countries. There are also additional problems in regard to sources and their utilization. For example, I was not able to fully decipher the 1959 census results until 1969-1970, especially in regard to ethnic composition, because those results, published in 1962, were inadequate for a thorough analysis. To accomplish the latter it was necessary to collate bits and pieces of data published during the decade following the census. A similar situation exists with the 1970 census results, of which the important volume 4 became available in 1973. Several crucial bits of data had yet to be published by mid-1975. Finally, not all tabulations in the 1970 census were made on the same basis as were those in 1959. For example, age groups 0-9 and 10-19 were used in some tables, 0-10 and 11-19 in others.

A very important change has been made in official statistics, furthermore, in regard to immigration in Soviet Estonia. This is apparent from a 1973 publication of the Central Statistical Bureau in Tallinn (CSBESSR, 1973), in which the annual beginning-of-the-year population figures from 1960 onward differ from those of earlier official accounts. The 35,000 figure given for immigrants in 1969 (which was calculated by myself and others on the basis of the earlier reported total population in 1969, the census count of 1970, and the known natural increase in 1969) has been distributed over the whole decade of the 1960s. The total number of immigrants for the intercensus period essentially remains unchanged, as do the absolute figures for births, deaths, and natural increase. But the change in the beginning-of-the-year population altered the figures for vital rates in all years. Thus, the figures reported herein are in some cases slightly different from those given in my earlier writings (Parming, 1972a, 1972b, 1972c). In general, I have used herein the most recent data available. If major discrepancies exist, these will be pointed out. While I have made an attempt to compare 1959 with 1970 figures where appropriate, this was not possible in all cases for the reasons cited. In order to conserve space, I have referred throughout this chapter to my three earlier articles on Soviet Estonian demography.

It must be noted that, while extensive attention has been given by Soviet Estonian scholars to various historical subjects, urbanization, and population geography, there has been virtually no comment on the changes wrought by World War II. The massive Soviet deportations, the flight westward, and the immigration of Russians from 1945 to the present have had important demographic consequences which cannot be ignored, and our analysis begins with these subjects. While there is no general history of Estonia's population, a glimpse at its growth is offered by figure 1.

Figure 1

Estonia's population 1200 – 1976

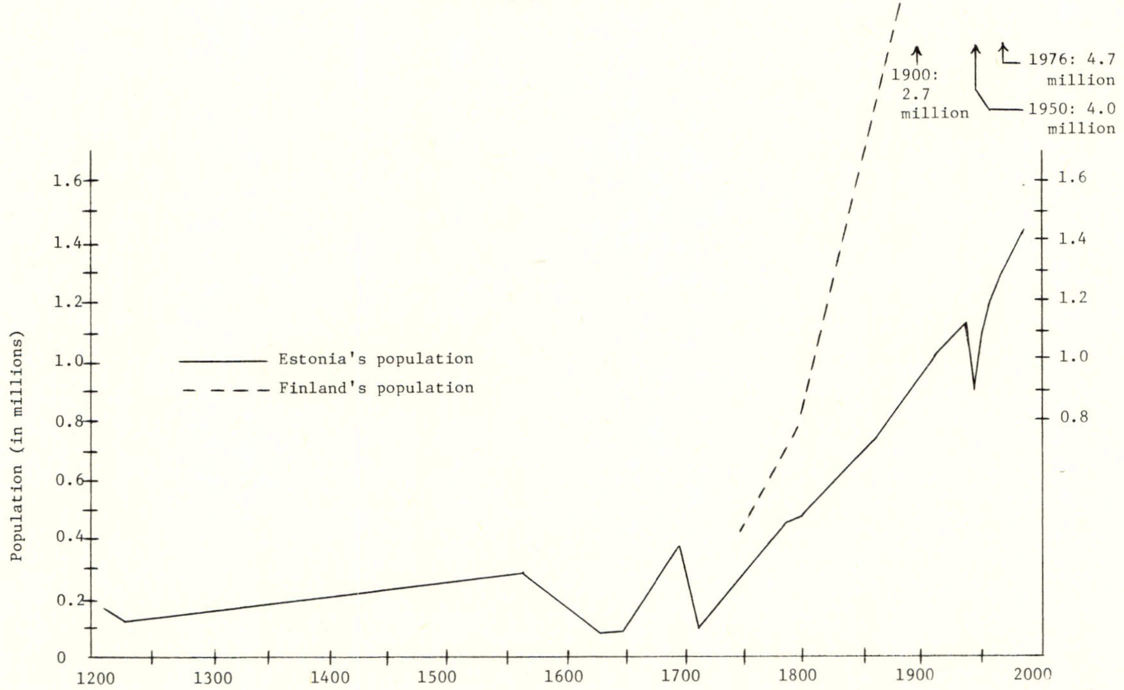

Population Losses, 1939-1949

As a consequence of World War II, especially as a result of the sovietization of society, Estonia suffered severe population losses between 1939 and 1949. These losses were caused by resettlement, deportations, executions, flight, and territorial transfers. These processes, in turn, had a serious effect on the ethnic, social, and age composition of the population.

Soon after the conclusion of the Molotov-Ribbentrop Pact of 1939, which divided northeast Europe into Soviet and German spheres of influence, the two countries reached an agreement for the resettlement of the Baltic German communities. About 13,000 of Estonia's 16,400 Germans thus left Estonia for Germany in the winter of 1939-1940 (Angelus, 1955, 1956; Weiss, 1956; Loeber, 1972). The Germans in Estonia had been primarily concentrated in the upper echelons of society and were especially influential in large economic enterprises and the professions. However, because of wartime conditions and the imminent sovietization of Estonia, the Germans' departure had no serious domestic consequences. A followup resettlement after Estonia's incorporation into the Soviet Union involved about 7,000 people. Of this latter group, about 4,000 were actually ethnic Estonians.

During the German occupation of Estonia (1941-1944), large numbers of another Estonian ethnic group, the Swedes, were officially resettled in Sweden, mostly in 1943-1944 (Aman, 1961; Geijerstam, 1951). Their departure likewise had no great effect on social and economic processes in Estonia. Again, a number of the departing "Swedes" were actually ethnic Estonians—perhaps as many as 2,100 (see Parming, 1972a:55n). While the resettlement of Germans and Swedes increased the demographic importance of the ethnic Estonians in Estonia, this fact had no significance politically or otherwise. The fate of Estonia's Jewish group, numbering 4,400 in 1934, has been largely unexplored. Amitan-Wilensky (1971:347) suggests that 1,000 Estonian Jews remained in Estonia when the Germans occupied the country in 1941 and were thereafter executed by the German authorities. But Kulischer (1943) reported that most of Estonia's Jews fled to the Soviet Union in 1941. Presumably they returned after the war, since in 1959 the Soviet census showed 5,400 Jews in Estonia.

The most significant population loss through forced transfer or politically motivated flight involved the ethnic Estonians, who had comprised 88 percent of the country's population in 1939. Some ethnic Estonians departed for Western countries as early as the winter of 1939-1940, but the first sizable flight took place in 1942-1943, when many fled to Finland to avoid German military service. This flight had involved up to 6,000 people by 1944 (Parming, 1972a:55). Most were men, and they formed a voluntary regiment in the Finnish army (Uustalu and Moora, 1974). A massive flight occurred in the late summer of 1944, when Soviet forces were about to reenter Estonia; this flight appears to have involved about 70,000 people, of whom up to 17,000 perished (Parming, 1972a:55-56). This group of refugees included most of the country's intellectuals, cultural figures, and other societal leaders who had survived the Soviet occupation of 1940-1941 and the German occupation of 1941-1944. However, a study by the Swedish government attests that, except for the high percentage of intellectuals, the refugees were socioeconomically representative of prewar Estonia. At the war's end, almost 100,000 former Estonian citizens were living in Western countries as political refugees who refused to return to Soviet-ruled Estonia.

Executions and deportations of Estonian citizens by Soviet authorities began almost immediately after the annexation of Estonia in mid-1940 and reached their climax in mid-1941. Surveys undertaken immediately after the Soviet departure in 1941 indicate that in one year of Soviet rule about 2,000 Estonian residents were executed for political reasons and another 19,000 were forcibly deported to inner Russia (Parming, 1972a:54). While the executed and deported were generally statistically representative of Estonian society, both socioeconomically and ethnically, the process decimated the ranks of native leaders in all areas of life. Indeed, the generation of national leaders who had founded the Republic of Estonia and overseen its development in the interwar period was virtually annihilated. Additionally, about 33,000 Estonian residents fled to the Soviet Union upon the Soviet withdrawal in 1941 (Parming, 1972a:55). While it seems that most of the latter group returned to Soviet Estonia in late 1944 or 1945, there is little evidence to suggest that many of the deported people survived to return.

Soviet authorities conscripted about 33,000 young Estonian

men into the Red Army in mid-1941. It appears that the
overwhelming majority of them perished in forced-labor
battalions or in the ranks of the Red Army's Estonian Rifle
Corps (Parming, 1972a:54-55). Another 5,600 men who were
transferred intact from the Estonian army to the Red Army in
1940 cannot be considered a population loss; almost all of them
defected to the Germans during the first few battles in 1941,
and after a brief period in German prison camps they returned
to Estonia.

Losses during the German period have never been scruti-
nized. Soviet sources routinely inflate these figures by including Russian prisoners of war and Jews from other countries
who were executed in concentration camps in Estonia by the
German authorities. It may be estimated that about 6,000
Estonians were executed by the Germans between 1941 and
1944; this figure includes local Jews and local Communists
(Parming, 1972a:55). The number of Estonians sent to Germany as industrial and agricultural laborers is unknown but
largely irrelevant, because most reappear in the statistics as
political refugees at the conclusion of the war. About 3,000
Estonians who were forcibly evacuated by retreating German
forces in 1944 returned voluntarily to Estonia, as did a few
hundred refugees, once the war was over (Parming, 1972a:55-
56). Another unknown is the number of Estonian men who
died as volunteers or draftees in German military units,
although a figure of 25,000 might not be an unreasonable
estimate. For example, the line regiments of the Estonian
Legion (the Twentieth Waffen SS Division) were trapped in
Estonia by Soviet encirclement, and the new units formed in
Germany (largely from among refugees) suffered heavy losses
in Silesia and were trapped in Czechoslovakia. There is no
known study of civilian deaths in the war.

A study of Soviet radio broadcasts in late 1944 suggests that
further deportations occurred then and involved approximately 30,000 people (Parming, 1972a:56). However, the single
largest deportation occurred in the spring of 1949 in conjunction with the collectivization of agriculture. Citing a Soviet
Estonian official through third parties, an exiled Estonian
writer reported that the deportation involved 80,000 people
(see Parming, 1972a:57). Elementary-school enrollment data
presented in Parming (1972a:58) substantiate the assertion that
the deportation was sizable. This is further confirmed by recent

comments in volume 4 of the *Estonian Soviet Encyclopedia* under the term *kulak*. The entry states in part that "during the period of collectivization, the kulaks were liquidated; most of the kulaks were sent in 1949 to the farther regions of the Soviet Union" and that in 1939 the kulaks had comprised 13 percent of the farm population. The fact that there were 760,400 rural people in Estonia in 1939 would, indeed, suggest that 80,000 people were deported in 1949.

Deportees were allowed to return to Estonia after Khrushchev's de-Stalinization speech in 1956, but it is not known how many did so, or how many had even survived the harsh conditions of Siberia for so many years. An analysis of population changes between 1939 and 1959 suggests that up to 145,000 ethnic Estonians perished in Estonia or in the Soviet Union as a consequence of Soviet repression or in the Red war machine.

The wartime losses formed an important backdrop for subsequent demographic changes for several reasons. First, the losses included a very large share of the country's upper and middle classes, its professional people and intellectuals. Second, the depopulation process so reduced the number of males in the population that this factor in itself hampered population recovery. Third, the total loss of adults created a labor-force vacuum which subsequently could be eliminated only through immigration. Finally, the depopulation foundations of immigration led to the ethnic restructuring of society. (The vast changes wrought between 1939 and 1959 are reflected in the age structure of ethnic Estonians, as shown in table 5.) In 1934 there were 992,500 ethnic Estonians in Estonia; in 1959 there were 892,700. However, the latter figure includes many Russian-Estonian immigrants from the post-1944 period.[1] By 1970 the number of ethnic Estonians had risen to 925,000, an increase that appears to reflect in part the continuing immigration of Russian-Estonians.

A further population loss was incurred through the administrative transfer of territory from the Estonian SSR to the Russian SFSR in January 1945 (Riismandel, 1953). The transfer included all areas east of the Narva River in the northeast corner of Estonia and most of the former province of Petseri in the southeast corner. While it is true that most of the residents of these areas were Russians, the new border in the southeast hardly followed ethnic settlement patterns. Because maps in Soviet Estonian publications depict the new southeast border in an inconsistent manner, it is difficult to assess the true extent of the territorial and (hence) population losses. On the basis of maps, ethnographic and ethnolinguistic materials, and 1922 and 1934 census results updated for migration, births, and deaths, I would estimate that the transferred areas in 1939 had 71,500 people, of whom 15,800 were ethnic Estonians and almost all of the rest Russians.[2] This, of course, represents a "theoretical population," since no one can ascertain how many of these residents survived the war and resided in their former homes in 1945 nor how many remained there after the transfer.

After the war, however, Estonian population losses were counterbalanced by the immigration of other Soviet people, primarily Russians. Before examining these patterns of immigration, attention must be given to the processes of urbanization.

Urbanization

By 1959 the Estonian SSR was the most urbanized Soviet republic, with 56 percent of the population residing in cities and towns. By 1973 this proportion had risen to 67 percent. While a great deal of Estonia's postwar urbanization reflects the consequences of industrialization, other factors, including historical trends, are also significant. Patterns of urbanization and of the growth of cities are summarized in figure 2 and in tables 1 and 2. These data show that Estonia between 1870 and 1970 experienced a steady rate of urbanization until 1945, at which time there was an abrupt increase in the rate. This accelerated rate has been maintained up to the present time. As is shown in figure 2, the urbanization of ethnic Estonians appears to have progressed at a fairly constant rate, while the urbanization of the total population increased abruptly after the war.

During World War II there was a sharp decline in the urban population for a number of reasons. First, the resettled Germans were primarily an urban group. Second, the Soviet deportations of 1940-1941 influenced urban groups more than the rural population. Third, urban residents were overrepresented among the refugees fleeing westward. Finally, while World War I largely spared Estonia, in terms of major battles

Table 1

Estonia's total, urban and rural population,
1922 - 1976
(at beginning of each year, except as noted, in thousands)

Year	Total population	Urban population	Percent urban	Rural population	Percent rural
1922*	1,107.1	301.6	27.2	805.5	72.8
1934*	1,126.4	349.8	31.1	776.6	68.9
1939**	1,134.4	367.6	32.4	766.8	67.6
1950	1,096.7	516.1	47.1	580.6	52.9
1951	1,104.0	548.4	49.7	555.6	50.3
1952	1,129.8	579.5	51.3	550.3	48.7
1953	1,141.3	599.1	52.5	542.2	47.5
1954	1,150.2	622.0	54.1	528.2	45.9
1955	1,157.3	634.1	54.8	523.2	45.2
1956	1,162.5	640.3	55.1	522.2	44.9
1957	1,174.4	653.1	55.6	521.3	44.4
1958	1,184.7	662.7	55.9	522.0	44.1
1959*	1,196.8	675.5	56.4	521.3	43.6
1960	1,209.1	690.7	57.1	518.4	42.9
1961	1,222.2	709.5	58.1	512.7	41.9
1962	1,236.3	736.6	59.6	499.7	40.4
1963	1,249.8	757.4	60.6	492.4	39.4
1964	1,267.1	776.7	61.3	490.4	38.7
1965	1,284.8	798.0	62.1	486.8	37.9
1966	1,297.3	814.6	62.8	482.7	37.2
1967	1,308.7	828.6	63.3	480.1	36.7
1968	1,319.4	843.3	63.9	476.1	36.1
1969	1,334.3	859.7	64.4	474.6	35.6
1970*	1,356.1	881.2	65.0	474.9	35.0
1971	1,373.9	900.6	65.6	473.3	34.4
1972	1,391.2	920.7	66.2	470.5	33.8
1973	1,405.2	937.5	66.7	467.7	33.3
1974	1,418.0	954.3	67.3	463.7	32.7
1975	1,428.7	968.1	67.8	460.6	32.2
1976	1,438.0	982.4	68.3	455.6	31.7

Notes: *Denotes census counts in 1922 in December, in 1934 in March, and in 1959 and 1970 in January. ** In September.

Sources: For 1922 and 1934: RSK, 1938:5; for 1939: Parming, 1972a:57, 68; for 1950-1973: CSBESSR, 1976:27.

on Estonian soil, World War II did not. The major cities, especially Tallinn, Tartu, and Narva, suffered extensive damage during both the Russian withdrawal in 1940 and the reentry in 1944, a fact that increased the likelihood of civilian casualties. Narva, for example, on the path of major fighting in 1944, was virtually razed; it had been Estonia's third-largest city. According to a Soviet-Estonian writer on the topic

Table 2

Population of selected Estonian cities, 1922 – 1976 (in thousands)

City	1922 (Dec.)	1934 (Mar.)	1939 (Sep.)	1940 (Jan.)	1950 (Jan.)	1959 (Jan.)	1970 (Jan.)	1976 (Jan.)
Tallinn	127.6	152.9	162.9	159.6	212.4	281.7	362.7	407.8
Tartu	50.3	58.9	58.4	58.7	unk.	74.3	90.5	98.7
Narva	26.9	23.5	25.3	24.0	unk.	27.6	57.9	70.6
Pärnu	18.5	20.3	22.6	21.8	unk.	36.1	46.3	49.9
Viljandi	9.4	11.8	12.7	12.9	unk.	17.9	20.8	21.9
Valga	9.5	10.8	10.1	10.4	unk.	13.4	16.8	18.5
Rakvere	7.7	10.0	10.1	10.4	unk.	14.3	17.9	19.3
Võru	5.1	5.3	6.4	6.6	unk.	10.7	15.4	16.5
Haapsalu	4.3	4.6	5.5	4.8	unk.	8.6	11.5	13.3
Kuressaare	3.4	4.5	5.0	4.8	unk.	9.7	12.1	13.5
Tapa	2.4	3.8	3.7	3.8	unk.	8.0	10.0	10.4
Kohtla-Järve	–	–	–	–	unk.	56.1	68.3	71.2
Sillamäe	–	–	–	–	unk.	8.2	13.5	15.5
Kiviõli	–	–	–	–	unk.	10.4	11.2	11.1
Total urban Population	301.6	349.8	367.6	362.7	516.1	675.5	881.2	982.4

Notes: Columns will not yield total urban population because not all urban settlements are shown in the table. The years 1922, 1934, 1959, and 1970 in the table show census figures. The 1922, 1934, 1939, and 1940 figures for Tallinn include the population of Nõmme, a suburb absorbed by Tallinn during the Soviet period. The name Kuressaare was changed after the war to Kingissepa. In 1945 part of the city of Narva, all of the city of Petseri, and several smaller towns in the province of Petseri were in the territory administratively transferred from the Estonian SSR to the Russian SFSR. All figures in the table are for the territorial boundaries existing at the time (that is, the Republic of Estonia in 1922, 1934, 1939, and 1940; the Estonian SSR afterward).

Sources: For 1922-1950: Parming, 1972a:68; for 1950-1973: CSBESSR, 1976:27, 28.

(Kaufmann, 1963), as a consequence of World War II, Estonia's urban population was reduced by up to 38 percent.

In 1922, 27 percent of Estonia's population was urban; by the second census in 1934 this proportion had risen to 31 percent. Demographic data suggest that urbanization was beginning to increase rapidly just before World War II as the economy recovered from the depression and began to shift from an agricultural to an industrial base. For a number of reasons, urban population in Estonia during the interwar years grew as a result of migration from rural areas. The best works on the topic are by Kruus (1920), Kant (1935), and Pullat (1972). It should be noted that the importance of migration to urban population growth has been retained up to the present time. The contemporary increase in urban areas is due largely to the postwar immigrants.

The four major determinants of urban population growth since 1945 have been collectivization, economic reorganization, administrative expansion, and immigration. The last three factors are closely interrelated. The full impact of collectivization on urbanization has not been analyzed in Soviet Estonia, and it is impossible to do so in the West because of the inadequacy of available data. Yet one finds frequent suggestions in Soviet Estonian sources that "agricultural reorganization" during the first five postwar years stimulated migration to towns and cities, a suggestion supported by the accounts of postwar refugees and tourists. Indeed, since postwar immigration alone cannot have accounted for the very sharp increase in the urban population between 1945 and 1950, collectivization—carried out in a very brutal manner within the space of a few months—must have had some impact.

Economic reorganization from an agricultural to an industrial base (as described by Järvesoo in chapter 4 of this book) has provided both pull and push factors of a traditional nature. Thus, in the Soviet intercensus period 1959-1970, 19 percent of urban population growth was due to migration from rural to urban areas (Parming, 1972b:53). As has been the case elsewhere in the world, urban migration has drained the rural areas of young adults. For example in 1959, among ethnic Estonians, 42.7 percent of the rural population were aged 45 or older; the figure was 34.1 percent for the urban population. At the same time, 38.2 percent of the urban residents were aged 20-44, while the comparative figure for rural residents was

28.2 percent. Indeed, although the total rural population was larger than the urban population (474,354 to 418,255), in the 20-44 age group the opposite was true (159,598 to 133,811). (See age-structure tables for 1959 in Parming, 1972a:69.) That these trends have persevered into the 1960s is suggested by 1970 census data.

As shown by Parming (1972a:69), the age structure of the urban population for the non-Estonians follows the same pattern as that for the ethnic Estonians. One of the consequences of these patterns of migration and immigration is that, during the last fifteen years or so, natural increase has been greater in the cities than in rural areas (Vissak, 1967). However, this finding is entirely due to the different age structures of the urban and rural populations, Age-specific birth rates remain higher in the rural areas.

The administrative expansion of cities included both municipal boundary extensions and major economic reorganization. While the oil-shale basin in northeast Estonia (between Narva and Rakvere) had a very small population in 1939, by 1959 the newly created cities there (Kohtla-Järve, Sillamäe, and Kiviõli) contained 74,700 people, or 11 percent of all of Estonia's urban residents. This increase reflects the vast expansion of the oil-shale industry in the region after the war. The growth of cities has also involved the extension of municipal boundaries. Tallinn, for example, absorbed not only small suburbs after the war but also the formerly separate city of Nômme, prewar Estonia's fifth-largest city. However, administrative expansion has appreciably decreased in importance as a factor in the growth of the urban population. During the intercensus period (1959-1970), the administrative expansion of municipal boundaries accounted for only 4 percent of the urban population increase (Parming, 1972b:53). No new towns or cities have been created for some time.

Without question, immigration has been the single most important factor in Estonia's urban population growth since World War II. (I refer here to population movement directly from outside the Estonian SSR into its cities, a movement covered in greater detail later in this chapter.) As figure 2 suggests, such movement must have been influential in urban growth in the immediate postwar years. This trend was first confirmed by 1959 census data which indicated that, while non-Estonians constituted 25 percent of the population of the

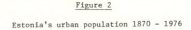

Figure 2

Estonia's urban population 1870 - 1976

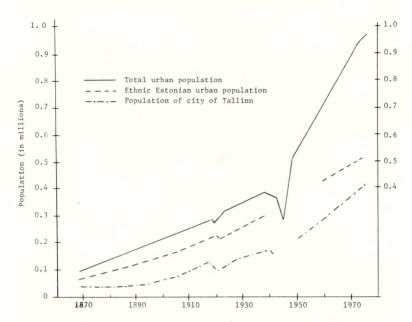

Estonian SSR, they accounted for 38 percent of its urban population. Data from 1959 further show that ethnic Estonians were 47 percent urban and non-Estonians were 85 percent urban (see Parming, 1972a:63-65, tables). In 1970 non-Estonians comprised 32 percent of the total population, and 42 percent of the urban population. Estonians in 1970 were 54 percent urban; non-Estonians were 88 percent urban.

The immigrants are concentrated in the urban areas between Tallinn and Narva along the northern coast. As Laas (1963) puts it, "the representatives of our brotherly peoples who have arrived in our country have settled mostly in the northern and northeastern cities." The *Estonian Soviet Encyclopedia*, vol. 2 (ENE, 1970:72), points out that of Tallinn's population in 1959, 60 percent were ethnic Estonians. In 1934 this figure had been 86 percent (RSK, 1938:24)—a percentage which would have appreciably increased by 1945 because of the departure during the war years of most of Estonia's Germans and Jews, since both groups had been highly concentrated in Tallinn's population of 162,900 in 1939. Intercensus data (1959-1970) show that virtually all of the immigrants moved directly into the urban centers, accounting for fully 45 percent of all urban growth during the period (Parming, 1972b:53).

Natural increase provided 32 percent of the urban growth during the intercensus years (Parming, 1972b:53). It is important to remember that this growth pattern is largely attributable to the presence of the immigrants, who are mostly young adults, and who marry earlier and tend to bear more children per family than do ethnic Estonians. While 1959 census data indicated that only 25 percent of the total population was non-Estonian, in the urban population this proportion was 38 percent, and in the key reproductive age group in the urban areas (20-34) it varied from 44 percent to 48 percent (Parming, 1972a:63, table). The differentials in Estonian and non-Estonian age structures, marital patterns, and fertility rates have had an obvious impact; in the urban age group 0-9 in 1959, half of the children were non-Estonian. Since the non-Estonians are concentrated on the northern coast, if contemporary elementary-school enrollment data were available, controlled for ethnicity, in all probability they would show that in most northern cities non-Estonian children are a majority; in the oil-shale basin and in Narva, it is quite likely that the ethnic Estonian child would be an exception altogether.

Immigration

In 1939 Estonia's population totaled 1,133,917. Given known losses during the period 1939-1945, it may be estimated that in early 1945 there were about 830,000 people in the present territorial area of the Estonian SSR. Volume 2 of the recent *Estonian Soviet Encyclopedia* places this figure at 854,000 (ENE, 1970:69).[3] Official Soviet data for 1950 show 1,096,700 people in the Estonian SSR. In making a direct comparison of 1945 and 1950 data, if we take into account the deportation of 80,000 people in 1949, we can see that the increase in population between 1945 and 1950 was sizable.

Some of this increase can be attributed to the return of emigrés and deportees, the relocation of former inhabitants of territory transferred to the Russian SFSR in 1945, and the increase in the birth rate during the five-year period 1945-1949 (see table 8). However, even liberal estimates of these three factors leave a sizable percentage of the increase unexplained. Most of the population increase of the first five postwar years was due, in fact, to immigration. On the basis of incomplete data, it may be estimated that about 180,000 immigrants were involved. The fact that the immigrants were mostly in the fertile age groups provides another reason for the large postwar increase in the birth rate.

Several factors preclude a full analysis of this early immigration, given the lack of available data. Both the exact fate and the statistical treatment of the approximately 129,000 deportees from 1940 to 1949 remain unknown.[4] Moreover, up to 180,000 ethnic Estonians were living permanently in the Soviet Union prior to World War II; it is impossible to ascertain how many of the postwar immigrants came from this group. Thus, it is unknown whether the 96,000 ethnic Estonians reported to have been living in the Soviet Union outside the Estonian SSR in 1959 (the number was 82,000 in 1970) represent remnants of the deportees and their offspring or remnants of the prewar ethnic Estonian population of the Soviet Union and their offspring.

From 1950 onward, either official data are available for immigration or they are readily calculable from other data. Net migration in Estonia for the period 1920-1970, with comparative figures for natural increase, is summarized in table 3. That the postwar immigrants are largely non-Estonian is discernible from a comparison of the ethnic composition of the population in Estonia during three census years: 1934, 1959, and 1970. Since the basis of determining ethnicity has remained more or less constant (individual choice—or, for a child under legal age, the father's ethnicity), such a comparison provides a fairly honest picture of change. The applicable data are presented in table 4. In controlling the 1934 population for the present territorial area of the Estonian SSR and comparing this figure to 1959 and 1970 census data, the most remarkable difference, other than the decrease in the number of Estonians, is the phenomenal increase in the number of Russians—from 41,700 in 1934 to 240,000 in 1959 and 335,000 in 1970. Also noteworthy is the increase in the number of Ukrainians and White Russians. Some of the growth in the Russian population undoubtedly represents the relocation of people who formerly inhabited the northeast corner of Estonia, which was trans-

Table 3

Natural increase and net migration in Estonia
1920 - 1975

Year	Natural increase	Net migration	Year	Natural increase	Net migration
1920	-10,300	unk.	1950	4,500	2,800
1921	- 1,700	19,300	1951	5,400	20,400
1922	4,900	16,300	1952	5,300	6,200
1923	3,900	5,500	1953	5,700	3,200
1924	5,700	1,700	1954	6,900	200
1925	4,500	- 400	1955	7,100	-1,900
1926	3,800	- 3,200	1956	6,900	5,000
1927	1,900	- 2,900	1957	6,500	3,800
1928	300	- 1,800	1958	6,600	5,500
1929	2,300	- 700	1959	6,800	5,500
1930	- 1,100	- 700	1960	7,400	5,700
1931	2,900	- 200	1961	7,200	6,900
1932	1,400	500	1962	6,500	7,000
1933	3,100	1,300	1963	6,000	11,300
1934	1,700	- 700	1964	6,900	10,800
1935	1,500	100	1965	5,400	7,100
1936	1,000	800	1966	4,800	6,600
1937	600	- 300	1967	5,000	5,700
1938	1,600	- 600	1968	5,600	9,300
1939	2,000	800	1969	5,600	16,200
1940	1,500	-13,400	1970	6,400	11,400
1941	- 1,000	- 4,100	1971	7,100	10,200
1942	- 6,000	-93,200	1972	6,200	7,800
1943	- 1,100	- 1,000	1973	5,700	7,100
1944	- 3,500	-13,200	1974	6,100	4,600
1945	unk.	-70,000	1975	4,800	4,500
1946-1949	unk.	unk.			

Data Sources: Parming, 1972a:57; CSBESSR, 1976:28, 30; [compare
this to data in Parming, 1972a:60].

ferred to the Russian SFSR in 1945. However, most of the
population in the transferred territories resided in the southeast corner of Estonia, and private sources of information
indicate that there was no sizable movement of population
from that area into Estonia proper, of either ethnic Estonians
or Russians. Even if all of the population in the transferred
territories had been relocated in Estonia, the increase in
Estonia's Russian population through immigration remains
dramatic.

Table 4

Ethnic composition of Estonia's population
1934 - 1970

Ethnic group	1934a	1934b	1959	1970
Estonians	992,520	977,200	892,653	925,157
Russians	92,656	41,700	240,227	334,620
Latvians	5,435	4,000	2,888	unk.
Germans	16,346		–	–
Swedes	7,641		–	–
Jews	4,434		5,436	5,288
Poles	1,608		2,256	unk.
Finns	1,088		16,699	18,537
Ingrians	841		–	–
Ukrainians	–	34,600	15,769	28,086
Byelorussians	–		10,930	18,732
Tatars	–		1,535	unk.
Lithuanians	–		1,616	unk.
Other/unknown	3,844		6,782	25,659
Totals	1,126,413	1,057,500	1,196,791	1,356,079

Notes: The 1934a data are Estonian census figures for the territorial
area of the Republic of Estonia; the 1934b data are the former adjusted
for the territorial area of the Estonian SSR by the writer. The 1959
and 1970 data are Soviet census figures. In Soviet population statistics,
Ingrians are classified as Finns. During the period 1941-1944 about
16,000 Ingrians from the Soviet Union proper resettled in Estonia.

Sources: For 1934a, 1959: Parming, 1972a:61; for 1970: CSBUSSR, 1973:15.

As the data in table 3 indicate, immigration was highest in
the early 1950s, in the first half of the 1960s, and after 1968. The
most important cause of immigration is probably related to
industrialization and the size of the local labor force (see
Parming, 1977a). Soviet executions, deportations, and military mobilizations of 1940-1949 involved about 164,000 people, and the politically motivated flight westward another
117,000. To these losses in population must be added military
and civilian war casualties. It is obvious that the loss of
population in relation to total prewar population size was
extremely high. The rapid postwar industrialization created a
vast demand for labor which could hardly be met from inside
Estonia, under the circumstances.

The oil-shale industry is reported to have been initially
developed by German prisoners of war. Yet its full expansion,
as was the case with other areas of industry, was completed

only through the utilization of imported or migrating Russian workers. The ethnic Estonians, given their high educational level, would in any case have been unlikely to fill the working-class positions. As it was, the first deportations and the political flight depleted the ranks of the professional, technical, and white-collar labor force, thus permitting rapid upward occupational mobility for the remaining natives. This upward mobility was further stimulated by industrialization, which created thousands of new positions requiring managerial, technical, or other white-collar skills and an expanded educational apparatus to provide training in these skills. Hence, the immigrants filled the lower industrial positions, and, as most commentators have noted, the very highest positions as well. The middle ground remained the domain of the natives.

It is beyond the scope of this chapter to explore the question of whether or not industrialization was undertaken by Moscow to stimulate labor movement and hence to facilitate demographic Russification. While such a theory is plausible, it must be also kept in mind that before the war Estonia was already importing seasonal labor from Poland and Lithuania because of a labor shortage. Yet the present level of industrialization should have been possible with native population resources, had World War II not interrupted the society. In 1939 Estonia had 1,134,000 people, a level that was not reached again until mid-1952. In the absence of large-scale immigration, given the likelihood of a small postwar baby boom, Estonia's population in the mid-1960s probably would have achieved the same level as a result of natural growth. Most Western newsmen visiting Estonia have noted that the sizable immigration of Russians irritates the natives appreciably. Moreover, an intriguing issue has been raised by ethnic Estonians in contemporary Soviet Estonia: Why have the authorities not facilitated the immigration of Mordvians and Karelians, two Finno-Ugric peoples in the Soviet Union closely related to the Estonians, instead of Russians? An overview of the natives' attitudes on immigration is provided by Parming (1976); see also Küng (1973).

The most remarkable demographic characteristic of the immigrants is their age composition. The predominance of young adults has resulted in a very high rate of natural increase, because of high age-specific birth rates and low age-specific death rates. That most of the immigrants are in the fertile age groups is evidenced by several factors. For example, a Soviet Estonian official noted in 1967 that almost all the immigrants were of working age (Allik, 1967). Even more convincing proof of this fact is found in the comparison of the age structures of Estonians and non-Estonians in 1959 and 1970 in table 5.

That immigration cease is a desire often expressed by Soviet Estonians. However, whether this will occur is another matter. As data in table 3 indicated, immigration has varied so much from year to year that predictions are difficult. Although immigration slackened during 1967 and early 1968, leading to optimism both in the West and in the Estonian SSR, 1969 turned out to be the second-greatest year of immigration since 1950 (after 1951), and 1970 ranked third. Indeed, the five-year period 1968-1972 saw the largest sustained influx of immigration since the immediate postwar period.

Many observers have begun to point out that since the Russian rate of natural population increase, because of lower fertility, is not as high as it once was, fewer Russians will be available to migrate anywhere because of labor shortages in the Russian SFSR. However, such a viewpoint ignores several important considerations. First, although a situation is developing that might dictate the general unavailability of people for migration, this does not preclude population movement to specific localities. Second, it must be kept in mind that the Soviet Union has a very inefficient pattern of labor utilization for an advanced industrial country. While concern has been expressed by Soviet authorities in recent years about a declining rural labor force, this is a relative matter. The Soviet system of agriculture and agricultural productivity necessitates maintaining a sizable rural labor force merely in order to feed the society. The same conditions prevail in industry. If economic and managerial reforms—which at times are discussed and which sometimes are implemented experimentally—are ever undertaken, the Soviet Union will find itself with a large labor surplus, which can, of course, be redirected to any part of the country.

A third and major factor that will influence the size of the labor force available for relocation in the future is related to the manner in which the population explosion in Central Asia will be resolved. The first birth-cohorts of this regional baby boom, which is not unlike the growth of third-world countries, will imminently begin to enter the labor force. The local economy,

Table 5

Age structure of the Soviet Estonian population in 1959 and 1970
(in thousands)

Age group	1959						Percent Estonian at age level
	Ethnic Estonians		Non- Estonians		Total Population		
	Number	%	Number	%	Number	%	
0 - 9	126.2	14.1	63.0	20.7	189.2	15.8	67
10 - 19	128.3	14.4	40.0	13.2	168.3	14.1	76
20 - 29	132.5	14.8	69.3	22.8	201.8	16.9	66
30 - 39	114.5	12.8	59.5	19.6	174.0	14.5	66
40 - 49	109.2	12.2	31.0	10.2	140.2	11.7	78
50 - 59	121.4	13.6	20.8	6.8	142.2	11.9	85
60+	160.5	18.0	20.4	6.7	180.9	15.1	89
Totals	892.6	100%	304.1	100%	1,196.7	100%	75

Notes: *These figures are approximations, because the 1970
Soviet census gave the age breakdown for ethnic Estonians
in the Estonian SSR by age groups 0-10 and 11-19. Adjustments
by writer. Figures in the "number" columns will not yield
"Totals" shown, and percentage columns will not yield 100%
because of rounding. In the Soviet 1970 census data the
number of ethnic Estonians shown by age group does not yield

as it is currently organized, will not be able to absorb large
numbers of new workers. It is not likely that the Soviet Union
will make major capital allocations to this region for industrial
expansion because of its proximity to China. There remain two
possibilities of labor migration: Russians who have moved or
been sent to the area might be withdrawn in order to make
positions available for the natives, or the natives can emigrate.
In any case, the Soviet Union faces an emerging dilemma of
major proportions because of this situation, and its resolution
could easily lead to some type of labor migration.

A Moscow decision which in the long run should act to slow
down immigration in Estonia involves capital allocations for
industry. The most recent economic plans have foreseen a

Table 5

Age structure of the Soviet Estonian population in 1959 and 1970 (in thousands)

1970						
Ethnic Estonians		Non-Estonians		Total Population		Percent Estonian at age level
Number	%	Number	%	Number	%	
*132.6	14.3	*65.5	15.2	198.1	14.6	*67
*127.1	13.7	*73.9	17.2	201.0	14.8	*63
122.8	13.3	72.7	16.9	195.5	14.4	63
132.1	14.3	82.6	19.2	214.7	15.8	62
116.8	12.6	67.7	15.7	184.5	13.6	63
99.5	10.8	33.0	7.7	132.5	9.8	75
194.3	21.0	35.4	8.2	229.7	16.9	85
925.2	100%	430.9	100%	1,356.1	100%	68

the total given. I have assumed that the census "total" is correct and made a small adjustment (1,800) in the 60+ age group.

Data Sources: Parming, 1972a:63; CSBUSSR, 1972a:72-73; 1973:382.

slowdown in Baltic industrial expansion, which fact should slow immigration by reducing the need for new industrial labor. Yet some immigration will continue, given the attractions of Estonia's Western culture and high standard of living.

Whatever the future immigration pattern, Estonia's ethnic structure has been extensively altered during the Soviet period. It must be kept in mind that immigration was nearly as large as natural increase between 1950 and 1959 (50,700 and 61,700, respectively) and even larger between 1960 and 1969 (86,600 vs. 60,400). From 1970 to 1972 immigration was again greater than natural increase, 29,400 to 19,700. Indeed, since 1962 immigration has exceeded the natural increase during every year. For the period 1950-1972 as a whole, immigration has

Table 6

Marriage per 1,000 females in fertile
age groups in Soviet Estonia in 1959

	16-19	20-24	25-29	30-34	35-39	40-44	45-49
Total population	52	410	711	757	734	622	596
Ethnic Estonians	42	367	668	721	712	653	599
Russians	81	496	791	818	781	688	594

Source: Parming, 1972a:71.

outrun natural increase 166,700 to 141,800. Furthermore, as the following section of this chapter demonstrates, the fact that Estonians and non-Estonians in the Estonian SSR have appreciably different rates of natural increase works to the Estonians' disadvantage.

Factors Influencing Population Growth

There are cogent demographic reasons for separating ethnic Estonians from non-Estonians in analyzing fertility in the Estonian SSR. The most overriding consideration concerns the significant difference in age structures noted earlier (table 5). The second major reason deals with marriage patterns, shown in the data for 1959 in table 6. (Unfortunately these data are not presently available for 1970.) Clearly, Russian women marry at an earlier age and at a greater rate than Estonians, especially during the key fertile ages 20 to 39. Age-specific birth rates are given in table 7. (Again, such data are presently unavailable for 1970.) A hidden but very important consequence of differential marriage patterns is reflected in the fact that, while non-Estonians constituted 25 percent of both the total and female populations of the Estonian SSR in 1959, non-Estonian females made up 39 percent of all married women between the ages of 20 and 39 (Parming, 1972a:72). Marriage is an important variable here because most of the children are born in wedlock.

Table 8 summarizes historical and contemporary data on vital rates and natural increase in Estonia. It appears that, in

Table 7

Age-specific birth rates for women of fertile ages in
Soviet Estonia, 1958 - 1959

Age group	Birth rate	Age group	Birth rate
15 - 19	20.1	35 - 39	41.9
20 - 24	122.3	40 - 44	12.0
25 - 29	119.1	45 - 49	0.9
30 - 34	72.9		

Source: Parming, 1972a:71.

regard to fertility, the Estonians had completed the demographic transition prior to extensive industrialization. Figure 1
suggests that the reason for the declining rates must be sought
in the eighteenth and nineteenth centuries, when the area was
officially under czarist administration but was in fact ruled by a
local Baltic German elite. While such an examination is
beyond the scope of this chapter, it should be kept in mind that
many of the social factors which bear on fertility, especially
those related to family formation, date back to this period.
Thus, a low rate of marriage and a high average age of marriage
for females are cultural patterns inherited by the ethnic Estonians of the Estonian SSR from earlier times.

Four important demographic trends which bear either on
population growth in general or on fertility in particular, and
which directly reflect changes during the Soviet period, are the
reduction of the infant death rate, the general increase in life
expectancy, the emergence of a very high divorce rate, and the
prevalence of abortion as a birth-control method. The decrease
in infant death rates (see table 9) and the increase in longevity
(table 10) clearly reflect the general improvements in health
conditions, better access to medical care, and higher standard
of living effected during the last two decades of Soviet rule in
Estonia.

A brief examination of the divorce rate is pertinent. The
Estonians are the least-married ethnic group in the Soviet
Union (Mereste, 1969); thus a high divorce rate could easily
bear on fertility, given the fact that most children are born in

Table 8

Births, deaths, natural increase and vital
rates in Estonia   1880 - 1975

Year	Births	Crude birth rate	Deaths	Crude death rate	Natural increase	Rate of natural increase
1880-1884	–	31.7	–	22.4	–	9.3
1897-1899	–	29.1	–	19.3	–	9.8
1901-1908	–	28.0	–	19.1	–	7.9
1910-1914	–	25.0	–	18.6	–	6.4
1915-1919	–	19.3	–	25.1	–	-5.8
1919	18,456	17:3	28,800	27.0	-10,344	-9.7
1920	19,625	18.4	21,363	20.0	- 1,738	-1.6
1921	22,067	20.3	17,143	15.8	4,924	4.5
1922	22,255	20.2	18,401	16.7	3,854	3.5
1923	22,347	20.1	16,630	15.0	5,717	5.1
1924	21,441	19.2	16,918	15.2	4,523	4.0
1925	20,445	18.3	16,680	14.9	3,765	3.4
1926	19,977	17.9	18,047	16.2	1,930	1.7
1927	19,705	17.7	19,356	17.4	349	0.3
1928	20,064	18.0	17,785	16.0	2,279	2.0
1929	19,110	17.1	20,178	18.1	- 1,068	-1.0
1930	19,471	17.4	16,610	14.9	2,861	2.5
1931	19,509	17.4	18,077	16.1	1,432	1.3
1932	19,742	17.6	16,641	14.8	3,101	2.8
1933	18,208	16.2	16,472	14.7	1,736	1.5
1934	17,305	15.4	15,853	14.1	1,452	1.3
1935	17,891	15.8	16,864	14.9	1,027	0.9
1936	18,222	16.1	17,594	15.6	628	0.5
1937	18,190	16.1	16,614	14.7	1,576	1.4
1938	18,453	16.3	16,496	14.6	1,957	1.7
1939	18,450	16.3	16,940	15.0	1,510	1.3
1940	18,000	16.1	19,000	17.0	- 1,000	-0.9
1941	16,000	15.0	22,000	20.6	- 6,000	-5.6
1942	18,993	18.7	20,097	19.8	- 1,104	-1.1
1943	16,000	15.9	19,500	19.4	- 3,500	-3.5
1944	unk.	unk.	unk.	unk.	unk.	unk.
1945-1949	unk.	20.6	unk.	unk.	unk.	unk.

Table 8

Births, deaths, natural increase and vital
rates in Estonia 1880 - 1975

Year	Births	Crude birth rate	Deaths	Crude death rate	Natural increase	Rate of natural increase
1950	20,279	18.4	15,817	14.4	4,462	4.0
1951	20,730	18.6	15,354	13.7	5,376	4.9
1952	21,111	18.6	15,817	13.9	5,294	4.7
1953	20,146	17.6	14,420	12.6	5,726	5.0
1954	20,909	18.1	13,981	12.1	6,928	6.0
1955	20,786	17.9	13,638	11.7	7,148	6.2
1956	19,660	16.8	12,783	10.9	6,877	5.9
1957	19,509	16.5	13,026	11.0	6,483	5.5
1958	19,598	16.5	12,971	10.9	6,627	5.6
1959	19,938	16.6	13,130	10.9	6,808	5.7
1960	20,187	16.6	12,738	10.5	7,449	6.1
1961	20,230	16.5	13,036	10.6	7,194	5.9
1962	19,959	16.1	13,495	10.9	6,464	5.2
1963	19,275	15.3	13,251	10.5	6,024	4.8
1964	19,629	15.4	12,754	10.0	6,875	5.4
1965	18,909	14.6	13,520	10.5	5,389	4.1
1966	18,629	14.3	13,800	10.6	4,829	3.7
1967	18,671	14.2	13,699	10.4	4,972	3.8
1968	19,782	14.9	14,225	10.7	5,557	4.2
1969	20,781	15.5	15,150	11.3	5,631	4.2
1970	21,552	15.8	15,186	11.1	6,366	4.7
1971	22,118	16.0	15,038	10.9	7,080	5.1
1972	21,757	15.6	15,520	11.1	6,237	4.5
1973	21,239	15.0	15,573	11.0	5,666	4.0
1974	21,461	15.1	15,393	10.8	6,068	4.3
1975	21,360	14.9	16,572	11.6	4,788	3.3

Data Sources: Parming, 1972b:48; Parming, 1972a:57-58; Palli, 1968;
CSBESSR, 1976:30, 31 [compare this data to Parming, 1972a:60].

Table 9

Infant death rate in Estonia 1922 - 1972

Year	Death rate	Year	Death rate
1922–1924	119.1	1965	20.2
1925–1929	108.4	1966	20.0
1930–1934	97.2	1967	19.2
1935–1939	85.1	1968	18.3
1955–1959	40.9	1969	16.9
1960–1964	27.1	1970	17.8
		1971	17.6
		1972	15.8

Data Sources: Parming, 1972b:53; CSBESSR, 1973:37.

Table 10

Life-table life expectancy in Estonia
1932 - 1934 and 1965 - 1966

Age	Men		Women	
	1932–1934	1965–1966	1932–1934	1965–1966
0	58	66	64	74
10	52	58	58	66
20	44	49	50	56
30	36	40	42	46
40	28	35	34	37
50	21	23	25	28
60	14	16	17	19
70	9	10	11	12
80	5	5	6	6

Data Source: Parming, 1972a:76.

wedlock. Indeed, the relationship between family dissolution and fertility could be strong, since 21 percent of the divorces in 1959-1960 and 26 percent of those in 1966-1967 involved couples married less than four years, an important period in family history in terms of procreation (Mereste, 1969). Data on the divorce and marriage rates are summarized in table 11. It would appear from these figures that Soviet Estonia has one of the highest divorce rates in the world.

Table 11

Marriages and divorces in Estonia 1930 - 1975

Year	Number of marriages	Number of divorces	Marriages per 1000 people	Divorces per 1000 people	Divorces per 100 marriages
1930	8,897	697	8.0	0.6	7.8
1933	8,425	766	7.5	0.7	9.1
1940	10,182	1,186	9.6	1.1	11.6
1950	10,456	671	9.5	0.6	6.4
1951	10,103	763	9.0	0.7	7.6
1952	9,484	944	8.4	0.8	10.0
1953	9,738	783	8.5	0.7	8.0
1954	11,083	1,104	9.6	1.0	10.0
1955	11,927	1,434	10.3	1.2	12.0
1956	12,354	1,589	10.6	1.4	12.9
1957	13,088	2,117	11.1	1.8	16.2
1958	12,655	2,528	10.6	2.1	20.0
1959	12,101	2,404	10.1	2.0	19.9
1960	12,146	2,544	10.0	2.1	20.9
1961	11,924	2,512	9.7	2.0	21.1
1962	11,054	2,532	8.9	2.0	22.9
1963	10,933	2,771	8.7	2.2	25.3
1964	10,821	3,133	8.5	2.5	29.0
1965	10,567	2,966	8.2	2.3	28.1
1966	11,272	4,149	8.7	3.2	36.8
1967	11,578	4,187	8.8	3.2	36.2
1968	11,858	4,164	8.9	3.1	35.1
1969	12,247	4,417	9.1	3.3	36.1
1970	12,373	4,379	9.1	3.2	35.4
1971	12,514	4,354	9.1	3.1	34.8
1972	11,794	4,632	8.4	3.3	39.3
1973	12,200	4,554	8.6	3.2	37.3
1974	12,277	4,740	8.6	3.3	38.6
1975	12,443	4,845	8.7	3.4	38.9

Data Sources: Tomberg, 1935:261; CSBESSR, 1973:35; 1975:30.

The rapid rise in divorces does not reflect a changing legal structure; obtaining a divorce in Estonia has been relatively easy for fifty years or so. Rather, Soviet Estonian researchers of the phenomenon suggest that the two most important factors are the high rate of female employment and the housing shortage. The former presumably leads to a conflict between marital and occupational roles, as happens elsewhere in the contemporary industrialized world. However, a more important cause of family strain is the critical housing shortage, which continues to the present day. To find a one-room apartment housing a couple or a whole family is not atypical, especially in the cities. Often even this small space is shared by a couple with parents or other relatives. Theoretically, it might be concluded that the traditional Estonian neolocal nuclear family has been forced into an extended-family mold, with the resulting structural strains finding release in divorce.

Divorce is increasingly viewed as a major social problem (along with alcoholism) by local social-science observers and the press because of its impact on adults, children, and the whole society. In regard to the society as a whole, two important negative consequences are low fertility and neglect in child rearing. The latter is seen as a cause of delinquency and of other social behavior judged undesirable. A few years ago, for example, a University of Tartu psychiatric medicine textbook discussed problems related to adult sex life in single-room apartments inhabited also by children or other relatives. More recently, in the late 1960s and early 1970s, a study group at the University of Tartu compiled a 194-page book entitled *Pere-konnaprobleemid* [Family Problems, 1972], a collection of research papers based on an extensive survey of 984 women obtaining abortions in Tartu. The first sentence of the book states: "The family is the basic cell of society." The cover depicts a couple with three children.

During the last few years, several books on sex and family life have been written in or translated into Estonian. Medical candidate Hubert Kahn's *Abielu tervishoiust* [On Marital Health], which appeared in 1970, is a good example of the former type of work. While Kahn's book, too, emphasizes that the family is the basic cell of society, it additionally deals with the psychosocial significance of the institution. Kahn's 128-page work, the first on this topic ever published in Soviet Estonia, covers such subjects as the physiology of sex, marital hygiene, fecundity and pregnancy, birth control, sexual problems, sexual perversions, and venereal disease. Fifty thousand copies were printed—a very large quantity in a society with only 255,000 Estonian-speaking adults between the ages of 20 and 39.

An even more widely printed work (80,000 copies) was the 1974 abbreviated translation from Finnish of *Sukupuo-lielämän tietokirja*, which appeared under the title *Avameelselt abielust* [Frankly about Marriage]. It is, in fact, a 221-page marital handbook. The first section focuses on sex and marriage, covering such topics as the physiological development of the sexes, menstruation, masturbation, foreplay, and pregnancy. The second section is devoted to the regulation of birth, the third to extramarital sexual activities, the fourth to sexual problems, and the fifth to sexual deviance and perversion. The appearance of such works during the last several years, in addition to many articles in the press, indicates not only a concern about family formation and stability but also a determination to resolve family-related problems.

Yet one of the major causes of both family problems and lowered fertility is beyond the control of the commentators; namely, the housing shortage. The importance of this factor emerges in studies dealing with abortion. Two major abortion studies have been published in Soviet Estonia during the past decade. The first was conducted in the early 1960s in Tallinn by Roosileht (1968), and the more recent by a study group at the University of Tartu in the late 1960s (Blumfeldt, et al., 1972). Because the main conclusions of the two studies are similar, the material here is drawn from the more recent one. (See Parming, 1977b, for a discussion of abortion.)

The Tartu study provides all type of data on abortion, including the reasons why women have abortions. It should be noted, first of all, that since abortion was legalized in 1955 (Roosileht, 1968) and made available on demand, it has become a leading birth-control method. Of the 984 women who sought abortions in the Tartu study, 40 percent of the married urban women and 24 percent of the married rural women had terminated their first pregnancies by abortion (Tiit and Kornet, 1972:147). Of the unmarried women, 80 percent had terminated their first pregnancies through abortion. Table 12 provides some data on the extent to which abortion serves as a birth-control method in the study sample. The prevalence of abortion undoubtedly reflects the unavailability of other birth-control devices, even though the Kahn book discusses such methods as IUDs, condoms, and pills. For the women interviewed, abortion represented a conscious decision not to have a child or another child. The reason most frequently cited by women as to why they were resorting to abortion was the smallness of their living quarters; for women who already had one or more children, this became the overriding consideration

Table 12

Number of abortions reported by women
in Tartu who sought abortions between 1967 and 1969

First abortion	31.8%
Second	24.8
Third	18.3
Fourth	10.0
Fifth	6.4
Sixth or more	8.7

Data Sources: Tiit and Kornet, 1972:150
[based on survey of 984 women seeking abortions].

(Kornet, 1972:166, 168). The study revealed that the living
space for the modal subject was only four to six square meters
(Tiit and Kornet, 1972:146). Of the urban women in the study,
10 percent shared a room, 53 percent lived in a single room,
24.5 percent had two rooms, and only 17 percent had more
space than this (Kornet, 1972:169). About two-thirds of the
married couples aged 20-25 had less than seven square meters
of living space per person (Astel, Kornet, and Tiit, 1972:215-
216). The latter authors insist that for the three-child family
there must be more than thirty square meters of living space—a
far cry from existing conditions.

Among other important factors influencing the decision to
abort were the unavailability of child-care centers, inadequate
family income, and unmarried status. Fully 53 percent of the
women surveyed did not want to stay home but wanted to
continue working (Kornet, 1972:171). (It is plausible that if
Estonian women withdrew in large numbers from the labor
force, this would enhance the demand for immigrant labor,
since most Estonian adults are either employed or in school.)
The women surveyed also had a lower average income than
that reported by Tartu women in general (Astel, Kornet, and
Tiit, 1972:235). According to the latter source, another factor
might be that sexual activity for females begins, on the average,
almost two years before marriage.

Table 13

Sizes of selected age groups of ethnic Estonians
in Estonia, 1934, 1959 and 1970

Age	Males		Females		Total		
group	1934	1959	1934	1959	1934	1959	1970
10-19	71,200	64,500	69,600	63,800	140,900	128,300	127,100
20-29	88,900	64,800	88,500	67,700	177,700	132,500	122,800
30-39	70,800	48,900	81,700	65,600	151,900	114,500	132,100
40-49	55,900	44,900	69,600	64,400	125,100	109,200	116,800

Notes: 1970 census data are not available for ethnic Estonians by sex.

Data Sources: RSK, 1938:11-13, 24-25; Parming, 1972a:63-65; and Table 5,
this chapter.

Table 14

Sizes of selected age groups of ethnic Estonians
in Soviet Estonia in 1959 by sex, and selected
sex ratios

Age group	Number of males	Number of females	Ratio of males to females
20-24	31,327	32,929	1.02
25-29	33,474	34,774	.79
30-34	27,398	34,687	.62
35-39	21,466	30,946	.62
40-44	19,227	27,181	.94
45-49	25,633	37,188	.69
50-54	25,500	36,769	.63
55-59	23,343	35,785	---

Note: Sex ratios were calculated on the basis of
figures joined by arrows.

Source: Parming, 1972a:64-65.

Divorce and abortion are not, however, the only factors delimiting births. Another important variable related to family formation is the differential sex composition of the ethnic Estonian population in the Estonian SSR. It must be kept in mind that the military mobilizations of 1940-1944 by both the Soviets and the Germans resulted in sizable losses of men. Normally, these mobilized age groups would have been active in family formation from 1945 to 1959. In 1934 there were 215,600 ethnic Estonian males in the country in the age group 20-49; in 1959 this number was only 158,600. The number of females aged 20-39 also decreased, in absolute terms, from 170,200 to 133,300. Pertinent data are summarized in table 13 (1970 data were not available).

Important also is the ratio of males to females; the basic data for 1959 are presented in table 14 (here, again, 1970 data were unavailable). Comparing the ratios of females in 1959 who would have been in the critical reproductive years between 1945 and 1959 (those who in 1959 were aged 20-39) and males five years their seniors, we note an exceedingly unbalanced sex composition. In conclusion, the differential histories of fertility and marriage, the effects of the war on the numbers of females and males among the ethnic Estonians, and the predominantly young-adult status of immigrants—all these factors clearly lead to differential vital rates.

Differential Growth

During the intercensus period 1959-1970 the number of ethnic Estonians in Soviet Estonia increased by less than 4 percent while the number of non-Estonians increased by more than 40 percent. This imbalance was caused foremost by immigration—which, as noted earlier, for the period 1950-1972 was larger than the natural increase, and which almost entirely involved non-Estonians. However, the imbalance was also caused in part by differential rates of natural increase, reflecting both a differential age structure and differential behavior in regard to family formation.

It is almost axiomatic that a population consisting largely of young adults, as is the case with the non-Estonians in Soviet Estonia, will have a low death rate because of low age-specific mortality. Further, such a population has a potential for a high

Table 15

Differential vital rates in Estonia: 1933, 1958 and 1969

	1933			1958			1969		
	Birth rate	Death rate	Natural increase	Birth rate	Death rate	Natural increase	Birth rate	Death rate	Natural increase
Estonians	15.9	14.5	1.4	14.6	12.4	2.2	15.0	13.3	1.7
Non-Estonians	18.2	15.6	2.6	21.4	6.2	15.2	16.0	6.6	9.4
Total population	16.2	14.6	1.6	16.5	10.9	5.6	15.5	11.3	4.2

Data Sources: For 1933, calculated on the basis of data in Sõrmus, 1935:58; for 1958 and 1969, calculated on basis of 1959 and 1970 census data by method noted in Parming, 1972a:73, 76.

birth rate, and in Soviet Estonia the non-Estonians have realized this potential. It must be kept in mind that the ranks of young adults in this group are continually reinforced by immigrants. While vital rates are not given by ethnic group in official Soviet Estonian statistics, it is possible to compute these fairly accurately for years close to the censuses. The appropriate data for 1958 and 1969 are shown in table 15, with 1933 data added for comparison.

Table 15 indicates a noteworthy decline in the crude birth rate of the non-Estonians, from 21.4 in 1958 to 16.0 in 1969. However, this decline most likely reflects a peculiarity of the non-Estonian age structure, not a basic change in fertility patterns. From table 5 it may be seen that the non-Estonian age group 10-19 was disproportionately small in 1959; the members of this particular age group would have been in their high-fertility years during the intercensus period. The 1970 data in table 5 show that the 10-19 age group was then sizable— indeed, 85 percent larger than the same age group was in 1959. This age group now forms the key reproductive sector. Immigration data (table 3) suggest that all non-Estonian age groups grew sharply in the late 1960s and early 1970s. Data on births (table 8) similarly indicate an upturn after 1969. The year 1971 had a greater absolute number of births than any other year in Estonia after 1923; 1970 and 1972 ranked, respectively, third and second. Even 1969 had a greater number of births than any year of the postwar Soviet period after 1954 and 1955. There is nothing to suggest that this increase in births may be attributed to anything other than the fact of immigration. Indeed, if we look at all the age groups in the population which would have been in the key reproductive sector during the intercensus years and the decade after 1970—that is, people aged 10-49—we find that between 1959 and 1970 the number of Estonians increased from 484,500 to 498,800, or by 3 percent; while the number of non-Estonians increased from 199,800 to 296,900, or by 49 percent.

The second half of the 1960s was a relatively advantageous period for the increase of ethnic Estonians, primarily because in 1959 76 percent of the females in the age group 10-19 were ethnic Estonians—the highest percentage of all age groups under 40. From table 14 it is evident that the sex ratios among ethnic Estonians in the key reproductive sector during the 1960s were appreciably more favorable to increasing the rate of family formation than had been the case with preceding (that is, older) age groups. This relative advantage is unlikely to continue, however, because of the rapid increase in fertile-aged non-Estonians from the late 1960s onward. Indeed, if we compare the percentages of ethnic Estonians in each age group in 1959 with comparative figures in 1970, we notice that the situation is rapidly deteriorating from the viewpoint of the ethnic Estonians (see table 5). The next Soviet census probably will indicate an even more striking change, because 21 percent of the ethnic Estonians in 1970 were age 60 or older. This age group in 1970 was 85 percent ethnic Estonian. During both the 1959 and 1970 censuses, the general rule was that the younger the age group, the less it was composed of ethnic Estonians.

The prognosis of trends in many respects borders on conjecture, because the data required for refined calculations are not available and cannot be derived from existing data. Even demographic predictions undertaken with the most sophisticated techniques and the best available data are not known for their accuracy. Major developments which might act to delimit the validity of demographic predictions in the case of Soviet Estonia are: (1) an abrupt increase in the number of ethnic Estonians as a result of their immigration from other regions of the Soviet Union (potentially 82,000 people in 1970), (2) a slowdown or reversal in the immigration of non-Estonians, (3) significant shifts in the marital patterns of both ethnic Estonians and non-Estonians, with concomitant changes in the birth rates of each group, and (4) the reinstitution of deportation by the central authorities.

Because the likelihood of any of these occurrences is unknown, prognoses are exceedingly difficult. Nevertheless, given recent and present trends and the age structures of ethnic Estonians and non-Estonians, differential growth is likely to persevere and even intensify. By the end of the present decade, the percentage of the Soviet Estonian population which is ethnic Estonian could easily decrease to 60 percent, and by 1990 to 50 percent.

Social Consequences of Demographic Change

Of all the trends and changes in Soviet Estonia's population since 1940, the most important is the changing ethnic composition of the population. This population change irritates the natives, stimulates anti-Russian attitudes, symbolizes and in some cases leads to Russification of other sectors of society, and affects the maintenance of the native culture. This issue is likely to remain the leading domestic controversy within Soviet Estonia (albeit one that is not officially discussed to any great extent) during the decades ahead. It is pertinent to point out here that immigration and birth-rate differentials do not tell the full story of the non-Estonian presence in Soviet Estonia. Two "temporary but permanent" population groups do not appear in official population statistics: the troops of the Red Army garrisoned in Soviet Estonia and shoppers/tourists. While any individual in one of these groups is in Soviet Estonia only temporarily, the groups as entities are there permanently.

Some of the broad issues related to demographic change, in terms of its consequences to society, have been covered in Parming (1972c). Only time will tell whether the native Estonians' fears of Russification are justified. However, two matters merit mention here. First, when ethnic composition shifts to a substantial degree, there are significant cultural consequences. The host society can hardly assimilate a great number of newcomers in a brief period of time. This is especially true of the Estonian SSR, where most immigrants are members of the ethnic group dominating Soviet society and its central power structure. For example, it may be quantitatively shown that the percentage of newspapers, periodicals, and books published in Estonian has declined along with the percentage of the population which is ethnic Estonian. The capital city of Tallinn is already in many respects a bilingual city—while in 1970 44 percent of its population was non-Estonian (32 percent of it was Russian), in 1934 only 14 percent of the city was non-Estonian. Finnish tourists have reported to me that in areas of northeast Estonia it is impossible to get along with only a knowledge of Estonian. Indeed, most available information indicates that bilingualism and biculturalism are unidirectional—the natives must learn Russian.

Second, the high concentration of Russians along the northern coast creates fear in some segments of the ethnic Estonian population because of past Soviet behavior. In 1945, the southeast and northeast corners of the former Republic of Estonia had been detached from the Estonian SSR and administratively transferred to the Russian SFSR, with the rationalization that most inhabitants of those areas were Russian. Although Estonia in modern times was a sovereign state for only two decades, its territory has been administratively intact since 1917. Any future border alterations—say, along the northern coast—would have serious ramifications for Estonia. This region, from Tallinn to Narva, contains a large share of industry, a major harbor, and important natural resources (especially oil shale).

Another undesirable consequence of the demographic change is the increasing tendency of ethnic Estonians to use the Russian immigrants as scapegoats. In many respects, these immigrants have come to symbolize Moscow's rule in Estonia. Hence they are blamed—justifiably or not—for such problems as the housing shortage. Indeed, Russians have become the butts of innumerable ethnic jokes. Virtually everything wrong in Soviet Estonia is dismissed by the natives as "VV"—*vene värk*, or "Russian stuff."

Yet one of the most remarkable trends, be it ever so small, in Soviet Estonian population processes is related to the choice of ethnic identity among the children of the intermarried. A study by Terentjeva (1970) among children of the intermarried between 1960 and 1968 found that in Tallinn, when such children reach the age of 16, most opt for an Estonian identity. If the presently low rate of intermarriage among Estonians should increase, and if the identity-choice trend persists, the number of ethnic Estonians will increase more rapidly than may otherwise be predicted. Hence, while there is a continual fear of Russification, as a result either of Soviet policy or of Russian influx, social reality on its own modest scale is proceeding in the opposite direction.

Notes

1. The number of Estonians in Russia has never been accurately determined. However, excluding losses in the Stalinist purges, the number should have been close to 180,000 on the eve of World War II. Losses had been high during the early years of sovietization. See, for example, the studies of Ilmar Arens in the series *Commentationes Balticae*, published in Bonn by the Baltisches Forschungsinstitut (vol. 10/11, part 1; vol. 12/13, part 1; and vol. 14/15, part 1). Other sources on this subject are Nigol (1918), Haljaspôld (1939), and Raun (1958). More than 40,000 Estonians living in Soviet Russia had been repatriated to Estonia in the early 1920s as a result of an option provided by the peace treaty of Tartu between the Republic of Estonia and Soviet Russia.

2. Most of the "ethnic Estonians" in the southeast corner of the transferred territory were *Setud*, Estonians who had historically formed a buffer zone between Estonia and Russia and who consequently had been partially Russified. In interwar Estonian population statistics, the *Setud* were often listed separately as a subcategory of Estonians. In 1934 there were 14,961 of them among 992,520 Estonians, and of this number 13,400 lived in the province of Petseri (RSK, 1938:24).

3. The figure of 830,000, which represents my own calculations, and the *Encyclopedia*'s 854,000 were not reached by the same method. The latter source underestimates or ignores the extent of such factors as Soviet deportations, the westward flight, and losses of Estonian men in the Red Army. Many of these losses were passed off as being a consequence of the German occupation. However, sources currently available in the West do not agree with the conclusion that there was a huge population loss during the German occupation period. On the other hand, most of the losses attributable to Soviet activities can be substantiated from primary and secondary sources. Furthermore, it is not clear whether the *Encyclopedia* figure

takes into account the population of the transferred territory. Survel (1947:51) cites a May 14, 1946, Tallinn radio broadcast as stating that Estonia's population had been reduced by one-fourth. This would imply that about 850,000 people had been lost by 1946.

4. Theoretically, deported people should be enumerated in subsequent censuses in the territories in which they were relocated. However, it cannot be assumed that this was, in fact, done. Indeed, data for the period 1945-1950 are not completely available. In regard to the number of ethnic Estonians, this data vacuum lasted until 1959, by which time many surviving deportees had returned to Soviet Estonia.

References

Allik, H.

1967   "Kôige tähtsam, kôige peamine" [The Most Impor-
        tant, the Most Significant]. *Rahva Hääl*, May 19, p.
        2.

Aman, Viktor

1961   "Estlandssvenskarna under andra Varldskrieget.
        Over flyttningen till Sverige," in *En bok om Est-
        landssvenskar*, ed. Viktor Aman et al. Stockholm:
        Kulturgoreningen Svenska Odlingens Vanner.

Amitan-Wilensky, Ella

1971   "Esthonian Jewry," in *The Jews in Latvia*, ed. M.
        Bobe et al. Tel Aviv: Association of Latvian and
        Esthonian Jews in Israel.

Angelus, Oskar

1955   "Ümberasumine Saksamaale" [Resettlement to Ger-
        many], in *Eesti riik ja rahvas Teises Maailmasôjas*
        [The Estonian State and People during World War
        II], ed. Richard Maasing et al. Stockholm: EMP.

1956   *Tuhande valitseja maa* [Land of a Thousand Rulers].
        Stockholm: EMP.

1968   "Die Russifizierung Estlands." *Acta Baltica 7*.
        Königstein: Institutum Balticum.

Astel, H., E. Kornet, and E. Tiit

1972 "Tartlannad ja raseduse katkestanud tartlannad. Statistiline vôrdlus," in *Perekonna-probleemid* [Family Problems], ed. A. Blumfeldt et al. Tartu: Tartu Riiklik Ülikool.

Blumfeldt, A., et al., eds.

1972 *Perekonna-probleemid* [Family Problems]. Tartu: Tartu Riiklik Ülikool.

CSBESSR (Central Statistical Bureau of the Estonian SSR) [*Eesti NSV Ministrite Nôukogu juures asuv Statistika Keskvalitsus*]

1957 *Eesti NSV rahvamajandus* [The National Economy of the Estonian SSR]. Tallinn: Eesti Riiklik Kirjastus.

1960 *Nôukogude Eesti saavutusi 20 aasta jooksul: statistiline kogumik* [Achievements of Soviet Estonia during Twenty Years: A Statistical Compendium]. Tallinn: Eesti Riiklik Kirjastus.

1968 *Eesti NSV rahvamajandus 1967. aastal* [The National Economy of the Estonian SSR in 1967]. Tallinn: Kirjastus Statistika.

1970a "1970. aasta üleliidulise rahvaloenduse eelkokkuvôte Eesti NSV kohta" [The 1970 Soviet Census Preliminary Summary for the Estonian SSR]. *Rahva Hääl*, June 21, p. 3.

1970b *Eesti NSV rahvamajandus 1969. aastal* [The National Economy of the Estonian SSR in 1969]. Tallinn: Kirjastus Statistika.

1973 *The National Economy of the Estonian SSR in 1972* (title translated from Russian). Tallinn: Eesti Raamat.

1976 *Eesti NSV rahvamajandus 1975* [The National Economy of the Estonian SSR in 1975]. Tallinn: Eesti Raamat.

CSBUSSR (Central Statistical Bureau of the Soviet Union, Moscow)

1962a *Census of the Soviet Union, 1959, Volume on the*

Estonian SSR (title translated from Russian). Moscow: Statistical Press.

1962b *Census of the Soviet Union, 1959, Summary Volume on the USSR* (title translated from Russian). Moscow: Statistical Press.

1972a *Census of the Soviet Union, 1970* (title translated from Russian), vol. 2. Moscow: Statistical Press.

1972b *Census of the Soviet Union, 1970* (title translated from Russian), vol. 3. Moscow: Statistical Press.

1973   *Census of the Soviet Union, 1970* (title translated from Russian), vol. 4. Moscow: Statistical Press.

Dahlstrøm, Edmund

1956   "Estonian Refugees in a Swedish Community," in *Minority Problems*, ed. Arnold Rose and C. Rose. New York: Harper and Row.

Dreifelds, Juris

1971   "Characteristics and Trends of Two Demographic Variables in the Latvian SSR." *Bulletin of Baltic Studies*, no. 8 (Winter), pp. 10-17.

Eesti Komitee (The Estonian Committee in Sweden)

1947   "Estonian Refugees in Sweden." Mimeographed bulletin dated November 27.

Ehrlich, R.

1960   "Eesti NSV väikelinnaliste asulate arenemisbaasist" [On the Basis of Development of Small Urban Settlements in the Estonian SSR], in *Eesti Geograafia Seltsi Aastaraamat 1954-1955* [Yearbook of the Estonian Geographical Society for 1954-1955]. Tallinn.

ENE *(Eesti nôukogude entsüklopeedia*

1968- [The Estonian Soviet Encyclopedia], 8 vols. Tallinn.
1976

Ernits, Erich

1966a "Pôgenikud sôjaaegsel Saksamaal" [The Refugees in

Wartime Germany], in *Eesti saatusaastad 1945-1960* [Estonia's Years of Fate, 1945-1960], vol. 4, ed. Richard Maasing et al. Stockholm: EMP.

1966b   "Pôgenikud pärast kapitulatsiooni" [The Refugees after Capitulation], in *Eesti saatusaastad 1945-1960* [Estonia's Years of Fate, 1945-1960], vol. 4, ed. Richard Maasing et al. Stockholm: EMP.

Foe, Jean J.

1969   "Les refugiés étrangers en Finlande durant la Seconde Guerre Mondiale." *Revue d'histoire diplomatique*, no. 4.

Geijerstam, Sven

1951   "Flyktingarna i Sverige." *Bra att veta*, no. 6.

Grabbi, Hellar

1967   "Eesti rahvastiku loomuliku juurde kasvu probleemid" [The Problems of Estonia's Natural Increase]. *Mana*, no. 32, pp. 82-83.

1968   "Ka kodumaal väljendub mure eesti rahva olemasolu pärast" [Worry about the Continued Existence of the Estonian People Exists also in the Homeland]. *Eesti Päevaleht*, February 21.

Haav, K.

1968   "Abielu, perekond" [Marriage, Family]. *Edasi*, July 24.

Haljaspôld, Herbert

1939   "Estonians outside Estonia." *Baltic Times*, September 27.

Hark, Kustas

1965   "Aschaffenburgi laagri 'metrikaraamat' kôneleb" [The Record Book of the Camp at Aschaffenburg Speaks]. *Meie Tee*, 35, no. 3-4: 43-45.

Holmogorov, A.

1973   *Nôukogude rahvuste arengujooned* [The Developmental Outlines of the Soviet People]. Tallinn: Eesti Raamat.

Horm, Arvo

1961   "Estonians in the Free World," in *Aspects of Estonian Culture*, ed. Evald Uustalu et al. London: Boreas.
1965   "Suur pôgenemine" [The Great Flight], in *Tammine rahvas 2* [The People of Oak], vol. 2, ed. Madis Üürike et al. Stockholm: Eesti Komitee.
1971   "Balternas flykt till Sverige 1940-1945. Organiserade räddningsaktionen," in *Symposium om Balterna i Sverige*. Stockholm: Baltiska Institutet.

Jänes, Harri

1966   "Urbaniit" [The Urbanite]. *Sirp ja Vasar*, April 8, pp. 6-7.

Kaasik, N.,

1947   "The Baltic Refugee in Sweden: a Successful Experiment." *Baltic Review* (Stockholm) 2 (December).

Kaelas, Aleksander

1950   *Human Rights and Genocide in the Baltic States.* Stockholm: Estonian Information Centre.
1956   *The Colonial Policy of the Soviet Union in Occupied Estonia.* Stockholm: Estonian National Council.

Kahn, Hubert

1970   *Abielu tervishoiust* [On Marital Health]. Tallinn: Valgus.

Kant, Edgar

1934   *Problems of Environment and Population in Estonia.* Tartu: Mattiesen.
1935   *Bevölkerung und Lebensraum Estlands.* Tartu: Akadeemiline Kooperatiiv.

Kaufmann, Voldemar

1963 "Väikelinnade arengust Eesti NSVs" [On the Development of Towns in the Estonian SSR]. *Eesti NSV Teaduste Akadeemia Toimetised: Ühiskonnateaduste Seeria* 12, no. 2: 107-120.

1965 "Eesti NSV tööjõuresurssid" [Labor Resources of the Estonian SSR]. *Eesti Kommunist* 21, no. 8: 36-44.

1966a "Muudatused rahvastiku rakendatuses Eestis 1934. ja 1959.a. rahvaloenduste andmeil" [Changes in the Utilization of Estonia's Population on the Basis of the 1934 and 1959 Censuses]. *Eesti NSV Teaduste Akadeemia Toimetised: Ühiskonnateaduste Seeria* 15: 3-15.

1966b "Rahvastiku probleemidest Pärnu Rajoonis" [On Population Problems in the Region of Pärnu]. *Pärnu Kommunist*, July 19.

1967a "Rahvastiku dünaamika ja seda mõjutanud seaduspärasused Eestis 20 sajandi esimesel poolel (1897-1959)" [Population Dynamics and Its Causal Principles in Estonia during the First Half of the Twentieth Century, 1897-1959]. Unpublished dissertation, Tallinn Polytechnic Institute, Tallinn.

1967b "Eesti NSV rahvastiku rakendatusest" [On the Utilization of the Population of the Estonian SSR]. *Majandusteadus ja rahvamajandus. 1966 aastaraamat* [Economic Science and the National Economy, 1966 Yearbook]. Tallinn: Eesti Raamat.

1968a "Demograafia ja rahvaiive" [Demography and Natural Increase]. *Õhtuleht*, October 13.

1968b "Rahvaiibe olukorrast Eesti NSVs" [On the State of Natural Increase in the Estonian SSR]. Mimeographed paper presented at the conference "Rahva tervishoiu aktuaalseid probleeme," Tallinn, May 15-16.

1970 "Eesti NSV rahvastiku juurdekasvust rahvaloenduse andmeil" [On the Growth of the Population of the Estonian SSR, Based on the Census]. *Õhtuleht*, August 19.

King, Gundar J.

1970   "Comments on the Current State of Baltic Demographic Research." *Bulletin of Baltic Studies*, no. 4 (December), pp. 3-4.

King, Gundar J., and Juris Dreifelds

1973   "Demographic Changes in Latvia," in *Problems of Mininations*, ed. Arvids Ziedonis et al. San Jose, Calif.: Association for the Advancement of Baltic Studies.

Kiviaed, Voldemar

1966   "Esterna i Sverige bildar samhälle," in *Svenska minoriteter*, ed. David Schwarz. Stockholm: Aldus/Bonniers.

Köörna, A.

1967   "Rahvastik ja tema arenemine" [Population and Its Development]. *Eesti Kommunist*, no. 2, pp. 87-90.

Koppel, Evi, and Ene Tiit

1970   "Abiellumus Tartus 1968. aastal." [Marriage Rates in Tartu in 1968]. *Nôukogude Eesti Tervishoid* 13, no. 2: 142-147.

Kornet, E.

1972   "Raseduse katkestamise motiividest" [On the Motives for Terminating Pregnancy], in *Perekonnaprobleemid* [Family Problems], ed. A. Blumfeldt et al. Tartu: Tartu Riiklik Ülikool.

Krepp, Endel

1955   "Rahvaarvust Eestis" [On the Size of the Population in Estonia], in *Eesti Üliôpilaste Seltsi Album 12*, ed. Leo Urm and Madis Üürike. Stockholm: Eesti Üliôpilaste Selts.

1959   "Rahvastiku probleemist" [On the Problem of Population], in *Kodumaa küsimused 1* [Questions about the Homeland, 1]. Stockholm: Eesti Rahvusnôukogu.

1960   "Eesti maa ja rahvas 1944-1959" [The Estonian Land and People, 1944-1959], in *Eesti Üliôpilaste Seltsi*

Album 12, ed. Leo Urm and Madis Üürike. Stockholm: Eesti Üliôpilaste Selts.

Kruus, Hans

1920　*Linn ja Küla Eestis* [The City and Village in Estonia].
Tartu: Noor Eesti.

Kulischer, Eugene M.

1943　*The Displacement of Population in Europe.* Montreal: International Labor Office.

Kumernius, Otto

1965　"Esternas evakuering fran Finland." *Aret Runt*, nos.
2 and 3.

Küng, Andres

1973　*Saatusi ja saavutusi* [Of Fate and Achievements].
Lund: Eesti Kirjanike Kooperatiiv.

Laas, Kaljo

1964　"Rahvastiku paiknemisest Nôukogude Eestis" [On
the Location of Population in Soviet Estonia]. *Eesti
Geograafia Seltsi Aastaraamat 1963* [Yearbook of
the Estonian Geographical Society for 1963]. Tallinn.

1965　"Muutustest Eesti NSV rahvastiku paiknemises ja
asulastikus" [On the Changes in the Locations and
Settlement of the Population in the Estonian SSR].
Unpublished dissertation, Tallinn Polytechnic Institute, Tallinn.

1967a　"Eesti NSV rahvastik möödunud seitseaastakul"
[The Population of the Estonian SSR during the Past
Seven Years]. *Majandusteadus ja rahvamajandus
1966* [Economic Science and the National Economy,
1966 Yearbook]. Tallinn.

1967b　"Maarahvastiku formeerumise territoriaalsetest iseärasustest Eesti NSVs" [On the Peculiarities of
Territorial Formation of the Rural Population in the
Estonian SSR]. *Kaasaja maakorraldus*, no. 2, pp. 54-
56.

1968a　"Pilk rahvastikukaardile" [A Glimpse at the Population Map]. *Horisont*, no. 4, pp. 7-8.

1968b "Kui kaugel me siis oleme" [How Far Are We Then? (in intensifying demographic research)]. *Edasi*, November 20.

1968c "Kas elanike arvu on vôimalik prognoosida?" [Is It Possible To Prognose the Population Figure?]. *Küsimused ja vastused* 10, no. 3: 15-17.

1969a "Môtteid demograafiast" [Thoughts on Demography], in *Kalender 1969*. Tallinn: Eesti Riiklik Kirjastus.

1969b "Eesti NSV rahvastik möödunud seitseaastakul" [The Population of the Estonian SSR during the Past Seven Years], in *Majandusteadus ja rahvamajandus 1967-1968 aastaraamat* [Economic Science and the National Economy, Yearbook for 1967-1968]. Tallinn: Eesti Raamat.

1969c "Demograafia arengust ja uurimisprobleemidest Nôukogude Liidus" [On the Development of Demography and Research Problems in the Soviet Union]. *Eesti NSV Teaduste Akadeemia Toimetised: Ühiskonnateadused* 18, no. 3: 277-279.

1971 "Rahvastiku iibest ja tööjôu resurssidest" [On the Natural Increase of the Population and Labor Resources]. *Eesti Kommunist*, October.

Laas, Kaljo, and Harri Paalberg

1967 "Uued linnad Eesti NSVs" [New Cities in the Estonian SSR]. *Tehnika ja Tootmine*, no. 5, pp. 199-200.

Lemberg, Adelaida

1967 "Russification in the Baltic States." *Baltic Review*, no. 33 (January), pp. 32-41.

Loeber, Dietrich A., comp.

1972 *Diktierte Option. Die Umsiedlung der Deutsch-Balten aus Estland und Lettland, 1939-1941*. Neumünster: Karl Wachholtz Verlag.

Luts, A.

1966 "Abiellumistest Vôru rajoonis" [On Marriages in the Region of Vôru], in *Etnograafiamuuseumi aastaraamat 21* [Yearbook of the Ethnographic Museum, vol. 21]. Tallinn: Valgus.

Maasing, Richard, et al., eds.

1954- *Eesti riik ja rahvas Teises Maailmasôjas* [The Estoni-
1962   an State and People during World War II], 10 vols.
       Stockholm: EMP.

Madise, Juhan

1966   "Emigratsioon Saksamaalt" [Emigration from Ger-
       many], in *Eesti saatusaastad 1945-1960* [Estonia's
       Years of Fate, 1945-1960], vol. 4, ed. Richard Maas-
       ing et al. Stockholm: EMP.

Madissoon, H.

1942   "Eestie rahvas—kui palju ja kui vähe teda on olnud?"
       [Estonian People—How Many and How Few Have
       There Been?]. Interview, *Eesti Sôna*, May 17.

Mereste, Uno

1969a "Elada täisväärset elu" [To Live a Full Life]. *Edasi*,
       September 5, 6, 9, 10.
1969b *Rahvastiku-teadus ja rahva loendus* [Population
       Science and the Census]. Tallinn: Eesti Raamat.

Müürsepp, P.

1968   "Môtteid inimkonna tulevikuperspektiividest (rahva
       juurdekasvust)" [Thoughts on the Future Perspec-
       tives of Mankind, Population Increase]. *Sirp ja
       Vasar*, August 9.

Naan, Gustav, ed.

1975   *Nôukogude Eesti: Entsüklopeediline teatmeteos* [So-
       viet Estonia: An Encyclopedic Reference Work].
       Tallinn: Valgus.

Ney, Gottlieb

1968   "Auswirkung der Sowjetisierung auf das Siedlungs-
       wesen in Estland," in *Acta Baltica 7*. Königstein:
       Institutum Balticum.

Nigol, August

1918   *Eesti asundused ja asupaigad Wenemaal* [Estonian
       Settlements and Localities in Russia]. Tartu: Posti-
       mees.

Oras, Ants

1948   *Baltic Eclipse.* London: Victor Gollancz.

Paalberg, Harri

1966a   "Linna perspektiivsest elanike arvust" [On the Prospective Number of Inhabitants in Cities]. *Ehitus ja
Arhitektuur,* no. 2, pp. 3-6.

1966b   "Eesti NSV linnade elanike arvu dünaamikast" [On
the Dynamics of the City Population of the Estonian
SSR]. *Eesti NSV Teaduste Akadeemia Toimetised:
Ühiskonnateaduste Seeria* 15: 287-297.

1967   "Eesti NSV linnade peamised arengusuunad ja neid
mõjustavad tegurid" [The Major Developmental
Directions of the Cities of the Estonian SSR and
Factors Which Affect These]. Unpublished dissertation, Tallinn Polytechnic Institute, Tallinn.

1968a   "Linnad täna ja homme" [Cities Today and Tomor-
row]. *Noorte Hääl,* September 19.

1968b   "Eesti suuremate linnade arengusuunad" [The Developmental Direction of the Larger Estonian Cit-
ies]. *Eesti Kommunist,* no. 11, pp. 17-23.

1968c   "Linnastumine Eesti NSVs" [Urbanization in the
Estonian SSR]. *Tehnika ja Tootmine,* no. 9, pp. 466-
468.

1969   "Linnastumine kui ülemaailmne protsess" [Urbani-
zation as a Worldwide Phenomenon]. *Tehnika ja
Tootmine* 13: 356-358.

Palli, Heldur

1968   "Läbi sajandite" [Through the Centuries]. *Horisont* 2
(April): 9-14.

1973   *Ajaloolise demograafia probleeme Eestis* [Problems
of Historical Demography in Estonia]. Tallinn: Eesti
NSV Teaduste Akadeemia Ajaloo Instituut.

Parming, Tönu

1970   "Eestlaste   ümberrahvustumine   Põhja-Ameerika
Ühendriikides" [The Assimilation of Estonians in the
United States]. *Mana,* no. 37, pp. 14-38.

1972a   "Population Changes in Estonia, 1935-1970." *Population Studies* 26 (March): 53-78.

1972b "Rahvastikuteadusest ja rahvastikust Eestis Nôuko-gude ajastul" [On Population Studies and Population in Estonia during the Soviet Period]. *Tulimuld* 23, no. 1: 42-57.

1972c "Soziale Konsequenzen der Bevölkerungs-Veränderungen in Estland seit 1939," in *Acta Baltica 11*. Königstein: Institutum Balticum.

1976 "Contrasts in Nationalism in the Soviet Baltic." Paper presented at the Fifteenth Annual Conference of the Southern Slavic Association at the University of Virginia, Charlottesville, Va.

1977a "The Historical Roots of Nationality Differences in the Soviet Baltic," in *Nationality Group Survival in Multi-Ethnic States*, ed. Edward Allworth. New York: Praeger.

1977b "Abortion in a Soviet Republic." Unpublished manuscript.

Parts, Anton

1958 "Eesti-vene piiri muudatusest ja piiritagustest eest-lastest" [On the Change in the Estonian-Russian Border and on the Estonians on the Other Side of the Border]. *Tulimuld* 9, no. 3: 144-146.

Pennar, Jaan, Tönu Parming, and P. Peter Rebane

1975 *The Estonians in America 1627-1975*. Dobbs Ferry, N.Y.: Oceana.

Pullat, Raimo

1967 "Urbaniseerimise sotsioloogilisest ja demograafilis-est aspektist" [On the Sociological and Demographical Aspect of Urbanization]. *Ehitus ja Arhitektuur*, no. 5, pp. 3-5.

1968 "Rahvastiku kohta on vaja täpseid andmeid" [It Is Necessary to Have Exact Figures for the Population]. *Eesti Kommunist*, no. 5, pp. 62-65.

1969 *Môeldes ideaalsele linnale* [Thinking about the Ideal City]. Tallinn: Eesti Raamat.

1970 "Esimene demograafiakoolkond Eestis" [The First School of Demography in Estonia]. *Eesti NSV Teaduste Akadeemia Toimetised: Ühiskonnatea-dused* 19: 99-101.

1972a "Eesti linnarahvastik 18. sajandi lôpust 1940. aastani. Ajaloolisdemograafiline uurimus" [Estonia's Urban Population from the End of the Eighteenth Century to 1940: A Historical-Demographic Study]. Unpublished dissertation, Estonian Academy of Sciences, Tallinn.

1972b *Eesti linnad ja linlased 18 sajandi lôpust 1917. aastani* [Estonia's Cities and Urban Population from the End of the Eighteenth Century to 1917]. Tallinn: Eesti Raamat.

Purre, Arnold

1964 "Teine punane okupatsioon Eestis. Aastad 1944-1950" [The Second Red Occupation in Estonia, 1944-1950], in *Eesti saatusaastad 1945-1960* [Estonia's Years of Fate, 1945-1960], vol. 2, ed. Richard Maasing et al. Stockholm: EMP.

1968 "Eesti rahvastik okupeeritud Eestis" [The Estonian Population in Occupied Estonia], in *Eesti saatusaastad 1945-1960* [Estonia's Years of Fate, 1945-1960], vol. 5, ed. Richard Maasing et al. Stockholm: EMP.

1972 "Ethnischer Bestand und Struktur der Bevölkerung Sowjetestlands im Jahr 1970." *Acta Baltica 11.* Königstein: Institutum Balticum.

Raun, Alo

1958 "Eestluse statistikat Nôukogude 1926. a. rahvaloenduse andmeil" [Statistics on Estonians on the Basis of the 1926 Soviet Census]. *Mana* 3, no. 4: 55-60.

Riismandel, Väino J.

1953 "Eesti maa-ala Vene halduse all" [Estonian Lands under Russian Administration]. *Tulimuld* 4, no. 2: 102-108.

Roosileht, August

1968 "Artifitsiaalsest abordist ja selle vastu vôitlemisest" [On Artificial Abortions and Fighting against Them]. *Nôukogude Eesti Tervishoid* 11, no. 2: 104-107.

RSK (Riigi Statistika Keskbüroo) [State Central Statistical Bureau]

1938   *Rahvastikuprobleeme Eestis* [Population Problems in Estonia], vol. 4 of the 1934 census. Tallinn: Riigi Statistika Keskbüroo.

Seppel, Viktor

1968   "Seisuga 15. jaanuaril kell 00.00" [The Status at 00.00 o'Clock on January 15]. *Horisont* 2 (April): 29-33.

Sibul, Karl

1954   "Eesti pagulased DP-dena Saksamaal" [Estonian Refugees as Displaced Persons in Germany], in *Minevikust tulevikku* [From the Past into the Future], ed. Helmut Hagar et al. Stockholm: EÜS Pôhjala.

Smogorzewski, K. M.

1950   "The Russification of the Baltic States." *World Affairs*, October.

Sôrmus, R.

1935   "Eesti ja eesti vähemusrahvused" [Estonia and Its Minorities], in *Tähiseid: Eestluse aastaraamat 1935* [The Signs: Estonian Yearbook for 1935], ed. E. Roos. Tartu: Eesti Rahvuslaste Klubi.

Survel, Jaak

1947   *Estonia Today.* East and West Series. London: Boreas.

Taagepera, Rein

1969   "National Differences within Soviet Demographic Trends." *Soviet Studies*, April, pp. 478-489.

Tamre, Asta

1967   "Mida räägib teie perekonnast demograafia?" [What Does Demography Say about Your Family?]. Interview in *Rahva Hääl*, May 6, p. 3.

Tarmisto, V.

1959   "Rahvastik, asulastik" [Population, Settlement Patterns], in *Eesti NSV: andmete kogumik* [The Estonian SSR: A Compendium of Facts], ed. V. Tarmisto. Tallinn: Eesti Riiklik Kirjastus.

Tarmisto, V., and M. Rostovtsev

1956   *Eesti NSV: majandusgeograafiline ülevaade* [The Estonian SSR: An Economic-Geographic Overview]. Tallinn: Eesti Raamat.

Terentjeva, Ludmila

1970   "How Do Youths from Binational Families Determine Their Nationality?" (translated from Latvian by Gundar J. King). *Bulletin of Baltic Studies*, no. 4 (December), pp. 5-11. Originally appeared in *Zinatne un tehnika*, no. 8 (August 1970), pp. 10-12.

Tiit, Ene, and E. Kornet

1972   "Sünnituste arvu môjutavatest teguritest" [On Factors Influencing the Number of Births], in *Perekonna-probleemid* [Family Problems], ed. A. Blumfeldt et al. Tartu: Tartu Riiklik Ülikool.

Tepp, L.

1968   "Rahvastiku kujunemine pole rahvuse omapära" [Population Development Is Not a Characteristic of Nationalities]. *Edasi*, November 11.

Tomberg, G.

1935   "Abielulahutused 1929-33. a." [Divorces during 1929-1933]. *Eesti Statistika Kuukiri*, no. 162 (May), pp. 260-264.

Tonsiver, Heino

1970   "Iive—sündimus—suremus" [Natural Increase, Birth Rate, and Death Rate]. *Ôhtuleht*, February 7.

Tork, Juhan

1965   "Pagulase uned ning mured ja maailmakriis" [The

Refugee's Worries and Dreams and the World Crisis], in *Eesti Üliôpilaste Seltsi Album 15*, ed. Rein Taagepera. Toronto: Eesti Üliôpilaste Selts.

Uustalu, Evald, and Rein Moora

1973   *Soomepoisid* [The Finnish Boys]. Toronto: Soomepoiste Klubi Torontos.

"Vaatleja" [The Observer]

1967   "Mis sünnib okupeeritud Eesti rahvaga?" [What Is Happening with the Population of Occupied Estonia?]. *Meie Tee* 37, no. 5-6: 68-72.

Vahter, Leonhard

1960   "Influx of Russians into Estonia." *Baltic Review*, no. 20 (July), pp. 13-17.

Vanderer, Rudolf

1967   "Kui palju on eestlasi praeguses Eestis?" [How Many Estonians Are There in Contemporary Estonia?]. *Meie Tee* 37, no. 9-10: 145-146.

Vernant, Jacques

1953   *The Refugee in the Post-War World*. London: George Allen and Unwin.

Vissak, S.

1967   "Iive, iive, iive—kas pole pole meilgi muretsemisväärset?" [Natural increase, natural increase, natural increase—Have We Too Not Something to Worry About?]. *Edasi*, April 18. Reprinted in *Mana*, no. 32 (1967), pp. 82-88.

Volkov, L.

1969   "Eesti NSV perspektiivne asustussüsteem" [The Prospective Settlement System of the Estonian SSR]. *Tehnika ja Tootmine* 13, no. 3 (March): 115-119.

Weiss, Helmut

1956   "Järelümberasumine" [The Followup Resettlement],
        in *Eesti riik ja rahvas Teises Maailmasôjas* [The
        Estonian State and People during the Second World
        War], vol. 3, ed. Richard Maasing et al. Stockholm:
        EMP.

Specialized Periodicals

Eesti Statistika Kuukiri [The Estonian Statistical Monthly]

Official publication of the Estonian State Central Statistical
Bureau. Appeared semimonthly and later monthly through
mid-1940. The best statistical source for Estonia between 1918
and 1940. Articles as well as current statistics.

Statistische Berichte für Estland

Official publication of the German occupation forces in
Estonia, published in Tallinn, 1941-1944. Some data on vital
rates and marriages.

Statistische Berichte für das Ostland

Official publication of the Reichskommisariat für das Ostland in Riga during the German occupation years. Occasional
useful population data for 1941-1944.

2

Nationalism, Collaborationism, and New-Leftism

Rein Taagepera

Attitudes toward Soviet rule in Estonia have been affected by various conflicting considerations. It is important to recall that the advent of Soviet rule did away with independent statehood, rather than continuing czarist Russian rule or taking directly over from the Germans or other foreigners. It is known in Estonia that a government in exile exists, and that the United States has not recognized the Soviet annexation of Estonia. Both the influx of immigrants and Moscow's control are resented. Joining the Communist party was considered treason by many until 1956; since then, feelings have been mixed. But Soviet power in Estonia is uncontested. The high average age of Estonians and the low number of 15- to 25-year-olds makes for caution rather than bravado. Even people who dislike the regime do not always look forward to the prospect of turbulent change.

By Soviet norms, the Estonians are doing rather well. The standard of living is higher than that of any other Soviet republic except neighboring Latvia. Estonians have better than average incomes, more spacious housing, and a greater choice of consumer goods. They also have a quasi-official status as a "laboratory republic," one where various techniques and administrative methods are first tested (see Kahk, 1967:10, and Taagepera, 1975a). For example, Estonia received polio vaccinations before the Russian SFSR. Its collective and state farms have been shifting to less centralized (and more profitable) management patterns. Also, Estonia is in the forefront of the wide-scale computerization of the economy and civil administration.

However, by their own standards the Estonians are not doing so well, since their comparisons are with West European rather than Soviet norms. According to Soviet bookkeeping, Estonia's per-capita national product is higher than that of Finland. But most Estonians feel, and many know, that they have vastly less purchasing power than the Finns. Restrictions on travel and on intellectual and political activities are felt more acutely in Estonia than in Russia. The fact that Estonia, as a "Soviet Scandinavia," attracts Russian vacationers and immigrants makes matters worse, since this influx threatens to crush the very Western character of the republic which attracted the Russians in the first place.

The Soviet government to some extent recognizes the special Western character of Estonia and makes minor concessions to it. Thus, Finnish television can be legally viewed in Estonia. It is the only part of the Soviet Union where non-Communist television programs can be seen (and understood). Translations of Western books and performances of Western plays and musicals are more accessible in Estonia than in Russia. Estonians also manage to travel abroad more frequently than do Russians, but much less frequently than is the practice in Western Europe. The direct route by ship between Tallinn and Helsinki is used almost exclusively by Finns, a fact that constantly reminds the Estonians that it is easier to get into Estonia than out.

Among the various ways in which Estonians have tried to cope with the Russian presence are nationalism, collaborationism, and new-leftism. The last two responses will receive the most attention in this chapter because they are less widely known. Selective collaboration is an avenue that minimizes short-term national losses but introduces the risk of gradually degenerating into total mental capitulation. The other little-known response might be termed "ultra-Marxism"—accepting the Russian-imposed Marxist ideology but modernizing it along the lines of the Western new left. While collaborationism represents a passive response, ultra-Marxism is the most dynamic response observed in Estonia since the defeat of the postwar anti-Communist guerrilla movement, although it has no relationship to the latter. The debate on collaboration has been described more fully in Taagepera (1975b) and that on the new left in Taagepera (1976).

Nationalism and Dissent

Nationalism may manifest itself in many areas—culture, politics, or economics—and may be expressed in ways ranging from booing at sports events to active and militant defiance of an established authority.

Some forms of nationalism are officially tolerated by the Soviet regime. Cultural nationalism has become widely accepted in contrast to the situation in Stalin's days (see Taagepera, 1970 and 1973a). Demands for the acknowledgment of the existence of the works of deceased or exiled non-Communist writers culminated in 1968 and were largely successful. Thus, there is no basic contrast between the review of Estonian literature by Nirk (1970) in Soviet Estonia and that of Mägi (1968) in exile. Demands for purity of the language have been addressed even in the official journal *Eesti Kommunist* (1970, no. 2, p. 76). Around 1968 demands were made that music and art must be "national" (i.e., folklore-inspired), but such extreme requests have since decreased. The mammoth song festivals (attended in 1969 by 250,000 people, one-quarter of all the Estonians in Estonia) are a prime example of a cultural safety valve for nationalism: traditional Estonian songs predominate; visiting Finnish choruses get large ovations and Russian choruses scant applause; the public and the choruses demonstratively repeat a certain patriotic song after the close of the official program (see *Estonian Events*, 1969, no. 15, p. 3).

Economic nationalism is almost forced upon the local officials by excessive centralization. Often this attitude represents localism more than nationalism, for it is indistinguishable from similar home-rule demands made in Siberia or even in the Moscow oblast. But the Soviet Estonian establishment has also occasionally objected to immigration, and the desire to avoid problems on the home front has motivated the local party's first secretary, Käbin, to effectively shelter moderate nationalism from Moscow's suspicions. Cooperation with other Baltic republics in culture and economics has increased beyond what was allowed in the 1950s, an expression of an internationalism which is not adverse to nationalism.

It must be kept in mind that not all manifestations of dissent in Estonia are nationalist in origin or content. For example, Estonia has been the focus of some unionwide quests for civil rights which are not nationalist except to the extent that civil rights include national rights. In 1969 the Union of Fighters for Political Freedom, led by naval officers, was crushed in Tallinn. One-fourth of the thirty-one people arrested were Estonians (*Khronika*, 1969, no. 9; *New York Times*, October 24, 1969). The widely circulated "Program of the Democratic Movement" could have been the work of the same group; it shows signs of non-Russian and probably Baltic authorship (*Khronika*, 1969, no. 10; *Radio Liberty Dispatch*, May 20, 1970). An earlier 1968 anonymous memorandum issued by "numerous members of the ESSR technological intelligentsia" also soft-pedaled the national issue and concentrated on all-union problems of civil rights and of rapprochement with the West (*Münchner Merkur*, 1968, no. 306; *Frankfurter Allgemeine Zeitung*, December 18, 1968). Residents of Estonia have been arrested for sympathizing with Solzhenitsyn (*Khronika*, 1971, no. 18) and for protesting against the invasion of Czechoslovakia (*Frankfurter Allgemeine Zeitung*, October 9, 1968). At a party organization meeting called to endorse the invasion, University of Tartu Communists refused to do so, and a faculty member blurted out: "In the house of the hanged man one does not speak of rope." He received only a light reprimand because of his previous good record and because of the general atmosphere of the moment (Taagepera, 1973b).

Hippie behavior and new-leftist manifestations emerged as other forms of nonnational protest, as did a poet's decision to publish his esoteric verses in Sweden when he could not do so in Estonia (see *Estonian Events*, 1969, no. 17, p. 3). The publication of Jewish works shunned elsewhere in the USSR immediately after an anti-Jewish campaign (see *Estonian Events*, 1972, no. 31, p. 1, and 1972, no. 21/22, p. 1) had the same connotations. Consumer protest against the shortage of goods is also not nationally motivated, but in Estonia such protest quickly becomes anti-Russian when the shortage of goods is seen as being caused by exports to Russia or by excessive purchasing by Russian tourists. Tourists interested only in shoes, sausages, and textiles were scored in a Lithuanian short piece (by V. Žilinskaite) reproduced in *Sirp ja Vasar* (September 3, 1971). In a story by V. Ilus (*Looming*, 1968, no.

11, pp. 1656-1664), the main motive of a Russian who had decided to move from the Moscow oblast to Estonia was that "they have all sorts of sausages in the store. But we had only one type." The sorest spot is the housing shortage, which is widely viewed as caused by or made worse by preferential treatment given to Russian immigrants. Thus, any dissent or dissatisfaction is liable to be turned against the Russian content of the formally Soviet rule.

Even high Soviet Estonian officials are liable to crack jokes making fun of Russians and their alleged lack of culture. (A personally witnessed sample: The Czechs wanted to create a ministry for maritime affairs. When reminded that their country is landlocked, they replied: "So what? After all, Russia has a ministry for cultural affairs.") In streetcars and other public places Russians are "routinely" cursed at, according to numerous visitors, with apparently decreasing concern for consequences. Students have carried signs with unorthodox slogans and sung nationalist songs during officially organized demonstrations (see *Estonian Events*, 1969, no. 16, p. 2, and 1971, no. 27, p. 1). After the Czechs won a televised Soviet-Czech ice-hockey match on April 20, 1972, several hundred Tallinn Polytechnic Institute students shouted "We won!" and took to the streets (for details, see *Estonian Events*, 1972, no. 35, p. 2). Some were arrested and many more were expelled.

The prevailing mood of Soviet Estonians whom the author has met is well expressed by a U.S. press quote: "If we were just left alone, we could do better" (*Christian Science Monitor*, September 17, 1969). However, many are disturbed by the thought of a violent change of regime. Behind the friction between technocrats and intellectuals lurks a deeper cleavage: that between those who were deported around 1949 and those who helped to deport them. While the latter obviously have a vested interest in the regime's survival, the specter of a potential "white terror" frightens everyone. Mati Unt, a young and rather unorthodox Soviet Estonian writer, described how a drunken "patriot" had declared Unt personally responsible for, and fit to be executed because of, everything that had happened under Soviet rule, even though Unt was a small child during the years of political transition (M. Unt, "Tühirand: Love Story," *Looming*, 1972, no. 5, p. 707).

If Russian bossism could be subdued by implementing true federalism within the Soviet framework, many critics might cease to toy with the dangerous idea of getting Estonia entirely out of the Soviet Union. On the other hand, fusion into a Russian-speaking "Soviet nation" is completely unacceptable—Moscow's increasing insistence on "accelerated fusion" only aggravates the existing discontent.

In 1967 Estonia's main cultural weekly published an innocuous-seeming poem about a kindergarten teacher, Masha (a Russian name), who was good at heart but ineptly bossed the children (all with Estonian names) instead of teaching them. The initials of the children formed the Estonian word for "nation." Also, Estonia's main cultural monthly commemorated the fiftieth anniversary of the October revolution with a poem that started: "And yet I keep thinking about a *small* country." It then discussed at length Estonia's role in the world, and only in the few last lines remembered to add that the country was now "tacking" with the "October wind." Other poets openly polemicized against the idea of the eventual fusion of Soviet nations and languages or proclaimed their faith in the durability of Estonia. For a while there seemed to be some belief that all of these matters could be resolved through debate with "Auntie Masha." Then came the invasion of Czechoslovakia.

Poetic criticism faded—perhaps because censorship became stronger, but also because there was loss of faith in such methods. Instead, the formation of the underground Estonian National Front was reported by *Khronika* (1972, no. 25). Little was known about this national front, except that it demanded a referendum on Estonia's self-determination and had published several issues of an underground magazine, *Eesti Demokraat* [Estonian Democrat]. In addition to the Soviet external and internal crackdown of 1968, the 1970 census may have given a boost to such underground activity: Estonia was found to have 30,000 more people than had been estimated, and all of them were Russians. Estonians were still 75 percent of the population in 1959, but by 1970 the percentage had dwindled to 68 percent, and immigration was, if anything, on the increase. From the viewpoint of the intellectuals, 5,000 years of Finnic language (as suggested by archeological evidence) and 800 years of West European culture in Estonia were seriously threatened by this trend. As for the common man, he began to find that Russian immigrants were moving into the new housing he was scheduled to get, that Russian tourists were less interested in looking at monuments than in raiding the stores for scarce goods, and that the bureaucracy was being manned increasingly by people who did not understand his language.

It does not seem that the Soviet regime actively organized this immigration, with its overtones of cultural genocide. It has simply allowed it to happen, as it allows Estonia to have its Estonian-language universities, press, television, and theaters. But Moscow has also insisted on economic centralization, even if this runs counter to local interests, cultural or ecological. By all accounts, Estonia is already overindustrialized. But the fake "progress" represented by ever-proliferating factory smoke-stacks and immigrant workers continues, despite popular resentment and timid remonstrations from the few Estonian-born party leaders.

The hopes of those Estonians who believed that problems could be worked out within the Soviet framework have been repeatedly dashed. The Stalinist deportations and purges still remain the absolute low point, a period which young Estonian intellectuals consider a "historical gap" in the country's cultural development. But hopes for de-Stalinization have not been fulfilled. Around 1956 many young Estonians began to join the Communist party—an act that had previously been widely considered to constitute national treason. They hoped to achieve something by agreeing to play the game according to the Russian rules. They partly believed in Marxist ideals and hoped to implement true federalism. But while Khrushchev vacillated between greater autonomy and recentralization, under Brezhnev the policy has been one of slow but steady centralization. On February 14, 1973, Estonians read in *Rahva Hääl*, their principal daily, that recentralization of the economy under Moscow's control "enhanced the rights of the union republics." Auntie Masha was indulging in Orwellian double-speak, eleven years ahead of 1984. Talking to Moscow about true federalism within the Soviet Union was like talking to a wall. But a political return to the Western world seemed unrealistic and, in view of the West's recent problems, perhaps less attractive than it once did. There remained another alternative: a Communist Estonia *outside* the Soviet Union.

In 1971, the idea of an Estonian "people's democracy" according to the pattern of Poland or Bulgaria was openly attacked for the first time in the Soviet Estonian press (A. Lebbin, *Eesti Kommunist*, 1971, no. 5, p. 37). By 1972, Soviet

Estonia's Byelorussian-born president had joined in the attack, which was formally directed against the Estonian anti-Communist exile "establishment" (A. Vader, *Eesti Kommunist*, 1972, no. 5, p. 3). However, the real target must have been within Estonia itself, since the exiles are predominantly hostile to the idea of a people's democracy. Indeed, Soviet Estonia's president concluded his attack by acknowledging that "manifestations of national uppishness and narrowmindedness can sometimes be observed among us."

An Estonian "people's democracy" actually existed briefly in 1940 as a way station toward Estonia's annexation by the Soviet Union. Khrushchev possibly toyed with the idea of reestablishing it before the Hungarian revolution gave him pause. Yet, in Estonian Communist party circles, the matter kept reappearing. Several independent sources confirm that in 1967 Vambola Pôder, foreign information chief of the Estonian Communist party, ridiculed the idea of a people's democracy in a talk he gave to Communist writers. However, in the discussion that followed, several writers voiced the opinion that a separate Estonia was worth serious thought. The open Soviet criticism of such thoughts since 1971 can have two meanings. In the wake of the 1968 disappointments, the talk of a people's democracy even in Estonian party circles may have become so widespread that it could no longer be officially ignored. But it may also be that the Soviets are gradually coming to accept the idea. There are precedents for the belief that overt attacks serve as a transition phase in change. The outlook for an Estonian people's democracy has been discussed in more detail by Taagepera (1972 and 1973b).

After an unusually subdued 1973, a remarkably active period of political initiative (and repression) began in late 1974. In the space of twelve months, at least ten political *samizdat* texts reached the West—probably more than during the preceding twenty years combined. Among them were these:

1. Memoranda to the United Nations secretary general and the General Assembly, signed by the Estonian National Front and the Estonian Democratic Movement. Both memos were dated October 24, 1972, but they were first published in the West (*Baltic Events*, October 1974) two years later. Both demanded restoration of Estonia's independence through U.N.–supervised elections.

2. A report of mathematician Olev Meremaa's harassment

after he demonstrated openly in support of Sakharov, Solzhenitsyn, and human rights on May 1, 1974.

3. Memoranda to Kurt Waldheim and to the world press,
dated December 1974, reporting the arrest in Tallinn of four
people accused of writing the 1972 memos, and repeating the
demand for U.N.–supervised elections. The Democratic
Movement and the National Front again signed the Waldheim
memo, while "A Group of Estonian Patriots" signed the other
one.

4. Two letters (dated December 19, 1974) addressed to
friends and to world opinion by Sergei Soldatov, who expected
subsequently to be (and was) arrested, confirming his support
of "the 1972 moral and political renaissance program" and
other "democratic documents" calling for "nonviolent, peaceful evolution."

5. A letter (dated February 10, 1975) released by the "Estonian Patriotic and Democratic Movement," analyzing Russification and asking exiles to use the Voice of America as their
main communication link with Estonia.

6. A memo titled "To all Governments Participating in the
Conference on Security and Cooperation in Europe" signed by
"Representatives of the Estonian and Latvian Democrats" and
dated Tallinn-Riga, June 17, 1975. This first Latvian-Estonian
joint memo called for a détente that was "real, not an illusory
one," and that was based on respect for human and national
rights. Restoration of independent Baltic states was demanded.

7. "Quo vadis, Estonian Nation?"—an unsigned and un-
dated manifesto (received in 1975) addressed to fellow Estonians, analyzing Russification and calling for the generation of a
new national elite.

These texts almost certainly were written in Estonia, judging
from style, vocabulary, information content, Soviet reaction,
and independent confirmation of facts. Items 6 and 7 are the
least certain. The authors clearly were different, since style and
emphasis vary. A brief analysis of the contents of these
communications is given in Parming (1976).

In November 1975, after a year-long trial, four persons were
sentenced to five or six years in prison because sending letters
to the United Nations was considered to be "anti-Soviet
agitation and propaganda": Kaljo Mätik, Mati Kiirend, Sergei
Soldatov, and Artjom Juskevitsh (see *Helsingin Sanomat*,

November 13, 1975, p. 25, and November 18, 1975, p. 19). All
four were engineers; their ages ranged from thirty-six to forty-
three. The last two had Estonian mothers but Russian or
Ukrainian fathers—an eloquent testimony to the attraction of
Estonian culture and the home-rule movement. The movement
probably includes only a few dozen activists, in view of the
tight police control and of the minimal hopes for success. Since
their sacrifices do not yield tangible results, the majority of the
population opts for personal security through passive collaboration. The price to be paid is analyzed in the next section.

If I Cannot Beat Them, Should I Join Them?

"I am a dumb country woman. And the question I will ask
you is likely to be dumb. But give me a straight answer: Do you
stand in your life and doings on clear grounds and at the right
place?" This is the question an Estonian mother asks her son,
who has become a general in the Russian army, in a short story
published by Jaan Kross (1971a) in Soviet Estonia.

The son has acquired fame by crushing a dangerous revolt
against the empire. Therefore the mother wonders what would
happen if Estonians should revolt and her son should be sent in
to quell this uprising, too. The son shoots back: "So do you
think that I should have tried to lead an Estonian revolt, and
have myself executed?" By helping the Russian empire to crush
rebels elsewhere, the son has achieved a position where he can
(and does) humiliate his former bosses. He can also help his
parents. But beyond this he can do nothing, not even to save a
sympathetic countryman caught while trying to escape to
Finland. And he faces the question: "But who am I, in reality?"

Needless to say, the setting is historical—1783, to be exact.
An Estonian-born General Michelson indeed helped to subdue
Pugatshov. But the problem presented is timeless: Should a
talented member of a downtrodden group free himself as an
individual by joining the oppressive establishment, or should
he seek collective liberation for his whole group even when the
odds against group success are overwhelming?

Another example from Soviet Estonian literature further
illustrates the dilemma: A painter who has become famous in
the West returns to Estonia, only to find that his achievements
carry no weight in the eyes of the local artistic establishment,

which is composed not really of artists but of craftsmen. They treat him as a foreigner, although he is locally born while many of the craftsmen are immigrants. They ask him to prove his ability by working under them and by passing an exam. To everyone's surprise, the painter accepts the humiliating terms because "in order to take it in a tragic vein, one should first take it seriously. But this matter makes one laugh." His artistic level is so much superior to that of the local masters that he feels confident that he can indulge their primitive demands without making any concession to artistic standards, which matter most to the painter himself.

This is the subject of another short story by Kross (1970); and the painter in question is Michel Sittow, who returned from the Spanish court to Tallinn in 1506. But are the bosses, who are stupid enough to make stupid demands, always stupid enough to be circumvented? If one can laugh about a problem, can one always laugh the problem out of existence? No, says a construction engineer in the Soviet Estonian press: We do laugh and make jokes about the senselessness of our paper-work, but the reports still have to be in by the deadline (*Sirp ja Vasar*, September 15, 1972). Clearly, one has to make compromises. However, when does one reach the point at which all available energy is spent in compromising and circumventing, and nothing is left for creative activity? Let us proceed.

The editor of an Estonian newspaper is dead tired of having his paper continually prostituted (as he says) by foreign bossing and censorship. The bosses are possibly just as tired of trying to catch all of his ever-recurring bits of nationalism, and some of them offer to pay him if he desists. He badly needs the money. He reasons in the following way about his paper, his "daughter," as he says: "They have turned her into their whore anyway, long ago. . . . And I cannot help it." So why not accept money for what has been happening anyway? "Can't we purify it through the proper use of it?" the editor asks about the bribe money. But the rumor that he has sold out soon breaks loose and will haunt him the rest of his life, along with the lives of his progeny.

This is the topic of a third short story by Kross (1971b). The alleged sellout occurred 100 years ago; the central figure was J. W. Jannsen, the publisher-editor of the first permanent Estonian-language newspaper. The rumor did go around that Jannsen was receiving money from the Baltic German establishment, and reportedly some proof of this was recently found by V. Miller (1972). Kross made Jannsen's act seem understandable, if not justifiable: Jannsen could have, but did not, abandon his people, as did General Michelson. The money enabled Jannsen to keep the paper going, and a prostituted paper for the Estonian reading public presumably was better than no paper, or than a paper edited by the German establishment. Or was it?

An intensive reevaluation of Jannsen had begun in Soviet Estonia several years before Kross published his story. The underlying issue appeared to be this: Should an oppressed population refuse to cooperate in any way with the oppressor and instead aim at a grand confrontation, with possibly disastrous results? Or should the oppressed population formally adopt the oppressor's religion and customs, call conquest "liberation," and then methodically proceed to exploit the very opportunities resulting from these concessions in attitude? Estonia confronted this problem a century ago.

For Estonians, it is a question not only of compromise between Marxism and other lines of thought. It is also a matter of compromise between "Marxism with a human face" and the other variety. This issue was brought to a head during Stalin's purges, but it is contemporary enough to interest even writers who were adolescents at that time.

Enn Vetemaa, born in 1936, described in his short story "Musician" (1967) the slow alcohol poisoning of a writer who had played the official tune in 1949 against his own teacher. He even had a good reason: had he not led the attack, someone else might have done it even more brutally. The musician's first name, Ruuben (Reuben), is that of the biblical Joseph's eldest brother, who talked the others into casting Joseph into a pit without first slaying him. Ruuben's stratagem of playing wolf, in order to save the sheep from real wolves, backfires both in the Bible and in Vetemaa's story (in which the professor dies during a police interrogation). Estonia is often called Maarja- maa, the land of St. Mary, in poetry—and, incidentally, it is so called in Vetemaa's story. The name of the denounced professor's daughter also is Maarja. She forgives the musician and patiently sleeps with him whenever he happens to return from other women to her familiar grounds. But the musician is slowly eroding under the burden of the sort of guilt which does

not haunt true scoundrels. And Maarja is sterile. Toward the
end of the story, two persons with the names of the biblical
Reuben's parents are introduced—Jakob and Lea. Their shack
supplies a moment of respite to the musician, since they
represent a tie both to the innocent past and to a more fruitful
future.

Feelings of guilt for an even more passive offense were
expressed by a poet who had been an adult in 1949 and who
slowly died of cancer in 1969—August Sang. In a poem which
was broadcast but (to the best of my knowledge) not published,
he inveighed against Stalinist henchmen and wondered whether "the past will not repeat itself." But then he asked himself
what he had been doing in 1949 to stop the game:

> And be it that it would have been
> completely hopeless enterprise—
> for senselessness perhaps is sometimes
> the only thing that still makes sense.

Since he had not taken any action, Sang concluded:

> I know that I am guilty, too:
> my crime is that I stayed alive.

This is a bit too strong. He also expressed this "secret guilt"
(about not speaking up) in his published work (Sang, 1963).
But in the same collection, he also uttered the diametrically
contrary thought:

> To die for great ideas—that is simple.
> But life demands some compromises.

Sang did not make accusatory noises, in 1949, like Vetemaa's
musician. He did not publish from the beginning of the Soviet
rule in 1940 until 1963. Should he have continued his silence?
Or should he have broken it even earlier?

The new generation of writers is aware that it has avoided the
musician's offense "thanks to their birthdate" and maybe only
temporarily (as expressed by Vetemaa, 1967:40). The pressures
on them are less brutal. In fact, they are sometimes of the same
type one finds in the United States:

You tried to convince me
that roads are softly curved.

.   .   .   .

You said why does one have
to give a straight "no" or "yes"

when one can as well smile
and leave it unsaid.

.   .   .   .

You tried to explain to me
something simple and yet impossible.

The preceding lines are by Helgi Muller (1963), born in 1932,
from a poem dedicated "to U.L." A poet with those initials,
Uno Laht, worked in the State Security Ministry (MVD) in the
late 1940s and twenty years later wrote about "solitary abandoned farms" representing "your hidden distress, Estonia" (in
Looming, December 1968). "Where are those peasant men and
women?" Laht asked, suggesting that flight to the cities was the
answer. Another partial answer is revealed in the works of a
number of other Soviet Estonian writers: innocent people—
nay, whole villages—were deported by the MVD at the time
Laht was working there. One is reminded of a character in
Vetemaa's story, Tiit, who was in the forefront of the purges in
1949, and who fifteen years later was in the forefront of the
rehabilitation (often posthumous) of his erstwhile victims. One
is also reminded of the Stalinist's portrait in Sang's unpublished poem:

And with his glance he seems to tell me
"Someone must do the dirty jobs.
I did my share. But what of you?"

Those young writers who have most seriously tried to resist
the establishment's pressures might have the fewest illusions
about their prospects of success. Johnny B. Isotamm, with a
past of imprisonment and more recent charges of hippieism,
wrote in his first published volume in 1971:

me johnny b
in the past fighting the wall
bloodying his eyebrows at the wall

now sitting in the shadow of the same wall
and scratching my back against the wall

in the future lording it on the top of the wall
important disgusting and fat.

A similar evolution was described earlier by August Sang (in *Looming*, February 1967). Vetemaa himself joined the Komsomol at the ripe age of twenty-five—perhaps significantly, one year before his first poetry book was published. Once this step was taken, joining the Communist party followed rather quickly, at age 28.

To be honest without compromise, and to have an impact on society—these tend to be mutually exclusive objectives in any society. The completely honest individual will be completely isolated because, given the complexity of issues, every person is likely to assign slightly different fingerprints to the personal concept of ideal honesty. Common action requires compromises. Reform groups traditionally have splintered into powerlessness when they insisted on purity, or have grown into new oppressive forces when they sacrificed principles for revolutionary efficiency. This is a dilemma faced by every American presidential candidate as well as by the most powerless political prisoner on any continent. But some contexts make this dilemma more acute than others. The problem of political collaboration in *past* situations has visibly become a major source of *present* preoccupation among some Soviet Estonian writers. Yet, while these writers pondered the extent to which Russian Marxism could be accepted, other Estonians toyed with the idea of being more Marxist than the Soviet establishment.

Playing Their Game, Only More So

In Eastern Europe (including the Soviet Union), many young people have been equally repulsed by their own Marxist establishment and by the type of opposition that could be labeled backward-looking and "reactionary." To these people, the "ultra-Marxist" emulation of the Western new left offered a progressive-looking way to oppose the establishment. Insofar as Estonia is largely urbanized, has a high percentage of college students and graduates, and enjoys relatively extensive Western contacts, it could be expected to be more likely than most Soviet republics to rethink the meaning of Marxism in the postindustrial world. In addition to the official Soviet version of Marxism, which obviously is worded and interpreted to suit the specifically Russian objectives of the Soviet regime, there also is a national motivation to go beyond the official creed. This section will describe what Estonians learned about new-left unrest in the West, through official channels, and how they responded.

The ambivalent reaction of the Soviets toward the new left is exemplified by the contents of two successive pages in the same issue of the main Soviet Estonian daily, *Rahva Hääl*, on July 2, 1969. On one page, J. Sitkovski stated that "there exists also an 'ultra-leftist anticommunism' propagated by people like H. Marcuse and his numerous followers among Western students and intellectuals."

> Herbert Marcuse's criticism of capitalism is acid and exposing. But the trouble lies in that he directs his criticism equally against the socialist countries, and, in particular, against the Soviet Union. Arguing in favor of a "single industrial society" theory, Marcuse equates the American and the Soviet regimes. Thus his criticism bears the seal of anticommunism.
>
> . . . Discounting the proletariat as a revolutionary force, Marcuse raises into this position *déclassé* elements, unstable and ideologically unhardened youth, bohemian tramps who in his opinion have not yet lost the ability to commit revolutionary acts. To the steady and methodical struggle of the communists to attract wide circles of workers, Marcuse substitutes petty bourgeois forms of struggle such as adventurist revolt, provocations, and isolated guerrilla uprisings (Sitkovski, 1969).

Yet, on the following page of the same daily, these "petty bourgeois" tactics are applauded:

the United States is not able to regulate its internal problems. Everywhere in the country there are great anti-war manifestations and youth demonstrations . . . . The National Guard bayonets are directed against the students at Berkeley.

Sitkovski's article offers a typical example of what the Estonian reader learned about Western student unrest through the central Soviet news channels. Occasionally, more direct reports became available. The youth monthly *Noorus* (1970, no. 5) featured a remarkably cool firsthand report by Jaak Kangilaski about his talks with Western youth during a trip through France and the United States. Kangilaski reported that the new left criticizes the old left (including the Western Communists) for placing too much emphasis on the economic struggle and parliamentary action while ignoring the problems of the individual. Ho Chi Minh, Che Guevara, and Mao Tse-tung were reported to be the main heroes of the new left, whose admiration for the revolutionary movement of the third world Kangilaski deemed exaggerated (without specifying whether this applied to Mao alone or also to Guevara). In May 1968, the French new left had played an "important and, in the opinion of French communists, a basically harmful role," because it had led the students to indulge in adventures which the workers could not support, observed the young Estonian reporter.

Along with disassociating themselves from the new-left revolt in the West, Soviet Communists have felt a need to explain this rejection in Marxist terms. A "petty bourgeois" explanation satisfies some but sounds implausible to others because the new left is so blatantly antibourgeoisie. The term *"déclassé,"* used by Sitkovski, implicitly suggests that the new radicals do not belong to any of the traditional social classes. The theory proposed by the French philosopher Roger Garaudy is that the intellectuals are becoming a revolutionary force separate from the working class, although the two are going to act together as "a new historical bloc." Garaudy's ideas were discussed in the Estonian press while he was being gradually excluded from the French Communist party. In particular, L. Remmelgas noted in *Sirp ja Vasar* (February 20, 1970) that "even in our midst one can note during the discussion of those problems a dangerous similarity with Garaudy's

nondialectical and non-working-class-oriented thoughts."
Along with a *pro forma* condemnation of Garaudy, Remmelgas gave quite a fair description of Garaudy's line of reasoning.

To the Soviet establishment, the most worrisome question
implicit in Garaudy's thesis is: Are the intellectuals becoming a
distinct social class? The idea suggests itself spontaneously to
anyone who attempts extrapolations from the *Communist
Manifesto* in the light of present technological developments.
According to the *Manifesto*, the age of great discoveries
expanded the role of the bourgeoisie, who assumed "a most
revolutionary part." Then the industrial revolution called into
existence the modern working class, which had become the
only "really revolutionary class" by the time the *Manifesto* was
written. But now the existence of a new technological revolution is recognized both by the West (which calls it the "second
industrial" or "technetronic" revolution) and by the Soviets
(who call it the "scientific-technological revolution"). Given
this fact, one may wonder whether a new revolutionary class
should not arise according to the very pattern presented in the
Communist Manifesto. The new-leftist unrest of the intellectuals may then be interpreted as the first show of strength by this
class.

Up to now this unorthodox idea has been expressed in
Estonia only in a negative form, in assertions that the intellectuals are *not* a separate class. But this very insistence on
denying a proposition that no one has explicitly advanced is
akin to indirect affirmation. In an article by N. Moltšanov in
Sirp ja Vasar (March 6 and 13, 1970) the denial is repeated
periodically in a way reminiscent of Marc Antony's "But they
are all honorable men" in Shakespeare's *Julius Caesar*. Moltšanov's argument is that as the scientific-technological revolution proceeds, the number of educated people (intelligentsia)
increases, and it becomes hard to simply assign them to the
existing classes. So a common and specific denominator for
this "group" is needed.

> However, in contrast to the bourgeoisie or the working
> class the intelligentsia is of course not a class but a social
> grouping which in principle can be formed out of people
> who belong to different classes but who are brought
> together by their level of education and who may thus

acquire specific psychological characteristics (Moltšanov, 1970).

In earlier times the intellectuals came mainly from middle-class homes and remained middle class. But now the expanded intelligentsia has become another target for exploitation, and feels alienated. Yet its new-left anticapitalist actions are self-contradictory and show immaturity: "This proves once more that the intelligentsia has its own psychology but that it never has had and never can have its own class ideology" (Moltšanov, 1970). What it does have is a bewildering mix of bourgeois and working-class tenets which expresses a vigorous protest but lacks any positive program. Because the ideas of justice, truth, and humanism are working-class monopolies, says Moltšanov, the exploited intelligentsia has no other choice but to join forces with the workers. It will be the workers' most important ally, but still a subordinate ally—because, on its own, "the intelligentsia has not seized and cannot seize power since it is not a separate class."

Moltšanov's argument that educated people constitute a distinct "social grouping" is presented powerfully and convincingly, while the contention that they should not be called a "class" boils down to transparent circular reasoning.

The discussion thus far has concerned the reaction of the Soviet Estonian press to the new-left phenomenon in the West. But the phenomenon also spread to Eastern Europe. As in the West, youth protest in Eastern Europe has expressed itself in two different ways. One way is to become apolitical, to drop out of the society and retire to hippiedom. The other way is to become a radical "Marxist revivalist"—to reject the policy of offering material incentive to workers, demand "absolute democracy," and admire Mao and Guevara. While they prefer to call themselves ultraleftists, the outlook of the East European group is manifestly similar to that of the new left in the West (see, e.g., *Economist*, March 14, 1970).

There have been some contacts between East European ultraleftists and Western new leftists. The Husak regime asserted that a Czech student opposition group was inspired by West German new leftist Rudi Dutschke (*Economist*, January 24, 1970). But the prize goes to the British Communist J. Aldridge, who explained the whole Czech "spring of 1968" in terms of a Western-inspired uprising of intellectuals against the working class. Estonia's *Rahva Hääl* chose to reproduce this thesis (June 30, 1970).

According to Aldridge, British political leaders incited the Czech intellectuals to carry out "a revolution against the true revolution." It was "a perspectiveless revolution of individuals, an anarchist revolution of the educated." While Aldridge insisted that it was incorrect to think that the whole Czech people consisted of "dissatisfied intellectuals only," he implied that all or most intellectuals were dissatisfied—indeed, to the point of revolt:

> The problem of 1968 is not only Czechoslovakia's prob-
> lem but concerns us English also. When analyzing the
> 1968 events in Czechoslovakia one cannot help but ask
> oneself: What is the role of the educated in the society? Do
> they have the right to determine the fate of the other
> people? Can they present their demands in a form that
> ignores the nature of the socialist-capitalist antagonism?
> (Aldridge, 1970).

Such questions also puzzled the Estonian philosopher Gustav Naan, but he viewed them in terms of tension between intellectuals and bureaucrats. Known in the Soviet Union as a rather daring philosopher of science, Naan has since 1965 increasingly pondered the role of scientists and that of intellectuals in general.

In an essay in the Estonian literary-social monthly *Looming* (November 1969), Naan ostensibly discussed modern bourgeois society, making a distinction between the bourgeois and proletarian "classes," which account, respectively, for about 2 percent and 30 percent of the total population. The rest of the population does not belong to these two classes, but rather belongs to the bureaucratic and intellectual "strata." Bureaucracy, he asserted, has a conservative and stabilizing role in society, while intellectuals have an anticipatory and renovating role; they are critical and individualistic. The regulatory role between these two antagonistic (though equally useful) "strata" belongs to the tiny ruling class and to the proletarian "people" (who are only about 30 percent of the total population). According to Naan, the system usually gets out of equilibrium as a result of a bureaucratic overtightening of screws rather than of an excess of intellectual freewheeling. Yet the creativeness of the intellectuals is becoming increasingly indispensable to both the society and the ruling class. Not only are intellectuals the originators of all ideologies (including Marxism), the gray matter of the brain has become the world's most important strategic raw material. As a result, "the intellectuals are becoming the most exploited social stratum" (presumably depriving the industrial workers of that distinction, although Naan does not spell it out).

Comparing British stability with czarist Russian failure, Naan implicitly suggests (with the help of copious quotations from Marx and Lenin) that the Soviets are depriving themselves of crucial stabilizing factors by their overheavy dependence on bureaucracy, by treating would-be reformers as subversive, and by not tolerating an autonomous press and a loyal opposition party. His peculiar mix of Marxist and bourgeois thinking is different from that of Western new-left ideologues. But his insistence on a new and crucial role for the intellectual "stratum" is unmistakable. And he does not imply that this role is limited to the non-Soviet world.

Naan's views were strongly disputed soon afterward by M. Makarov (*Looming*, March 1971), who ostensibly criticized some Western Communist views but actually countered Naan's theses point by point. Makarov charged that "such ideas were a major component of the Czechoslovak counter-revolution during which Zd. Mlynar said the intellectuals would liberate the society from the 'hostile bureaucratic class' . . . represented by the Communist Party leaders." Naan apparently received a reprimand after he repeated his views on the new role of intellectuals even more explicitly at a 1970 or early 1971 closed meeting. But the text of this talk kept circulating in Estonia, and in late 1972 (see *Sirp ja Vasar*, October 6, 1972, p. 15) Naan again publicly discussed the role of the intellectuals.

Has there been any sign that the Estonian intellectuals are assuming an active new role (apart from discussing the possibility of doing so)? What could be expected, given Estonian conditions, is either an apolitical dropping out of society or a Guevara-oriented ultraleftism.

Dropping out means rejecting the existing social privileges

rather than fighting for them. Hence, the early peaceful brand
of hippie in America managed to shock both the bourgeoisie,
who had their share of the economical pie, and the workers,
who were struggling to get a piece of it—the hippie retorted
that the pie was not worth having. The Estonian literary
establishment faced a limited problem of the same type around
1970. Instead of fighting to get their poetry published, like the
young poets of 1960, members of the new crop were not
interested in getting into print past the official gatekeepers—
they preferred to publish private "forty-nine-copy" albums.
(Private publications in Soviet Estonia are those of which
fewer than fifty copies are printed.) In an unprecedented review
of such "unofficial poetry" in an official literary magazine, the
establishment's reaction was described as follows:

> It is said that the fifth generation is behaving scandalous-
> ly. They allegedly have no ambition at all, and . . . do not
> want to get enmeshed with professional writing. So to say
> non-professional, absolutely free doing their own thing,
> the most independent form of esthetic self-realization (U.
> Laht, *Looming*, June 1970).

Although he admitted that the activity of the young poets
was associated in the mind of the "public" with long hair, and
that the poets had been branded by some as "the local variety of
the hippie movement," Laht did not believe that a true hippie
movement could take place in Estonia, except as a superficial
fad, because "our social structure avoids the nonsense of over-
saturated consumerism where the oppression by things subjects man, and giving them up may look like one way out."
Samples of poetry from the private albums, as quoted by Laht,
show a surrealism which might have offended the petty-
bourgeois mentality of the Soviet Estonian establishment, but
they contain hardly anything which would not have been
published for political reason in the official journals. Laht
considers the following sample from Johnny B. Isotamm as
mere showing off:

> We do not understand each other, my dear
> we talk different languages, my dear
> You've got an artificial brain *made in USSR*.

Isotamm reluctantly made his peace with the literary establishment in 1971. Although hippie attire (including long hair and the wearing of crosses) persists in Estonia, there is little protest content left.

Also appearing in Estonia were other ultraleftist symptoms. Two poems praising Che Guevara appeared almost simultaneously in the winter of 1969-1970—one in Hungary, the other in Estonia. The Hungarian defiantly told his critics that Guevara was the model for "us ultras" (*Economist*, March 14, 1970). The Estonian poem was by Arvi Siig, who had written the poem about Auntie Masha. His poem "Che" (in *Looming*, January 1970) is worth quoting in full:

Che, Che Guevara!
The world is black—black.
The glory of revolution
is only
a line out of its miscellania.
Jan Hus must have perished in the same way,
although in a different way.
The black and white list will
contain your name, Che Guevara.

There was a promise of dawn.
Winds and clouds were restless.
In the jungle
and at the top of the stone jungle
the new day flashed.
Over your body they march again,
as they marched
into a certain small country—
the troops of the world gendarme.

Let's get a dictator!
On with the puppet show!
Democracy?
We know that dialectics!
There is no justice without power:
and power will get you—
into the sandpit!

only the buried ones
make no mistakes.

Dominican Republic or Babylon?
The world—the graves of the worthiest.
With a fresh cross on the grave
freedom is cursing the lie.
At the end of the twentieth century
mourning the light
as if it were still B.C.
I lower my head

The poem may be taken as a mere Soviet diatribe against the
United States. Only in this way, of course, could it be published, in spite of its praise of Che Guevara—whom the Soviet
establishment abhors without daring to admit it, except in an
indirect way (see Kangilaski's report, discussed earlier). But the
marching of foreign armies "into a certain small country"
makes one think not only of the American intervention in the
Dominican Republic but also of the more recent Soviet
intervention in Czechoslovakia, the country of Jan Hus, whom
Siig compares with Che. If American interventionism alone
were at issue, there would be no ground for the total pessimism
expressed in the poem's final lines, since the Soviet Union
would supply a beacon of hope. Siig clearly is assigning the role
of the "world's gendarme" jointly to the American and Soviet
establishments in a typical new-left manner.

Other manifestations of unrest among the Estonian intellectuals would not qualify as "new left" by Western standards but
may be part of the same phenomenon, modified by the specific
conditions prevalent in the Soviet Union. In contrast to the
"new left of the students," it could be called the "new left of the
academicians." (Sakharov's memoranda are a prime example.)
Assuming a worldwide unrest of the intellectual class (or
"stratum," in Naan's euphemistic terminology), different sections of this class might be the first to protest in different
countries. In America, students are materially insured via their
parents and can afford to revolt, while the academicians have
too much to lose. In the Soviet Union, only somebody with a
national standing can protest and actually be heard. The main
document of the Estonian "new left of the academicians"
(other than Naan's essays) is the aforementioned "memo of the

Estonian intellectuals" of 1968. More far-reaching than Sakharov's, this memorandum argues in favor of Western-type
political freedom.

Press attacks against the new left continued in Estonia
throughout 1971. Their methods were considered fascist (*Rahva Hääl*, May 6, 1971), and they were even accused of murder-
ing Communist students in Chile (M. Makarov, *Looming*,
March 1971). By 1972 offers were being made to coopt the rank
and file of the by now disintegrating Western student movement, provided that it adopted some "Communist-led positive
changes" (V. Merkin, *Eesti Kommunist*, July 1972). Ultra-
Marxist voices in Estonia faded along with the worldwide ebb
of the new left. From the vantage point of the mid-seventies,
the new left may seem to be a phenomenon of the past, just as
worker unrest may have seemed during the post-Luddite
period. However, new leftism is bound to reemerge in one form
or another if it is viewed as a symptom of the rise of a new social
class—the "thinking class," consisting of massive numbers of
college-educated people with limited job opportunities (see
Taagepera, 1971a and 1971b). The social foundation for ultra-
Marxist thought and action continues to exist in Estonia.

Conclusions and Prognosis

By the end of the 1950s the young Estonian elite was
increasingly accepting Marxism as an inevitable and suitable
medium for personal and national development. The policy of
working within the Soviet legal framework was called by some
the *leedu tee* ("Lithuanian path") because Lithuanians were
viewed as the most successful practitioners of this approach.
The movement spread in the early 1960s and reached its peak in
early 1968. This was the time of confident declarations, in
poetic form, that matters could be worked out with the
Russians in a friendly and mutually satisfying way. But the
invasion of Czechoslovakia caused a crisis in Estonia. Hope
and enthusiasm were replaced by hopelessness and dejection.
The "Lithuanian path" lost its persuasive and unifying power.
After discussion of collaborationism peaked in 1969-1970,
evaluation of Kross's collaborationist characters (especially of
General Michelson) has been increasingly negative. New
leftism briefly became a focal issue in 1970, just prior to its

worldwide eclipse. Attacks against the idea of an Estonian people's democracy have not been heard since 1972. The U.N.-oriented self-determination movement of the Estonian National Front may have reached its peak in 1975. Are humanists and nationalism in Estonia back to where they were ten years ago? Not quite.

Perhaps the major achievement has been a negative one—there has been no purge, probably thanks to a levelheaded evaluation of mutual interests by both dissidents and Estonian Communist party leaders. Given past Soviet practice, it is almost unbelievable that the poets and intellectuals who said and wrote the heady stuff of 1967-1970 are still free and being published. Have they been coopted by the regime? In some sense, definitely. However, the national power base is intact—in contrast to the situation in the 1950s, when the older generation had not been coopted but had been physically and/or mentally broken (as were August Sang and Vetemaa's musician). Western contacts have been maintained at the 1968 level. Skill in handling the Soviet system has increased, while the aura of progressiveness of the Soviet version of Marxism has been destroyed by the ultra-Marxists. National culture is stronger and more Western-oriented than it was ten years ago. During the same decade, Russian immigration has continued relentlessly. Immigration may eventually begin to weaken Estonian national culture, if it continues; but during the remaining years of the twentieth century it will only serve to irritate the Estonians' national feelings.

What about the future of humanistic and national dissent in Estonia? Perhaps the answer is to be found in one Soviet Estonian's personal reaction to a long-range action program in which this person recognized the concept of the "Lithuanian path." His first reaction was negative, in view of the concept's failure in 1968. The second reaction was: "There is no other path, after all." After a period of dejection, the slow and patient work within the Soviet legal framework will continue, with ebbs and flows reflecting the USSR-wide and worldwide tolerance of dissent. It will continue until the Soviet regime either acknowledges that its own political stability would be best served by granting meaningful federal autonomy (including autonomy for the Estonian Communist party organization) or until the Estonians have been pushed out of their native territorial area to a greater extent than the Welsh have been in theirs. There is no other path.

References

Estonian Events

1967-   Bimonthly newsletter edited by R. Taagepera (Uni-
1975   versity of California, Irvine). Title from 1973 on:
         Baltic Events.

Isotamm, Johnny B.

1971   (with J. Sang, J. Üdi, and T. Liiv). *Närvitrükk* [Nerve
         Print]. Tallinn: Loomingu Raamatukogu.

Kahk, J.

1967   *Soviet Estonian Science*, Ten Aspects of Estonian
         Life Series. Tallinn: Eesti Raamat.

Khronika

1968-   *Khronika tekushchikh sobytii.* Underground bi-
1972   monthly, Moscow.

Kross, Jaan

1970   *Neli monoloogi Püha Jüri asjus* [Four Monologs
         regarding St. George]. Tallinn: Loomingu Raamatu-
         kogu.
1971a   *Michelsoni immatrikuleerimine* [The Immatricula-
         tion of Michelson]. Tallinn: Loomingu Raamatuko-
         gu.
1971b   "Pöördtoolitund" [Swivel Chair Lecture]. *Looming*,
         January, pp. 3-38.

Mägi, A.

1968   *Estonian Literature.* Stockholm: Baltic Humanitar-
         ian Association.

Miller, V.

1972   *Minevikust tulevikku* [From the Past toward the
         Future]. Tallinn. (Cf. *Sirp ja Vasar*, August 4, 1972,
         p. 5.)

Moltšanov, N.

1970   "Lääne intelligents: minevik, olevik, tulevik" [Western Intelligentsia: Past, Present, Future]. *Sirp ja Vasar*, March 6 and 13.

Muller, Helgi

1963   *Tähesärk* [Star Shirt]. Tallinn: Eesti Riiklik Kirjastus.

Naan, Gustav

1969   "Vôim ja vaim" [The Power and the Spirit]. *Looming*, December, pp. 1856-1878.

Nirk, Endel

1970   *Estonian Literature*. Tallinn: Eesti Raamat.

Parming, Tönu

1976   "Contrasts in Nationalism in the Soviet Baltic." Paper presented at the Fifteenth Annual Meeting of the Southern Slavic Association, University of Virginia, Charlottesville, Va.
1977a "Developments in Nationalism in Soviet Estonia since 1964," in *Nationalism in Eastern Europe and the USSR during Brezhnev and Kosygin*, ed. George Simmonds. Detroit: University of Detroit Press.
1977b "Historical Roots of Nationality Differences," in *Nationality Group Survival in Multi-Ethnic States*, ed. Edward Allworth. New York: Praeger.

Pennar, Jaan

1968   "Nationalism in the Soviet Baltics," in *Ethnic Minorities in the Soviet Union*, ed. E. Goldhagen. New York: Praeger.

Sang, August

1963   *Vôileib suudlusega* [A Sandwich with a Kiss]. Tallinn: Eesti Raamat.

Siig, Arvi

1970   "Che." *Looming*, January, pp. 98-99.

Taagepera, Rein

1968   "The National Differences within Soviet Demographic Trends." *Soviet Studies* 20: 428-489.
1970   "Nationalism in the Estonian Communist Party." *Bulletin of the Institute for the Study of the USSR* 1: 3-15.
1971a   "The Revolt of the Thinking Class." *Queens Quarterly* 78, no. 1: 19-29.
1971b   "Revolt of the Thinking Class." *The Nation*, May 31, pp. 681-684.
1971c   "The 1970 Soviet Census: Fusion or Crystallization of Nationalities?" *Soviet Studies* 23: 216-221.
1972   "On the Status of Estonia." Unpublished study prepared on the occasion of the European Security Conference.
1973a   "Dissimilarities between the Northwestern Soviet Republics," in *Problems of Mininations*, ed. Arvids Ziedonis et al. San Jose, Calif.: Association for the Advancement of Baltic Studies.
1973b   "Estonia: Uppity Satellite." *The Nation,* May 7, pp. 585-588.
1973c   "The Soviet Nations." *Journal of Baltic Studies* 4: 97-112.
1975a   "Estonia and the Estonians," in *Handbook of Major Soviet Nationalities*, ed. Zev Katz. New York: Free Press.
1975b   "The Problem of Political Collaboration in Soviet Estonian Literature." *Journal of Baltic Studies* 6, Spring: 30-40.
1976   "The Impact of the New Left on Estonia." *East European Quarterly* 10, no. 1: 43-51.

Vetemaa, Enn

1967   *Pillimees* [Musician]. Tallinn: Loomingu Raamatukogu.

3

Soviet Nationality Policy and the Estonian Communist Elite

Jaan Pennar

This chapter covers two related topics: Soviet nationality policy and the Estonian Communist perspective of it; and how this policy has been implemented by the Communist party of Estonia within its own ranks. The latter includes an effort to describe, within the limits of available data, the Soviet Estonian Communist elite. Although both topics are approached from a historical perspective, much of the analysis deals with contemporary developments. It will be shown that the Estonian interpretations of Soviet nationality policy are conceived in a more rational, if not more liberal, vein than is commonplace elsewhere in the Soviet Union, and that the Communist party of Estonia is becoming increasingly Estonified despite the heavy Russian presence in both the rank and file and the top leadership. Of necessity, the attention accorded to Soviet nationality policy is minimal.

The Estonian Perspective

Historically, Estonian Communists have called for close cooperation with their Russian counterparts, albeit in a proletarian, internationalist sense. "Our banner," declared the Bolshevik committees of Estonia and Tallinn in January 1918, "is not separation from Russia, but the closest and most brotherly union with the working people of Russia. The Revolution has linked us. . . . Our toilers in the city and the countryside should not forget for a moment that they are members of the international community of workers" (*Rahva Hääl*, December 16, 1972).

Johannes (Ivan) Käbin, first party secretary in Estonia, recalled the 1918 declaration during the 1972 celebrations of the fiftieth anniversary of the Soviet Union. "These lines," added Käbin, "excite one even today with their spirit of internationalism!" Parenthetically, in December 1917 Lenin had proposed to Jaan Anvelt, an Estonian Communist leader, that the Estonian Communists declare a formally independent socialist republic so as to forestall an imminent German occupation of the country. Estonian Communist leaders thought this tactic would not be successful, although some preliminary steps were taken; for example, the establishment of the Estonian Workers Commune in Narva in 1919 (Rudnev, 1970:98-100). Be this as it may, Käbin's speech in 1972 was not studded with references, customary on such occasions, to the role of the great Russian people in the multinational family of the Soviet Union. The Russians were not called "elder brothers," nor were they hailed as "first among equals." Rather, Käbin stressed the theme of unity among Soviet nationalities.

By contrast, the Soviet party leader Leonid Brezhnev, also speaking on the occasion of the fiftieth anniversary, chose to pay homage to the Russian republic as "the first among equals" (*Pravda*, December 22, 1972). He was careful to qualify this statement, however, by adding that this was the way it was "justifiably" referred to by the peoples of "our multinational country." The nationality problem, Brezhnev suggested further, had been "fully, finally, and forever" solved in the Soviet Union on the basis of the Leninist legacy, which he then proceeded to outline. A brief analysis of that legacy is pertinent.

Lenin had little precedent to draw on when it came to nationalism and its manifestations. To be sure, Marx had spoken of Irish autonomy and Engels had supported the independence of Poland, but basically the theory of class struggle overlooked ethnic consciousness and conflict as a distinct phenomenon, suggesting that its solution was to be found in proletarian internationalism. But, as Lenin discovered in his attempt to forge the Russian Social Democrats into a viable Bolshevik party, nationalism could not be wished away by merely applying the Marxist theory of class struggle.

Basic decisions on the subject were laid down at the Second Congress of the Russian Social-Democratic Labor Party in 1903, which is perhaps best known for the split in the ranks of the party which occurred there. Of the two factions, the Bolsheviks and the Mensheviks, the latter supported a broad-based party organization as opposed to Lenin's concept of a steeled and unitary vanguard party. Earlier, a federal approach stressing national and cultural differences, advocated by the Jewish Bund, had also been rejected by Lenin. The party was to remain single and unitary. It is thus incorrect to refer to an Estonian Communist party. The proper terminology should be the Communist party of Estonia, denoting merely the territorial subdivision of a unitary party organization.

But Lenin at the Second Congress also chose to support the formula adopted at the First Congress in 1898 in support of "the right of self-determination of all nations entering the state structure." Having achieved his main goal—unitary party organization—Lenin could now afford to support the principle of self-determination, to which he attached less importance. As was the case with Estonia in 1917, the principle was to be applied largely as a temporary measure on the road to socialism. Furthermore, it was assumed that the significance of the principle of self-determination would diminish once a world system of socialism had been established. Advocacy of self-determination was also good politics, because national tensions were becoming more and more obvious both in Russia and in other parts of Europe.

Other niceties affecting nationalism were not overlooked by the Second Congress of 1903. A resolution was adopted which called for the right to an education in one's mother tongue (education in czarist Russia was conducted almost exclusively in Russian) and which also proposed that the "mother tongue" (for example, Ukrainian) be placed on a par with the state language (that is, Russian) in all local public and governmental institutions.

These decisions, made near the turn of the century, provided the foundation for the Soviet nationality policy of today. However, in reviewing Lenin's statements and observations afterward, it is clear that he was rather unsure about the whole subject.

Nationalism was really an obstacle to Lenin's ultimate goal of world socialism. Thus, before 1917 Lenin had asserted, in effect, that the assimilation of the great Russian and Ukrainian proletariat was an "unquestionably progressive" development, and that the "process of assimilation of nationalities through capitalism constitutes a tremendous historic progress" (Low, 1958:60-61). But as a tactician, he could not overlook the rising tide of nationalism: "The socialists cannot achieve their great goals without struggling against any oppression of nations" (Lenin, 1936:206). He finally reconciled the right to self-determination and secession with a "free, voluntary and not a forcible rapprochement and merger of nations" (Lenin, 1942:254). This formed the rationale for the creation of the Soviet Union in 1922.

Whether what emerged as the Soviet federation was exactly what Lenin had in mind is difficult to ascertain. He was ailing during the debates. It is known, however, that he harbored considerable suspicions in regard to Stalin, who, as commissar of nationalities, was the leading figure in the drafting of the new constitution. At least one idea of Stalin's was discarded— that of establishing the then-existing Soviet republics as mere autonomous units within a centralized Soviet Russian state. Lenin insisted upon the retention of several attributes of sovereignty. He was particularly concerned that the Russians should not gain the upper hand, which he considered would represent a reversion to prerevolutionary days and thus would render a Communist future for the rest of the world less attractive. "It would be unforgivable opportunism," Lenin noted, "if, on the eve of . . . [the] emergence of the East and at the very beginning of its awakening, we were to undermine our authority there by the smallest rudeness and injustice with regard to our own *inorodtsy* [non-Russians]" (Lenin, 1957:558-559).

These last lines were written at the time that the Soviet Union was established in 1922. They set the stage for Lenin's dissatisfaction with Stalin. The latter played a key role at the Twelfth Party Congress in 1923, which concerned itself with the nationality question. Since Lenin was unable to participate in its proceedings, owing to his illness, its resolutions reflected a compromise on the nationality question. In a way, they dealt much more with local Soviet conditions than with the world-wide importance that nationalism may have had in Lenin's vision of a universal socialist society. When the congress resolved to describe Russian chauvinism as the main danger, and local nationalism as a minor threat, to the building of Soviet socialist society, it really limited itself to Soviet conditions exclusively and forgot the rest of the world. Together with other measures taken by the party at the time, the resolutions on the nationality question adopted by the Twelfth Congress paved the way for "socialism in one country." Stalin himself managed to be elected the party's secretary general at the congress, which placed him in a key position in the forthcoming power struggle.

Basically, however, the resolutions reflected Lenin's position that Russian chauvinism represented the main danger to the country. The result was that throughout most of the 1920s local nationalism was encouraged under the slogan *korenizatsiya*, or nativization. Educational efforts took priority, and schools and universities switched to using the local languages. Together with the New Economic Policy, which favored private farming and other small-scale enterprise, *korenizatsiya* established a Soviet base for local nationalism which, by 1933, Stalin was declaring to be a greater threat than Russian chauvinism. From then until the death of Joseph Stalin in 1953, Russian nationalism gained the upper hand in Soviet nationality policy. While the Khrushchev period at first witnessed a readjustment of balance between the Russians and other nationalities of the Soviet Union, it eventually saw a regression to an overemphasis of Lenin's views regarding the rapprochement and subsequent merger of nations, with the Russian language in the dominant position as *lingua franca*.

Lenin's legacy is subject to current debate in the Soviet Union. The basic issue deals with the linguistic and cultural heritage of the non-Russians versus the increasing usage of Russian and eventual assimilation. Some authors, such as Ivan Dzyuba, suggest that current Soviet nationality policy is a far cry from what Lenin had in mind. Dzyuba, who tried to prove his argument statistically in regard to the Ukraine, never received a public hearing in the USSR. Rather, his work was published abroad. Others have adopted a more defensive stance.

At an interrepublican conference held in Tallinn, Estonia, in November 1969, it was noted: "Nowhere did Lenin speak of the disappearance of national differences, national languages and cultures in near historical perspective. The existence and the further development of national languages and national cultures can in no way be regarded as a hindrance to the victorious path in the construction of communism" (*Sovetskaya Estonia*, November 28, 1969). As for the use of the Russian language as a means of communication between different nationalities, it would be "utterly false to regard this as a manifestation of national nihilism."

Estonian researchers have generally adopted a rational approach to Soviet nationality policy. Thus, Klara Hallik, a lecturer on Marxism at the Tallinn Polytechnic Institute, suggests that internationalist feelings cannot be achieved without first taking into account positive national feelings: "A correct evaluation of the progressive traditions of one's own nation permits a better understanding of the existence and interests of other nations" (Hallik, 1969:27). According to her, socialism, as a matter of fact, heightens national pride. This leads to the conclusion that national feelings should be handled with care. Among her other observations are the following: "The higher the level of national culture, the more multifaceted its relations with the spiritual creative power of other nations. A successful internationalization of a national culture is possible only when it is blooming itself" (Hallik, 1969:33). Hallik follows this up by citing examples of non-Russian cultural influences on the Soviet scene. She goes so far as to suggest that the Uzbeks should further the unity of the peoples of Central Asia: "Why should not the national art of the Uzbek people, having a rich cultural heritage, become in the future the center of cultural unity of the peoples of its language group?" (Hallik, 1969:35).

Hallik is disturbed by the idea of "denationalization" which has currency in Soviet discussions on the nationality problem. There is, she claims, a "methodological error" in simplifying the mutual dependence of class and national relations: "The classes disappear but the nations remain and continue their development. This is reason enough for not transferring the national question mechanically into juxtaposition with the changing class relations in a socialist society" (Hallik, 1970:128). In other words, the "greater part of nationalist style, prejudices, illusions, feeling and habits . . . are related to non-political consciousness." Therefore, "the Soviet people now and also in the foreseeable future represent a belonging of the individuals in a multinational structure wherein the relations between separate nations are regulated by principles of socialist internationalism" (Hallik, 1970:129). She further takes issue with alleged assimilatory tendencies, based on evidence supplied by the 1959 census which shows that 10.5 million non-Russians consider their native language to be Russian. She suggests that 56.5 percent of these are Ukrainians and Byelorussians, to whom a linguistic switch is relatively easy. But, more important, "assimilation is related primarily to national extraterritoriality, because among all of those who regard their native language as that of another nation, 90 percent live outside their own republic" (Hallik, 1970:134). She concludes, as a result, that the "assimilatory ghost" has been blown way out of proportion.

Hallik stuck to her arguments even when the 1970 census revealed that a total of 14.7 million people in the USSR conversed in a language other than their mother tongue, 13 million of them in Russian. She made allowance for the small nationalities, among whom 6 to 7 percent had become assimilated, as well as for some instances of mixed marriages. But Hallik stressed that the major nationalities in the union republics continued to use their own languages "by almost one-hundred per cent," and that if any assimilation took place anywhere it was not on account of "social and national pressure from the outside" (*Kodumaa*, March 8, 1972).

Hallik's negative emphasis on assimilation might reflect an attempt of the party to soothe the fears, expressed by Estonians both in the Estonian SSR and abroad, that they are slowly being subjected to Russification. Frequently cited as justification of that fear are census data. For example, a comparison of 1959 and 1970 census figures shows a decrease of ethnic Estonians from 74.6 to 68.2 percent in the republic's population, mostly as a result of Russian immigration. Another figure often cited, showing the effects of World War II, is the absolute decline of Estonians living in Estonia and the rest of the Soviet Union from 1,144,000 in 1939 to 1,007,000 in 1970. The proportion of Russians in Estonia increased, during the same period, from about 8 percent to almost 25 percent. To make the last figure look more palatable, a Soviet Estonian economist suggests that almost half of the Russians in Estonia are conversant in Estonian (Talvar, 1972).

No data are available along these lines about other union

republics, but it would seem unlikely that such a high proportion of Russians are "going native" anywhere else in the USSR.
At best, nationalities in the Caucasus and Central Asia can
boast of a much higher birth rate than the Russians, which has
enabled them to double their populations since the 1926
census. The probable reason for the "assimilation" of Russians
in Estonia is the fact that the republic is both culturally and
economically among the most advanced in the USSR. This
statement does not necessarily presuppose that the republic
will remain in such an exalted position in the long run.

While Soviet Estonian literary critics may complain about
the ill effects of Russian usage on the Estonian language,
Soviet researchers closer to the seat of power hail the spread of
Russian in the USSR. Even the assimilatory tendencies are
looked upon positively in this connection.[1] As a matter of fact,
the Twenty-fourth Party Congress, which met in 1971, decided
that a new historical community had been created—the Soviet
people—wherein Russian plays the role of the language of
"inter-nation intercourse." Political and economic unity were
also emphasized.

These aspects were given renewed emphasis on the eve of the
fiftieth anniversary of the Soviet Union by Pyotr Masherov,
first party secretary in Byelorussia and an alternate member of
the Politburo. According to Masherov, the process of the
"drawing together of nations" is taking place most intensively
in the field of economic relations. In other words, republican
boundaries are losing their significance. At the same time, "our
society is becoming increasingly homogenous from the social
standpoint" (Masherov, 1972:26). He feels that one of the more
important tasks which remains is to create "in all of the
country's republics conditions *facilitating and stimulating as
much as possible the working people's mastery of the Russian
language, along with their own native tongues*" (Masherov,
1972:29).[2]

The Estonian Communist Party and Its Elite

Political integration in the Soviet Union is, of course,
maintained by the Communist party. Although the Bolsheviks
were quite active in Estonia before 1917, the establishment of
an actual Communist party of Estonia dates to November

1920. Unlike other Western czarist provinces (Finland, Latvia, Lithuania, and Poland) the Estonian Social Democrats had no separate party organization but were part of the Russian Social Democratic Labor party. One of the reasons for this might have been that the southern half of Estonia was administratively part of the czarist province of Livonia, which also included northern Latvia. In addition, there were large numbers of Estonian workers in St. Petersburg and, conversely, Russian workers in Tallinn. Moreover, the Menshevik faction was quite strong among Estonian Social Democrats.

The multinational nature of the Bolsheviks in Estonia is exemplified by the Tallinn party organization in 1917, which included 2,302 Estonians, 523 Russians, and 357 Latvians. Altogether, the Soviets claimed 10,000 party members in Estonia in 1917 (Pankseyev, 1967:63). Although a large number of Estonian Communists fled to Russia when the Germans occupied the country in 1918, the figure appears too high and probably includes the rebellious Russian soldiers and sailors stationed in Estonia at the time. No more than 700 Communists were counted in Estonia in 1920.

During the years of the Republic of Estonia, declared in 1918, the Communist party, whose proclaimed goal was to end the republic, was subject to official harassment, but it attracted new members. Among those who perished during the early 1920s was Viktor Kingisepp, an Estonian party leader and intellectual who had been active in revolutionary activities since his student days in St. Petersburg. In December 1924 Estonian Communists attempted a coup in Tallinn at the instigation of the Comintern, to whom the party was subordinate. The failure of the move caused greater hardships for the party and a drop in its membership. It continued to operate in Estonia under the guise of various leftist fronts, but without much success. By the 1930s there remained but a few hundred members in the party. Most of the imprisoned Estonian Communists were amnestied in 1938.[3] By 1940, on the eve of the Soviet takeover of Estonia, the party claimed only 133 members (Pankseyev, 1967:81).

However, there was a large number of Estonian Communists in Soviet Russia during the 1920s and early 1930s. The figure cited for 1927 is 3,700 (Liebman, 1970:96). The Stalinist purges not only decimated the rank and file of these party members but also robbed the leadership of a number of its outstanding members, including Hans Pöögelmann and Jaan Anvelt, both of whom had been quite active in the Comintern.

Thus, when Stalin's emissary Andrei Zhdanov called upon Konstantin Päts, the president of the Republic of Estonia, in the summer of 1940, to install a new pro-Soviet cabinet, it contained not a single known Communist. For the one-party elections which followed, only thirty party candidates could be mustered for the eighty electoral districts.[4] However, within a few months of the transfer of political power, most of the nonparty Estonians in government had been coopted into the Communist party. Thereafter, party membership grew steadily, and by the time of the German invasion of the Soviet Union it had reached 3,751 (Pankseyev, 1970:28).

The war led to a decimation of both party leaders and the rank and file. Altogether, seventeen out of thirty-three Central Committee members and six out of nine of its bureau members perished during the war years (Pankseyev, 1967:211). An important factor here was the animosity of the Estonian population toward the party. On the one hand, the populace viewed the party members as traitors who had forfeited Estonian independence to the Soviet Union. On the other hand, prior to the outbreak of Soviet-German hostilities, Soviet authorities had deported about 19,000 Estonian residents and executed about 2,000 within the space of weeks; this in itself was cause for intense hatred of the collaborators. Many party members were killed by the Estonians even before the Germans reached the area.

A major, although probably unintended, role in recreating a postwar party fell to the Red Army's Estonian Rifle Corps. Formed in 1942, the corps drew upon Estonians conscripted in the spring of 1941 as well as on the survivors of the Communist Estonian *hävitus pataljonid* ("destruction battalions"), the Soviet Estonian militia, and Estonians born and reared in Russia proper, in addition to some Russians (about 10 percent). About 30,000 men found their way into the ranks of the corps. The Estonian Rifle Corps suffered heavy casualties, fighting initially on the Central Front and subsequently in Estonia and Latvia. Recent reminiscences of some of its medical personnel indicate that the wounded alone numbered 19,600 (*Kodumaa*, September 20, 1972). About 1,000 of its men defected to the German side in 1942 (Parming, 1972a:54).

The important point is that a significant number of leaders in the present Soviet Estonian elite, not only in the Communist party but also in the arts and professions, were at one time or another associated with the Rifle Corps. They include, by way of example, Valter Klauson and Edgar Tônurist, premier and first deputy premier of Estonia, respectively; Leonid Lentsman, the head of the trade unions council; Uno Laht, a well-known Soviet Estonian poet and humorist; academician Gustav Naan, chief editor of the *Estonian Soviet Encyclopedia*; Kaarel Ird, director of the Vanemuine theater in Tartu; and Alexander Pankseyev, director of the Estonian Institute of Party History, who, despite his Russian-sounding name, traces his origin back to Estonian settlers in Siberia.

The Rifle Corps was commanded by an Estonian born in Russia, Lt. Gen. Lembit Pärn. His chief political officer (commissar) was August Pusta, another Russian-born Estonian who subsequently settled in Estonia. The total number of Communists in the Rifle Corps during its existence has been estimated at close to 6,000. Early in 1945 the corps had 2,818 party members and 2,436 candidate members (Pankseyev, 1967:199). Estonian party membership outside the corps at the time was about half this number. By 1947 the corps veterans comprised 96 percent of the district party and executive secretaries in Estonia and 83 percent of the leadership of the local soviets. More than 600 veterans were assigned to plants and factories as directors and engineers, and 52 went to higher educational institutions as professors and lecturers (*Kodumaa*, September 20, 1972).

During the immediate postwar years, these new party cadres faced an Estonian population which was suspicious of, if not outright hostile toward, Soviet rule. As in Lithuania during the same period, but not to the same extent, in the Estonian countryside there was active resistance to Soviet rule, and in the southern districts there was extended guerrilla warfare. Juhan Smuul (1922-1972), an Estonian writer who won the Lenin Prize, recalled that during the few months he spent in the South Estonian town of Vôru after the war, "the bandits killed in the surrounding communities tens of party members and komsomols" (*Sirp ja Vasar*, February 25, 1972). This apparently inspired him to write a poem eulogizing Stalin, something he felt slightly apologetic about in a later autobiographical essay. Officially called "bandits," the guerrilla fighters were popularly known as the "brethren of the forest." Recently there has been greater understanding shown toward them by some Soviet Estonian authors. For example, they are called "pawns in a game" instead of the more traditional "bandits" (*Estonian Events*, February 1969:6).

The "forest brethren" had the support of the rural population of Estonia, and in a way their struggle was one of the farmers against collectivization. The resistance ceased in 1950, by which time collectivization was completed. A large number of the *kulak* farmers had been deported in 1949. Whether deportation had to occur with collectivization was subject to considerable debate within party circles. But in the end it was apparently decided that one cannot build a new socialist society with the help of the former class enemy (cf. Pankseyev, 1967:405-407).

Popularly, however, the deportations of 1949 merely connoted Stalinism. This was brought home with greater force by a directive of the Central Committee of the All-Union Communist party in 1950, which took the Estonian Communist leadership to task for failure to stem "bourgeois nationalism." The Central Committee of the Communist party of Estonia was convened and a party purge followed. The then first party secretary in Estonia, Nikolai Karotamm, was relieved of his post and Johannes Käbin was named his successor. For Käbin, this apparently became an appointment for life. In 1970 the *Estonian Soviet Encyclopedia* noted, however, that since "the plenum took place under conditions of the cult of personality, many accusations in the directive [of 1950 convening the Central Committee] had no grounds" (vol. 2:7).

Although Käbin owed his promotion to Stalin, he could relate also to both Khrushchev and Brezhnev because basically he sprang from the same mold—the party bureaucracy. Born in 1905 in northeastern Estonia, he soon moved with his family to a farm near Petersburg. In 1923 Käbin found himself in Leningrad as a worker. In 1926 he began his training in Marxism-Leninism, which culminated in his graduation from the Institute of Red Professors in Moscow in 1938. A party member since 1927, Käbin began his party career in 1931. In 1941 he was assigned to Estonia as deputy head of the party department of propaganda and agitation. This led, after the war, to the directorship of the Estonian Institute of Party History, then to one of the Communist party of Estonia secretarial posts, and finally to his appointment as first secretary. Under Käbin's leadership the Communist party of Estonia grew considerably, but simultaneously it slowly increased its Estonian component (see table 1).

During the postwar years, the Estonians did not become a majority in their own party until the mid-1960s. This fact was not necessarily due to any restrictions placed on the Estonian Communists; rather, it reflected still another form of national resistance to sovietization. However, as perceptions of political reality changed, spurred on by such events as the abortive Hungarian uprising in 1956, party membership became more attractive, as a means both of furthering personal ambition and of wielding some power (possibly even in the interest of Estonian ethnicity).

The 52.3 percent of Estonians in the party in 1970 still fell short of the Estonian share in the republic's population at the time, which was 68.2 percent. As if to compensate for these percentages, the Estonian party and government elite has a much stronger Estonian presence. In 1971 more than 80 percent of the membership of the Estonian party's Central Committee were ethnic Estonians. For cabinet ministers and their deputies, the figure reached upward of 90 percent (cf. *Estonian Events*, June 1971:7). This had not always been the case. In 1960 the Central Committee membership was just over 70 percent Estonian, which was close to the Estonian share (74 percent) in the total population at the time.

Such elective local bodies as the Supreme Soviet of the Estonian SSR and the local soviets have consistently included a high percentage of Estonians (see table 2). While the usual role of such bodies in the Soviet Union is merely to ratify decisions made higher up, the standing commissions of the Supreme Soviet of the Estonian SSR recently gained some power in drafting legislation, or, at least, in conducting hearings. Thus, the Commission on Education and Culture, which convenes more frequently than the required quarterly meetings, has discussed such educational matters as the introduction of the compulsory study of Russian and Estonian in the republic's schools. This was done in coordination with the Supreme Soviet of the USSR in Moscow (see Laulik, 1973).

The recent Estonification of the party and government leadership seems to reflect a conscious policy—an attempt to demonstrate to those who fear the Russification of Estonia that their concern is groundless. While it can be safely assumed

Table 1

Ethnic composition of the Communist Party of Estonia

Year	Total members	Estonians		Russians		Others	
1941	2,036	unk.	(85-95%)	unk.		unk.	
1946	7,139	3,436	(48.1%)	unk.		unk.	
1952	21,173	8,799	(41.5%)	unk.		unk.	
1956	22,524	10,047	(44.6%)	unk.		unk.	
1961	37,848	18,604	(49.1%)	unk.		unk.	
1967	61,722	32,088	(52.0%)	22,912	(37.1%)	6,722	(10.9%)
1970	70,195	36,729	(52.3%)	25,895	(36.9%)	7,571	(10.8%)

Sources: Pankseyev, 1967; Institut Istorii, 1971; Eesti nõukogude entsüklopeedia [Estonian Soviet Encyclopedia], vol. 2, 1970.

Table 2

Ethnic composition of selected elective bodies in
Soviet Estonia, 1959 and 1966 - 1967

| | 1959 | | | 1966 - 1967 | | |
	Estonian	Russian	Other	Estonian	Russian	Other
Estonian SSR represen- tatives to Supreme Soviet of the Soviet Union	unk.	unk.	unk.	80%	17%	3%
Supreme Soviet of the Estonian SSR	86.4%	11.2%	2.2%	85.4%	12.4%	2.2%
City, town, and rural district soviets	88.3%	unk.	unk.	89%	8.7%	2.3%

Sources: For 1959: Sovetskaya Estonia, December 19, 1959; for 1966-1967: Parming, 1972b.

that the party leadership is much less nationalistically inclined than the population as a whole, party leaders appear most likely to support and favor those plans and goals which are acceptable both in Moscow and among the local population.

The social origins of the Communist party in Estonia are shown in table 3. The categories "workers" and "farmers" used in the table allow for considerable leeway. The Soviet-Estonian party historian, Alexander Pankseyev, suggests that if strict occupational criteria were applied, only 137 party members would have qualified in 1945 as "workers" and only 2 as "farmers" instead of the figures used, 939 and 90, respectively (Pankseyev, 1967:226-227). In spite of conscious attempts to increase the number of party members shown statistically to have proletarian origins, the number in the category "employee" in the party in Estonia has always exceeded the all-union party's average. As noted in the table footnote, the term "employee" has a rather broad meaning and includes almost all people not involved in manual or agricultural work.

Another area in which the party in Estonia exceeds the corresponding all-union party figure is in the percentage of female members. The educational level of Estonian Communists is also higher. By 1970 more than one-fifth (22.43 percent) had received some higher education, and a majority (59.84 percent) had received a complete or partial secondary education (Pankseyev, 1971:81).

The picture which emerges of the party in Estonia is that of an educated, white-collar organization with a dominant number of Estonians in leading positions. But Estonian "dominance" is not necessarily synonymous with "power."

The leadership of the Communist party of Estonia is centered in the secretariat and the bureau of its Central Committee. The secretariat is composed of five members—Johannes Käbin, first secretary; Konstantin V. Lebedev, second secretary; and Fedor S. Ushanev, Karl Vaino, and Väino Väljas, secretaries. Of the five, two are Russian (Lebedev and Ushanev). Lebedev, as second secretary, by virtue of his position represents the party secretariat in Moscow. Until 1971 Lebedev headed the Baltic-Byelorussian sector for party organizational work in Moscow.

Käbin left Estonia as a child and did not return until he was thirty-five. Considered to be more Russian than Estonian during the early years of his career in Estonia, he has, neverthe-

Table 3

Social origins of the members of the Communist Party of Estonia

Year	Total members	Men (%)	Women (%)	Workers (%)	Farmers (%)	"Employees" (%)*
1941	2,036	unk.	unk.	1,219 (59.9%)	340 (16.7%)	477 (23.4%)
1945	2,409**	1,932 (80.2%)	477 (19.8%)	939 (39.0%)	90 (3.7%)	2,237 (57.3%)
1951	18,897	14,569 (77.1%)	4,328 (22.9%)	7,146 (37.8%)	1,825 (9.7%)	9,926 (52.5%)
1956	22,524	16,050 (71.3%)	6,474 (28.7%)	7,685 (34.1%)	2,573 (11.4%)	12,266 (54.5%)
1961	37,848	27,452 (72.7%)	10,396 (27.3%)	13,547 (35.8%)	5,462 (14.4%)	18,839 (49.8%)
1967	61,722	42,326 (68.6%)	19,396 (31.4%)	22,865 (37.0%)	8,283 (13.5%)	30,574 (49.5%)
1970	70,195	unk.	unk.	26,462 (37.7%)	9,177 (13.1%)	34,556 (49.2%)

Notes: * "Employees" is a broad party statistical category which includes almost everyone who is not a worker or farmer. Basically, it is equivalent to the American term "white collar." ** 1945 figures do not include members of the Estonian Rifle Corps.

Sources: Pankseyev, 1967; Institut Istorii, 1971; Eesti nõukogude entsüklopeedia [Estonian Soviet Encyclopedia], vol. 2, 1970.

less, shown tolerance toward things Estonian if they promote the general economic and cultural level of the republic. Little is known about either Ushanev or Vaino, except that the former has been secretary in charge of agriculture since 1955 and the latter has been secretary in charge of industry since 1960. Vaino is a Russian-born Estonian.

The bright young star in the party secretariat is Väino Väljas, who is a "home-grown" Estonian Communist. Born in Estonia in 1931, Väljas made his career via the Komsomol. A graduate of Tartu University, he became first secretary of the Komsomol in Estonia while still a student and, subsequently, first secretary of the Tallinn City Party Committee. He was elected a party secretary in 1971.

The Central Committee's bureau consists of eleven members. In addition to the five members of the secretariat listed above, the bureau's members are Nikolai Johanson, first secretary of the Tallinn City Party Committee; Valter Klauson, chairman of the Estonian SSR Council of Ministers; Leonid Lentsman, chairman of the Estonian SSR Council of Trade Unions and a former second secretary (1953-1964); Otto Merimaa, chairman of the People's Control Committee; Edgar Tônurist, first deputy chairman of the Estonian Council of Ministers; and Artur Vader, chairman of the Estonian Supreme Soviet (Vader is hence the "president" of the republic) and a former second secretary (1964-1971).

Of these latter six bureau members, only Tônurist and Johanson are "home-grown" Estonian Communists. Most of the others were born and grew up outside Estonia. Klauson, born of Estonian parents near Petersburg, obtained his engineering and party education in the Soviet Union between the wars. Lentsman was born in the Crimea and Vader in Byelorussia, both presumably of Estonian parentage. Since both were second secretaries in Estonia over a period of several years and were subsequently assigned to other posts in the republic's party hierarchy, it would seem that the post of second secretary is not necessarily so powerful as is commonly assumed.

Even though most members of the party elite in Estonia are of Estonian ancestry, many have a "Russian orientation" as a result of having grown up in the Soviet Union before World

War II. Given this background, the elite appears well suited for the role of mediator between the central decision-making organs in Moscow and the people at the receiving end in Estonia. The leaders know the language used—both literally and figuratively—at both ends of the transmission belt.

It would almost seem that Käbin, owing to his long tenure as first secretary, has established something of a personal fiefdom in Estonia. He feels on a par with the party leaders in the Kremlin, where he is regarded as a peer. He has spoken up on policy at such public forums as the USSR Supreme Soviet, suggesting changes where appropriate. He is listened to; and when some incoherent or inapplicable all-union directive is issued, he may disregard implementing it in Estonia. This happened occasionally during the Khrushchev era, according to personal communications received by this writer. Over the years, Käbin has shown increasing tolerance toward ethnic Estonian idiosyncrasies, apparently because this has aided him in improving the economic performance of the Estonian SSR. Indeed, Käbin's performance in this regard has helped bring Estonia into the forefront among Soviet republics.

Under the leadership of Käbin and others in the party hierarchy, Soviet nationality policy is being applied in Estonia in a rational manner so as to make it more palatable to the population at large. Its theoretical conceptualization underplays the Russian impact which is evident in everyday life. And in its practical application the Estonian Communists are given a seemingly disproportionate share in running their republic.

It may be concluded that a Leninist nationality policy is being enforced in Estonia. While this policy might satisfy certain national aspirations under Soviet conditions, those conditions hold in check national manifestations which may run counter to the Marxist philosophy which guides them. Soviet political culture tolerates virtually no deviation from the norm. Thus, if Estonian Communists were to express a desire for greater autonomy for their republic more strongly than suits the party leadership in Moscow, they would surely be slapped down. More serious manifestations of nationalism are therefore in conflict with party doctrine and may, as a result, build up a potential for future discontent.

Notes

1. Cf. A. M. Gindin and S. G. Markin, "Tvorcheskoe razvitie Leninskoi natsionalnoi politiki v rezheniyakh XXIV syezda KPSS." *Voprosy istorii KPSS*, no. 7 (1971), p. 27.

2. Ibid., p. 29 (emphasis in the original).

3. An English-language source on the Communist party in Estonia during the period 1918-1940 is Tönu Parming's "The Estonian Communist Party during the Period of the Republic" (paper presented at the Fifth Conference on Baltic Studies, Columbia University, May 1976). English-language sources on the 1924 coup are Johnson (1961), Lipping (1976), and Neuberg (1970). In early 1938 Estonia amnestied almost all political prisoners, both Communists and rightists who had attempted to seize power in the early 1930s.

4. O. Kuuli and A. Reserv in *Eesti Kommunist*, no. 7 (July), 1968, according to *Estonian Events*, September-October 1968, p. 8.

References

Dzyuba, Ivan

   1968   *Internationalism or Russification?*. London: Weidenfeld and Nicolson.

Gindin, A. M., and S. G. Markin

   1971   "Tvorcheskoe razvitie Leninskoi natsionalnoi politiki v rezheniyakh XXIV syezda KPSS." *Voprosy istorii KPSS*, no. 7, pp. 17-30.

Goldhagen, Erich, ed.

   1968   *Ethnic Minorities in the Soviet Union*. New York: Praeger.

Hallik, Klara

   1969   "Rol kulturnykh svyazei v ukreplenii druzhby sovetskikh narodov." *Kommunist Estonii*, no. 9 (September), pp. 27-35.

1970   "Rahvused tänapäeva sotsiaalses progressis" [Nations in Contemporary Social Progress]. *Looming*, no. 1 (January), pp. 124-137.

1972   "Rahvuslik ja internatsionaalne ehk mônda rahva elujôust" [National and International or Something about a Nation's Vitality]. *Kodumaa*, no. 10 (March 8), pp. 2-3.

Institut Istorii Partii pri TsK KP Estonii

1967   *Nekotorye voprosy Organizatsionno-partiinoi raboty*. Tallinn: Eesti Raamat.

Johnson, Stephen N.

1961   "The Coup d'Etat That Failed." *Baltic Review*, no. 22.

Küng, Andres

1973   *Vad Händer i Baltikum?* [What's Happening in the Baltics?]. Stockholm: Aldus/Bonniers.

Laulik, H.

1973   "Ajame juttu rahvasaadikuga ja rahvasaadikuist" [Talking to a People's Deputy and about People's Deputies]. *Kodumaa*, July 4, pp. 12-13.

Lenin, V. I.

1936   *Sochineniya*, third ed., vol. 18. Moscow: Partizdat TsK VKP (b).

1942   *Collected Works*, vol. 19. New York: International.

1957   *Sochineniya*, fourth ed., vol. 36. Moscow: Gosudarstvennoe Izdatelstvo Politicheskoi Literatury.

Liebman, A.

1970   "Eestimaa Kommunistlik Partei Kommunistliku

Internatsionaali Koosseisus" [Communist Party of Estonia as Part of the Communist International], in EKP Keskkomitee Partei Ajaloo Instituut, *Töid EKP ajaloo alalt*, vol. 5. Tallinn: Eesti Raamat.

Lipping, Imre

1976   "The Coup of 1 December 1924 in Estonia," in *Yearbook of the Estonian Learned Society in America*, vol. 5. New York.

Low, Alfred D.

1958   *Lenin on the Question of Nationality*. New York: Bookman.

Masherov, P.

1972   "O nekotorykh chertakh i osobennostyakh natsionalnykh otnoshenii v usloviyakh razvitogo sotsializma" [On Certain Features of Nationality Relations in the Conditions of Developed Socialism]. *Kommunist*, no. 15 (October), pp. 15-33.

Neuberg, A.

1970   *Armed Insurrection*. London: NLB.

Pankseyev, A. K.

1967   *Na osnove leninskikh organizatsionnykh printsipov* [On the Basis of Leninist Organizational Principles]. Tallinn: Eesti Raamat.

1970   *V edinom stroyu k obshchei tseli* [In a Single Formation toward the Common Goal]. Tallinn: Eesti Raamat.

1971   "Izmeneniya k olichestvennogo i kachestvennogo sostova Kompartii Estonii posle 23 syezda KPSS," in Institut Istorii Partii pri TsK KP Estonii, *Nekotorye voprosy organizatsionno-partiinoi raboty*. Tallinn: Eesti Raamat.

Parming, Tönu
1972a "Population Changes in Estonia, 1935-1970." *Population Studies* 26 (March): 53-78.
1972b "Soziale Konsequenzen der Bevölkerungs Veränderungen in Estland zeit 1939," in *Acta Baltica 1971*. Königstein: Institutum Balticum.

Pennar, Jaan, et al.
1971 *Modernization and Diversity in Soviet Education—With Special Reference to Nationality Groups.* New York: Praeger.

Rudnev, D.
1970 *V. I. Lenin ja Eesti* [V.I. Lenin and Estonia], in EKP Keskkomitee Partei Ajaloo Instituut, *Töid EKP ajaloo alalt*, vol. 4. Tallinn: Eesti Raamat.

Rutkis, Janis, ed.
1967 *Latvia Country and People.* Stockholm: Lettiska Nationella Fonden.

Smuul, Juhan
1972 "Autobiograafia." *Sirp ja Vasar*, no. 8 (February 25), p. 4.

Taagepera, Rein
1970 "Nationalism in the Estonian Communist Party." *Bulletin of the Institute for the Study of the USSR* 1: 3-15.

Talvar, H.
1972 "Tähelepanekuid rahvastiku palgejoontest" [Observations on Population Characteristics]. *Kodumaa*, no. 20 (May 17), pp. 4-5.

Part 2
Economic and
Societal Processes

4

The Postwar Economic Transformation

Elmar Järvesoo

During the past three decades of Soviet rule, Estonia has been transformed from an agrarian to an industrial society. The Estonian SSR today is the Soviet Union's most industrially advanced and most urbanized component republic; it also enjoys the highest standard of living. This chapter focuses on the major economic changes which have taken place during the post–World War II period. Although the discussion will emphasize developments in the Estonian SSR, at times it is necessary to take note of trends in the Soviet Union as a whole, since the economies of the various republics are integral and planned components of the economy of the USSR.

The Prewar Economy and Wartime Changes

While still predominantly an agrarian country, with about one-half of its population engaged in farming, Estonia on the eve of World War II had passed the threshold of sustained economic growth, development, and industrialization. The land reform of 1919 had radically restructured agriculture. While during czarist years the typical rural person operated property rented from the Baltic German–owned estates or was a laborer on such an estate, by the mid-1920s the bulk of the rural population lived on family-owned and -operated farms. In the production of basic foodstuffs, the Republic of Estonia

131

quickly became self-sufficient. After the initial difficulties of agricultural reorganization had been overcome, an ever-increasing amount of dairy products, bacon, and eggs was exported. Total agricultural output almost doubled between 1918 and 1940, and milk production tripled.

Industrial organization and production also underwent extensive readjustment during the interwar decades, with objectives redefined to more fully meet domestic needs, especially in regard to consumer goods. Before World War I, 53 percent of the total industrial output had been textile products, primarily for the Russian market. Engineering and metal works contributed another 10 percent and the alcohol distilling and brewery industry 6 percent. Since Soviet Russian markets were largely closed to Estonian industrial products during the interwar period, textile plants and the Tallinn shipyards and railroad works operated under capacity. Much of the equipment in these enterprises had been evacuated to Russia in 1918 in anticipation of the German occupation, and it was never returned.

The narrow industrial base was broadened by expanding the finished textile-goods industry in addition to food-processing, beverage, paper and wood-pulp manufacturing, and other industries. Of special significance were the pioneering efforts undertaken in oil-shale mining and processing, as well as in phosphate mining. Estonia was thereby able in the 1930s to export considerable amounts of oil, while simultaneously reducing imports of gasoline and coal. During the second half of the 1930s, when the transformation from an agrarian to an industrial economy was truly launched, there was a mix in which state, private, and cooperative enterprises all played important roles. State-owned plants predominated in the oil-shale industry (although foreign capital was also present), timber production, wood-pulp manufacturing, peat processing and electricity generation. On the other hand, more than 90 percent of milk and all export bacon was processed by cooperative firms, and about 40 percent of retail trade represented consumer cooperatives, which were also pioneers in modernizing store design and trading facilities. Independent grocers in 1937 organized their own cooperative wholesale purchasing agency to better compete with the popular consumer cooperatives. Agricultural production, however, was fully in the hands of family farms.

An important development during the interwar period was the emphasis placed on a supportive infrastructure for economic development. Agricultural research and education also became significant, and many of the postwar gains reflect the benefits of prewar policies. Also, as a result of the development of a chemical and oil-shale industry, Estonia made advances in certain areas of scientific research which proved valuable to postwar developments. Furthermore, while the Estonians were almost fully literate in the late nineteenth century, great advances were made in public education during the interwar years. By the 1920s the population of Estonia had one of the highest educational levels in the world, not an unimportant foundation for the postwar technologically based industrialization. While the Estonian SSR today is the Soviet Union's most economically advanced republic, in a relative sense it already held this position in 1940, at the outset of the Soviet period.

Integration of the economy into the Soviet system proceeded rapidly after the incorporation of Estonia into the USSR in 1940. The overpowering presence of the Red Army guaranteed that nationalization of the entire economic system would take place smoothly and peacefully, without violence or overt resistance. The early sovietization process is covered in greater detail by Kareda (1947), Ekbaum (1949), and Järvesoo (1973). The bulk of the early policies caused an economic slowdown and a decline in the standard of living. The outbreak of German-Soviet hostilities in mid-1941, and the ensuing German occupation of Estonia through late 1944, temporarily interrupted the sovietization process. The wartime activities also caused major damage to the economy. The retreating Red Army in 1941 burned and blew up bridges, power stations, small plants, and even agricultural facilities. Most of the railroad stock, locomotives, and trucks were evacuated to the Soviet rear. The German period saw emphasis placed only on those economic sectors which would contribute to the war effort; hence there was no general recovery between 1941 and 1944. The German army, in its 1944 retreat, also caused destruction to the economic plant, as did the Soviet army's extensive use of artillery and aerial bombardments against the major cities, including the use of incendiary explosives.

By the time the war had ended, Estonia had lost a large part of its textile, paper, and pulp mills, and the oil-shale industry was in ruins. Transportation was paralyzed, and agricultural production had declined to about one-half of the prewar level. Residential housing in the major cities had suffered severely. It has been estimated that about 38 percent of the 1941 residential space was lost during the war (Sepre, 1945). Loss of population was also huge. Soviet and Western analysts agree that between 1939 and 1945 Estonia's population declined by about 25 percent. In an economic sense, particularly significant was the extensive loss of scientific and technical personnel and the middle class per se; the bulk of those who had not been executed or deported during the first year of Soviet rule in 1940-1941 fled to the West in 1944.

The speed of the postwar economic recovery was uneven in tempo, and it reflected priorities assigned in Moscow. Residential construction was assigned one of the lowest priorities of all, a situation that was further aggravated by the sizable immigration of labor during the first five postwar years from the Russian SFSR. Since much of this early immigration was related to the restructuring of the oil-shale industry, it may be presumed that the bulk of investments made in residential housing during the first postwar decade was for construction in the oil-shale region. Indeed, within the space of a few years major cities arose where there had been only villages before the war. By 1959 the three cities of the oil-shale basin (Kohtla-Järve, Sillamäe, and Kiviôli) accounted for 11 percent of the total urban population in the Estonian SSR.

Although food supply levels were critical, little emphasis was placed on agricultural recovery. The situation was not helped by the feared specter of collectivization, which struck in 1949. The coerced collectivization of agriculture resulted in the deportation of an estimated 80,000 rural people, about 12 percent of the total rural population at the time. As economic entities, the collective farms in the Estonian SSR were, as in the rest of the Soviet Union, a failure. Their creation reflected the prevailing agricultural policy and ideology of the Soviet Communist party; moreover, collectivization apparently was seen as the only means of ending guerrilla resistance to postwar Soviet rule. Although the Estonian rural population had not, even in the face of the brutal deportation, destroyed crop inventories or animals, as had occurred in the Ukraine two decades earlier, agricultural production was already in a sad state of affairs in late 1944 and early 1945 because of the "socialist land reform" executed then. This policy resulted in the creation of tens of thousands of economically unviable farms, typically with ten to twelve acres of arable land. At the same time, the regime brought increasing pressure on the farmers to join collectives, which further delimited production. The slow agricultural recovery reflected both the generally unsound agrarian economic policy (including organization and management) of the Soviet Union and the central government's suppression of the agricultural sector of the economy as a means of accumulating capital and directing resources toward industrialization.

The highest postwar priority in recovery was accorded to industry, particularly to oil-shale mining and processing, electricity generation, and textiles. Frequently, recovery proceeded with surprising speed. The oil-shale industry, which was placed under the direct control of the All-Union Ministry of the Coal Industry and was thereby integrated into the Soviet northwestern energy supply system, had been reconstructed by 1946. Its rapid expansion followed thereafter. Oil shale was now seen, not as a source of petroleum products for Estonia, but as a raw fuel source for use in generating electricity and as a source of household gas for the Soviet northwestern region as a whole. In late 1948 a pipeline was completed linking Leningrad to the Estonian oil-shale industry, and 78 million cubic meters of gas were piped. The pipeline was extended westward to Tallinn in 1953. The thermal electricity-generating plants, which used oil shale as well as peat for fuel, also had reached their prewar capacities by 1946, as had the textile industry. During the five-year period 1946-1950, the growth rate in industry was reported as 36 percent per year. In agriculture it was only 10 percent.

Full recovery did not really occur until the 1960s, and the advances made at the end of that decade and in the early 1970s are noteworthy. The main indicators of the economic transformation and of economic growth and development are shown in tables 1 through 5. The data presented in this chapter are all from official Soviet sources. Although the bulk of the data cannot be verified by observers in the West, tourists and visiting journalists confirm that the Estonian SSR is today a highly industrialized and urbanized society, that in many areas

Table 1

Change in average annual growth rates in Soviet
Estonian industry and agriculture, 1951 – 1975

	Industrial output	Agricultural output	
		Total	Socialist sector
1951–55	+14.4%	–1.85%	– 1.7%
1956–60	+11.4%	+8.35%	+13.2%
1961–65	+ 9.9%	+1.90%	+ 5.2%
1966–70	+ 8.6%	+2.50%	+ 3.2%
1971	+ 8.1%	+5.40%	+ 6.6%
1972	+ 6.3%	–7.77%	– 5.6%
1973	+ 5.9%	+6.4%	+ 8.1%
1974	+ 7.1%	+8.6%	+ 9.6%
1975	+ 7.6%	unk.	+ 5.1%

Sources: Eesti NSV rahvamajandus, 1974:75, 128; Narodnoe
Khoziaistvo SSSR, 1975:310; Rahva Hääl, January 29, 1974,
January 26, 1975, and January 24, 1976.

of economic organization and management it is appreciably
more advanced than the rest of the Soviet Union, and that it
has the highest standard of living of all Soviet republics.

There is no reason to doubt the rank order of Soviet
republics in regard to economic indicators in official statistics.
However, Soviet economic data are difficult to evaluate
because of the nature of the index numbers. Change is often
shown in percentages, with no indication of the index base.
Soviet Estonian officials are likely to use 1940 as a general base
index year so as to demonstrate the extent of economic
development during the Soviet period of rule. However, the
index figures often are based on only part of 1940's output
data, because Estonia did not become a Soviet republic until
early August. Even if the whole year were used as a base,
because of the impact of the war on the Estonian economy the

Table 2

Selected basic indicators of economic development
in Soviet Estonia, 1960 - 1974

	1960	1965	1970	1974
National income, Estonian SSR	100	143	205	253
National income in USSR	100	137	199	251
Industrial employment	100	126	138	141
Industrial output	100	160	242	316
Agricultural employment	100	84	77	74
Agricultural output	100	110	125	136
Retail sales, Estonian SSR, rubles per capita	521	635	956	1,111
Retail sales, USSR, rubles per capita	367	454	639	780
Retail price index, all goods	100	101.1	100.7	100.8
Retail price index, foods	100	104.9	104.9	107.1
Retail price index, industrial goods	100	96.6	95.4	93.5

Sources: Eesti NSV rahvamajandus, 1976:58, 85, 131, 139, 255-6, 265;
Narodnoe Khoziaistvo SSSR, 1975:573, 628.

use of 1940 as an index year to show relative growth from the period of the "bourgeois republic" is misleading. In this chapter, we are concerned primarily with postwar changes, not with the relative changes from prewar times to the present.

Economic Growth and Structural Changes, 1950-1960

During the decade following the collectivization of agriculture (in 1949), industrial growth in Soviet Estonia mirrored the overall Soviet policy of forced development. As noted, many industries recovered from wartime damage during the latter half of the 1940s, and during the 1950s annual industrial production more than tripled. The year 1960 was a landmark in Estonia's economic history—in that year, for the first time, rising industrial employment exceeded declining agricultural employment (164,000 people were employed in industry and 158,500 in agriculture). By 1974 232,200 people were employed

Table 3

Distribution of labor in Soviet Estonia by
major industrial sectors, 1960 - 1974

	1960	1965	1970	1974
Manufacturing	31.5%	34.3%	35.2%	34.3%
Agriculture and forestry	26.5%	20.3%	16.0%	14.5%
Transport and communication	9.2%	9.9%	9.3%	9.5%
Construction	7.4%	7.9%	9.3%	9.4%
Trade	6.4%	7.3%	8.3%	8.9%
Health care	4.5%	4.6%	4.8%	5.0%
Education, arts, and sciences	7.7%	8.8%	9.8%	10.5%
All others	6.8%	6.7%	7.3%	7.9%
Totals	100.0%	100.0%	100.0%	100.0%

Source: Eesti NSV rahvamajandus, 1976:237.

Note: Labor force used in private household farming is not
included.

in industry and about 117,000 in agriculture (*ERM*, 1976:131,
238). Industrialization was, of course, accompanied by rapid
urbanization. The rural population in the present territory
declined from 700,300 in 1940 to 460,600 in 1975, while the
urban population increased from 354,100 to 920,700 during the
same period.

It should be noted that a very large share of the industrial
labor force, and thereby the urban population, represents
postwar immigration. The ethnic Estonian population of the
Estonian SSR was 47 percent urban in 1959 and 54 percent
urban in 1970. Hence, from the more restrictive viewpoint of
the natives, the urban-industrial turning point in development
actually occurred in the late 1960s. In regard to immigration, it
might be added that many of the major labor-intensive industries are under the control of all-union ministries and agencies
in Moscow. While the native Estonians have faced persistent

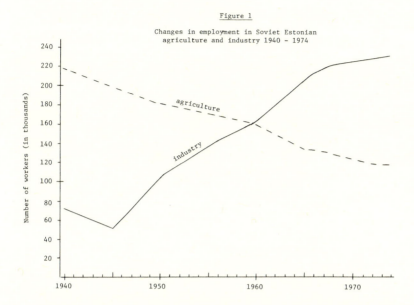

Figure 1

Changes in employment in Soviet Estonian agriculture and industry 1940 – 1974

restrictions in moving to the urban areas, these industries often recruit labor from the Russian SFSR. The industrialization of Estonia probably does not reflect a purposeful, centrally directed technique of Russification; however, rapid industrialization has caused large-scale immigration of Russians into the Estonian SSR—a major cause of friction and dissent.

The main characteristics of the present locational patterns of economic activities and industrial structure evolved during the decade of the 1950s. While the capital city, Tallinn, retained its leading position in industrial concentration and diversity, its relative weight declined, and four other important secondary industrial centers were developed. Narva, a northeast border city between the Estonian SSR and the Russian SFSR; Tartu, the old university city in the east-central region; and Pärnu, a port city in the southwest, are old industrial centers whose industrial output profiles were appreciably expanded and diversified. The oil-shale basin in the northeastern corner of Estonia emerged as a major industrial center during the postwar period. According to the latest available information, which is now a decade old but generally unchanged, about 43 percent of total industrial employment was in Tallinn, 12

Figure 2

Location of industry in Soviet Estonia

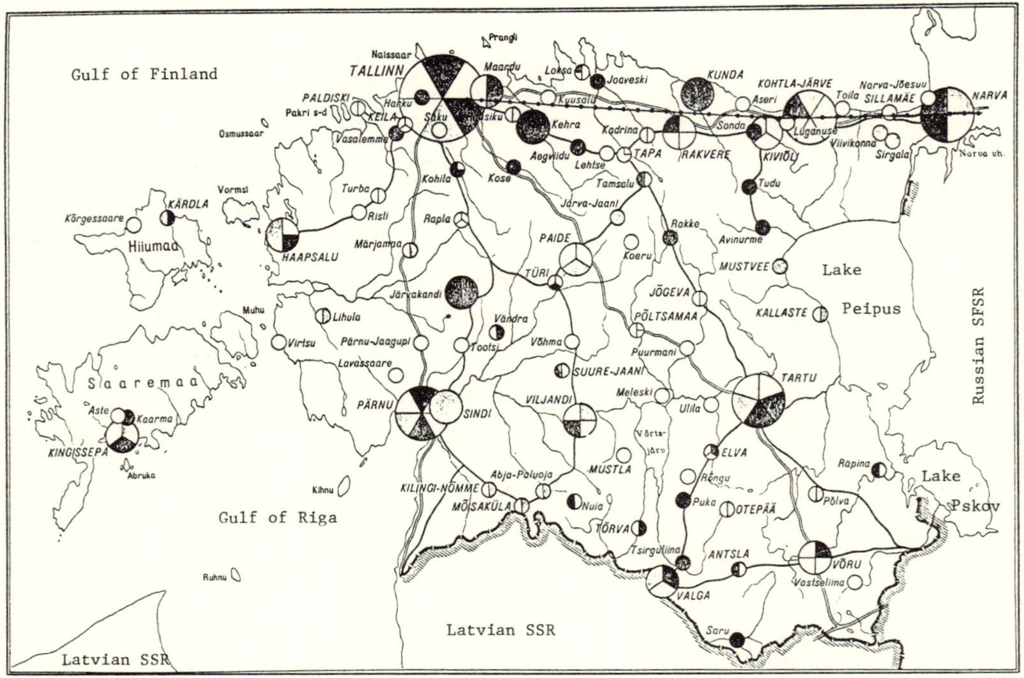

percent in Kohtla-Järve (the major oil-shale city), 9 percent in Tartu, 8 percent in Narva, and 5 percent in Pärnu (Veimer, 1967:237). Thus, 77 percent of all industrial employment is concentrated in only five urban centers (see figure 2).

Concentration of industrial output in larger and fewer firms is another feature of recent developments, although this has frequently been the result of combining smaller plants into a single administrative and financial unit so as to achieve better control. The tendency toward higher concentration of production is also reflected in the declining significance of the cooperative sector in both industry and agriculture and the corresponding rise of the state sector. After the initial nationalization of the manufacturing and service industry, a group of smaller enterprises was usually combined into a producer and service cooperative, *artel*, while another part of the cooperative sector was made up of industrial enterprises belonging to the collective farms or agricultural *artels*. Between 1950 and 1960 the cooperative share of industrial production declined from 12.6 percent of the total to 5.5 percent, while the output of the state-owned sector increased from 87.4 percent to 94.5 percent. The decline reflects primarily the industrial output of the consumer cooperatives (*ERM*, 1974:73).

The postwar industrialization obviously required huge capital inputs. Capital outlay for all investment purposes went up from 364 million rubles during 1946-1950 to 625 million in 1951-1955 and to 1,019 million in 1956-1960 (*ERM*, 1974:226). The benefits of the increased capital outlays were felt most noticeably during the 1960s, a decade of remarkable economic growth in Estonia. (It should be noted that statistical reporting has improved considerably since 1960.) In 1960, industrial output accounted for 60 percent of the republic's gross national product, agriculture for 21 percent, and construction activity for 9 percent. Personal incomes continued to rise during the 1950s, although slowly; housing facilities showed modest improvement; and the overall standard of living continued slowly to improve.

Table 4

Average monthly earnings of workers and employees in selected economic
areas in Soviet Estonia, 1960 - 1974 (in rubles)

	1960	1965	1970	1974	Increase, 1960–1974
All wage earners	81.9	99.9	135.3	153.9	88%
Industry (production personnel)	92.6	107.1	146.7	166.4	80%
Agriculture	62.8	80.5	125.5	153.3	144%
sovkhoz workers only	54.4	75.1	117.2	150.8	177%
kolkhoz workers only	41.8	67.5	126.2	158.5	278%
Forestry	55.4	81.0	106.8	130.1	136%
Transportation	87.6	108.6	153.2	178.0	103%
Communications	62.1	73.1	99.0	113.6	82%
Construction (production personnel)	97.3	120.4	169.0	196.5	102%
Trade and eating places	61.9	80.9	103.5	111.0	79%
Housing and communal services	60.3	78.2	106.6	119.6	99%
Health care and physical education	60.8	83.4	99.7	109.0	79%
Education	73.1	97.8	111.1	129.0	76%
Science and research	80.3	102.3	134.0	154.6	92%
Banking and insurance	70.7	85.2	110.6	127.6	80%
Government	87.3	115.2	128.8	137.2	57%

Source: Eesti NSV rahvamajandus, 1976:180, 187, 243.

Table 5

Development of industrial production
in Soviet Estonia, 1960 - 1974

	1960	1965	1970	1974
Output index	100	164	242	316
Labor force index	100	126	138	141
Labor productivity index	100	128	178	227

Source: Eesti NSV rahvamajandus, 1976:82, 85, 88.

Economic Growth and Development since 1960

As is evident from tables 1–5, economic growth continued during the 1960s, although at a slower rate than during the preceding decade. After a brief interlude of regional economic councils (*sovnarkhoze*s) during the Khrushchev era, when all industries were administered by local authorities (Estonia was one of fifty economic regions), a large segment of Estonian industry was again subordinated directly to the all-union ministries in Moscow. The republic authorities have little to say in regard to production plans, output disposition, or management in such enterprises, which in 1974 accounted for 30 percent of all industrial output. This includes the entire oil-shale industry, most electricity generation, pulp and paper manufacturing, fisheries and fish processing, and some leading engineering and metalworking plants.

One of the most important characteristics of the 1960s was economic reform. Officially known as the "new planning and incentive system" in the West the reforms were better known under the term "Liebermanism." Such reform essentially involved the abandonment of a great many plan-fulfillment indices in favor of one main indicator—profits—as the ultimate yardstick for economic success. A large share of profits which formerly had to be turned over to the state could now be retained by the enterprises to be used for incentive payments to employees, capital investment for modernization, and expansion of production. Under the new system, local managers nominally had much more freedom in decision making, although within the central planning framework. In Estonia, an astonishing 98 percent of industrial output comes from enterprises operating under the new planning and incentive system.

While development of heavy industry and producer-goods output continued, the emphasis since 1960 has been on consumer goods and services. It appears that 1973 was the watershed which tipped the balance toward consumer goods in Estonia. Improvement in personal incomes and in the standard of living during the late 1960s and early 1970s has been a major aspect of the most recent economic changes, and the gains may be characterized as truly spectacular (see table 4). National income more than doubled in Estonia during the 1960-1970 years; average monthly wages went up from 82 rubles to 135 rubles (a gain of 65 percent), and some low-income groups gained considerably more. Retail sales per capita went up from 521 to 956 rubles (a gain of 83 percent). The level of retail sales in the Estonian SSR is at present nearly 50 percent higher than the Soviet Union's average. Retail prices during the period remained almost stable, although there was a small shift in the price structure. Aggregate food prices have gone up only about 5 percent since 1960, while the prices of industrial products declined by the same amount, resulting in a mere 0.7-percent increase in total retail prices.

Major Agricultural Changes

Before proceeding to a more extensive discussion of industrialization, some attention must be given to changes and trends in agriculture. Advanced industrial societies either must have very efficient agricultural economies (which employ few people but produce large quantities of food for those in the industrial, service, and other sectors of the economy) or must import large quantities of basic foodstuffs. The Estonian SSR has, at present, one of the most highly developed agricultures of any Soviet republic. However, agricultural production did not equal the 1938-1939 pre-Soviet level until the early 1960s, a decade after industry had recovered. The lowest point was reached during the first few years of the 1950s. Since 1960, agricultural developments have been noteworthy. For a more extensive discussion of the early Soviet years and the ensuing changes, see Ekbaum (1949) and Järvesoo (1973, 1974, 1975).

The early weakness of postwar Estonian agriculture reflects the combined effects of collectivization and of the policy decision to direct the maximum amount of capital and resources to the industrial recovery. There were, of course, also the consequences of wartime destruction with which to contend. More important, collectivization in 1949 destroyed the most successful group in agricultural life, the so-called *kulak*s, who were nothing more than family farmers in Estonia. A policy that eliminates 12 percent of the rural population in the space of a few weeks can do nothing but lead to a dire decline in the production of food. Furthermore, there was no managerial precedent in Estonia for operating large agricultural enterprises, which the new collectives were. Clearly, the existing

Soviet model offered nothing in the way of a successful precedent. For example, the concentration of production required the construction of large buildings and facilities for housing animals, feeds, and food processing. The architects and construction engineers, however, had no access to existing advanced Western facilities so as to learn what to do or what not to do. Thus, much of the new physical plant during the early postwar construction period was obsolete at the outset, if not outright inefficient. Further, the enterprises were frequently run by party functionaries with little expertise in agricultural organization, production, or economics.

A highly concentrated, modern agriculture requires various supplies and equipment, such as fertilizers, tractors, and combines. These were not available in adequate quantity in any case, and resources were utilized inefficiently because of the organizational structure. Finally, because the general economic policy favored industry, agricultural wages were so low as to provide little incentive for work. During the late 1940s and early 1950s the bulk of the key foodstuffs continued to be produced in the "private sector," the plots of land allocated to *kolkhoz* and *sovkhoz* workers.

General trends in agriculture are summarized in tables 6–9. The main trends during the 1960s merit some attention. First, there was a continuation of the late 1950s' pattern toward the reduction in the number of *kolkhoz*es and *sovkhoz*es in favor of fewer but larger units (table 6). Second, there was a steady increase in capital and resource allocations to the agricultural sector of the economy. For example, mineral fertilizer use, which already had increased from 151,000 tons in 1950 to 301,000 tons in 1960, further increased to 672,000 tons in 1970 and 773,000 in 1974. The fertilizer application rate is thereby approaching a ton per hectare of planted cropland. (In 1974, Estonia applied 194 kilograms of plant nutrients to a hectare of planted cropland, or 170 pounds per acre—nearly four times the all-union average, which was 55 kilograms per hectare, and about one-third more than that of the United States.) Third, there was a dramatic increase in agricultural wages and in the general quality of rural life during that decade (see table 4). And finally, an increasing impact was made by agricultural research and education.

Enrollment in the university-level Estonian Agricultural Academy increased from 2,273 in 1960 to 3,746 in 1974. The

Table 6

Number and sizes of socialist farms, labor force employment in the socialist
sector of agriculture, and number of livestock in Soviet Estonia, 1950 - 1974

	1950	1955	1960	1965	1970	1974
Number and sizes of socialist farms						
Sovkhozes						
Number of farms	127	97	144	157	171	153
Sown area per sovkhoz (in hectares)	270	579	146	1,611	1,851	2,631
Workers per sovkhoz	98	177	304	315	302	341
Kolkhozes (excluding fishing)						
Number of farms	2,213	908	648	467	292	196
Sown area per kolkhoz (in hectares)	263	705	702	900	1,314	2,134
Members in working age	60	113	108	122	170	233
Agricultural labor force (in thousands)						
Agricultural total	177.9	--	158.5	133.4	122.5	117.4
In sovkhozes	18.3	--	47.6	52.5	53.2	53.6
In kolkhozes	155.0	--	103.2	80.9	68.9	63.8

Livestock numbers (in thousands)	1940	1950	1955	1960	1965	1970	1974
Dairy cattle	528	462	--	494	610	692	788
Hogs	319	297	--	587	592	688	816
Sheep and goats	325	274	--	267	175	165	176
Horses	203	163	--	66	40	31	23
Poultry (in millions)	n.a.	2.04	--	2.83	2.51	3.68	4.40

Source: Eesti NSV rahvamajandus, 1976:125, 131, 167, 179.

number of graduates rose from 358 in 1960 to 531 in 1970, but
dropped to 481 in 1974 (see *ERM*, 1976:329). Further, the
number of scientific personnel in agricultural research institutes increased from 154 in 1960 to 301 in 1974; in veterinary
science the number rose from 35 to 64 (*ERM*, 1976:336). The
number of specialists with university education in *kolkhoz*es
and *sovkhoz*es increased from 1960 to 1974 as follows: agrono-
mists, from 183 to 494; livestock specialists (zootechnicians),
from 163 to 537; veterinarians, from 111 to 400; engineers,
from 49 to 354 (*ERM*, 1976:132).

However, in spite of noteworthy progress in large-scale
production, the private sector still supplies a disproportionately large share of many key foodstuffs—since 1965, about 20
percent of all products marketed. In crop production, the
private sector's market share was about 30 percent, in livestock

Table 7

Distribution of arable land, potatoes and vegetables,
milk cows, and hogs among major land-user groups in
Soviet Estonia, 1956 – 1974 (in percentages of the total)

	Arable land			Potatoes and vegetables			Milk cows			Hogs		
	1956	1960	1974	1956	1960	1974	1956	1960	1974	1956	1960	1974
Socialized sector												
Sovkhozes*	12	30	49	9	18	33	9	19	40	22	33	50
Kolkhozes	81	64	46	53	42	31	44	40	38	26	39	42
Private sector												
Kolkhoz members	6	3	2	29	40	36	36	41	22	30	28	8
Workers and employees	1	3	3	9			11			12		

Note: *Includes other state farms, but not other land users.

Sources: Eesti NSV rahvamajandus, 1956:74, 75, 85, 86, 107, 108; Eesti NSV rahvamajandus, 1976:126, 144, 145, 147, 167, 168.

products 18-19 percent. By 1971, the figures had increased to 37 percent in crop production and 27 percent in livestock production; in 1973 the figures, respectively, were 24 percent and 27 percent (*ERM*, 1976:142). Although in the Estonian SSR the contribution of the private sector has generally been declining and is lower overall than in the rest of the Soviet Union, it still contributes about 40 percent of potatoes, 29 percent of milk, 25 percent of meat, and 35 percent of eggs. In regard to vegetables, the private sector's contribution is higher—50 percent—and in regard to fruits and berries, 80 percent to 90 percent. Thus, in many respects, in spite of noteworthy achievements in the adoption of a "socialist agriculture," the overall success of the system in satisfying food demands leaves quite a bit to be desired from an economic viewpoint.

During recent years mechanization has continued to advance. By 1974 there were 19,176 tractors in Soviet Estonia (or 1 per 120 acres of arable land), 3,325 grain combines, 2,125 field choppers, and 10,900 trucks. Overall, about twenty horsepower of mechanical power was available per farm worker. All *kolkhoz*es and *sovkhoz*es were supplied with electricity, and major operations in soil preparation, grain and potato planting, and grain and potato harvesting were virtually 100 percent mechanized. More than 99 percent of the dairy cows in the socialist sector were machine milked.

Indeed, within the Soviet agricultural system—which, in

Table 8

Average annual outputs and production plans of major crops, leading livestock
products, and average annual governmental procurements of livestock products
in Soviet Estonia, 1946 - 1975

	1946–1950	1951–1955	1956–1960	1961–1965	1966–1970	1971–1975	Plan for 1971–1975
Major crops							
(in thousands of tons)							
Grain and pulses	527	314	316	476	705	901	930
Potatoes	1,097	936	1,127	1,254	1,336	1,238	1,518
Vegetables	122	105	116	101	126	128	143
Hay	unk.	696	801	748	873	784	unk.
Root crops (feed)	unk.	121	126	433	634	293	unk.
Leading livestock products							
All meats (dressed							
weight, 1,000 tons)	43.4	58	81	100	126	150	160
Milk, 1,000 tons	459	559	750	849	1,009	1,090	1,136
Eggs (millions)	80	140	195	230	300	431	382
Wool (tons)	579	542	638	558	394	427	unk.
Governmental procurements							
of livestock products							
Livestock & poultry							
(live weight,							
1,000 tons)	11	25	55	98	142	188	unk.
Milk (1,000 tons)	113	228	443	602	805	958	unk.
Eggs (millions)	12	16	31	67	141	258	unk.
Wool (tons)	99	278	248	190	---	---	unk.

Sources: Eesti NSV rahvamajandus, 1976:153, 170, 176; Rahva Hääl, January 24, 1976.

Table 9

Kolkhoz gross income and indivisible funds
per kolkhoz member household, 1965 - 1974

	1965	1970	1974
Kolkhoz gross income per year:			
USSR average, in rubles	1,160	1,590	1,760
Estonian SSR	1,600	2,730	3,190
Index, Soviet Union = 100	138	172	181
Indivisible funds (fixed assets):			
USSR average, in rubles	2,750	4,180	6,210
Estonian SSR	5,780	9,480	15,600
Index, Soviet Union = 100	210	228	242

Sources: Narodnoe Khoziaistvo SSSR, 1974:423; Eesti NSV rahvamajandus,
1976:179-180.

Table 10

Gross product per man-day in Soviet Estonian agriculture
and in other selected Soviet republics

	sovkhozes		kolkhozes	
USSR average	11.96 rubles (=100)		9.63 rubles (=100)	
Estonian SSR	19.23	(161)	18.66	(195)
Latvian SSR	15.64	(129)	12.99	(135)
Kazakh SSR	13.36	(112)	12.42	(130)
Lithuanian SSR	13.04	(109)	11.93	(124)

Source: Sel' skoe khoziaistvo SSSR, 1971:496, 592.

comparison with those of other industrially advanced countries, continues to be relatively inefficient—Soviet Estonia is an important exception. Farmers' incomes, production intensity, and land and labor productivity are among the highest in the union, while the cost of production of leading farm commodities is the lowest. Estonian *sovkhozes* are operating at profit without governmental subsidies; they were all placed on the "self-management" system as early as 1967 during the economic reform. In the Soviet Union as a whole, only 49 percent of the *sovkhozes* were operating without subsidies by the end of 1973; the goal was to transfer them all to self-management by 1975.

Labor productivity has reached a high level in Soviet Estonia as a result of mechanization and high-intensity farming, as the figures in table 10 show (*Sel' skoe khoziaistvo*, 1971:496, 592). In 1971 labor productivity in Estonian *kolkhozes* was nearly double the all-union average and was the highest of any union republic. In *sovkhozes*, where labor productivity is in general higher than in *kolkhozes*, Estonia also led the Soviet Union with a total 61 percent higher than the all-union average. These relationships have been persistent for the past decade. According to Tônurist (1974:235), one man-year in Estonia produced 4,996 rubles of farm output, compared with 2,576 rubles in the Soviet Union as a whole. (The Estonian SSR was also ahead of the Leningrad and Moscow oblasts.)

The Soviet central planners expect Estonia to further develop its present dairy-beef-hog-poultry farming. Published directives for the Tenth Five-Year Plan (1976-1980) stipulate a 17-percent increase in average annual gross farm output. Specific growth goals are 38 percent for meat, 16 percent for milk, and 8 percent for eggs (*Rahva Hääl*, November 19 and 20, 1976).

Since the existing socialist farms (*sovkhoz*es and *kolkhoz*es) are said to have now achieved their planned long-range sizes and boundaries, the construction of future production and population centers, *kolkhoz* and *sovkhoz* villages, has started and will continue. Soviet, including Estonian, geographers, economists, architects, and construction engineers have recently been busy planning and designing the pattern of the future farm land use, production organization, and rural settlements—one of the most ambitious and expensive schemes after collectivization. Unfortunately, relatively little has been published with regard to specific plans. Publications deal mostly with planning principles and methodology. The general plan is to concentrate scattered rural populations into large *kolkhoz* and *sovkhoz* villages, along with large-scale production facilities—the socialist farmsteads.

During the 1971-1975 five-year-plan period, ten large experimental dairy farms, each with 800 to 1,000 milk cows, were scheduled to be built. These are now completed, and new experiences are being reported. Also, the construction of seven large industrial-type hog farms and two poultry "factories" was planned. The first section of the largest hog farm, near Viljandi, designed for finishing 44,000 hogs a year, was completed and put into use early in 1974. New poultry farms, one near Tallinn and the other in Tamsalu, are also in operation (Järvesoo, 1975). The Tallinn Poultry Factory, which has reached its planned capacity of 400,000 laying hens and produces 100 million eggs annually, has become a showplace for foreign visitors.

Information is scarce about the future population centers (*kolkhoz* and *sovkhoz* villages, agrotowns, and rural resettlement projects). There seems to be subdued disagreement and debate about the proposed multistory, multiapartment, urbantype housing. This settlement pattern clearly limits the use of household plots and the keeping of livestock; rural people do not like this. It is indicated that the planned primary population centers would include about 500 to 1,000 people, the secondary centers about 200 people. Existing larger rural towns are frequently preferred as sites for future *kolkhoz* and *sovkhoz* villages. Urban amenities and services are projected to be parts of such rural settlements (Järvesoo, 1974).

The construction of giant farm complexes and the resettlement of the population into agrotowns is a long-range project because of the immense investment required. The presently completed and planned farms are considered experimental. Serious warnings have been expressed in recent publications about going too fast without adequate experience. At the same time, there are signs that Moscow is showing impatience because of too-slow progress. Another recommendation in the current five-year plan calls for the construction of farm-related industries by *sovkhoz*es and *kolkhoz*es, the agroindustrial complexes, so as to alleviate seasonal unemployment in rural areas and better serve local consumers (see Tônurist, 1974:84-180).

Why are the Soviet authorities bestowing such privileges upon a peripheral area? Without the conscious and purposeful preferred allocation of needed and scarce farm inputs—such as machinery, fertilizers, and feeds—Estonian agriculture could not have achieved its present status. It appears that Moscow found in the Baltic countries both an advanced agricultural industry and a highly educated labor force, a combination which offered good possibilities for experimentation with an intensive type of farming. The results of such experimentation could then be used to construct a development model for the less advanced regions of the Soviet Union. This idea was explicitly stated in Moscow's *Pravda* on June 18, 1972, in the article "Estonskii eksperiment," written by Mikhail L. Bronštein, an economics professor at the University of Tartu.

The Estonian Economy in Soviet Plans

The Estonian economy, after more than three decades of Soviet rule, has been fully integrated into the overall Soviet economy. Soviet economic objectives in Estonia are concisely stated in the directives of the five-year plans. The completed 1971-1975 five-year plan required Estonia to:

raise industrial output by 36–39 percent; assure further development of electrical machinery and equipment industry, of instrument and appliances industry, including other machine-building branches that require limited amounts of metals, of light, meat and dairy industries.

To raise by 1975 oil-shale mining output to 26 million tons, electrical energy generation 1.4 times, instrument and appliance output 1.5 times and fisheries output 1.4 times.

Finish construction of the Estonian (New Baltic) electric power plant and begin construction of the Tallinn heating and power plant. Accelerate the construction of new oil-shale mines for supplying with fuel the Baltic and Estonian power plants. Expand the capacities for producing construction fiberboard from low quality lumber and from woodworking residues.

Secure further agricultural development and specialization in dairy and beef production, bacon pig raising and potato production. Drain 210,000 hectares of swampy and waterlogged soils and carry out other land improvement works on 150,000 hectares. Establish 130,000 hectares of improved, high yielding meadows and pastures.

Expand the commercial port facilities and the railroad yard facilities in Tallinn. (*NLKP* 24:319-320).

Goals for the current five-year plan are similar, although growth rates are generally lower, in line with all-union plans.

In summary, these plan assignments stipulate further expansion of industrial production—particularly in oil-shale chemistry and electrical, engineering, precision, and measuring instrument production—and further intensification of agricultural production, mainly livestock farming and potato output. However, it is noteworthy that, for the current five-year period, projected industrial growth in Estonia (26 percent) is considerably below the growth rate projected for the Soviet Union as a whole (35–39 percent, including a 38–42 percent increase in producer goods and 30–32 percent in consumer goods). Consumer goods are expected to increase by 30 percent (*Rahva Hääl*, November 20, 1976).

Soviet regional specialization is based on the principle of

comparative advantage, on availability of natural and human resources, and on historical development. Estonia is endowed with significant oil-shale deposits, the exploitation of which had already begun before the Soviet period. Soviet planners have been interested in developing the Estonian oil-shale basin into a significant energy source for the entire Soviet northwest and the Baltic region. The region lacks other, more economical energy sources for such large industrial centers as Leningrad, Riga, and Tallinn. Also, Estonia has significant deposits of phosphorites. Present fertilizer output exceeds local needs, and plans call for the further development of phosphorous and nitrogen fertilizer output. There are also ample raw materials for portland-cement manufacturing, oil-shale ashes for cinder blocks and panels, and clay for bricks. The textile industry has old historical roots, and so also have the wood-pulp and paper manufacturing industries. A well-educated and skilled labor force allows the development of precision and measuring instrument production.

In the ensuing sections of this chapter, major sectors of the economy will be considered in greater detail, with emphasis on developments since 1960. The discussion will begin with the manufacturing industries, one of the fastest-growing sectors, whose output is claimed to have increased more than three times since 1960, whose total employment has increased about 40 percent, and whose labor productivity has more than doubled (see table 5).

Light Industry

Soviet Estonian light industry includes the textile manufacturing, garment, leather, and footwear industries. It employs the largest proportion of the labor force, accounting for about 25 percent of industrial employment in 1970 (a comparative figure is about 17 percent for the Soviet Union as a whole). The textile industry has a 150-year history in Estonia. While its relative importance has declined recently, its output volume has seen a steady rise. The output value of light industries ranks second only to the food-processing and beverage industry, accounting for 24 percent of total industrial output in 1970 (Ritso, 1972:98). Table 11 summarizes developments since 1960.

Light industries suffered very heavily during World War II.

Table 11

Development of light industries in Soviet Estonia, 1960 - 1974

	1960	1965	1970	1974
Gross output index	100	130	191	223
Total employment index	100	120	118	114
Labor productivity index	100	109	161	195
Cotton fabric, millions of square meters	108	127	193	170
Linen cloth, millions of square meters	6.7	7.1	6.9	5.8
Woolen cloth, millions of square meters	4.6	4.9	5.9	7.2
Topcoats, raincoats, 1,000	788	762	838	474
Women's dresses, 1,000	348	789	1,270	1,479
Men's and boys' dress shirts, 1,000	n.a.	1,428	1,725	1,686
Knitted underwear, millions	5.6	7.1	13.7	12.5
Leather shoes, millions of pairs	3.9	5.7	6.9	6.0
Rubber shoes, millions of pairs	1.9	1.7	1.9	1.9
Socks and stockings, millions of pairs	8.5	9.3	8.3	12.5

Source: *Eesti NSV rahvamajandus*, 1976:82, 88, 105, 107-109.

The withdrawing Red Army in 1941 burned all of the large textile plants, including the largest cotton mills in Tallinn and Narva. German occupational forces were not interested in reconstruction; they operated only the smaller plants which had escaped destruction, using local raw materials such as flax and wool. In the first postwar year, 1945, the output in textile manufacturing was only 12 percent of the prewar output in cotton yarn and threads, 4 percent in cotton fabrics, 55 percent in woolens, 37 percent in linen fabrics, 9 percent in rayon, and 18 percent in knitwear. But during the next few years the old textile plants were rebuilt, and by 1950 the prewar level of output had been surpassed except in the production of rayon fabric. From then on, light-industrial output has expanded rapidly, and recent growth rates have exceeded the average of the Soviet Union. Over the period 1956-1970 light-industrial output in Estonia tripled, while the Soviet Union as a whole experienced a 2.4-time increase. Particularly rapid was the growth in output of cotton fabrics, knit goods, and leather footwear. In cotton fabric manufacturing, Estonia ranks fifth among the Soviet republics (after the Russian SFSR, Uzbekistan, the Ukraine, and Azerbaidjan). Estonia produces more than 60 percent of the cotton cloth in the three-republic Baltic region. In per-capita production, Estonia ranks first in this area. In 1970, Estonia produced 5.6 times the Soviet average yardage of cotton fabric per capita, 3 times as much knit underwear, 2.1 times as much knitwear, 1.8 times as much linen fabric and leather footwear, 1.7 times as much ready-made clothing, and 1.6 times as much woolen fabric. It was relatively easy to repair the war damages and expand the output of the historically well-developed production base.

For the 1976-1980 five-year period, a modest growth of 18 percent has been projected for light industry in Estonia—lower than the total (26–28 percent) projected for the Soviet Union, and also somewhat lower than the actual growth rate during the previous five-year period.

During the 1960s (the seventh and eighth five-year periods), considerable capital outlays were made for light industry. Physical plants were expanded and machinery and equipment renovated in Narva, Tallinn, Pärnu, and elsewhere. Recently, the woolen mill at Sindi (established in 1832) was extensively reconstructed and expanded. Modernization of plants and greater specialization has increased labor productivity.

A considerable part of light-industrial output is of high quality and attractive design; Estonian products are in strong demand all over the Soviet Union and are even marketed abroad. About 80 percent of cotton fabric output, nearly 60 percent of knit goods, and nearly 40 percent of socks, hosiery, and ready-made garments are shipped to other republics. Cotton and linen fabrics, terry cloth and towels, and woolen scarves are exported both to other areas of the USSR and abroad. At the same time, there is an unsatisfied demand in the Estonian SSR for a variety of such minor dry goods as leather and fur articles, rugs, headgear, and some special types of men's and women's shoes (Ritso, 1972:99).

In the garment and fur industry, Estonia is a net exporter. The House of Fashion in Tallinn has become a notable fashion center for the Soviet Union, and its fashion magazine *Siluett*, published in both Estonian and Russian editions, enjoys a wide circulation in the Soviet Union, particularly in Leningrad and Moscow.

Since most of the raw materials for textiles has to be shipped in—cotton and wool from distant Central Asia, flax fiber from Byelorussia and the Ukraine—and because textile manufacturing is labor intensive in an environment of tight labor supply,

questions are evidently being raised regarding the propriety
and economics of the Estonian textile industry, particularly its
further expansion. Furthermore, domestic Soviet demand for
Estonian products is declining as other parts of the Soviet
Union are industrializing, and competition in foreign markets
is stiff.

Machine Building and Metalworking

Employment in the machine-building and metalworking
industries comprises about 21–22 percent of the total industrial
labor force. This proportion increased rapidly from about 16
percent in 1958 to nearly 22 percent in 1964 and has remained
at that level, although the number of people employed increased by about one-fifth (to about 50,000) between 1964 and
1970. In the Soviet Union as a whole, 33 percent of industrial
employees were in machine building and metalworking in
1970.

Engineering industries also have a notable tradition in
Estonia, developing rapidly after the turn of the century.
Before World War I, output was heavily concentrated in
shipbuilding, railroad cars, and railroad equipment. Current
machine-building output is much more diversified, and includes electric motors, rectifiers and transformers, excavators,
trailer homes, electric cables, oilfield and refinery machinery,
farm machinery, and a variety of smaller consumer durables.
All of these items are produced largely for nonlocal needs and
are being exported to foreign countries. Tallinn is the overwhelming leader in engineering industries, representing 78
percent of the total output (Rei, 1972:21). Electronic and other
equipment accounts for 36 percent of the industry total, other
machines for 21 percent, metal products and structures for 15
percent, and machine and equipment repairs for 28 percent.

Expansion of machine building and metalworking continued at a rapid rate until recent years, as is evident from table
12. Total output in 1974 was nearly six times higher than 1960
output, while employment in this sector nearly doubled. In
overall long-range Soviet planning, Estonia has been assigned
the role of producing precision and measuring instruments,
electric motors and appliances, electronic equipment, and
automation-control instruments—all products requiring small
amounts of heavy raw materials but a high level of skilled-

Table 12

Development of machine-building and metalworking
industries in Soviet Estonia, 1960 - 1974

	1960	1965	1970	1974
Gross output index	100	215	383	564
Total employment index	100	154	177	190
Labor productivity index	100	140	216	296
Electric motors				
(.25 to 100 kilowatts), 1,000	216	258	294	292
Transformers, 1,000 kilowatts	774	4,072	6,244	4,006
Excavators	339	880	1,680	1,835
Trailer homes	316	1,079	1,418	---
Electric cable, 1,000 kilometers	25.7	41.5	46.2	51.4
Radio sets, 1,000	16.9	25.8	10.1	18.0
Oilfield and refinery equipment,				
1,000 tons	7.0	7.8	10.8	20.9

Source: Eesti NSV rahvamajandus, 1976:82, 88, 98-100.

labor input—and providing competent research and development institutions.

The Volta electric-motor manufacturing plant in Tallinn has all-union significance. It currently produces about 5 percent of all electric motors, more than 300,000 of the Soviet Union's total of 6.4 million. Fifteen years ago this proportion was a higher 10 percent. Although this plant was recently renovated and expanded, excessive fragmentation of the industry among various administrative agencies is considered a serious disadvantage.

For the current five-year period, another 40-percent expansion of output is foreseen for machine building—the highest projected growth rate among all the industrial sectors (*Rahva Hääl*, November 20, 1976).

Food Processing

The food-processing industry developed rapidly during prewar years, when Estonia became a significant exporter of dairy and meat products. The domestic market for processed food products also expanded noticeably. During the Soviet period, food processing has further expanded, particularly in the area of food canning. Concentration into fewer and larger industrial plants has been an evident trend, and small plants have closed or been absorbed by larger firms.

Food-processing industries currently employ about 14 percent of the industrial labor force (some 35,000 people). Gross output increased by 175 percent during the 1960-1974 period, while employment went up by about 38 percent (nearly proportional to the overall rise in industrial employment), as is evident in table 13. Food-processing industries produced nearly one-third of the value of all industrial output.

Agriculture and fisheries are the most important sources of raw materials for food processing. Milk output recently reached the prewar level of a little over 1 million tons a year, while beef and pork output is considerably above the earlier levels. A larger proportion of milk and meat produced is marketed, while on-farm consumption has decreased. The farm population has also declined by about one-half from its prewar level, and there is probably less direct selling of milk and meat from farms to nonfarm rural people, who are now supplied mostly through regular retail channels. Home baking is rapidly disappearing. Combined with rapid urbanization, all of these factors have contributed to the growth of the food-processing and beverage industries, the output of which currently exceeds the prewar level and shows a steady increase in most product lines. The most notable growth is in the output of canned foods, cheese, bakery products, sausage, and whole milk products (table 13). While before World War II a large proportion of dairy butter was exported, the export share has sharply declined. But cheese exports have increased, as has the export of canned foods (mostly canned fish products). The fish catch has increased rather spectacularly—partly as a result of the activities of the Tallinn-based ocean fishing fleet of Ocean, the all-union fishing firm—in line with the Soviet overall effort to exploit ocean resources more extensively. While in 1950 only 4 million cans of fish were marketed in Estonia, in 1970 the total reached nearly 104 million standard cans.

Further growth is projected in the food-processing industries, in livestock output, and in fishing activities in the Baltic Sea, North Sea, and all the world's oceans. Growing Soviet and especially Estonian incomes will guarantee a demand for any increase in such output in the foreseeable future. Projected growth rates in the 1976-1980 five-year period are 31 percent for the meat and dairy industries and 18 percent for all food-processing industries (*Rahva Hääl*, November 20, 1976). The fishing industry must increase output by 19 percent.

Table 13

Development of food-processing industries
in Soviet Estonia, 1960 - 1974

	1960	1965	1970	1974
Gross output index	100	150	215	275
Total employment index	100	120	133	138
Labor productivity index	100	124	158	199
Fish catch, 1,000 tons	82	181	291	unk.
Meat (dressed weight), 1,000 tons	55.1	65.1	98.6	122.2
Sausage products, 1,000 tons	16.7	21.4	31.7	38.3
Whole-milk products, 1,000 tons	138.4	179.8	235.2	286.2
Dairy butter, 1,000 tons	17.2	21.6	21.6	27.1
Cheese (whole-milk) 1,000 tons	3.2	4.8	8.9	10.3
Canned foods, millions of standard cans	61.9	95.6	151.3	231.0
Bakery products, 1,000 tons	18.4	27.9	35.4	40.8

Source: Eesti NSV rahvamajandus, 1976:83, 89, 110-113.

It is projected that most of the increase in output must come from increased labor productivity, since available local labor resources are nearly exhausted. Concentration and reconstruction of the dairy plants and meat-packing plants will continue, as will the broadening of the assortment of dairy products, which is still considered unsatisfactory. There is also room for expanding the output of canned and frozen fruits and vegetables so as to satisfy the demands of the local market. Official policy also calls for a reduction in the output of hard liquors (but an expansion in the production of beer, wine, and nonalcoholic beverages), since drinking is a serious problem in the Soviet Union.

Forestry, Woodworking, and Pulp and Paper Manufacturing

Growth of the wood-based industries is to some extent limited by the availability of local raw material. During the war and early postwar years, exploitation of local forests considerably exceeded productive capacity; hence the sustained yield. In recent years some 30–35 percent of industrial timber needs have been satisfied by imports from the Russian SFSR. Growth is based primarily on structural shifts toward a greater variety of processed products. Since 1960 the industry's gross output has about doubled (see table 14), with only a modest 13-percent increase in employment (to about 23,000 people, or 10 percent of total industrial employment). Of the total employed, about 10,000 were working in wood processing, 9,000 in lumbering operations, and 4,000 in wood-pulp and paper manufacturing. The latter are among the oldest industries in Estonia; the oldest paper mill in Tallinn dates to 1677 (Renter, 1958:21). Per-capita output of timber-based industries exceeds by far the Soviet averages: in pulp and paper production by 4.6 times; in furniture, plywood, and fiberboard output by 2.9 times; in particle-board output by 2.3 times. Further growth is not considered expedient.

Lumbering operations have changed radically since the war. While logging and hauling of round wood used to be a winter-season side employment for farm people, it is now a specialized industry with a year-round labor force, and timber cutting and hauling operations are now largely mechanized. Improvements in lumber harvesting technology have increased labor productivity.

Of the productive forest land, 57 percent belongs to the state, 40 percent to agricultural *sovkhoz*es and *kolkhoz*es, and 3 percent to other institutions. It is evident that only state forests are managed and utilized efficiently; *sovkhoz* and *kolkhoz* forests are poorly managed for various reasons. As a result, the productivity of the latter is low, and cutting quotas are not always met. About 40 percent of the timber harvest is still used for fuel, an uneconomical utilization of a valuable and scarce resource. But progress has been made, and will continue to be made, toward the more efficient use of processing and wood-working residues.

Woodworking is the leading sector of the wood-based industry, accounting for more than one-half of the total output value. Furniture manufacturing accounted for 52 percent of woodworking output in 1970, an increase from 41 percent in 1961. Furniture production has been expanding rapidly, encouraged both by exports and by demand in the local market. High-quality Estonian furniture of modern design has found ready markets in distant parts of the Soviet Union as well as in foreign countries. About 40 percent of furniture output is exported. Seven large, specialized, and well-mechanized workshops account for 90 percent of the furniture output. But

Table 14

Development of forestry, woodworking, and pulp and
paper manufacturing in Soviet Estonia, 1960 - 1974

	1960	1965	1970	1974
Gross output index	100	136	181	227
Employment index	100	108	113	113
Labor productivity index	100	126	159	200
Timber and firewood cut, million solid meters	2.0	1.9	2.3	2.3
Sawn wood, 1,000 cubic meters	891	730	798	891
Plywood, 1,000 cubic meters	23.1	28.8	32.6	36.0
Particle board, 1,000 cubic meters	.4	13.8	22.8	17.7
Wood pulp, 1,000 tons	95.1	112.1	118.1	120.9
Paper, 1,000 tons	86.8	94.5	105.0	103.6
Cardboard, 1,000 tons	10.3	14.4	12.8	10.6
Fiberboard, million square meters	----	1.92	2.15	3.16
Skis, 1,000 pairs	374	468	539	590
Pianos	188	397	332	420

Source: Eesti NSV rahvamajandus, 1976:82, 88, 101–103.

narrow specialization limits variety, leaving parts of the local demand unsatisfied. Given the limited furniture imports, there is thus a gap between supply and demand and the local furniture market. Despite some reservations (because of the relatively long hauls for exports), furniture-manufacturing traditions and strong export demand for Estonian furniture provide justification for further expansion of the industry, a fact reflected in the 40-percent increase projected in the 1971-1975 five-year plan (Lugus, 1972:91). Estonia also has a reputation for producing high-quality, modern store fixtures and furniture for retail establishments. These are designed and manufactured by the Wholesale Society of Consumer Cooperatives (ETKVL), and 80 percent of the output is exported. Estonian pianos have earned a good reputation in Soviet concert halls, and some are exported to Western Europe.

A significant new growth industry during the recent five-year plans has been fiberboard and particle-board manufacturing. In Püssi (northern Estonia), a 22-million-ruble plant is under construction with a planned capacity for producing 10 million square meters of hard fiberboard and 100,000 solid meters of particle board per year. It is said to be one of the largest firms of its type in Europe.

Ski manufacturing is another wood industry in which Estonia excels. Two ski-manufacturing plants, one in Tallinn, the other in Pärnu, currently produce more than .5 million pairs of high-quality laminated competition skis, of which 80–85 percent are exported. The special competition skis are reputed to be the best in the Soviet Union. Brisk demand has encouraged the expansion of ski output and exports. Consequently, the last five-year plan provided for an output goal of 840,000 pairs per year by 1975. Both ski-manufacturing plants were reconstructed and expanded during that period.

Pulp and paper products have traditionally been an important export item. About 65–70 percent of pulp output and 40–48 percent of paper is shipped out of Estonia—although there is a local paper deficit, which has frequently limited the output of the printing industry. Considerable quantities of low-quality paper for book printing are imported from Latvia. Only very modest output increases are projected for pulp and paper, apparently because raw materials and water resources are limited. At present, about 45 percent of raw material for paper manufacturing is imported from the Russian SFSR and the Karelian ASSR. Also imported are 50 percent of plywood logs, 65–70 percent of poles, and 40 percent of mine props. The overall goal for forestry, woodworking, and pulp and paper industries is a growth rate of 24 percent during the 1976-1980 five-year plan (*Rahva Hääl*, November 20, 1976).

The main problems of the forestry, woodworking, and pulp and paper manufacturing sector appear to be the fragmentation of forest management among various agencies, the incomplete utilization of harvested timber, and the inefficient organization and performance of some segments of the industry, such as sawmills. The fact that local timber resources are limited places an effective restriction on the further quantitative growth of the industry. More efficient utilization of timber resources and a shift toward high-quality products are opportunities which the wood-based industries must exploit in the future.

Fuel Industry and Energetics

Fuel production currently employs about 17,000 workers (about 8 percent of total industrial employment). While employment has been rather stable over the last decade, output of

Table 15

Development of the fuel industry and electrical and thermal
energy generation in Soviet Estonia, 1960 - 1974

	1960	1965	1970	1974
Fuel industry				
Gross output index	100	166	238	328
Employment index	100	111	110	111
Labor productivity index	100	149	219	296
Oil-shale mined, million tons	9.2	15.8	18.9	27.3
Peat for fuel, 1,000 tons	467	670	972	637
Peat briquets, 1,000 tons	100	177	299	279
Household gas, million cubic meters	433	515	581	568
Electric and thermal energy generation				
Gross output index	100	388	657	911
Employment index	100	178	240	248
Labor productivity index	100	218	275	367
Electric energy, billion kilowatt hours	1.9	7.1	11.6	16.0
Thermal energy, billion calories	.6	1.6	3.8	4.7

Source: Eesti NSV rahvamajandus, 1976:82, 88, 97.

the industry has grown considerably, mostly because of mechanization and the increase in labor productivity (see table 15). The fuel industry in Estonia employs approximately twice the amount of labor, on a relative basis, as the Soviet Union's average. More than half of the labor force is in the oil-shale industry. Steadily expanding fuel-peat production is another peculiarity of the utilization of fuel resources in Estonia.

Systematic work was begun on oil-shale exploration and research under the leadership of an unstinting enthusiast, Märt Raud, a civil engineer. In 1919 oil-shale mining was initiated in an attempt to alleviate the fuel shortage caused by difficulties in importing coal. In 1924 the first oil-cracking plant opened at Kohtla-Järve after a small experimental plant, in operation since 1921, had shown promise. Thus, a slow but steady growth of Estonia's oil-shale industry began. By 1940 the output of oil-shale mining had risen to nearly 2 million tons a year, and about 200,000 tons of crude oil and some 20,000 tons of gasoline were produced.

Usable oil-shale deposits occur in north and northeast Estonia, between Rakvere and Narva, in an area of about 3,000 square kilometers, and continue into the Russian SFSR east of the Narva River, where Slantsy, the center of the Russian oil-shale industry, is located. Explored oil-shale resources in Estonia amount to about 10 billion tons (*ENE*, vol. 6, 1974:305). Industrially usable reserves have been estimated at 8.6 billion tons, or, in terms of oil, about 1.7 billion tons—considerable even at the international level.

During Soviet rule the oil-shale industry has been under direct Moscow administration, and it has been developed forcefully and wastefully. Because the Soviet northwestern industrial region lacks other, more efficient energy sources, during the postwar period the task of filling the energy gap fell to the Estonian oil-shale industry, even though today the region is connected by direct pipelines to inner Russian and Ukrainian oil and natural-gas sources. While during the prewar years the production emphasis was on oil and gasoline and direct use in thermoelectric power plants was of secondary significance, this emphasis has changed. In the immediate postwar period the first priority was the production of household gas, initially for the Leningrad area. In 1948, when a direct pipeline was built from northeast Estonia to Leningrad, 78 million cubic meters of gas was produced. By 1960 this figure was 433 million cubic meters, and since 1970 nearly 600 million cubic meters per year (see table 15).

Since the late 1950s the emphasis in the oil-shale industry has been shifting toward electric-energy production in large thermal power plants. In 1955 construction was begun near Narva of the 1.6-million-kilowatt Baltic Thermoelectric Plant. The first 100,000-kilowatt generator went into operation in November 1959, and full capacity was reached in February 1966. In 1967 the plant produced 7.5 billion kilowatt hours of electrical energy, or about 89 percent of total electricity output in Estonia. The plant is literally a "mine-mouth" station, supplied with shale from the nearby Sirgala mine. It burns about 10 million tons of shale a year, pulverized for better burning. After this first giant was completed, construction of an equal-capacity twin power plant was begun a few miles to the southwest. Here, the first generator went into operation in June 1969 and the full 1.6-million-kilowatt capacity was reached in August 1973.

Oil-shale mining output has grown steadily, mainly to supply fuel for the two giant power stations. Production was 27.3 million tons in 1974, of which about 20 million tons was used by the two power plants. While earlier plans contemplated constructing three giant thermoelectric power plants, developments in nuclear energy and the construction of a new nuclear power plant near Leningrad have modified those plans and obviated the need for a third oil-shale power plant. Consequently, oil-shale mining is now expected to level off at about 25–26 million tons a year. Recently, construction was started on the 300,000-kilowatt Iru thermoelectric power and heating plant near Tallinn, which will use oil as fuel.

Both underground and strip mining methods are being used to extract oil shale. Strip mining is preferred because it is cheaper, even at new production sites where oil-shale veins are 300 feet or more underground. Although an extra price has to be paid for grading and restoring the landscape, reforestation experiments on strip-mined areas have been successful.

Some unresolved problems bear on the future development of the oil-shale processing industry. Shale oil and gas are more expensive than mineral oil and natural gas, and they cannot successfully compete as a fuel with the latter, which abound in the Soviet Union. The prospects are considered brighter for using shale oil and gas as raw materials in the local chemical industry. The peculiar characteristics of shale oil and gas are said to give the former some advantages over petroleum and natural gas in certain chemical industries. Also, shale-processing methods, particularly oil cracking, are undergoing changes as old plants are deteriorating and being reconstructed.

In addition to oil shale and its derivatives, peat bogs are an important potential fuel resource in Estonia. Peat bogs in this climatic zone are frequent and extensive, and their systematic exploitation for thermoelectric generation and home heating began during prewar years. The first peat briquet manufacturing plant was established at Tootsi in 1938. During the Soviet period fuel-peat production has been greatly expanded, particularly during the last decade, and another briquet plant was built in Toila (northern Estonia). More than .5 million tons of peat and .3 million tons of briquets a year were produced in recent years (see table 15).

It is noteworthy that about 40 percent of harvested timber is still being used as fuel, particularly in rural areas and in homes. For towns and cities, central steam and electric heating systems have been projected for expansion in newly built city residential areas and, eventually, in new rural settlements, the agrotowns.

Electrical and thermal energy production is closely related to the fuel industry. This relatively small but important sector employs only about 6,000 people (less than 3 percent of industrial employment). While employment has increased two and a half times since 1960, gross output had increased more than nine times by 1974 and labor productivity had approximately tripled (see table 15). Particularly rapid was the growth in electrical energy: more than eightfold during the 1960-1974 period, when the two giant thermoelectric power plants went into operation. There will be some increase in the future, since the Estonian power plant did not reach its full capacity until August 1973. But, in general, electricity output will level off. Growth for the 1976-1980 period is expected to be 11 percent. About 80 percent of the electricity generated is exported from the republic.

Building Materials

The production of building materials currently employs about 15,000 people, nearly 6 percent of total industrial employment (see table 16). Gross output has more than tripled since 1960, encouraged by the strong demand for building materials generated by lively construction activity. Several new building-material plants have been established, and some old ones reconstructed and appreciably expanded.

Leading building materials in Estonia include cement, lime, bricks, concrete construction panels, fiber-glass padding, and sheet glass. Also, local limestone ("marble"), crushed rock, gravel, and sand are important. Plywood, particle board and fiberboard were listed under forestry products.

The old Kunda cement plant (established in 1870) has been reconstructed and its capacity expanded. As a result, its output, 101,000 tons in 1960, has grown to more than 1 million tons annually. Further expansion is under way.

New types of building materials are being manufactured from oil-shale cinder and flyash (cinder blocks and panels, insulation panels). To use such otherwise bothersome indus-

Table 16

Development of the building-materials industry
in Soviet Estonia, 1960 – 1974

	1960	1965	1970	1974
Gross output index	100	185	278	366
Employment index	100	118	130	146
Labor productivity index	100	156	208	251
Portland cement, 1,000 tons	101	675	964	1,046
Lime, 1,000 tons	190	187	196	209
Bricks, millions	310	281	332	296
Concrete construction panels, 1,000 cubic meters	192	428	699	908
Fiber-glass padding for insulation, 1,000 cubic meters	97	132	172	212
Asbestos sheets, million unit sheets	unk.	44	61	64
Sheet glass, 1,000 square meters	1,832	1,916	1,932	2,101

Source: Eesti NSV rahvamajandus, 1976:82, 88, 103–105.

trial residues, building-materials manufacturing is frequently combined with thermoelectric plants (Narva, Ahtme), phosphate mining (Maardu), and woodworking industries (Valga, Tartu, Pärnu). The two thermoelectric giants near Narva produce, from burning about 20 million tons of oil shale a year, about 10 million tons of cinder and flyash. The latter, which consists mostly of lime, is used extensively for liming acid soils, but this need is limited locally to a maximum of a half-million tons per year. A small amount of flyash is also used for manufacturing portland cement at Kunda, but the bulk goes for manufacturing various kinds of prefabricated construction panels and blocks. A smaller building-material manufacturing plant is operating at Ahtme. The Narva building-materials *kombinat* was recently completed in order to use part of the cinder and flyash from the two thermoelectric giants. Yet less than 10 percent of the oil-shale ashes find utilization at present (Öpik, 1973:18-23). Preparations are being completed to use this material for liming Russian soils in conjunction with regional agricultural development.

In general, Estonia is well supplied with principal building materials for current and future needs. At present, considerable quantities of building materials are exported: 90 percent of ground limestone, 78 percent of roofing materials, 30–35 percent of cement and fiber glass, 23 percent of asbestos, and 13 percent of lime (Aader, 1972:62). At the same time, imported building materials include crushed rock, high-quality cement, fireproof bricks, gypsum boards, gypsum, ceramic tile, sewer pipe, and foam-rubber plastic materials. Since construction activity was expected to increase by 40 percent during the 1971-1975 five-year plan, a corresponding expansion of the local building-materials output was needed. While most raw materials were available in sufficient quantities for such an expansion, some raw materials had to be imported. The 1976-1980 five-year plan calls for a 21-percent increase in building-materials output.

Poor quality is admittedly a characteristic of Soviet construction, and substandard building materials play a part. Thus, the need to improve the quality of building materials, particularly of standard prefabricated and finishing construction details, is of great concern. There is a general shortage of plastic construction materials and a poor selection of floor coverings, paints, insulating materials, metal parts, and finished wooden construction details.

Chemical Industries

The leading chemical industries in Estonia are based on oil shale or related to mineral fertilizer manufacturing (see table 17). In the oil shale–based chemical industries, three types of raw materials are used: crude oil, gas, and kerogen, the organic matter of oil shale. The list of products of oil-shale chemistry is as long and impressive as that of the derivatives of any petrochemical industry: from asphalt for road construction to various pharmaceutical products, and from insect sprays and detergents to impregnating oils. This product mix has been changing over the years and will probably change further as market conditions change. Major products currently include impregnating oil and fuel oil, electrode coke, detergents and washing powders, resins and tanning substances, light aromatic carbohydrates, solvents, and naphthalene.

A nitrogen fertilizer plant completed at Kohtla-Järve in the late 1960s produced 347,500 tons of fertilizers in 1970 and had a projected output of 440,000 tons by 1975. An older fertilizer plant is in operation at Maardu (near Tallinn), where ground raw phosphate has been mined and produced since the early

Table 17

Development of chemical industries
in Soviet Estonia, 1960 - 1974

	1960	1965	1970	1974
Gross output index	100	165	244	325
Employment index	100	124	137	142
Labor productivity index	100	132	178	228
Sulphuric acid (monohydrid), 1,000 tons	132	152	173	195
Mineral fertilizers, 1,000 tons	465	804	1,326	1,543
Incl. ground rock phosphate, 1,000 tons	212	342	364	n.a.
Superphosphate, 1,000 tons	253	461	614	706
N-fertilizers, 1,000 tons	n.a.	n.a.	348	n.a.
Sulphur, tons	3,302	4,060	5,169	4,977
Lacquers and enamel paints, tons	548	1,711	1,974	3,717

Source: Eesti NSV rahvamajandus, 1976:82, 88, 98.

1920s, and construction of a superphosphate plant was started in 1940. The latter plant was completed during the Soviet period, but it is primarily using apatites from the Kola peninsula, not local phosphates, as raw material.

While the output of raw phosphate at Maardu has been greatly expanded (currently about 360,000 tons per year), it is used mainly either for mixing with superphosphate or as a phosphate fertilizer for acid soils. About half of the fertilizer output is currently exported. Future plans include production of combined-formula fertilizers and improvement of handling qualities. A new phosphate-mining site and enrichment plant is being contemplated for Toolse, probably during the late 1970s, to exploit the phosphate resources there. Toolse phosphate deposits are quite extensive: a 50-kilometer (20-square-mile) area where the ore vein is 2.5–3.0 meters (8–10 feet) thick contains approximately 10.5 percent phosphoranhydride, a percentage that can be easily enriched to 28–30 percent. The vein is accessible by inexpensive strip mining.

Finally, various consumer products of the chemical industries have earned good reputations in other Soviet republics. Such products include a wide range of cosmetic wares, paint pigments, textile dyes, hair dyes, hair sprays, window and furniture cleaning materials, and floor waxes. About 80 percent of such products are exported.

Retail Trade and Service Industries

From a Soviet viewpoint, the retail and service industries are considered nonproductive activities since they do not provide a material output. This peculiar view has relegated much of the tertiary economic and social activities, including trade and other services, to low priorities, and hence to large-scale neglect. In the annexed Baltic states, retail trade and service industries were well developed, and this tradition has kept them well advanced in comparison to the rest of the Soviet Union. Coupled with their better-developed consumer goods industries, their superior local distribution systems and service industries represent an important element of the higher standard of living found in the three Baltic republics.

Retail sales per capita in Estonia have consistently been about 40-45 percent above the Soviet Union average and are the highest among the union republics, with Latvia a close second. Per-capita sales after 1960 developed somewhat faster in Estonia than in the union as a whole, but lately Soviet growth has caught up. Per-capita sales in Estonia amounted to 1,111 rubles, while the average for the Soviet Union was 780 rubles (see table 18). Both per-capita sales rates have more than doubled since 1960.

State-owned retail establishments, servicing mostly urban areas, do about two-thirds of the total retail business; cooperative stores, primarily in rural areas, account for the remaining one-third. Sales in rural stores account for one-sixth and urban stores for five-sixths of the sales volume. (Per-capita sales in rural stores amount to only two-fifths of urban per-capita sales.) Sales of food products make up a little more than half of the sales, industrial products somewhat less. Finally, public eating places represent about one-tenth of the retail business.

There has been some increase in retailing facilities per 10,000 inhabitants since 1960, particularly in store floor space, seating places in public eating establishments, and number of public eating places. The number of retail shops shows a slight decline, however, as a result of larger store sizes (see table 18).

There is a nearly private sector within retail trade—the *kolkhoz* or collective farm markets, where mostly privately produced farm products are traded. Although its significance was considerable during the immediate postwar years, it has declined recently to less than 1 percent of the total retail trade

Table 18

Retail sales and structure in state and
cooperative systems in Estonia, 1960 – 1974

	1960	1965	1970	1974
Total retail trade, million rubles	634	820	1,305	1,581
Total retail trade index	100	130	206	249
Retail trade per capita				
In Estonia, rubles	521	635	956	1,111
In Estonia index	100	122	183	212
In USSR, rubles	367	454	639	780
In USSR index	100	124	174	212
Number of retailing establishments	3,603	3,857	3,920	3,954
Retailing establishments per 10,000 inhabitants	29	30	29	28

Sources: Eesti NSV rahvamajandus, 1976:253, 255, 256, 257, 276;
Narodnoe Khoziaistvo SSSR, 1974:628.

(7–8 million rubles per year). But *kolkhoz* markets supply a much larger share of some selected food products, such as potatoes, fresh fruits, berries, and vegetables. The decline of the *kolkhoz* markets is directly related to the decreasing scarcity of food and the disappearance of large differentials between state and free-market prices. Moreover, private producers can now sell or consign their surplus food products at current prices to local consumer cooperatives at a 10-percent commission fee. Although sales through these outlets are now considerably greater than sales through *kolkhoz* markets, the Estonian SSR Council of Ministers in 1976 reaffirmed their commitment to encourage the *kolkhoz* system.

Consumer services have been improving over the past decade, but they are still very modest and insufficient to meet demand. Value of services has more than quadrupled since 1960, but amounted to only 38 rubles per capita in 1974. A special agency, the Ministry of Consumer Services, was established to develop this much neglected sector.

Housing

Housing is another sector of the consumer economy that was grossly neglected for a long time. However, real improvements have been made since the late 1950s and early 1960s. Housing in Estonian cities and towns suffered extensively during World War II. Withdrawing Soviet armies burned many small towns in the summer of 1941. Further, in 1943 and 1944 the Soviet air force systematically bombed Estonian cities and towns with incendiary bombs, which caused extensive fires among wooden structures. Not until 1955 were the wartime housing losses recovered. But extensive urbanization had reduced the available per-capita floor area in cities and towns.

In rural areas, housing per capita has increased as a result of depopulation (deportation and migration to cities), while housing quality has been deteriorating. Repair materials for old farm dwellings are scarce, probably because the official goal is to resettle the rural population in agrotowns. But the latter scheme has made little progress because of the scarcity of funds and building materials. Only about 15 percent of the rural population lives in new rural settlements.

In cities and towns the housing situation is somewhat different. Considerable new construction has increased total urban housing space by more than 75 percent since 1960 and per-capita space by some 30 percent (see table 19). It is noteworthy that about one-fourth of all housing space is still owned privately, although this share is declining. As for housing conveniences, all urban apartments have electricity, six out of seven have running water and sewers, three out of four have household gas available, and about half have central or distant heating.

Housing space allocation policies are used to regulate urbanization. In the Baltic republics in particular, these policies favor Russian immigrants—who appear to get apartments without waiting, although waiting lists otherwise exist. That this is the case is reflected in the fact that most new residential areas of the larger cities are now predominantly Russian sections. Native migrants usually have to wait from two to three years for permission to move into the cities. Poor quality is the main problem in new housing construction, as is the case elsewhere in the Soviet Union. Available finishing materials are of poor quality, as are materials and workmanship related to plumbing and heating systems.

Table 19

Development of the service industry and of urban housing
facilities in Soviet Estonia, 1960 - 1974

	1960	1965	1970	1974
Service industry				
Number of consumer service				
establishments	1,368	1,920	2,166	2,100
Number of employees, thousands	n.a.	12.4	15.8	18.5
Total value of services provided				
million rubles	9.4	20.8	37.4	53.4
Value of services per capita, rubles	8	15	26	38
Number of selected service establishments				
Public saunas	n.a.	117	355	343
Barbers, hairdressers	n.a.	455	533	526
Shoe-repair shops	n.a.	143	132	109
Tailor shops	n.a.	228	229	225
Urban housing facilities				
Total housing facilities, million				
square meters of useful floor area	8.1	10.2	12.3	14.3
of the total, percent of private housing	25	26	24	22
Housing floor space per city dweller,				
square meters	11.4	12.6	13.6	14.8
Percent of housing supplied with:				
running water	67	77	84	87
sewer system	69	79	85	88
central or distant heating	18	35	48	56
electricity	100	100	100	100
household gas	27	51	71	78

Source: <u>Eesti NSV rahvamajandus</u>, 1976:287, 301, 302.

Transportation and Communication

In comparison with the rest of the Soviet Union, transportation and communication systems in Estonia are well developed, but still behind those of the densely populated countries in Western Europe. About 10,000 people are employed in communications and more than 57,000 in transportation, of which 41,000 are in motor vehicles, 11,000 in railroads, and 5,000 in sea transport. Total employment in this sector has increased by about one-fourth since 1960.

The increase in transportation and communication services

has been particularly rapid since 1960, no doubt as a result of income increases during this period. Improvements are also noticeable in the expansion of the highway system, particularly of hard-surfaced roads, in bus services, and in the volume of freight and passengers hauled by all modes of transportation. Many of these indicators more than doubled or tripled during the 1960-1974 period.

It is noteworthy that the number of telephones has more than tripled since 1960, while radio sets just about doubled. Television had a late start in the Soviet Union, but it has been catching up fast. Since television sets are rather expensive in relation to earnings, the rapid increase in their use reflects improved income over the last decade.

Economic Ties with Other Regions and Countries

In the modern world, the international division of labor and specialization do not allow even large countries to be fully self-sufficient. Small countries traditionally have a very high foreign trade rate—25 to 40 percent of the national product commonly goes for imports from other regions or countries. For the Estonian SSR, external economic ties are needed for two principal reasons: first, Estonia is relatively poorly endowed with industrial raw materials; second, under Soviet rule Estonia is an integral part of the comprehensive Soviet system, in which regional and international division of labor and concentration and specialization of production are purposefully sought through central planning. Because specialization frequently leads to the production of a narrow assortment of products in any given locality, an exchange is required to meet the local demands.

In 1966 the share of imports in the total consumption of the Estonian SSR exceeded 30 percent, whereas a total of 31 percent of the republic's output was exported. In 1961 the corresponding figures were 22 percent for imports and 21 percent for exports (Tulp, 1972:151). According to a 150-industry input-output table compiled in the mid-1960s, only 18 were of a purely local nature. The remaining 132 industries sold part of their output on an all-union or international scale.

Industrial development in Estonia is heavily dependent on imported raw materials, which account for 40-45 percent of the total used. It is estimated that more than one-fourth of all industrial input, including fuel, machinery, equipment, and raw materials, is imported (Tulp, 1970:149). Imported raw materials include ferrous and nonferrous metals, cotton, wool, timber and pulp, apatite, and chemical products. Practically all fuel oil, coal, and natural gas are imported. Among imported finished and semifinished products, the following are important: transportation equipment, cars, trucks, buses, railroad cars and locomotives, industrial machines and equipment, farm machinery and equipment, and various building materials. About one-third of all consumer goods are imported, including about one-fifth of all foods; all sugar, vegetable oil, rice, citrus fruits, and grapes; a large percentage of grains (mainly wheat); and 60 percent of wines.

Imports of manufactured consumer goods and foods accounted for about 40 percent of total imports in 1966; industrial raw materials, semimanufactured goods and fuel for about 27 percent; machines, equipment, and instruments for 24 percent (Tulp, 1970:151; Tulp et al., 1972:16-21). Geographically, about 45 percent of all imports came from the neighboring Russian SFSR, 16 percent from the Ukraine, 7 percent from Latvia, and 13 percent from foreign countries, primarily those of Eastern Europe (Tulp, 1972:156).

In exports, three aggregated sectors stand out: light-industrial products accounted for nearly 29 percent of the export value in 1969, food products for 26 percent, and machines and equipment for 19 percent. Also of importance are exports of electrical energy, paper and pulp, and various products of chemical industries, each of the three contributing about 4–5 percent to the total export volume (Tulp, 1972:155). Engineering and metalworking industries rely most heavily on exports; thus, 97 percent of machines and instruments and 90 percent of electrical appliances and instruments are exported. Other industries exporting large shares of total output include wood pulp and paper, 72 percent of output; mineral fertilizers, 71 percent; cotton cloth, 65 percent; fishery products, 57 percent; and various chemical products (pharmaceuticals and cosmetics), 56 percent (Tulp et al., 1972:35).

About half of the electrical energy produced in the Estonian SSR was exported to the Leningrad region and to the other Baltic republics before the second giant power plant was finished; in 1976 some 80 percent was exported. Of the

traditional dairy and meat industries, 35 percent and 26
percent of output, respectively, found outlets outside the
Soviet Union, primarily in Czechoslovakia, Cuba, and East
Germany. Garment and other textile industries exported 34–
39 percent of output and other nonspecified light industries 43
percent.

Geographically, the pattern of export destinations is similar
to the import pattern. The Russian SFSR received 48 percent
of the exports, the Ukraine 13 percent, and Latvia about 7
percent. Foreign countries took about 14 percent, with the
principal recipients being Czechoslovakia, Cuba, East Germany, and Great Britain (Tulp et al., 1972:76–77).

Standard of Living

While it is difficult to compare the standard of living in
Estonia with living standards in Western countries and the
Soviet Union, it can be said with certainty that living conditions have improved noticeably in the Estonian SSR, particularly since the 1960s. National income and personal consumption per capita are much higher in Estonia than in the Soviet
Union as a whole. Among the Soviet republics, Estonia and
Latvia have the highest national income and retail sales rates
per capita, about 40–50 percent above the Soviet average.
Total national income increased in Estonia during the 1960–
1974 period by 153 percent. Comparable figures are 151
percent for the Soviet Union and 155 percent in neighboring
Latvia. The agricultural population, *kolkhoz* farmers in particular, experienced the highest income increases, followed by
other low-wage earners. A relatively stable 73 percent of the
national income is being used for personal consumption.

Personal consumption for Estonia averaged 1,060 rubles in
1970; the average was 631 rubles in 1960. It is difficult to
evaluate the material standard of living provided by 1,060
rubles, which was equal to U.S. $1,117 at the official 1970
exchange rate but equivalent to only $270 to $350 on the
Western black money markets. Neither of these extremes
reflects the true value of the purchasing power of the ruble in
the Soviet Union, which is somewhere in between. Consumption and price structures in the Soviet Union are so different
from those in the West that making an objective comparison of

living standards is no simple matter. In the Soviet Union a large share of expenditures is imposed upon the residents by central planners and the government. Not only is education free, at the university level about three-fourths of the students who make satisfactory academic progress draw stipends which generally cover about half of their living expenses. Hospitalization and medical services are free. However, drugs must be paid for; they are said to be expensive and their availability is uncertain. Housing is relatively inexpensive if a minimally satisfactory apartment can be found in a government-owned and -subsidized building; such apartments, however, are scarce. Acquiring and operating a private dwelling is quite expensive. Despite some improvements in recent years, scarcity of housing is still considered the foremost everyday problem in the USSR. This is also the case in Estonia (Küng, 1973:93, 163).

The structure of personal-consumption expenditures and a comparison of typical earnings and prices may further define the standard of living. Only a rough breakdown of aggregate personal-consumption expenditures is available for recent years (*ERM*, 1974:72). Purchases of consumer goods account for 78.1 percent of the total, services (probably including transportation and housing) for 8.6 percent, obligatory and voluntary taxes and fees for 9.5 percent, and savings accounts and government bonds for 3.8 percent. Retail trade figures report that more than half of the personal expenditure is for food, a little less than half on various manufactured goods. Consequently, 41–42 percent of all personal income in the Estonian SSR is spent on food. (Comparable figures are 20–25 percent in West European countries and 16–17 percent in the United States.) Housing, certainly substandard by Western criteria, takes only 5–6 percent of income, about one-fourth the percentage spent in the West. There are very few privately owned cars (one per forty-eight residents) and motorcycles (one per fifteen residents), and public transportation is inexpensive. Many kinds of entertainment, such as movies, theaters, and concerts, are modestly priced, as are books, magazines, and newspapers. Increased savings—up from 1.7 percent of personal income in 1960 to 4.1 percent in 1972 and 3.8 percent in 1974—are frequently said to reflect shortages of goods, not a need or will to save.

Other good indicators of living standards are diet and public

Table 20

Selected indicators of the standard of living
in Estonia, 1960 - 1974

	1960	1965	1970	1974
Personal consumption in current				
prices, rubles per capita	631	749	1,060	1,198
index	100	118	167	190
Consumption of principal food- stuffs per capita:				
Meat, Estonian SSR, kilograms	68	63	73	77
" USSR, kilograms	40	41	48	55
Milk and dairy prod. Estonian SSR, kilograms	406	406	420	407
Milk and dairy prod. USSR kilograms	240	251	307	315
Eggs, Estonian SSR	190	164	241	259
" USSR	118	124	159	205
Fish and fish products, Estonian SSR, kilograms	17.7	22.7	29.5	27.4
Fish and fish products, USSR, kilograms	9.9	12.6	15.4	16.5
Sugar, Estonian SSR, kilograms	36.5	40.3	43.6	42.4
" USSR, kilograms	28.0	34.2	38.8	41.0
Vegetable oil, Estonian SSR, kilograms	4.6	6.6	6.7	7.4
Vegetable oil, USSR, kilograms	5.3	7.1	6.8	7.9
Potatoes, Estonian SSR, kilograms	181	199	151	155
" USSR, kilograms	143	142	130	121
Vegetables, Estonian SSR, kilograms	72	69	80	78
" USSR, kilograms	70	72	82	87
Cereal products, Estonian SSR, kilograms	145	129	112	105
Cereal products, USSR, kilograms	164	156	149	142
Medical care per 10,000 residents				
Number of physicians, Estonian SSR	23.9	29.5	33.1	36.0
" " " USSR	20.0	23.9	27.4	31.5
Hospital beds, Estonian SSR	94.0	110.1	110.2	111.0
" " USSR	82	96	110	115.8

Sources: Eesti NSV rahvamajandus, 1976:60, 74, 353; Narodnoe
Khoziaistvo SSSR, 1974:603.

and private health services. Table 20 compares major food
items consumed in Estonia with those consumed in the Soviet
Union, as well as the number of physicians and hospital beds
per 10,000 residents. While the Soviet food-consumption
pattern since 1960 clearly shows movement toward a "rich

man's" diet abundant in meat, milk, eggs, and fish, Estonian consumption rates of such items are noticeably higher. Consumption of such "poor man's" foods as starchy potatoes and cereals has been declining. Further qualitative diet improvements can be expected, considering the serious Soviet attempts to develop the livestock industry.

The low purchasing power of Soviet wages and salaries relative to the high prices of consumer goods—that is, the wage earners' low real income—in comparison to the high relative earnings in the United States is a favorite topic in popular magazines. Consideration of a few typical wage-price relationships is helpful in characterizing the situation in Estonia, although such relationships may be misleading because of the commonly low quality of consumer goods and the time spent in lines waiting to purchase them.

The minimum wage is still 60 rubles per month. A large proportion of clerical employees, typists, filing clerks, and service personnel is in the 60–80 rubles-per-month low-wage category. Many of the 280,000 pensioners get considerably less than the minimum wage. Elementary-school teachers' salaries until recently were 80–110 rubles per month, with the possibility of increase, after twenty-five years of service, to a maximum of 125 rubles. These rates also characterize the earnings of junior research workers and postal, banking, and insurance employees. Retail and wholesale clerks earn 80–120 rubles, store managers 120–200 rubles, taxi drivers 100–200 rubles, and skilled workers in industry 120–200 rubles a month. Physicians earn 140–200 rubles per month, high-school teachers 100–200 rubles, senior research workers 180–250 rubles, university assistants and associate professors 250–350 rubles, and professors 450–550 rubles.

Direct taxes are low. The income tax on a monthly wage of 100 rubles is about 8 percent, increasing along with salaries to a maximum of 13 percent. In considering personal earnings, it must be remembered that both husband and wife normally work. The employment rate in Estonia is the highest in the Soviet Union: 94 percent of all able-bodied people, including homemakers. Food prices are typically low for staple products but higher for fresh fruits and livestock products. Butter is 3.50 rubles per kilogram (2.2 pounds), meat and fish 3–4 rubles per kilogram, milk .26 rubles per liter (1.1 quart), eggs 9 kopeks apiece. It costs about 1 ruble a day to feed one person. To feed a family of four for a year would require 11 rubles more than the average wage earner's income after taxes.

Apparel, textile goods, and footwear used to be rather more expensive and of poorer quality than such items in the United States, but inflation in recent years has boosted American prices to about the Soviet level. However, quality differences still remain. A man's woolen suit costs 110–170 rubles; a pair of shoes with rubber soles 10–15 rubles; shoes with leather soles 25–35 rubles. A bicycle goes for 60–80 rubles, a motorcycle 1,300–1,500 rubles, a Moskvich passenger car 4,500 rubles, and a transistor radio 35–150 rubles.

Soviet statisticians place the standard of living in Estonia behind only the living standards of Switzerland, Sweden, West Germany, France, and the Benelux countries in Europe (Lember, 1973:4). Supposedly, it is higher than the standards of living in Finland, Norway, Denmark, Great Britain, and Italy. Such a ranking indicates wishful thinking on the part of the officials. Many modern household conveniences, such as electric ranges, refrigerators, and washing machines, are still scarce in Estonia, and only 15 percent of the rural population resides in newly built houses with electricity and other conveniences. Indeed, if one compares the gap between the material standards of living in Estonia and Finland in 1939 with that of the present, it has apparently widened rather than closed, even though the recent absolute gains in Estonia have been noteworthy.

Nevertheless, Estonia's material standard of living is probably higher than comparable standards in Mediterranean Europe, most of Eastern Europe, and all of the non-Western world. Finally, many intangibles that determine a standard of living cannot be empirically measured. Thus, while many Estonians presently have the financial resources (because of increased personal incomes) for foreign travel, the latter is politically restricted. According to Küng (1973), the limited possibility for travel abroad is a leading complaint about everyday life in Soviet Estonia.

Conclusions

Economic development under Soviet rule has been rapid, especially in regard to industrialization. However, while rapid economic growth has contributed to a rise in the standard of living, it has had negative side effects. Forced industrialization beyond the limits of the local labor force has contributed directly to the immigration of large numbers of non-Estonians, leading many natives to charge that industrialization represents a purposeful Russification policy.

Moreover, industrial development has been lopsided. Heavy industries have enjoyed a high priority in material, capital, and labor allocations, while many areas of consumer economics—for example, housing—have received too little attention. Many consumer products are of shoddy quality. Service industries were also neglected until quite recently. Industrialization and urbanization, as well as inadequate outlets for spending increased personal income and savings, have contributed to high levels of alcohol consumption. Alcohol problems are receiving increased attention in the local press, since greater consumption has contributed to increases in the divorce rate, motor-vehicle accidents, work and leisure accidents, and crime. Work discipline and labor productivity have suffered; absenteeism on "blue Mondays" is widespread.

Finally, industrialization has also led to pollution, especially along the northern coast and the oil-shale basin. Hence, while Estonia has become a leader in the Soviet economy, pioneering many types of manufacturing, marketing, and management techniques, it also appears to be, together with Latvia, the republic of the Soviet Union most beset by problems seemingly typical of industrially developed societies.

References

Aader, L.

1972   "Ehitusmaterjalide tööstus" [Building Materials Industry], in *Eesti NSV tööstus üheksandal viisaastakul* [Estonian SSR Industry during the Ninth Five-Year Plan]. Tallinn: Eesti Raamat.

Aasmäe, V.

1969   "O razrabotke sistemy territorial'nogo planirovania v kolkhozakh i sovkhozakh estonskoi SSR" [On the System of Collective and State Farms Territorial Planning in the Estonian SSR]. *Eesti NSV Teaduste*

Akadeemia toimetised, Ühiskonnateadused 18, no.
2: 133-142.

Abels, George
1945   "Nôukogude maareformi teostamine Eestis" [Imple-
        mentation of the Soviet Land Reform in Estonia], in
        Viis aastat Nôukogude Eestit. Tallinn: RK Poliitiline
        Kirjastus.

Antons, Richard
1960   *Pôllumajandusalaseid direktiive, seadusandlikke ja
        ametkondlikke akte* [Directives, Legal Acts, and
        Ordinances Regarding Agriculture], vols. 1 and 2.
        Tallinn: Eesti Riiklik Kirjastus.

Arman, E.
1961   "Kas üks vôi mitu kolhoosiasulat?" [One or More
        Kolkhoz Villages?]. *Sotsialistlik Pôllumajandus* 16,
        no. 14: 654-657.

Astaškin, A.
1961   "Rajoonide ja kolhoosiasulate planeerimise prob-
        leeme" [Problems of Planning Regional and *Kolk-
        hoz* Villages]. *Sotsialistlik Pôllumajandus* 16, no. 24:
        1105-1108.
1974   *Pereustroistvo estonskoi derevnii* [Reconstruction of
        Rural Estonia]. Tallinn: Valgus.

Bronshtein, Mihhail L.
1972   "Estonskii eksperiment," *Pravda*, no. 170 (June 18).

Brutus, L.
1960   "Eesti NSV sotsialistlikust industrialiseerimisest"
        [On Socialist Industrialization in the Estonian SSR],
        in *Nôukogude Eesti Majandus 1940-1960* [Soviet
        Estonian Economy 1940-1960]. Tallinn: Eesti Riiklik
        Kirjastus.

EE (Eesti entsüklopeedia 1–8)
1932   [Estonian Encyclopedia, vols. 1–8]. Tartu: Loodus.

Eesti NSV TA Majanduse Instituut

1970   *Eesti NSV rahvamajanduse aktuaalseid probleme* [Current Problems of the National Economy of the Estonian SSR]. Tallinn: Eesti Raamat.

Eesti NSV tööstus üheksandal viisaastakul

1972   [Industry of the Estonian SSR during the Ninth Five-Year Plan]. Tallinn: Eesti Raamat.

Ekbaum, Arthur

1949   *Destruction of Independent Farming in East Europe.* Stockholm: Estonian Information Centre.

ENE (Eesti nôukogude entsüklopeedia), vols. 1-8

1968-   [Estonian Soviet Encyclopedia]. Tallinn: Valgus.
1976

ERM (Eesti NSV rahvamajandus 1957)

1957   [The National Economy of the Estonian SSR in 1957]. Tallinn: Eesti Riiklik Kirjastus.

ERM (Eesti NSV rahvamajandus 1972)

1974   [The National Economy of the Estonian SSR in 1972]. Tallinn: Eesti Raamat.

ERM (Eesti NSV rahvamajandus 1974)

1976   [The National Economy of the Estonian SSR in 1974]. Tallinn: Eesti Raamat.

ERM (Eesti NSV rahvamajandus 9 viisaastakul: Ülesanded ja probleemid)

1972   [The National Economy of the Estonian SSR during the Ninth Five-Year Plan]. Tallinn: Eesti Raamat.

Instituut ekonmiki akademii nauk ESSR

1969   *Ekonomicheskie sviazi Estonskoi SSR v sisteme narodnago khoziaistva SSSR.* Tallinn: Eesti Raamat.

Järvesoo, Elmar

1973a   "Estonia: Economic Problems during the Independence Years, 1918-1940," in *Problems of Mini-nations*, ed. Arvids Ziedonis et al. San Jose, Calif.: Association for the Advancement of Baltic Studies.

1973b   "Progress despite Collectivization: Estonian Agriculture," in *Problems of Mininations*, ed. Arvids Ziedonis et al. San Jose, Calif.: Association for the Advancement of Baltic Studies.

1974a   "Agrotowns in Soviet Estonia." Paper presented at the Fourth Conference on Baltic Studies, University of Illinois, Chicago Circle Campus, May 16-20.

1974b   "Private Enterprise in Soviet Estonian Agriculture." *Journal of Baltic Studies* 5 (Fall): 169-186.

1975   "Giant Livestock Farms in Soviet Estonia." Paper presented at the Third Conference on Baltic Studies in Scandinavia, Stockholm, June 14-16.

1976   "Comparative and Real Income of the Farming Population in Soviet Estonia." Paper presented at the Fifth Conference on Baltic Studies, Columbia University, May 20-23.

Jeret, U.

1965   *Mööda tööstuslikku Põhja-Eestit. Kalevipoja aarete maal* [Along the Industrial North Estonia]. Tallinn: Eesti Raamat.

1967   *Industry and Building in Soviet Estonia.* Ten Aspects of Soviet Life Series. Tallinn: Eesti Raamat.

Kahk, Juhan, E. Laasi, and A. Ruusmann

1965   *Eesti talurahvas teel sotsialismile* [Estonian Peasants on the Road to Socialism]. Tallinn: Eesti Raamat.

Kareda, Endel

1947   *Technique of Economic Sovietization.* East and West Series, no. 3. London: Boreas.

1949   *Estonia in the Soviet Grip.* East and West Series, no. 5. London: Boreas.

Kasepalu, A.

1961   "Töötajate töölkäimise kauguse ja ajakulu sõltuvus majandite keskuste paiknemisest" [Commuting Distance and Time Related to Location of Farm Centers]. *Sotsialistlik Põllumajandus* 16, no. 19: 568-570.

Kaur, Uno

1962 *Wirtschaftsstruktur und Wirtschaftspolitik des Freistaates Estlands.* Bonn: Baltisches Forschungsinstitut. (Reprinted from *Commentationes Balticae* 8/9, no. 3: 83-256.)

Kraaving, E.

1961 "Pôllumajanduslike rajoonide ja majandite planeerimise küsimusi" [Problems of Planning Agricultural Regions and Farms]. *Sotsialistlik Pôllumajandus* 16, no. 5: 193-195.

Küng, Andres

1973 *Saatusi ja saavutusi: Baltikum tänapäeval* [Of Fate and Achievements. The Baltic Today]. Lund: Eesti Kirjanike Kooperatiiv.

Lageda, P.

1972 "Energeetika-, kütuse- ja keemiatööstus" [Energetics, Fuel, and Chemical Industries], in *Eesti NSV tööstus üheksandal viisaastakul.* Tallinn: Eesti Raamat.

Lember, E.

1973 *Eesti NSV: Elu-olu* [Estonian SSR: Everyday Life]. Tallinn: Eesti Raamat.

Lugus, O.

1970 "The Level and Prospects of the Forest Industry in the Estonian SSR." *Eesti NSV Teaduste Akadeemia toimetised. Ühiskonnateadused* 19, no. 1: 47-54.

1972 "Metsa-, puidu-, tselluloosi- ja paberitööstus" [Forestry, Woodworking, Pulp, and Paper Industry], in *Eesti NSV tööstus üheksandal viisaastakul.* Tallinn: Eesti Raamat.

Maamägi, Viktor, ed.

1971 *Eesti NSV ajalugu* [History of the Estonian SSR], vol. 3. Tallinn: Eesti Raamat.

Marksoo, A.

1972 "On Trends of Intrarepublican Migration in the Estonian SSR," in *Estonia: Geographic Studies.* Tallinn: Estonian Geographical Society.

Matin, Valentin, and Mihhail Bronshtein

1959 *Eesti NSV põllumajanduse kollektiviseerimine ning selle sotsiaalsed ja majanduslikud tulemused*[Collectivization of Agriculture in the Estonian SSR and Its Social and Economic Consequences]. Tallinn: Eesti Riiklik Kirjastus.

Meressoo, A., and L. Saat

1972 "Toiduainetetööstus" [Food Industry], in *Eesti NSV tööstus üheksandal viisaastakul.* Tallinn: Eesti Raamat.

Nar. Khoz. (Narodnoe Khoziaistvo SSR)

1973 [Statistical Yearbooks]. Moscow: Statistika, 1974. (See also earlier volumes.)

NLKP 23 Kongressi materjale

1967 [Materials on the Twenty-third Congress of the CPSU]. Tallinn: Eesti Raamat.

NLKP 24 Kongressi materjale

1971 [Materials on the Twenty-fourth Congress of the CPSU]. Tallinn: Eesti Raamat.

Öpik, I.

1973 "Soojuselektrijaamade heitmete ratsionaalse kasutamise probleeme" [Problems of the Rational Utilization of the Waste Products of Thermal Power Stations]. *Loodusuurijate Seltsi Aastaraamat* 62: 15-24.

Panksejev, Aleksandr

1961 *EKP võitlus töölisklassi ja talurahva liidu kindlustamise eest aastail 1944-1960* [Struggle of the ECP for Securing an Alliance between the Working Class and Peasants during the Years 1944-1960]. Tallinn: Eesti Riiklik Kirjastus.

Pôllumehe teatmik

1971   [Farmer's Compendium]. Tallinn: Valgus, 1970.

Rahva Hääl

1940-   [The People's Voice]. Main newspaper of the Com-
1977   munist party in the Estonian SSR. Tallinn.

Ratt, A.

1960   "Kolhoosi- ja sovhoosikeskuse paiknemist mõjuta
        vad tegurid ja nende majanduslik tähtsus" [Factors
        Affecting the Location of *Kolkhoz* and *Sovkhoz*
        Centers and Their Economic Significance], in *Nõuk-
        ogude Eesti majandus 1940-1960*. Eesti NSV Tea-
        duste Akadeemia Majanduse Instituut. Tallinn: Eesti
        Riiklik Kirjastus.
1961   "Majandi tootmisüksuse optimaalsest suurusest"
        [On the Optimal Size of the Farm Production Unit].
        Sotsialistlik Pôllumajandus 16, no. 22: 1017-1020.

Ratt, A., et al.

1964   "Pôllumajanduslike ettevõtete optimaalne suurus
        Eesti NSV-s" [Optimal Size of Farm Firms in the
        Estonian SSR]. *Pôllumajandus ökonoomika küsi-
        musi 4*. Tallinn: Eesti Raamat.

Rei, E.

1972   "Masinaehitus ja metallitööstus" [Machine Building
        and Metalworking], in *Eesti NSV tööstus üheksan-
        dal viisaastakul*. Tallinn: Eesti Raamat.

Renter, R.

1958   *Suurtööstuse tekkimine ja arenemine Eestis 19 ja 20
        sajandil (Suure Sotsialistliku Oktoobrirevolutsioo-
        nini)* [Origin and Development of Large-Scale Indus-
        try in Estonia during the Nineteenth and Twentieth
        Centuries (until the Great Socialist October Revolu-
        tion)]. Tallinn: Eesti Riiklik Kirjastus.

Ritso, L.

1972   "Kergetööstus" [Light Industries], in *Eesti NSV tööstus üheksandal viisaastakul.* Tallinn: Eesti Raamat.

Royal Institute of International Affairs

1937   *The Baltic States.* London: Oxford University Press.

Ruusmann, A.

1969   "Põllumajanduse kollektiviseerimine Eesti NSV-s" [Collectivization of Agriculture in the Estonian SSR]. *Nõukogude Kool* 27, no. 7: 485-489.

Sel'skoe khoziaistva SSR

1971   Moscow: Statistika.

Sepre, O.

1945   "Eesti NSV 1944/45. aasta rahvamajanduslikud saavutused" [Economic Achievements in Estonia during the 1944-1945 Fiscal Year], in *Viis Aastat Nõukogude Eestit* [Five Years of Soviet Estonia]. Tallinn: Poliitiline Kirjastus.

Soviet Economic Prospects for the Seventies

1973   Compendium of Papers Submitted to the Joint Economic Committee, Congress of the United States. Washington: U.S. Government Printing Office.

Taagepera, Rein

1972   "Inequality Indices for Baltic Farm Distribution, 1929-1940." *Journal of Baltic Studies* 3 (Spring): 26-34.

Tarmisto, V.

1969   "Territorial Concentration and Decentralization of Industry in the Soviet Baltic Republics." *Eesti NSV Teaduste Akadeemia toimetised. Ühiskonnateadused* 18, no. 3: 208-211.

1970a   "Tootmisharulise ja territoriaalse aspekti ühtsusest rahvamajanduse arendamisel ja juhtimisel" [The Unity of the Branch and Territorial Aspects in the Management and Development of National Economy]. *Eesti NSV Teaduste Akadeemia toimetised. Ühiskonnateadused* 19, no. 2: 208-219.

1970b   "Môningatest tootmise territoriaalse organiseerimise tulemustest Eesti NSV-s" [Results and Problems of Territorial Organization of Production in the Estonian SSR], in *Eesti NSV rahvamajanduse aktuaalseid probleeme.* Tallinn: Eesti Raamat.

1972   "On Some Specific Features of Intraregional Territorial Organization of Production," in *Estonia: Geographical Studies.* Tallinn: Estonian Geographical Society.

Tomingas, W.

1973   *The Soviet Colonization of Estonia.* New York: Kultuur.

Tônurist, Edgar

1967   *Eesti NSV põllumajanduse sotsialistlik rekonstrueerimine* [Socialist Reconstruction of Agriculture in the Estonian SSR]. Tallinn: Valgus.

1971   *Meie põllumajanduse täna ja homme* [Our Agriculture Today and Tomorrow]. Tallinn: Eesti Raamat.

1974   *Eesti NSV põllumajanduse industrialiseerimine* [Industrialization of Agriculture in the Estonian SSR]. Tallinn: Valgus.

Tulp, L.

1970   "Eesti NSV majanduslike sidemete arenguprobleeme" [Development Problems of Soviet Estonian Economic Relations], in *Eesti NSV rahvamajanduse aktuaalseid probleeme.* Tallinn: Eesti Raamat.

1972   "The Estonian SSR and Socialist Integration," in *Estonia: Geographical Studies.* Tallinn: Estonian Geographical Society.

Tulp, L., D. Rajango, and M. Vabar

1972   *Economic Ties of the Estonian SSR.* Tallinn: Eesti Raamat.

Vabar, M.

1972   "Foreign Economic Relations of Soviet Estonia," in
        Estonia: Geographical Studies. Tallinn: Estonian
        Geographical Society.

Veimer, A.

1967   *Eesti tööstuse arenemine seitseaastakul* [Develop-
        ment of Estonian Industry during the Seven-Year
        Period]. Tallinn: Eesti Raamat.

Vint, Endel

1971   *Intensiivse põllumajanduse majanduslik efektiivsus
        Eesti NSV-s* [Economic Efficiency of Intensive Agri-
        culture in the Estonian SSR]. Tallinn: Kirjastus
        Valgus.

5

The Struggle between the
State and the Churches

Vello Salo

The theoretical aim of the Communist party of the Soviet Union—the rooting out of any kind of religion—is identical in all parts of the country. But in practice there are many nuances and variations in specific localities. Some of these differences are due to such factors as the predominant religion found in a locality and the degree to which this religion, as an institution, is related to local ethnicity. Additionally, historical factors play a role. This chapter describes and analyzes the life of the churches in Estonia during the Soviet period.[1] (The term "church" is here used in a broad sense so as to include non-Christian communities.) In essence, the situation may be perceived as a struggle—the party is attempting to destroy religion, while the churches are trying to preserve it.

By 1940, the third major campaign of the Communist party to liquidate all churches in the Soviet Union had almost ended. When Estonia was absorbed into the Soviet system in 1940, the continuing Soviet campaign against religion was introduced there. However, this effort was interrupted by the German occupation. When Soviet forces reentered Estonia in late 1944, several aspects of the situation had changed. The most significant change was that the churches, in postwar Soviet society, had come to be considered possible political allies of the state and the party, especially in regard to foreign policy. Hence a more tolerant stance was adopted, even though the rooting out of religion remained a party—and thus a state—goal.

From the standpoint of official tactics, the postwar period in Estonia may be divided into three parts: From 1944 to 1956, the party used atheistic lectures and publications to fight religion. From 1957 to 1965 it attempted to replace such church ceremonies as baptism with new "antireligious" rites. From 1965 to 1977 "sociological investigations" of church activities were carried out. (For the last period, the beginning date is somewhat arbitrary and the ending date denotes the point at which this survey was concluded. This division is also valid when appraising the situation from the viewpoint of the churches.)

In many respects, the non-Soviet scholar has at his command far less material about the postwar period in Estonia (1944-1977) than about the first year of Soviet rule (1940-1941). The information gap is especially serious for the Stalinist period. Not only were refugees from this period few, there were few publications of any type in Soviet Estonia. Indeed, during this whole period only two useful works were published by the churches themselves: the 1947 *Apostlik-ôigeusuliste eestlaste kalender 1948: aastaks* [Estonian Orthodox Calendar for 1948] and the 1956 *Eesti Evangeeliumi Luteriusu Kiriku aastaraamat* [Yearbook of the Estonian Evangelical Lutheran Church]. Both contain statistical data about their respective congregations. Occasionally one may find official information on the Orthodox and Protestant churches in two Moscow journals, *Zhurnal Moskovskoi Patriarhii* and *Bratskij Vestnik*. But Estonian church leaders have been reluctant to reveal detailed information, and no written protests against the existing religious situation such as those issued by the Moscow Patriarchate and Lithuanian Catholics have emanated from Soviet Estonia. Furthermore, not a single piece of religious underground literature published in Estonia appears to have reached the West.

Religion in 1938 and Changes during 1939-1944

The last enumeration of churches, congregations, and clergy in Estonia was done in 1938 (*Eesti aadress-raamat, 1938-1939*:200-213). At that time, there were nine registered denominations with a total of 489 congregations and 467 clergymen. The Estonian Evangelical Lutheran church had 184 congregations (including 2 dependent congregations) and 191 clergy-men. The Estonian Apostolic Orthodox church had 157 congregations and 138 clergymen; the Old Believers (*staroo-bryadtsy*), respectively, 12 and 10; the Baptist church, 49 and 45 (including two assistant ministers); the Adventist church, 38 and 34; the Methodist church, 14 and 15; the Evangelical Christian Free Church Union, 17 and 17; the Roman Catholic church, 10 and 14; and the Jewish community, 8 congregations and 3 rabbis.

Additionally, the 1934 Estonian census provided information on religious affiliation, which was voluntarily reported. At the time, 78.2 percent of the population was Lutheran (874,026 people) and 19 percent were Orthodox and Old Believers. The other groups were rather small: 8,752 Baptists, 4,178 Evangelical Christians, 2,327 Roman Catholics, 2,310 Adventists, 1,242 Methodists, and 191 Pentecostals. In addition, 431 were members of six small Christian groups, 4,302 were Jewish, 7,093 reported themselves as being nonbelievers, and information was lacking on 8,292 persons. The census, all told, listed membership in seventeen Christian denominations and six non-Christian groups. Such religious groups as the Salvation Army were not included in the enumeration and tabulation.

The resettlement of almost all Baltic Germans and Estonian-Swedes during the years 1939-1944 meant a loss of almost 27,000 members, seventeen congregations, and sixty-five ordained clergymen for the Estonian Lutheran church. It must be pointed out that the church members in question were among the most active. This emigration had another important consequence: the Lutheran church became by default a national church—a circumstance which seems to have fortified it internally.

In the Estonian Orthodox church, the prewar weight of the Russians (38 percent of the membership in 1934) was greater than that of the Germans in the Lutheran church. A bloodletting comparable to the German-Swedish emigration did not hit the Orthodox church until 1945, at which time the altered northeast and southeast borders cut off about 71,000 citizens of the former Republic of Estonia. The great majority of these people was Orthodox, and they constituted twenty-four congregations, more than 15 percent of the congregations which the church had counted in 1938.[2] The congregations in question were, moreover, large and very active. The number of

Russians within the Estonian Orthodox church thereby diminished noticeably, although their influence was still considerable in the remaining fifteen purely Russian congregations, as well as in a number of mixed Russian-Estonian congregations. This situation had begun in 1940 to threaten the internal and external unity of the church, especially the future of the Estonian-speaking segment. The new 1945 boundary also cut off two Lutheran congregations (Petseri and Laura) and one dependent congregation (Kallivere).

The population changes also affected the clergy. The Lutheran church lost 162 pastors between 1939 and 1945—almost 85 percent of those in office in 1938. Of these, 25 were lost during the Soviet rule of 1940-1941 and 72 fled to the West in 1944 (Aunver, 1961b:102, 107). According to Veem (1960:31) there remained in Estonia at the end of 1944 only 79 pastors. (There had been 191 before the 1941 deportations.) The Orthodox church lost 69 priests between 1939 and 1944, or about 51 percent of the prewar figure; it lost 22 priests during 1940-1941, and another 22 fled to the West in 1944 (Hindo, 1970:21; Juhkam et al., 1961:189). The 1945 border changes involved another 25 Orthodox priests.

Thus, the two major churches in Estonia entered the postwar Soviet period with extraordinarily heavy losses that would have been difficult to overcome even under the most favorable of circumstances. The churches were struck further blows by the 1944-1945 and 1949 deportations, in terms of both clergy and members. It should be noted that the minority churches also suffered heavily.

July 1940–July 1941

The early campaign against the churches in Estonia was systematic, fast-moving, and progressively more brutal, although attempts were made to mask it with legality and to keep it secret from the public. The first steps were taken during the week before the formal annexation of Estonia. Within two months the churches had been deprived of their former economic bases, means for training new clergy, and opportunities to use the mass media. The period came to a close with mass deportations and murders in addition to wartime losses of people and buildings. However, the output of atheistic publications during this period was low (Salo, 1976).

Modifications in the manner of collecting church dues, instituted on June 30, 1940, were followed by the nationalization of all land and real estate, publishing houses, and bookstores. Measures soon followed depriving former clergymen of their pensions and requiring higher rents from the clergy as well as school taxes on their children, even though education, in principle, was supposed to be free.[3]

Religious instruction, which had been introduced into the school curriculum as the result of a 1923 referendum, was now abolished by a decree retroactive to August 1, 1940. Within a three-week period (August 13-31), the Faculty of Theology at the University of Tartu—the only Estonian institution for training Lutheran clergy and the only degree-granting theological faculty in the country—was closed, all its faculty members were dismissed, and about 70,000 volumes of religious and theological literature were destroyed in the university library.[4] Other institutions for the training of clergy were likewise closed, as well as the organ department at the Tallinn Conservatory (Raid, 1969a:69; Jürma, 1956:149).

Further, "church-based youth organizations and religious organizations sponsored from abroad, such as the Salvation Army, were closed down in August 1940. . . . [And] any kind of religious literature which through the religious inclinations of the people tends to support political goals inimical to the public interest was removed from sale" (Vimmsaare, 1970:10; see also Vassily, 1953:116-118, for the account of the French Jesuit Charles Bourgeois, who was allowed to remain in the country).

Religious radio broadcasts were gradually terminated (Vassily, 1953:112) and replaced by special atheistic programs (Vimmsaare, 1970:10). During the months of July and August 1940 a suppression of all periodicals was carried out; these included at least forty church publications.[5] The *Gazette of the ESSR People's Commissariat of Education* began publishing a list of forbidden books, which were removed from bookstores and libraries (Jürma, 1956:150). During this period no permit was granted for the publication of religious literature; nevertheless, three pamphlets, already in print, managed to appear. Congregations were required to turn over church archives to the Central Archives of the State (Raid, 1969a:83).

"On December 16, 1940, the criminal code of the Russian SFSR, which contains the main regulations of socialist law regarding religion and church, was put into effect in the Estonian SSR" (Vimmsaare, 1970:10). The unconstitutional police methods developed in the Soviet Union had actually been in effect since June. Among these was the frequent summoning of clergymen and members of their families to interrogation sessions, where efforts were made to press them into service as informers (Täheväli and Välbe, 1950; Chrysostomos, 1965-1968, vols. 1 and 2; Perlitz, 1944; Vööbus, 1950; Aunver, 1956:143).

These repressive measures, ironically, had a beneficial effect on the churches: discrimination on religious grounds created public sympathy for those persecuted, and the number of churchgoers rose considerably (Aunver, 1956:146). Some members of the clergy resigned from office, but none openly went over to the atheist side (Aunver, 1956:142; Raid, 1969a:82).

With the publication of the first issue of the journal *Ateist* [Atheist] in January 1941, the antireligious campaign entered a new phase. In the first months of the Communist regime, the execution of the campaign had been hampered by various organizational difficulties. These were now being overcome; hence the confiscation of cemeteries from congregations, a result of the general nationalization of land, was not started until February 1941. At the same time, the electricity rate for churches was increased to about fourteen times that charged to residences and offices.[6]

The forcible merger of the Estonian Apostolic Orthodox church with the Moscow Patriarchate took place in January 1941. This merger was carried out within a larger framework covering all East European areas recently annexed by the Soviet Union, Estonia being the last on that list (Aleksander, 1950:10-11).

The League of Militant Atheists, created in October 1940 by the Communist party, developed slowly and had little to show in the way of results (Raid, 1969a:71-78; Vimmsaare, 1970:11). Its activities consisted mainly of lectures and newspaper articles, both relying heavily on borrowed Russian materials. The official bibliography includes six antireligious pamphlets totaling 256 pages and 59,000 copies.[7] Moreover, six issues of *Ateist* appeared, totaling 6,000–10,000 copies. In order to keep people from going to church, an effort was made to schedule lectures and other activities to coincide with the times of church services (Raid, 1969a:76). There were scattered instances of disruption of church services and desecration of houses of worship (Aunver, 1961b:104).

The great deportation of June 13-14, 1940, marked the beginning of the most brutal phase of antireligious activity. Through murder, imprisonment, deportation, and conscription, the churches lost more than 60 members of the clergy, among them 4 bishops.[8] Of the lay leaders of the Lutheran church, 163 were deported and 27 murdered (Aunver, 1961b:103). For other denominations, exact data are lacking. At the outbreak of the Soviet-German war, most of the Jews in Estonia fled to the Soviet Union; this exodus ended, for all practical purposes, the religious activities of the Jewish community in Estonia. It is estimated that one-fourth of all the houses of worship in Estonia suffered damages as a result of war activity and willful destruction (Aunver, 1961b:105).

Prior to the return of the Soviet armies in the fall of 1944, about 70,000 persons escaped from Estonia. More than half of the remaining clergy also escaped. Their main motivation for fleeing was fear of more mass deportations, not, as the Soviet Estonian commentator Raid (1972:32) claims, "fear of public condemnation." That such fear was justified was evidenced by the deportations carried out immediately after the arrival of the Soviet armies (about 30,000 persons in the winter of 1944-1945) as well as by the catastrophe that followed barely four years later, in 1949, when about 80,000 were deported.

The renewed war action in 1944 inflicted heavy losses on the houses of worship. Of those belonging to the Estonian Lutheran church, only 92 out of 202 escaped damage (Aunver, 1961b:105; Veem, 1960:31). Again there occurred desecrations of churches by the Soviet armies (Veem, 1960:31).

The Stalinist Years, 1944-1956

The postwar years saw attempts to establish state control over the churches in order to exploit them for purposes of Soviet foreign policy (Chrysostomus, 1965-1968, vol. 3; Kolarz, 1963:15-18). Those years were also characterized by the relative apathy of the regime's atheistic campaign. Both observations were true throughout the entire Soviet Union (Raid, 1969b:80; Kolarz, 1963:15-18). In contrast to the situation in other parts of the USSR, in Estonia the absolute ban on all religious and theological literature which was enacted at the end of 1946 is still in force today.[9]

The Lutherans

In January 1945, a new leader had to be elected by the Lutheran church to replace Acting Bishop A. Eilart, who had been deported. A. Pähn was chosen for this post (Nelson, 1965:47); yet he too was soon imprisoned and exiled to inner Russia (Veem, 1960:31; Nelson, 1965:48). A formula of accommodation with the Lutheran church appears to have been reached after the renewed deportations in March 1949. Thus, Jaan Kiivit, who was elected bishop on October 23, 1949, was permitted to remain in office for a relatively long period, until 1967. On the other hand, the consistory of the church was forced to appoint A. Lepin, a representative of the ruling authorities, as its chief secretary.

After the regime closed down the theological institute which had functioned during the German occupation of 1941-1944, a theological examination board was permitted to supervise the private studies of ministerial candidates. The board made an effort to maintain the academic level of the former theological faculty at Tartu University. As a way of overcoming the shortage of clergy, assistant ministers, deacons, and lay preachers were appointed (Aunver, 1961b:108). The Council of Bishops voted to admit women as lay preachers on January 17, 1945 (Vimmsaare, 1969:63).

The Orthodox Church

It was relatively easy for Soviet authorities to resubjugate the Estonian Orthodox church, whose Metropolitan had fled to the Patriarchate of Moscow in 1944. The liturgy of reconciliation occurred on March 6, 1946. In the same month, Pavel (Dmitrovski), who did not have a command of the Estonian language, was named bishop of "Tallinn and Estonia." Bishop Isidor (Bogojavlenski), who was named after Pavel's death, did not speak Estonian either. As a result of the 1945 boundary alterations, the proportion of Estonian-language speakers to Russian-language speakers within the church membership was approximately six to one. The first Estonian to be appointed bishop after the war was Roman (Tang), who succeeded Isidor after the latter's death on December 18, 1949. He was transferred only eight months later, having been in office only from April 16 to December 20, 1950. After that, the see remained vacant for five years.

The Free Churches

Throughout the Soviet Union a campaign was launched in 1945 to unite all the Free Churches into the All-Union Evangelical Christian Baptist League (Nelson, 1965:157; Laks, 1965:81). The congregations refusing to join were threatened with closure, while those which agreed were allowed to organize correspondence courses to prepare ministers and choir directors under the supervision of a central examination board (which was, however, suspended after four years). They were also granted permission to publish a hymnal, but this remained only a promise until 1975 (Laks, 1965:84).

At first the united congregations thrived beyond expectations. (Indeed, the congregations' center in Tallinn was allowed to operate until 1960; a summary of this period is provided by Laks, 1965:82-85). Then, in the fall of 1950, the Council of Religious Affairs required all eight congregations in Tallinn to leave their churches and relocate in the city's largest medieval church, which was in urgent need of repairs. The faithful were sure that the authorities hoped to destroy the congregations through this move, but the work of restoration, 1950-1959, united them instead (Laks, 1965:87-93).

The Religious Resurgence

Lembit Raid, a Soviet Estonian author, reported a general upswing in the observance of church rites from the postwar period to about 1957 (see tables 1–3). This trend affected both the Lutheran and Orthodox churches. Raid pointed out: "To some extent the congregations were also enlarged by an increase in the number of young people. A certain revival could also be observed in the activity of the Roman Catholic Church.

Table 1

Number of people affected by church rites in
Soviet Estonia, 1945 - 1946

	1945	1946
Christenings (children)	4,897	7,804
Confirmants (youth)	3,215	8,039
Marriages (couples)	993	2,096
Burials (individuals)	12,535	13,228

Source: Raid, 1969b:68.

The Baptists, Adventists, Methodists and other religious organizations re-activated their missionary operations" (Raid, 1969b:68f).

According to Raid, the religious resurgence was due to the following causes: "(1) a rise in the level of religious feeling among a segment of the population during the war years; (2) the difficulties in healing the wounds of war; (3) the difficulties in building socialism." Furthermore, "the problem of traditions, of the observance of church rites, was placed skillfully in the forefront, especially in the Lutheran Church. Its importance grew to the point where such rites were even performed after the traditional age. . . . For example, of those participating in confirmation in 1957, 57 percent were over 18–19 years of age" (Raid, 1969b:71).

Composite rites were also put into use; for example, at the christening of a child, the parents would simultaneously be confirmed and wed by church rites. "The religious organizations showed special interest in the problems of youth, trying at every opportunity to have a say in these matters. This applies especially to the question of the moral upbringing of youth" (Raid, 1969b:11).

The atheist campaign was not intense during this period. In 1947 and 1954 not a single atheistic lecture was held, and in

1948 and 1949 only ten and ninety-four lectures, respectively, were given (Raid, 1969b:76).

Brisk activity developed among the Brethren, the Adventist-Reformists (who established a new nonregistered group in 1951), the Methodists, the Pentecostals, the "Union in Christ," and especially among the Jehovah's Witnesses. The last group even set up a printing office (it seems actually to have been only a mimeograph machine) and distributed periodically not only its own *Teataja* [Messenger] but also tracts in Estonian and Russian. On July 20–22, 1950, the convention of this denomination had 110 delegates participating (Nelson, 1965:63-65, 142, 188-200).

For the period 1944-1953 the official Estonian national bibliography, *Raamatukroonika*, enumerates twenty-six atheistic publications, of which fifteen appeared in the year 1953, totaling 128,850 copies and 1,125 pages. During the years 1945-1946 seven small church publications were issued, having a maximum of 64 pages each and totaling 7,300 copies and 241 pages. The Lutheran church issued no publications. During the years that followed, not a single religious publication appeared with the exception of church calendars, which were not allowed to contain texts (excepting the 1948 Orthodox church calendar).

The scarcity of clergy was one of the main problems of the churches, especially during the years 1945-1956 (i.e., until the return of a number of exiled pastors). During that period the Lutheran church had at its disposal only seventy or eighty pastors, aided by a dozen assistant pastors who had been ordained before completing the full course of studies (cf. Aunver, 1961b:107).

The Post-Stalin Period, 1957-1977

The immediate post-Stalin years, 1953-1957, were characterized by a flowering of church life. But the party counterattacked in 1957 with the so-called antireligious rituals and the active exploitation of the Estonian Lutheran church for purposes of Soviet foreign policy. As a result of the fourth antireligious campaign, launched by the party in 1959, there began a "sociological" period in atheistic literature (cf. Chrysostomus, 1965-1968, vol. 2:308-312).

Table 2

Total number of participants in Lutheran confirmation
and Komsomol summer camps in Soviet Estonia, 1953 - 1971

Year	Confirmation	Summer camp	Year	Confirmation	Summer camp
1953	3,500	—	1963	800	6,000
1954	5,800	—	1964	600	6,000
1955	5,900	—	1965	400	6,000
1956	6,100	—	1966	250	unk.
1957	9,200	39	1967	300	unk.
1958	8,400	2,299	1968	unk.	unk.
1959	6,200	6,300	1969	455	unk.
1960	3,800	6,950	1970	500	unk.
1961	2,400	7,000	1971	500	10,000
1962	1,400	5,200			

Sources: Raid, 1969b; Vimmsaare, 1969; and Ranne, 1972.

The Atheists

To describe the religious revival and the party's reaction to it, we cite again Lembit Raid, the Soviet Estonian historian of atheistic activity:

So strong was the influence of church confirmation in those years that even some ideologically insecure members of the Komsomol, as well as a few students at the institutions of higher learning, participated. Some young newly appointed teachers, graduates of pedagogical institutions, only recently appointed to their posts, also let themselves be pulled along. In the initial years of the communist summer camps, there were cases of young participants later also undergoing church confirmation.

It should be mentioned that the latter was not by any means the rule, but rather a question of rare exceptions. But it is apparent from the data presented [cf. table 2] that church confirmation culminated in the year 1957, having achieved a level of confirmations close to the prewar period. . . .

. . . the Komsomol organization created in 1957 a new youth tradition, the youth "summer days." This venture quickly achieved great popularity among the young people of the Republic and spread to all towns and regions (Raid, 1967:198).

The appeal of this youth program has varied over the years. For example, in 1965 only 17.4 percent of the eighteen-year-olds in the city of Tartu participated in the summer camps, which were designed to compete with confirmation as a rite of passage to adulthood (Baturin, 1970:34; cf. table 2). The "antireligious" rites" campaign by no means confined itself to countering confirmation, however. Efforts were made to create counterparts for other church ceremonies as well. Thus, a "child's name day" was substituted for baptism, and civil ceremonies replaced church weddings and funerals. Special efforts were made to combat the extremely popular religious memorial services at cemeteries. At first the church ceremonies were copied almost exactly; later, more original rituals were developed.

This campaign yielded remarkable results for several reasons: the active support of party and state institutions, the attraction of paid holidays for the participants in "youth summer days," the institution of rewards for participants in civil ceremonies and sanctions for participants at church rites, the substantial number of purely nominal Christians, the general secularization of society (noticeable also in other countries), and the launching of new, sufficiently attractive ceremonies and festivities. (See Salo, 1973, for details.) Table 3 gives some insight into trends in this area.

The Lutherans

Archbishop Kiivit's visit to Helsinki in 1955, his first trip abroad, marked a new phase: the harnessing of the Lutheran church for purposes of Soviet foreign policy. This visit was followed by a series of other trips: to England in 1955, to the United States in 1956, to the German Federal Republic in 1958, to Denmark in 1959. As a result, in 1963 the Lutheran Evangelical church in the Estonian SSR was admitted to the World Lutheran Federation and to the World Council of Churches, side by side with the Estonian Evangelical Lutheran church in exile. Fletcher (1973) gives a recent account of the role of religious bodies in Soviet foreign policy (see also Kolarz, 1963:263).

In connection with these developments, the Lutheran church was granted permission to publish one book, the title of

Table 3

Percentages of births, marriages and burials officiated
by the Church in Estonia, 1922 - 1974

Christenings	Weddings	Burials
1922 92.5%	93.6%	96.7%
1933 77%	78.0%	94.0%
1957 55.8%	29.8%	64.5%
1968 12.5%	2.6%	46.0%
1974 10.4%	2.9%	38.6%

Sources: Eesti Nõukogude Entsüklopeedia, Volume 2,
1970:119; Nõukogude Eesti, 1975:187.

which—*eesti Evangeeliumi Luteriusu Kiriku aastaraamat*
[Yearbook of the Estonian Evangelical Lutheran Church]—
is misleading, insofar as the Estonian Lutheran church was
not permitted during the 1944-1977 period to publish any religious material except this "yearbook." Further, the appearance of the year 1956 on the title page is peculiar, since the
book starts with a message dated 1957. Finally, although it
was distributed to ecumenical organizations abroad, the book
was not available in Estonia until 1969. Yet the work contains
theological and church-related articles and chronicles church
life until 1957.

Kiivit resigned in 1967—according to the official version, for
reasons of health. In reality, it seems that he fell victim to police
intrigue (cf. Laantee, 1968:7). His successor was Alfred Tooming, who was elected by the church council on October 12,
1967. Tooming continued his predecessor's visits abroad. In an
interview on Danish radio on August 25, 1969, Tooming stated
that the Lutheran church in Soviet Estonia had a membership
of 300,000. He admitted that the figure reflected a decline, but
insisted that many who stayed away from church were not
atheists. The bishop did not give precise reasons for the decline
in membership. Forty-seven churches were reported to be
active, with 125 clergymen (whose average age was sixty). Only

thirty students were preparing for the ministry. There was a shortage of textbooks, especially of Bibles. Their importation was not allowed, even at the request of the church. Eighteen-year-olds could be accepted for confirmation, but the confirmants were very few—only about 2,000 a year.

In the summer of 1972, issue no. 49 of *Kotimaa*, the organ of the Finnish Lutherans, published an interview with Archbishop Tooming which contained the following statements:

The Estonian Lutheran Church is celebrating an anniversary this year, since the theological institution of learning operating under the auspices of the Tallinn Consistory will be 25 years old. A total of 60 pastors have been prepared at this establishment. Among the students are many who already have some other profession.[10]

The Estonian Church has a shortage of clergymen. There are 150 congregations, but only 100 clergy (among them two women).[11] In addition, 30 lay preachers are also active.

Six times a year pastors come to hold services for the Finnish-speaking congregation in Petroskoi, which is served the rest of the year by lay preachers. Four hundred people partook of Holy Communion there at Pentecost.

The great interest on the part of congregation members toward Bible study appears as a new trend in our Church. In Tallinn's St. John's Church, where Mrs. Tooming serves as organist and choir director, a ten-minute session of Bible reading, introduced by organ music, is held every Wednesday at noon. The Sunday evening Bible lessons fill the 400-seat Church to capacity.

As a cooperative effort of the Lutherans, Baptists and Methodists, a new Estonian translation of the Bible is in progress. The Gospel according to St. Matthew, the Book of Psalms, and the First Book of Moses are almost completed. As to the timetable of the translation, the Archbishop knows not what to say. Prior to starting work, a promise had been received that the translation may also appear in print.

The Orthodox

Since the Orthodox do not now constitute an independent church in Estonia, their representatives have not made official visits abroad, nor have they granted interviews to Western journalists at home. Information about them is, consequently, sparse. Some data have, however, appeared in the exile-based Orthodox periodical *Jumala Abiga* [With the Aid of God]. According to the 1948 Orthodox calendar in Estonia, there were 133 congregations served by one bishop, eighty-four priests, and eleven deacons.

After the transfer of Roman (Tang), the only native Estonian bishop, on December 20, 1950, the Orthodox church in Estonia remained for five years without a shepherd. Bishop Joann (Alekseev), of Russian nationality, was not consecrated until December 25, 1955; on August 14, 1961, he was transferred to Gorki. The next appointee was the Tallinn-born (1929) Aleksei Ridiger, who was consecrated on September 3, 1961. He holds the post to this day, despite the fact that since 1964 he has also been the administrator of the affairs of the Moscow Patriarchate. In this capacity he has made numerous trips abroad. During the period 1958-1963, the Latvian Orthodox were also under the care of the Tallinn chief shepherd.

The training of Orthodox clergy takes place outside of Estonia in Russian-language educational institutions of the Moscow Patriarchate. According to Juhkam (1968:158), the church had in 1968 only fifty-five priests and six deacons to serve the ninety-eight existing congregations. In 1974 there were eighty-eight congregations, of which seventeen were Russian speaking, with approximately forty-five priests (*Nôukogude Eesti*, 1975:187).

The Methodists and Adventists

The only Methodist church within the Soviet Union is in Estonia; thus it has some significance in terms of foreign policy. A. Kuum, the superintendent, was able to participate in the World Conference of the Methodist Church in August 1971. According to Kuum, at that time there were fourteen Methodist congregations active in Estonia under the leadership of sixteen ordained ministers; membership growth for that year had been 155. Total membership in Estonia was about 2,200, of whom 1,153 were in Tallinn.[12]

A certain cooperation has developed between the Methodists and the Adventists. In the capital, the Adventists use the Methodist church; in Tartu, both congregations hold their services in the Orthodox church. The Adventists had thirteen congregations in 1972, with about twenty clergy and 1,700 members.[13]

The Evangelical Christians–Baptists

This church is very lively despite the closure of its Tallinn center by the authorities in 1959 (Laks, 1965:86, 121). Upon the retirement of A. Sildos, the senior presbyter's post was assumed by Robert Vôsu on December 14, 1969; Vôsu has made trips abroad and provided information about the life of his church. *Veckoposten*, the organ of the Swedish Baptists, noted on September 16, 1971, that there were eighty-two congregations in Estonia, with about 8,200 members. Bible study groups were especially popular, and in 1970 about 150 people were baptized. Estonian Baptists get along well with their Russian brethren, with whom they share church facilities.

According to a statistical survey in *Usk ja Elu* [Faith and Life], there were 9,595 baptized adults on January 1, 1946; as of January 1, 1966, there were 8,446. During those two decades, the church grew through 3,155 baptisms and 2,216 reaffiliations. At the same time, the church lost 4,491 members to death and 2,908 through withdrawal from membership (*Usk ja Elu*, no. 4, 1966:16).

The Atheists

The atheistic campaign became considerably more intense after the well-known 1963 speech of L. Iljitshov, in which he called for more scholarly research into atheism.[14] Since then there has been an increase in sociological investigations of religious life in Estonia; this has resulted in several dissertations. However, although such publications offer data on religious observances, none gives a complete picture of the contemporary religious situation or even of basic statistics. Even elementary information is missing about the numbers of congregations, clergy, and believers (Vimmsaare, 1969:5).

Therefore, since these studies reflect the goal-ideal of the party more than existing reality, the data given by their atheistic authors must be viewed with reservation.

Given this background, the publication of figures for the total number of Estonian congregations in volume 2 of *Eesti Nôukogude Entsüklopeedia* [Estonian Soviet Encyclopedia], which went to press three months before Vimmsaare's 1969 book came as a surprise. The encyclopedia notes that on January 1, 1969, there were 367 religious organizations in Estonia: 145 Lutheran (and 15 dependent) congregations, 87 Orthodox, 82 Baptist, 13 Adventist, 11 Methodist, 11 Old Believers, 2 Roman Catholic, and 1 Jewish. For the year 1974, the compendium *Nôukogude Eesti* [Soviet Estonia] (1975:187) gives the same figures except for the Lutherans (142 congregations) and Orthodox (88).

The current position of religious congregations is difficult. For example, the Swedish Lutheran Bishop Ragnar Askmark asserts that Estonian Lutherans annually pay 100,000 rubles to the state in rent for churches (*Östgöta Correspondenten*, August 7, 1970:5). Further, new regulations introduced by the state require congregations to deposit their collections in the state bank. This bank, in turn, maintains all records of financial transactions and disburses funds from church accounts on behalf of their congregations (see *Usurändur* [The Pilgrim], no. 3, 1967:12). Thus it would appear that some of the types of official pressure which were applied to the churches during the 1940-1941 period are being reintroduced.

The Communist party and its atheist organizations have a continuing advantage because of the state control over publishing. During the period 1954-1972, ninety-one atheist publications appeared (eleven of these in 1963) totaling 332,315 copies (42,700 in 1963) and 11,187 pages (2,359 in 1963). The churches were allowed to publish only the aforementioned yearbook (182 pages, number of copies printed not known). However, the three major denominations have regularly published liturgical calendars. Most of these contain no text, although some Orthodox calendars include liturgical texts.

The publication of a hymnal for the Baptists in 1975 (7,500 copies) was an exception. The two major churches have only prewar hymnals. As for the Bible, no part of it has been available in any form since 1944.

Conclusion

Considering the heavy human losses during the years 1939-1949 and the state of siege which has lasted, uninterrupted, for more than three decades, the churches in Estonia have survived surprisingly well. One should keep in mind the general trend of secularization, independent of the Soviet regime, which characterizes highly industrialized and urbanized societies. The Information Office of the Lutheran World Federation reported in 1968 that there were approximately 300,000 Lutherans in Estonia; 150,000 were confirmed church members (*LWB-Pressedienst*, no. 8, 1968; cited in *Baltischer Kirchlicher Brief*, no. 1, 1968:7). One hundred twenty-five pastors with 20–30 lay helpers served 147 congregations. There were signs of a revival of church life.[15] According to one Soviet author, almost one-half of the ministers of religious cults and more than two-thirds of all believers were Lutherans (Vimmsaare, 1969:5). Although the percentage of Russian believers has grown among the Orthodox and the Baptists, the total of ethnic Estonian church members could easily reach over 200,000, or nearly one-fourth of the total Estonian-speaking population. In 1969, about 250 clergy were active (cf. Bourdeaux et al., 1976:25). It might be noted that, in 1937, 272,340 Lutherans paid church dues; however, at that time religious activity did not involve any risk to professional, social, or family life.

The official number of congregations in 1974 is known to be 365. The number of Lutheran congregations that year corresponded in general to that of 1939, but the number of openly practicing Lutherans had decreased by one-half. In the Orthodox church, there was a striking decline in the numbers of both congregations and clergy, partly because of territorial alterations. The membership of the Baptists declined also (by 15 percent from 1946 to 1971). The Adventist membership remained, by and large, unchanged, while the Roman Catholic and Methodist memberships showed an increase. In 1974 there were in Estonia almost twice as many Methodists as there were in 1934. Only one Jewish congregation was left, although (according to the 1970 census) there were more Jews in Estonia than there were before the war.

The remarkable solidarity of church members is worth

stressing. During the entire period under discussion, only two clergymen—the Russian A. Ossipov and the Estonian V. Grünberg, both Orthodox—have openly forsaken religion and made antireligious statements in the press. The struggle between the Soviet state and the churches has strengthened and bound together the believers. Although it is impossible to give an exact figure for the number of believers, we may be sure that Christianity, not communism, is the largest popular ideological movement in Soviet Estonia, embracing at least one-fourth of the population.

After a generation of atheistic campaigning, the Communist party and the Soviet state are still expending considerable energy in their war against religion. Since 1957, their tactics have been more moderate and refined, consisting mainly of carefully disguised discrimination against believers. Open intrusion into church activities—for example, the violent interruption of a Lutheran service on April 6, 1975, which ended with the death of Pastor Rein Premet (see Veem, 1976:20)—and public derision of religion (see Shipler, 1977:10) are rare, but symptomatic.

The complexity of the situation is evidenced by the following comments, made by the highly placed writer V. Voina:

> According to the official statistics of the church, in Estonia the Lutheran Church loses every year thousands of members.
>
> If the process continues at the same tempo, then after fifteen years there will not be any left. . . . Is there reason for optimism? Yes and no. The thing is, that parallel with this process, there is a growth, not substantial, but nevertheless a growth, in the membership of the Baptists, Methodists, Adventists and Mennonites. If the losses of the Lutheran Church will continue to coincide with conversions into various other sects, then this does not give any basis for optimism (*Nauka i religija* [Moscow], no. 2, 1971:21-25).

One of the party's main arguments in justifying its efforts to fight religion is that the churches are opposed to progress. This reasoning, which was perhaps applicable to the Russian

Orthodox of the early 1920s, seems outdated to many Estonians. As one observer (quoted by Voina in the aforecited article) put it, "In Estonia, religious faith hinders the implantation of new things so little that such a persistent struggle against it resembles a war against windmills."

Notes

1. It is assumed that the reader is already familiar with such basic works on religion and church life in the Soviet Union as those by Bociurkiv (1975), Chrysostomus (1965-1968), Conquest (1968), Fletcher (1973), Kolarz (1963), Marshall (1968), and Struve (1967). Much of the information contained in this chapter was garnered from a great number of periodicals; most of these, as well as some other points of this survey, are covered in greater detail in Salo (1974b; in Estonian). For particular aspects see also Aunver (1961a), Laantee (1968), Veem (1960, 1975, 1976; on Lutherans), Hindo (1970; on the Orthodox, Laks (1965; on the Free Churches), and Salo (1973; on "antireligious rites," and 1976; on atheistic publications).

2. The congregations lost (names are written according to the Estonian form) through the transfer were Irboska Jumala Ema, Irboska Nikolai, Kolpino, Kriusha, Kulje, Lisje, Môla Kristuse Sündimise, Môla Onufri, Narva Jaanilinna, Narva Kolmainu, Narva Nikolai, Narva Znamenja, Nisô, Olga-Risti, Pankjavitsa Nikolai, Pankjavitsa Kolmainu, Petseri Neitsi Maria, Petseri 40 Kannataja, Petshkii, Salesje, Senno, Skamja, Shtshemeritsa, and Venküla. The old Petseri (Petchory) monastery, the site of the seminary, was lost, too, but the female convent of Pühtitsa remained and is still open today.

3. *Riigi Teataja* [State Gazette], no. 77, 1940, article 744; no. 89, 1940, article 865. See also *Eesti NSV Teataja* [Gazette of the Estonian SSR], no. 3, 1940, article 24 (compare this further to the same publication, no. 70, 1940, article 950, and no. 26, 1941, article 333); no. 15, 1940, article 157; no. 2, 1941, article 11; no. 27, 1940, article 315; no. 59, 1940, article 722. See also *Maarjamaa* [Land of Mary], no. 2 (20), 1971:15-17; Vööbus, 1950:21; and Raid, 1969a:69.

4. *Riigi Teataja* [State Gazette], no. 102, 1940, article 1011; no. 102, 1940, article 940. See also Vööbus, 1963:70-77; Oras,

1948:93; Jürma, 1956:150; and *Rahvaleht* [The People's News], September 3, 1940:3.

5. An accurate listing has never been published. The bibliographical reference work *Nôukogude eesti perioodilised . . .* (1968:193) listed twenty-three of the periodicals which were closed by referring to them as "periodicals of bourgeois Estonia which temporarily continued to be published after June 23, 1940."

6. *Eesti NSV Teataja* [Gazette of the Estonian SSR], no. 17, 1941, article 202; no. 22, 1941, article 281.

7. See *Raamatukroonika* [The Chronicle of Books] for 1940-1944.

8. Exact figures for all of the churches, especially the smaller ones, are not available. For the Lutherans, Aunver (1961a:104) places the losses at twenty-five; for the Orthodox church, Hindo (1970:21) claims a loss of twenty-two of whom one was a civilian casualty of war. The other churches lost at least fifteen clergymen (Aunver, 1961a:103), and the Roman Catholics lost one (Vassily, 1953:125; *Maarjamaa* [Land of Mary], no. 1, 1961:4-5). The bishops lost were the Lutheran Archbishop H. B. Rahamägi, the Orthodox Bishop Joann (Bulin), the Roman Catholic apostolic administrator, Archbishop Eduard Profittlich, and the Methodist superintendent and acting bishop, Martin Priikask (see Aunver, 1961a:102). Nothing has been revealed about their fate.

9. See *Zhurnal Moskovskoj Patriarhii*, no. 7, 1946:4; no. 1, 1950:19-20; no. 5, 1950:14, 18. See also Hindo, 1970:37-42; Chrysostomus, 1965-1968, vol. 3:141; and Kolarz, 1963:121-133.

10. This institution is the Theological Examination Board, established in 1946, which conducts correspondence courses. As the use of a mimeograph machine is not permitted, only typewritten study texts may be used. In June 1972 there were twenty-five students, according to a BBC interview. On its thirtieth anniversary (October 1976), twenty-two candidates were reported to be enrolled (*Vaba Eesti Sôna* [Free Estonian Word], December 2, 1976:1).

11. The women were ordained on November 16, 1967, and November 14, 1968, according to Vimmsaare (1969:64).

12. *Usurändur* [The Pilgrim], no. 6/7, 1971:11.

13. *Usk ja Elu* [Faith and Life], no. 1, 1965:16; *Eesti Päevaleht* [Estonian Daily], December 20, 1972:5.

14. *Kommunist,* no. 1, 1964:23-46; see also *Eesti Kirik* [Estonian Church], 1964:48.

15. A message directed to the 1976 Estonian World Festival in Baltimore by the Môtlevate Eestlaste Ühendus (approximate translation, Union of Thinking Estonians) from Soviet Estonia contains a strong protest concerning the state of religion in that country, but it was not identified with any particular church. The original text was published in *Maarjamaa,* no. 1, 1976:1-12.

References

Aleksander, Metropoliit

1950 "Tôde ülempiiskop Sergiusest" [Truth about Archbishop Sergius]. Interview in *Vikerlane,* no. 9, 1950.

Amitan-Wilensky, Ella

1971 "Esthonian Jewry. A Historical Summary," in *The Jews in Latvia,* ed. M. Bobe et al. Tel Aviv: Association of Latvian and Esthonian Jews in Israel.

Apostlik-ôigeusuliste eestlaste kalender 1948. aastaks

1947 [Calendar for Orthodox Estonians in 1948]. Tallinn: Rakendustrükiste Kirjastus.

Askmark, Ragnar

1970 "Kyrkligt strandhugg i österled" [Church Invaded in East]. *Östgöta Correspondenten,* August 7, 1970.

Aunver, Jakob

1956 "Kirik tagakiusamise all" [The Persecuted Church], in *Eesti riik ja rahvas Teises Maailmasôjas* [The Estonian State and People during the Second World War], ed. Richard Maasing et al., vol. 3. Stockholm: Eesti Majandus Produkt.

1961a "Religious Life and the Church," in *Aspects of Estonian Culture,* ed. Evald Uustalu. London: Boreas.

1961b *Aastate kestes. Kiriku- ja kultuuriloolisi vaatlusi 1924-1959* [In the Course of Years. Observations on Church and Cultural History, 1924-1959]. Uppsala: Eesti Vaimulik Raamat.

Baturin, I., ed.

1968   *Pika tee tähistest* [Landmarks on a Long Journey]. Tallinn: Eesti Raamat.

1970   "Noorte suvepäevade konkreetse sotsiaalse uurimuse kogemustest Eesti NSV-s" [On the Experiences of Concrete Social Research of the Youth Summer Days in the Estonian SSR], in *Ateism, religioon, sotsioloogia* [Atheism, Religion, Sociology], ed. Kuulo Vimmsaare. Tallinn: Eesti Raamat.

Bociurkiv, Bohdan R., and John W. Strong, eds.

1975   *Religion and Atheism in the USSR and Eastern Europe*. Toronto: University of Toronto Press.

Bontshevskij, U. J.

1971   *Kas leer on isaisade komme?* [Confirmation—a Tradition of Our Forefathers?]. Tallinn: Eesti Raamat.

1973   "Garantirovano konstitusiei." *Nauka i Religija*, no. 7.

Bordeaux, M.

1965   *Opium of the People*. London: Farber.

Bordeaux, M., H. Hebly, and E. Voss, eds.

1976   *Religious Liberty in the Soviet Union. WCC and USSR: a Post-Nairobi documentation*. Keston, England: Centre for the Study of Religion and Communism.

Bourgeois, Charles (see Vassily)

Chrysostomus, Johannes

1965-   *Kirchengeschichte Russlands der neuesten Zeit I-III.*
1968   München/Salzburg: Pustet.

Conquest, Robert

1968   *Religion in the USSR*. New York: Praeger.

Eesti aadress-raamat 1938-1939

1939   [Estonian Address Book for 1938-1939]. Tallinn: Riigi Statistika Keskbüroo. (Pp. 200-213 reprinted in *Maarjamaa*, no. 1, 1974, with indexes added.)

Eesti Evangeeliumi Luteriusu Kiriku aastaraamat

1956   [Yearbook of the Estonian Evangelical Lutheran Church]. Tallinn: Konsistooriumi väljaanne.

Eesti Statistika Kuukiri

1920-   [The Estonian Statistical Monthly]. Official publica-
1940   tion of the Estonian Central Statistical Bureau during the period of the republic.

Ehatamm, V., ed.
1976   *Nüüdisaja tavandeid* [Rites of Our Time]. Tallinn: Eesti Raamat.

Evangeeliumi Luteriusu Kiriku seadused Eesti NSV-s

1951   [The Laws of the Evangelical Lutheran Church in the Estonian SSR]. Tallinn: EELK Konsistoorium.

Evangeelsed laulud. Jumalateenistuse lauluraamat

1975   [Evangelical Songs: A Liturgical Hymnal]. Tallinn: Evangeeliumi Kristlaste-Baptistide Üleliidulise Nõukogu Presbüterite Nõukogu ENSV-s.

Fletcher, William C.
1973   *Religion and Soviet Foreign Policy, 1945-1970.* London: Oxford University Press.

Gerodnik, Gennadi
1962   "Uued traditsioonid ja religioon" [The New Traditions and Religion], in *Mõtisklusi usust* [Thoughts on Religion]. Tallinn: Eesti Riiklik Kirjastus.
1973   "Tebe vosemnadtsat" [You Are Eighteen]. *Sovetskaja Estonija*, no. 149, June 28.

Hindo, Nigul

1970   *Eesti Apostliku Õigeusu Kiriku seisukord kodumaal aastail 1940 kuni 1952* [The Situation of the Estonian Apostolic Orthodox Church in the Homeland, 1940-1952]. Unpublished manuscript.

Iljitshev, L.

1964   "Formirovanie nautshnogo mirovozzrenija i ateistitsheskoe vospitanie." *Kommunist* (Moscow), no. 1.

Juhkam, Martin

1968   "Kirik kommunistliku diktatuuri ahelais" [The Church in the Chains of the Communist Dictatorship], in *Eesti saatusaastad* [Estonia's Years of Fate], vol. 5, ed. Richard Maasing et al. Stockholm: EMP.

Juhkam, Martin, et al.

1961   *Eesti Apostlik Ortodoksne Kirik eksiilis 1944-1960* [The Estonian Apostolic Orthodox Church in Exile, 1944-1960]. Stockholm: Cultural Fund of the Estonian Orthodox Church.

Juhkentaal, Julius

1954   "The Pastor They Distrusted," in *Escape from Paradise,* ed. C. A. Smith. London: Hollis & Carter.

Jürma, Mall

1956   "Laastamine raamatukogudes" [Devastation in the Libraries], in *Eesti riik ja rahvas Teises Maailmasõjas* [The Estonian State and People during the Second World War], vol. 3, ed. Richard Maasing et al. Stockholm: Eesti Majandus Produkt.

Kiivit, Jaan

1963   "Die Estnische Evangelish-Lutherische Kirche. Gastvorlesung auf Einladung der Ev.-Theologischen Fakultät, Bonn, Februar 1961." *Lutherische Monatshefte*, no. 2.

1968 "Interview mit Erzbischof Tooming." *Junge Kirche*, no. 6.

Kinker, F.

1968 "Kultuurrevolutsiooni kaasaegsest etapist Nôukogude Eestis (kasutatud andmeid kuni 1965.a.)" [On the Present Stage of the Cultural Revolution in Soviet Estonia (English Summary)], in Tartu Riikliku Ülikooli Toimetised [Transactions of Tartu State University], vol. 202, *Töid NLKP ajaloo alalt 4* [Works on the History of the Communist Party of the Soviet Union, Part 4].

Kokla, Konstantin, ed.

1944 *Kiriklik kalender apostlik-ôigeusulistele 1944. aastaks* [Church Calendar for Apostolic Orthodox Estonians for 1944]. Tallinn: Eesti Apostlik-Ôigeusu Mitropoolia Sinodi väljaanne.

Kolarz, Walter

1963 *Die Religionen in der Sowjetunion.* Freiburg: Herder.

Koppermann, Maria

1972 *Minu 12 aastat Siberis* [My Twelve Years in Siberia]. Stockholm: Harta.

Küng, Andres

1973 *Estland zum Beispiel.* Stuttgart: Seewald.

Laantee, Karl

1968 "Atheism vs. Religion in Contemporary Soviet Society." *Lutheran Scholar*, April.

Laks, Johannes

1965 *Mälestusi eluteelt ja töömaalt* [Memoirs from the Way of Life and the Field of Action]. Toronto: Toronto Vabakoguduse Kirjastus.

Lebedev, E.

1970 "Rab bozhij Vladimir." *Molodezh Estonii*, no. 174, September 6, p. 2.

[Lukas], Maternus

1963 "Estland 1931-1941." Album Über die Tätigkeit der Kapuziner in Estland, im Archiv der Bayerischen Provinz des Kapuzinerordens. Unpublished manuscript.

Marshall, Richard H., Jr., et al.

1968 *Aspects of Religion in the Soviet Union, 1917-1967*. Chicago: University of Chicago Press.

Mezentsev, V. A., et al.

1964 *Vastused usklikele* [Answers to the Believers]. Tallinn: Eesti Riiklik Kirjastus.

Nelson, I.

1965 *Vagaduse varjus* [In the Shadow of Piousness]. Tallinn: Eesti Raamat.

Neumärker, Dorothea

1972 "In memoriam, Jaan Kiivit." *Kirche in Osten* 15: 163-172.

Nôukogude Eesti. Entsüklopeediline teatmeteos

1975 [Soviet Estonia: An Encyclopedic Compendium]. Tallinn: Valgus.

Nôukogude Eesti perioodilised väljaanded 1940-1960. Koondbibliograafia

1968 [Periodical Publications of Soviet Estonia, 1940-1960]. Tallinn: Eesti Raamat.

Oras, Ants

1948 *Baltic Eclipse*. London: Gollancz.

Perlitz, H.

1944   *The Fate of Religion and Church under Soviet Rule in Estonia, 1940-1941.* New York: World Association of Estonians.

Raid, Lembit

1967   "Olustikutraditsioon ja ateistlik kasvatustöö (1957-1965)" [Everyday Traditions and Atheistic Education, 1957-1965], in Tartu Riikliku Ülikooli Toimetised [Transactions of Tartu State University], vol. 203, *Töid NLKP ajaloost 5* [Works on the History of the Communist Party of the Soviet Union, Part 5].

1969a   "Eestimaa Kommunistliku Partei ateistliku kasvatustöö kogemustest aastail 1940-1941" [The Antireligious Explanatory Work of the Communist Party of Estonia in 1940-1941 (Summary)], in Tartu Riikliku Ülikooli Toimetised [Transactions of Tartu State University], vol. 233, *Töid NLKP ajaloo alalt 6* [Works on the History of the Communist Party of the Soviet Union, Part 6].

1969b   "Teaduslik-ateistliku propagandatöö arengujooni Eesti NSV-s sotsialismi ülesehitamise sôjajärgsetel aastatel (1945-1956)" [Development of Scientific-Atheistic Propaganda in the Estonian SSR during the Years of the Postwar Construction of Socialism (1945-1956)], in Tartu Riikliku Ülikooli Toimetised [Transactions of Tartu State University], vol. 238, *Töid NLKP ajaloo alalt 7* [Works on the History of the Communist Party of the Soviet Union, Part 7].

1970   "EKP tegevusest rahvahulkade ateistlikul kasvatamisel aastail 1961-1963" [Scientific-Atheistic Explanatory Work of the Communist Party of Estonia in 1961-1963], in Tartu Riikliku Ülikooli Toimetised [Transactions of Tartu State University], vol. 261, *Töid NLKP ajaloo alalt 8* [Works on the History of the Communist Party of the Soviet Union, Part 8].

Ranne, V.

1972   "Novye obryady i ikh mesto v dukhovnoj zhizni sovetskikh lyudej." *Voprosy nautshnago ateizma* 13 (Moscow): 181-197.

Risch, H.

1937   "Die estnische apostolisch-rechtgläubige Kirche." *Kyrios*, pp. 113-142.

Salo, Vello

1973   "La lotta contro le Chiese nell 'Estonia sovietica" [The Struggle against the Churches in Soviet Estonia]. *Russia Cristiana*, no. 130, pp. 53-62.
        "Antireligious Rites in Estonia after 1957." *Religion in Communist Lands*, no. 4/5, pp. 28-33.

1974a   "Antireligiöse Riten in Estland." *Acta Baltica* 13:40-52.

1974b   *Riik ja kirikud 1940-1974* [The State and Churches, 1940-1974]. Rome: Maarjamaa.

1976   "Atheistische Druckschriften in Estland 1940-1975." Manuscript, publication forthcoming.

1977   "Die Ostkirchen an der Ostsee." Manuscript, publication forthcoming.

Shipler, David K.

1977   "Soviet State Hems Churches with Laws and Ridicule." *New York Times*, January 4.

Struve, Nikita

1967   *Christians in Contemporary Russia*. New York: Scribner's.

Täheväli, A., and J. Välbe

1950   "Memorandum," cited by A. Kaelas in *Human Rights and Genocide in the Baltic States*. Stockholm: Estnisches Informationszentrum.

Uritam, R.

1970   "Tallinna kirikuskäijate demograafilisest koosseisust" [On the Demographical Composition of Churchgoers in Tallinn], in *Ateism, religioon, sotsioloogia* [Atheism, Religion, Sociology], ed. Kuulo Vimmsaare. Tallinn: Eesti Raamat.

Vahter, Leonhard

1964   "Aspects of Life in Estonia: Religious Persecution." *Baltic Review* (New York), no. 28, pp. 39-56.

Vassily, Hiéromoine [pseud. Charles Bourgeois]

1949   "Journal du hieromoine Vassili." *Études* 260-261:145-170, 332-350.

1953a   *Ma rencontre avec la Russie.* Buenos Aires: Renacimiento Cristiano. (Book form of preceding; we quote from this edition.)

1953b   *A Priest in Russia and the Baltic.* (English translation of preceding.) London: Burns, Oates, & Washbourne.

Veem, Konrad

1960   "Eesti vaba rahvakirik okupantide ikestuses" [The Free Estonian National Church of Estonia in the Yoke of the Occupants], in *EÜS Album 13*, ed. Leo Urm and Madis Üürike. Stockholm: Eesti Üliôpilaste Selts.

1975   *A Message to the Churches from the Estonian Evangelical Lutheran Church.* Stockholm: Estonian Evangelical Lutheran Church.

1976   "The Legislation on Religion of the Soviet Union and Soviet Estonia and Its Applications in Categorical Opposition to the Helsinki Declaration and the Report of the Fifth Section of the Fifth Assembly of the WCC." Mimeographed. Stockholm: Estonian Evangelical Lutheran Church.

Vimmsaare, Kuulo

1963   *Luteri kiriku ideoloogiast tänapäeval* [On the Contemporary Ideology of the Lutheran Church]. Tallinn: Eesti Riiklik Kirjastus.

1969   *Luterlus enne ja nüüd* [Lutheranism Before and Now]. Tallinn: Eesti Raamat.

1970   "Ateistliku môtte arengust Nôukogude Eestis" [On
        the Development of Atheist Thought in Soviet Esto-
        nia], in *Ateism, religioon, sotsioloogia* [Atheism,
        Religion, Sociology], ed. Kuulo Vimmsaare. Tallinn:
        Eesti Raamat.

Vimmsaare, Kuulo, ed.

1970   *Ateism, religioon, sotsioloogia* [Atheism, Religion,
        Sociology]. Tallinn: Eesti Raamat.

Voina, V.

1971   "Tysjatsha granej odnoj problemy." *Nauka i religija*,
        no. 2, pp. 21-25.

Vôôbus, Arthur

1950   *Communism's Challenge to Christianity*. Maywood,
        Ill.: Privately published.

1963   *The Department of Theology at the University of
        Tartu: Its Life and Work, Martyrdom and Annihila-
        tion*. Stockholm: Estonian Theological Society in
        Exile.

6

Physical Education and Sports

Reet Nurmberg-Howell

Physical education and sports maintain a position of high prominence in Soviet Estonia, as indeed they do throughout the Soviet Union. The Estonian people have a long tradition of participation in sports and other various forms of physical activity; consequently, the contemporary scene reflects, in part, the pre-1940 heritage. However, the magnitude of the total physical-culture movement and its political ramifications are results of the implementation of Soviet programs. For a more extensive discussion of the Estonian athletic and sports heritage, see Nurmberg (1972).

In the Soviet context, the term "physical culture" is very broad in scope, and the total physical-culture program encompasses the following: (1) physical eduction, those activities that are part of the formal school program in the general educational system, from preschool to secondary specialized and higher educational institutions and the Soviet army; (2) mass physical culture, for all citizens of the Soviet Union; (3) competitive sport, for the general populace; and (4) top sport, for the exceptionally skilled athlete (see Adamson, 1973).

The physical-culture movement, like all aspects of life in the Soviet Union, is directed, fostered, and controlled by the Communist party of the Soviet Union; hence its development has reflected the needs and desires of the party. Indeed, physical education is considered an integral part of the Soviet educational system, both in theory and in practice; thus it is subordinated to the general tasks of Communist education

223

(Tamjärv, 1952:7). Together with the Communist youth movement, physical education is intended to contribute to producing loyal and healthy citizens willing and able to defend their Soviet homeland. Also, physical education is seen as a way to strengthen the health of the masses, thus making for more efficient workers, and as an aid in the general moral, aesthetic, and intellectual development of individual citizens (Tamjärv, 1952:7).

The theoretical base of Soviet physical education dates back to Marx, who maintained that total education required a combination of intellectual, physical, and technical training (Morton, 1963:112). Theoretical aspects of physical education in the Soviet Union also draw on the teachings of Lenin, on Soviet pedagogy, and on Setsenov-Pavlov's materialistic physiology (Tamjärv, 1952:13). Hence, given its current political commitment and Marxist-Leninist theoretical base, physical education in contemporary Soviet Estonia is in some respects—particularly in theory—different from the way it was during the prewar years.

Sport in the Estonian SSR, as in all republics of the Soviet Union, is seen as playing an important role in the development of the "new Soviet man" (Morton, 1963:111), in whom spiritual wealth, moral purity, and physical fulfillment are harmoniously combined, and whose communistic ideas are accompanied by communistic deeds.[1] Thus the objective has been to utilize sport as a socializing force for producing more effective workers, defenders, and faithful followers of Communism. The two underlying principles of the sports movement are *massovost* (mass participation) and *mastestvo* (proficiency and achievement). Furthermore, like all other aspects of Soviet culture, sport is supposed to be socialist in content and national in form (Tamjärv, 1952:11). It is socialist in content to the degree that it has as its aim the cultivation of a mass international spirit, and it is national in form to the degree that sport is part of a national culture, particularly as expressed in indigenous physical activities, games, and contests (Tamjärv, 1952:11). In recent years an additional purpose has been assigned to sport; namely, that of counterbalancing the bad effects of alcoholism (Arusoo, 1973).

The preceding statements about the aims and philosophy of the physical-culture movement are proclaimed in newspapers, journals, and mass gatherings. Moreover, they have been promulgated in announcements from the Central Committee of the Communist party of the Soviet Union and the Council of Ministers of the USSR and are further evidenced by the new "GTO fitness program" (Rand, 1973:52-53). However, these pronouncements do not differ in any respect from those made in any other Soviet republic (except that the word "Estonia" is used in the Estonian SSR). Hence, with regard to philosophy—at least to the extent that it is written and professed—the physical-culture movement in Soviet Estonia follows the Soviet mode. In reality, most Estonians participate in physical activities for the traditional benefits of exercise and enjoyment and care little about the two major goals of the party for such activities: labor productivity and military preparedness.

The very nature of sport allows it to be used by the party to promote desired social, cultural, economic, and political ends. Although art, music, drama, and literature are similarly used, sport is understood, available to, and enjoyed by all people of all ages. Moreover, because most people participate in sports during their leisure time, they are automatically participating in leisure-time activities which are politically acceptable. Thus, sports acts as a means of social control. Also, the genuine enthusiasm and spontaneity which are generated by sports are exploited and directed toward politically inspired goals. For example, in competitive sport the individual inherently identifies with his team or group, which in turn leads to the development of a national identity. If an Estonian athlete achieves success in athletic competition, he brings credit first to the Soviet Union and only secondarily to the Estonian SSR.

The mass and communicative appeal of sport has been well recognized, and, although sport is in essence nonpolitical, it is used to achieve such nonsport objectives as political socialization, indoctrination, and integration. Certain kinds of leader-follower patterns can easily be encouraged through sports. These patterns provide some of the necessary conditions for socialization; for example, role models and a framework for primary social interaction. Furthermore, symbolic and propagandistic functions have been emphasized in the program; much pageantry, which invariably has political overtones, usually accompanies the competitions and athletic gatherings. Many athletic facilities have been built in Estonia, and often they are called "Komsomol" (as is one of the major stadiums in

Tallinn). However, the tendency to name facilities after Lenin, the Komsomol, etc. is not so pronounced in Estonia as it is in the Russian SFSR.

The very aims of the physical-culture movement encourage political indoctrination. Indeed, one of the purposes of physical culture is to utilize it as a means of "indoctrinating the masses of the population with Bolshevist theories, and thus fortifying Bolshevist domination" (Legostaev, 1951:40). Political discussions and lectures are considered an integral part of the training of athletes (Viirsalu, 1955:64), and political knowledge is important for athletic success (Tamjärv, 1952:7). As is the case with all people who are able to travel out of Estonia, only politically reliable athletes are permitted to travel and compete abroad. For example, in 1970, six sports officials were criticized in *Rahva Hääl*, the official newspaper of the party and government of the Estonian SSR, for not properly indoctrinating athletes and for permitting athletes who were politically weak to travel abroad.[2] Political indoctrination is also furthered through the sports newspaper *Spordileht* and the journal *Kehakultuur*, which carry, in addition to athletic news, articles devoted entirely to politics and political achievements and demands. The slogan "Kôigi maade proletaarlased, ühinege!" (Proletarians of all countries, unite!) appears on the first page of *Spordileht* (but no longer in *Kehakultuur*). It should be noted that Estonia is one of the few Soviet republics in which there are two regular sport publications, both of wide circulation. The wide circulation serves both to popularize physical culture and to spread the desired and approved political message.

However, the simplicity of sport and its emotional appeal have made it one of the best means of expressing nationalism by the Estonians. Intense pride is felt in the accomplishments of *meie vabariigi* (our republic's) athletes, especially those who have enhanced the reputation of Estonia in the international and all-union sporting arenas.[3] Included in the various sports games, which have been organized since the late 1950s, have been evenings devoted to traditional Estonian folk games. Also, there is some leeway in the prescribed all-union curriculum, and traditional folk dances are taught in the Estonian schools. There are other overt means of displaying nationalism through sports. Perhaps the most obvious is the use of the name "Kalev," a strong and powerful Estonian epic hero, for sports clubs, societies, and teams. Organizations by that name have been part of the Estonian sports scene ever since organized sports activities were initiated in Estonia. Kalev is such an accepted name that when discussions about what to call a new sports society formed specifically for the Estonian SSR were held in Moscow in 1943, no other name was mentioned. Today the Kalev Sport Society is the largest and most popular of all such societies in the republic. The world "Kalev" is tinged with nationalistic implications and generates emotional feelings among the populace. Increasingly during the last few years, nationalistic feelings have been openly displayed at athletic competitions. When Russian teams appear in the stadium or on the court, they are often received with jeers and whistles, the Estonian form of booing.[4] At meets, the public generally cheers for any non-Russian team—particularly if it is from a Western country, including the United States.[5]

The organization and administration of the Soviet Estonian physical-culture program follows the all-union model, and all-union changes have also been effected in Estonia. There is centralized governmental leadership and control of physical education; the responsibility lies with the Department of Physical Education in the republic-level Ministry of Education. However, the foundations of policy and program in Estonia are set by the Ministry of Education of the Russian SFSR. In theory, the physical-education curriculum is uniform throughout the Soviet Union. There is also a centralized body for the organization and administration of sports. In 1940 the existing Estonian Central Sports League and the provincial and individual sports leagues were disbanded, and a new central organization called the Committee for Physical Culture and Sport, affiliated with the Council of Ministers of the Estonian SSR, was formed. In 1959 this committee was abolished, and in its place was established the Union of Sport Societies and Organizations of the Estonian SSR, a public organization.

At the end of 1968, according to the directives of the Central Committee of the Estonian Communist Party and the Estonian SSR Council of Ministers, a new physical-culture and sports committee was formed by the Estonian SSR Council of Ministers. Although it has undergone three name changes since 1940, and the committee has changed from a state to a public and back to a state organization, there have been no changes in its structure or functions. The name changes have paralleled those at the all-union level, reflecting attempts by the government and party to more effectively organize and administer the physical-culture program. The purpose of the present committee is to strengthen the ties between the various sport societies and the trade unions, Komsomol, and other public and state institutions (Sisak, 1969:3) and to give the governing body of sport more authority, with the chairman being considered the equivalent of a minister in the government.

A fifteen-member council, of whom seven were to be political leaders, was established to preside over the newly formed committee in the hope that such a move would help strengthen the ties between the state and the sport movement. Under the committee's jurisdiction fall the city and regional organizations, the voluntary sport societies, the individual sport federations, and the physical-culture *kollektivs*. The republic-level body is responsible both to the Estonian SSR Council of Ministers and to the All-Union Physical Culture and Sports Committee at the USSR Council of Ministers. The finances for the committee come from the republic's annual budget, and virtually all requests, provided that they can be justified, are fulfilled. The committee is never lacking in funds. One of the positive features of the Soviet sport program has been centralized governmental financing. Many other countries—for example, Canada—are gradually adopting similar practices, although to a lesser extent.

Many of the leaders in the sport movement have responsibility for both the political organization and the sport program. For example, A. Green, deputy chairman of the Council of Ministers of the Estonian SSR, has directed the work of the Wrestling Federation for many years. Reginald Kallas, formerly head and secretary of the party section at the newspaper *Õhtuleht* and propaganda and agitation instructor for the Central Committee of the Estonian Communist party, is the editor of the sport newspaper *Spordileht*. The primary loyalty of such individuals is thus open to question.

The foundation, and the lowest rung, of the Soviet Estonian physical-culture movement is the physical-culture *kollektiv*, which is formed at the level of collective and state farms, factories, enterprises, businesses, institutions, and schools, both in urban and rural areas. The aim of the *kollektivs* is to athletically organize all people at their places of work, study, or residence. A nominal fee of thirty *kopeks* is charged for membership annually, but coaching and the use of facilities are free. Each of the physical-culture *kollektivs* belongs to one of the seven voluntary sport societies in Estonia: Kalev, Jôud, Noorus, Dynamo, Lokomotiv, Tööjôureservid, or Almavü. These societies are themselves based on certain types of occupations or professions. Thus, Dynamo is the society for members of the Security Police, Lokomotiv for the transportation workers, Tööjôureservid for the labor reserves, Jôud for the rural people, Noorus for schoolchildren, and Kalev for trade unions. Almavü (an acronym for the Army, Air Force, and Navy Volunteer Association) is an independent organization which is responsible for such activities as motor racing and underwater sports. Each of the seven sport societies is a republic-level branch of an all-union society. For funding, each is attached to a specific ministry; for example, Kalev to the Trade Unions Central League. The largest and most popular of these societies is Kalev, followed by Noorus and Jôud. Each sport society organizes annual championships at the local, regional, and republic levels, holds winter and summer *spartakiads* and sports games, conducts seminars, lectures, and courses, and runs summer camps and sport schools. Moreover, each is involved in competitions and other activities at the all-union level within its respective all-union society.

Additionally, each of the sports activities practiced in the Estonian SSR has a specific federation at the republic level which in turn is affiliated with a federation at the all-union level. The republic federations direct their specific activities through city and regional sections and their respective sections in the physical-culture *kollektivs*. In the 1970 *Kehakultuurlase Aastaraamat* [Yearbook for the Physical Culturist], the following sports are listed as being practiced in the Estonian SSR: rowing, underwater sports, auto sports, sambo wrestling, figure skating, modern rhythmical gymnastics, hunt shooting, soccer, cycling, ice hockey, ice ball, ice yachting, pentathlon, checkers, go-karting, sledding, track and field, speed skating, Greco-Roman wrestling, basketball, shooting, table tennis, field hockey, chess, motor sports, cross-country motor racing, motor ball, orienteering, boxing, yachting, riding, competitive fishing, Olympic gymnastics, badminton, skiing, sculling, tennis, weightlifting, swimming, free-style wrestling, motor boating, water polo, water skiing, fencing, diving, archery, volleyball, and handball (Laas, 1971:441-442). From this list it can be seen that most international sports are being practiced, though not all, of course, with equal intensity. However, golf, football, and baseball are not officially practiced sports in Estonia (nor elsewhere in the Soviet Union).

Since 1945, the sport program in Estonia has expanded in scope as such new activities as archery, go-karting, underwater sports, water skiing, fencing, and various types of motor sports have been introduced. Indeed, these sports have, in general, gained prominence among the people, and many all-union and European championships have been won. Success has been achieved particularly in underwater sports, in which more medals have been won than in any other sport. At the first world championships in 1973, Illa Raudik and Peeter Vaik were two champions on the winning Soviet team. However, the best was Vello Prangel, to whom ". . . Soviet underwater swimming owes its beginning and its international reputation" (Salmre, 1973:24). Since the early 1950s, fencing enthusiast Endel Nelis has promoted and developed fencing at his specialized sport school in Haapsalu. Recently, Svetlana Tširkova and Georgi Žazitski of the Estonian SSR reached international stature in fencing, winning Olympic and world championships. Although archery has been practiced as a competitive sport only since 1960, since then such Soviet Estonian archers as Eve Suits and Virve Holtsmeier have become among the best in the world. Indeed, the first-ever international archery competition was held in Tallinn in 1972. Because of their technical expertise, Estonians have also done quite well in the various motor sports.

Prior to World War II, heavy athletics (wrestling, weightlifting, and boxing) were major, well established, internationally successful sports in Estonia. However, after 1944 the popularity of these sports, particularly that of boxing, declined. Until the mid-1950s Johannes Kotkas, a 1952 Olympic gold medalist, and August Englas, a 1953 and 1954 world champion, maintained the prewar high performance level of Estonian wrestlers. Since then, however, wrestling has not maintained its prewar level. One reason for this apparent decline may be that growing world acceptance of the sport has greatly increased the number of participants, thus raising the quality of competitions. (An interesting comparison can be made with

Canada, whose wrestlers had likewise won numerous medals in the lighter divisions up to 1940. Since then, no Canadian wrestler has won an Olympic medal.) Another reason could be that coaching methods and training techniques in the Estonian SSR have not kept up with recent developments in the field. Moreover, the national popularity of any given sport tends to rise and fall, experiencing peak years as well as ebb years. This has been the case with weightlifting, for example. For many years after the war, this particular sport appeared to have lost its appeal to Estonian youth. No outstanding weightlifters emerged. Not until the late 1950s, with Tônu Tugar, Karl Utsar, and Jaan Talts, did weightlifting again come to the fore.

Shooting (pistol and rifle marksmanship), ice yachting, and chess were also popular and successful sports prior to the war. For some years after the war the sport of shooting was at a high level, and Estonians dominated the all-union championships. However, since then only Enn Rusi has been successful in international competition, and Estonians have never regained the world superiority and dominance which they attained and exercised in this field in the late 1930s. In contrast, ice yachting and chess have maintained a high level of both popularity and performance. Because of the quality of ice facilities in the bay of Tallinn, the majority of the Soviet ice-yachting competitions have been held there since 1960. In recent years, international victories have been achieved by Endel Vooremaa, Ain Vilde, and Helmut Leppik, who dominated the first world championships held in Detroit, Michigan, in 1973. World-caliber chess players include Paul Keres, Iivo Nei, and Maaja Ranniku, who have competed for the Soviet Union internationally. The consistently high level of chess over the years is primarily the result of one individual's expertise—that of Paul Keres—and of the longevity of competitive careers in this sport.

The traditional activities of track and field, basketball, volleyball, soccer, cross-country skiing, and modern rhythmical gymnastics have remained nationally the most popular, although not always the most internationally successful, sports. Attracting people at all age levels, these activities have drawn the greatest number of active participants. Moreover, these sports are emphasized at the sport schools; hence there is continuous development of young people in these activities.

The most popular and widespread of the aforenoted sports is generally considered to be track and field, which is one of the oldest sports in Estonia. Some of the top athletes in this sport have been Heino Lipp, Bruno Junk, Hanno Selg, Herbert Pärnakivi, Rein Aun, Tônu Lepik, Enn Sellik, and 1972 Olympic gold medalist Jüri Tarmak. When the world standings in track and field in 1970 were ranked according to performances in men's events, the USSR was ranked fourth. However, if the Soviet republics had been entered individually, the Russian SFSR would have been ranked fourth, the Ukraine fifth, Estonia fifteenth (and hence third in the USSR), Latvia seventeenth, Byelorussia eighteenth, Georgia twentieth, and Lithuania twenty-ninth (Alekors, 1970:270).

Basketball is the only one of the ball sports in which Estonians have experienced success. There is usually at least one Estonian on the Soviet national team; the Soviet team that toured America in 1971 had three members from Estonia. Joann Lossov, Ilmar Kullam, Jaak Lipso, Anatoli Krikun, Priit Tomsom, and Jaak Salumets have been some of the outstanding players. Estonian women volleyball and basketball players were members of Soviet national teams in the 1950s. Modern rhythmical gymnastics is another traditional activity which has continued to grow in popularity. For the average Estonian female, this is the most common physical activity, and women of all ages avidly take part in the numerous rhythmical gymnastics groups throughout the country. This style of gymnastics, introduced by Estonian women to the Soviet Union, has since become popular throughout the USSR. (Estonians, incidentally, have also popularized it elsewhere in the world through their postwar diaspora to Australia, North America, and Sweden.)

Although sailing and tennis were not practiced to any large extent prior to 1940, the bay of Tallinn has since become a very popular place for Soviet sailing competitions. The republic government has recently completed plans for a specialized boat center at Pirita. The most prominent sailor for Estonia is Aleksander Tšutselov, silver medalist at the 1960 Olympics. Although there is a severe lack of indoor tennis training facilities, Estonia has been the leading Soviet republic for many years in this sport—primarily because of the excellent coaching of Evald Kree and the performance of his outstanding pupil, Toomas Leius, who became the first Soviet tennis player to win at Wimbledon when he captured the junior men's singles title in 1959. In demonstrating a preference for and skills in such sports as sailing and tennis, which are Western-oriented, formerly aristocratic endeavors, Estonians perhaps are symbolizing through their sporting activities their Western orientation and separateness from the Soviet Union (Pennar, 1968:213).

Such activities as soccer, ice hockey, checkers, skating, cycling, table tennis, fishing, hunting, badminton, and swimming all have their ardent enthusiasts, and all are part of the sport picture of Soviet Estonia. The primary emphasis has been on the development of international sports; however, such Olympic events as gymnastics, downhill skiing, figure skating, diving, water polo, riding, and speed skating have never been developed to any appreciable extent and are considered minor activities. Although Ants Antson won a gold medal in speed skating at the 1964 Winter Olympics, that sport has not become widespread, primarily because of the lack of facilities for training. (Indeed, Ants Antson received his training outside Estonia.)

As noted, one of the two underlying principles of the Soviet sports program is *mastestvo* (sport proficiency). Victory in sport is considered to be a reflection of the superiority of both Soviet athletes and, in essence, the Soviet populace and political system. For example, after the Soviets entered the Olympic Games for the first time in 1952, the excellent performance of their athletes was said to be ". . . still another victory of our Soviet system."[6] Thus, the government and party of the Soviet Union and the Estonian SSR have emphasized and fostered the development of those sports that are thought to have the most international prestige. However, as we have seen, certain sports have not developed in Estonia despite great encouragement by the government. The topography of the countryside, the climate, the facilities available (particularly indoors), and the traditions of the past have determined which sports are popular and successful in Estonia.

Another factor influencing the development of certain sports in Estonia has been technological ability and craftsmanship. Indeed, it appears that Moscow has assigned to Estonia, along with Latvia and Lithuania, the "role of processor and technological specialist for which skills in designing, engineering, and mechanics are required" (Vardys, 1975:154). Sport has been one area in which this role has been manifested. In motor sports, the fact that the "Estonia" formula car, built by the Tallinn Auto Repair Factory, is accepted and used throughout the USSR has been one reason for the success achieved by Estonians in motor-car racing. Moreover, during the 1960s the go-karts for the USSR national team were built by this same Tallinn factory. The equipment made in Estonia for underwater sports is generally considered more advanced, efficient, and dependable than that produced in other Soviet or Eastern-bloc countries. As a result, Soviet Estonian under-water-sports athletes have captured more championship me-dals than have Estonian athletes in any other sport during the last ten years. Estonia-brand skis have become well known and are often used by Soviet national teams. Estonian boat builders are known for their efficiency and have introduced a new type of boat, the Optimist, for children's sailing. Estonian skill in craftsmanship was already apparent prior to 1940, particularly in the construction of ice yachts, rifles, and pistols. Indeed, sports calling for skilled workmanship and Western technical expertise have achieved exceptional success and popularity in Soviet Estonia.

In international competition, Soviet Estonian athletes, as members of USSR teams, had won by 1971 18 Olympic medals, 29 world medals, and 123 European championship medals. In comparing these totals with the 21 Olympic, 58 world, and 46 European championship medals won by repub-lic athletes prior to 1940, it is interesting to note that only in the European championships has there been an increase in medal achievement. This increase was primarily the result of Esto-nia's 33 first places in underwater sports. The main reason for the apparent decrease in international achievements during the Soviet period is that both the level of athletic performance and the number of countries competing have risen considerably throughout the world during the past twenty-five years; thus it is becoming harder and harder to win a world championship in any sport. Moreover, opportunities for Estonian participation in international competition have dwindled. Estonian athletes must now first defeat competitors from the other fourteen Soviet republics—an increasingly difficult task, particularly in such sports as wrestling, weightlifting, Olympic gymnastics, ice hockey, chess, and cross-country skiing. It has been argued on occasion that if a Russian athlete is equivalent in athletic performance to an Estonian, the Russian may be selected for political reasons as well as for reasons of Russian chauvinism. In spite of all of these factors, however, Estonian athletes have continued to do well in athletic competition.

Since 1945 Estonian athletes have competed internationally as members of the Soviet national teams and hence under the name "Soviet"—or, as such teams are often incorrectly called in the West, "Russian." However, Estonian republic-level teams can and do compete against such other East European countries as Bulgaria, Poland, Hungary, Czechoslovakia, and East Germany. Interestingly, since the early 1960s the uniforms of Soviet Estonian athletes have carried simply the name "Eesti" (Estonia) instead of the previous "Eesti NSV" (Estonian SSR) in all meets in which they are competing as representatives of the republic. In recent years, some official intercountry competitions with Western countries, such as Sweden and the United States, have been permitted. For example, Estonia has competed against Sweden in the decathlon and in basketball, both contests taking place in Sweden. In the summer of 1970, the Estonian basketball team defeated a touring American team. Also, there are close ties in the field of sports competition between Finland and Soviet Estonia. Finland considers the Estonian SSR separately from the rest of the USSR, and Estonia is one of the many countries with which Finland competes regularly at the international level (Laine, 1972). The opportunity to compete against foreign countries has steadily been increasing as the possibility of traveling beyond the Soviet Union has gradually been increased and as many more foreign teams are being invited to Estonia. To Estonians, the main incentive to be a top athlete is the opportunity to travel—that is, the opportunity to go freely to *välismaa* (abroad).

The emphasis on *mastestvo* and winning has made athletic competition an important aspect of the total sport program. Indeed, people are encouraged to participate in competition, particularly on the *kollektiv* level. Competitions in all sports are held at the local, regional, republic, and all-union levels. Considering the number of athletes competing in the all-union championships, the Estonians have done quite well, winning more than 2,000 medals between 1940 and 1971. The largest and most impressive of the athletic gatherings have been the all-union *spartakiads* (sport festivals), mass-scale, country-wide tournaments held quadrennially in Moscow. These festivals are intended to be displays of youth, vitality, health, and an "expression of the friendship of the peoples inhabiting the Soviet Union."[7] Although competitors from all of the republics participate in the all-union *spartakiad*, each republic holds an annual republic-level *spartakiad*. In Estonia, an interesting comparison may be made between these *spartakiads* and the *Eesti Mängud* (Estonian Games) of 1934 and 1939. In both instances, preliminary competitions and festivals were held in the counties and cities, and people throughout the entire country were involved. Parades of participants to the stadium near Kadrioru Palace were greeted by the top political leaders of the country—namely, Konstantin Päts in 1939 and Ivan Käbin in 1967. In 1939 some thirteen events were held, while in 1967 there were twenty sports. At both festivals, mass gymnastics performances were staged. Such displays have also been presented at the all-union *spartakiads*, as part of the national-traditional activities. It appears that such spectacles appeal to the Estonian people; thus they may be classified as being a traditional physical activity. In that they involved hundreds of people in exercises demonstrating both vigor and physical fitness, mass gymnastics displays coincide with the mass physical-culture emphasis of the Soviet physical-culture program.

Indeed, one of the most important aspects of the Soviet physical-culture program is its emphasis on mass participation. This emphasis is part of the goal of the total program in that it helps to lay the foundation for a Communist society; thus it should be part of the daily lives of all people.[8] One of the primary reasons for the mass-participation goal in the Soviet Union is related to achieving political integration. Through common recreational experiences which are easily and readily accessible to all, regardless of occupation or social status, class integration can be achieved. Besides this egalitarian aim, it is generally believed that sports prepare the new "Soviet man" to be healthy and physically ready for work and the defense of the country. Thus there is an ideological reason for the emphasis on mass participation and on the utilization of leisure-time activities in order to achieve political integration. Although mass physical culture represents a voluntary involvement for people in a state-sponsored activity, it is important from the health and fitness standpoint, and it also provides an opportunity to broaden the base from which top athletes will develop.

In Soviet Estonia the scope of the physical-culture program has been continually expanding since 1944, and numerous mass competitions, sports, games, and activities in which participation, not skill, is important have been organized regularly. Hiking, cross-country skiing, jogging, and *iluvôim-lemine* (modern rhythmical gymnastics) are some of the most important mass activities. Further, mass participation is encouraged by the "VTK" fitness program, the All-Union Sports Classification System, the sport societies and *kollektivs*, and the mass media. A very important aspect of mass physical culture has been *tootmisvôimlemine* (industrial fitness exercising), which is aimed at strengthening the health of workers so that their productivity will be higher (Okk, 1966:30). When the percentage of the total population involved in the physical-culture program was analyzed in 1966, it was found that Estonia had the second-highest percentage in the Soviet Union.[9]

It has been claimed that "massive development of physical culture in Estonia began only after the institution of Soviet rule" (Mandre, 1965:1). However, this is not correct. Mass participation in sport was a reality prior to the war; participation was available to all in a wide variety of activities, and sports clubs had been formed in cities, towns, villages, and rural areas. While it is indeed true that per-capita participation in physical activities is much higher at the present time than it was during the prewar period, even this finding warrants further analysis. Soviet and Estonian SSR literature which compares the prewar and postwar programs invariably uses 1940 as the comparison date. Such figures are misleading because 1940 was a war year, and many men were already mobilized into the armed forces. Moreover, the war overshadowed and affected all other activities. Also, these statistics do not take into account the prewar athletic clubs of the numerous Estonian youth organizations, which played a considerable role in the sport movement.

Furthermore, growth and development of athletics has been a worldwide phenomenon of the postwar period; mass participation and the proliferation of sporting activities and facilities have occurred in most countries, not only in the Soviet Union. Given the general receptivity to sports in Estonia, it could be conjectured that similar growth rates might have occurred in the absence of Soviet policies. The probability is that the growth rate and per-capita participation figures would have shown a marked increase in any case—as they did, for example, in the Finnish program.

Mass participation in physical activities has been stimulated by the implementation of two centrally organized and controlled award systems: the Gotov K Trudui-Oboronie (Ready for Labor and Defense) awards for general fitness and the All-Union Sports Classification awards for excellence in specific sports. The Ready for Labor and Defense program is translated into Estonian as *Valmis Tööks ja Kaitseks* and is abbreviated as VTK. When the VTK program was first implemented in Estonia and elsewhere in the Soviet Union, it had a paramilitary nature. However, since the scheme was reorganized in the late 1960s, there has been slightly less emphasis on military activities and more emphasis on recreational aspects. The aim of the new VTK program is "to promote sport on the widest scale among people of all age groups and bring promising athletes to the fore."[10]

The VTK fitness scheme was made an integral part of the school physical-education program, and all children are obliged to attain the two lowest levels while at school. As is the case in regard to other aspects of life in Soviet Estonia, specific quotas are set for the number of VTK badgeholders; hence there is considerable pressure on each physical-culture *kollektiv* to achieve its quota. Quota competitions are held between schools, businesses, clubs, cities, regions, and republics. According to 1972 statistics, the Estonian SSR was in thirteenth place in the number of VTK awardholders per capita (Latvia was ninth and Lithuania twelfth).[11]

According to the All-Union Sports Classification System, awards are given for excellence in particular sports. Standards for these awards are set nationally for five categories: Class C, Class B, Class A, Master of Sport, and Honored Master of Sport. The Master of Sport title is awarded for life and is accorded great prestige in the society at large. Many Estonian athletes have been awarded this title for exceptional athletic prowess. This title can be taken away from an athlete for disorderly or unsportsmanlike conduct or for incorrect political thinking. For example, Aleksander Gornakov, Estonia's top flyweight Greco-Roman wrestler, was stripped of his Master of Sport title for drunkenness the evening before a match with Leningrad.[12] Such exceptional coaches as Evald

Kree, Johannes Kotkas, and Fred Kudu, to name but a few, have received the Honored Coach title.

Although a picture of a well-developed, efficient, and successful physical-culture program in the Estonian SSR has generally been presented, there are many shortcomings and problems. Of major concern in the development of the program are two at times conflicting principles: *massovost* and *mastestvo*. Complaints are often expressed that there is insufficient effort to broaden the physical-culture base among the masses, and that, consequently, the goal of the physical-culture movement—that is, to make it a part of the daily life of each person—has not yet been achieved. Some critics say that too much effort and time is devoted to the development of top-caliber athletes (Adamson, 1973). Another major problem is related to athletic facilities; here lack of facilities, not finances, is the main concern. Many such projects are never completed because of construction problems and planning and organizational weaknesses. Some sports, such as tennis and rowing, are presently in dire need of indoor facilities. Although many new facilities have been built since 1944, these have not been sufficient to meet the needs and demands of the program.

The aims and objectives of Estonia's physical-education program are said to be the same as those in all other republics of the Soviet Union. Classes in physical education are compulsory in all school grades, including the first two grade levels of every higher-education institution. The content of the curriculum is essentially the same as such curricula elsewhere in the Soviet Union, with a few minor geographical adaptations. The one major Estonian exception to the uniform curriculum was the addition of two "sports hours" in 1972 to the regular class schedules in grades three and four. This plan is in effect only in Estonia. However, its effectiveness, and perhaps future implementation, will be considered by the education ministries of the other fourteen republics.

Participation in extrascholastic sports activities has been given considerable emphasis by educational authorities and by the physical-culture *kollektivs* which are part of the school sport society. Noorus societies have been formed at all schools. The better school athletes are selected to attend various sport schools, where they receive specialized coaching and have the benefit of excellent training facilities. The Soviet youth movement, which has been imposed on the Estonian youth, is closely connected with the educational system, and children are encouraged to join the Oktobrists, Pioneers, and Komsomol. These organizations, which provide recreation and sports activities for children, serve to propagate Communist ideology; hence Estonian children have not been very willing to join them. Pioneer camps, along with sport societies, sport schools, and city camps, provide recreational opportunities for schoolchildren during the summer. On the higher-education level, university students in Estonia belong not to the all-union student sports society, Burevestnik, but rather to the republic-level Kalev society.

Physical-education teachers and sports coaches receive their professional preparation at the Faculty of Physical Education of the University of Tartu and at the Tallinn Pedagogical Institute. Both institutions offer a four-year program which is the same as such programs in other Soviet institutions, except for a few changes to accommodate local conditions and traditions. Graduate work is possible at the University of Tartu, one of the four centers in the Soviet Union where theses in this field can be defended and advanced degrees awarded. Research work done in physical education and sports at the University of Tartu has received all-union acclaim, and in some areas, particularly sport endocrinology, it is considered to be the leading all-union center (Viru, 1972). In the Faculty of Medicine at the University of Tartu a sports medicine section, offering a six-year course leading to a doctor-coach degree, has been in existence since the late 1950s and was the first such program in the USSR. Because many students from other parts of the Soviet Union study there, it is the only section at the university where instruction is primarily in the Russian language. Another first in the Soviet Union was the *rakendus-sport* (applied sports) section at the University of Tartu, which offers specific athletic skills instruction for biology, geology, and geography students (Matvei, 1963:166).

If Soviet Estonian physical culture is evaluated objectively, several positive features must be acknowledged. Some of these features are the sport schools, the physical-fitness and sports classification award programs, compulsory physical education during the first two years of the university, similar professional preparation for sports coaches and teachers, industrial fitness programs, such mass-participation activities as hiking and cross-country skiing, and summer sport camps for school-children. Perhaps the two most positive aspects of the program are its extensive state support and its emphasis on developing the abilities of youth.

Apart from such traditional folk activities as folk dancing and *kurnimine* (cudgel throwing), the sport activities practiced in Estonia have been adopted from other countries. Germany, Sweden, Finland, the United States, Great Britain, and, more recently, Soviet Russia have exerted varying degrees of influence on the sports and physical-education programs in the country. Estonia's influence on the programs of these countries, on the other hand, has not existed apart from the activity of *iluvôimlemine* (modern rhythmical gymnastics). This form of movement was created by Ernst Idla in the 1920s for the Estonian people, to meet their needs and to suit their temperament. Since then, Idla and his students have spread this style of movement throughout Europe, North and South America, Australia, and New Zealand, as well as the Soviet Union.

In conclusion, then, sport in its broad context has always been an important aspect of people's lives and of the Estonian culture. However, changes in political rule have affected the philosophy, organization, and content of the sport program. The participation and scope of the programs, although difficult to assess accurately, have certainly increased. However, it cannot be said that this increase in participation and scope can be attributed to the Soviet organizational model, because this phenomenon has also occurred in most other countries of the world. Moreover, movements toward domestic mass-participation sports and success in international competition predate 1940.

Although the sport and physical-education programs have proclaimed Soviet political objectives, the majority of Estonians participate in them in order to fulfill their needs and desires for exercise, health, and recreation. Moreover, they have furthered, at least to some extent, national self-expression through sport. The Estonian people have continued to participate in physical activities which were already, prior to 1940, considered part of the Estonian culture, and Estonian athletes have continued to perform well in international competitions. Indeed, Estonians can be proud of their achievements in sport both at home and abroad, from the earliest organized sport activity in their country to the present day.

Notes

1. See "Terves kehas terve vaim" [A Healthy Mind in a Healthy Body], *Kehakultuur*, no. 6 (March 25, 1963), p. 164.
2. See *Estonian Events*, December 1970, p. 3.
3. See "Spartakiaad vaekusil" [The Scale of the Spartakiad], *Kehakultuur*, no. 24 (December 27, 1971), p. 739.
4. See "Kodumaa noorte venevaenulikkus" [Hostility of the Youth in the Homeland toward Russians], *Meie Elu*, January 20, 1972, p. 6.
5. See "Uurimus imperialismi ikkest Eestis" [A Study of the Yoke of Imperialism in Estonia], *Meie Elu*, July 21, 1972, p. 5.
6. See *Sovetskii Sport*, July 31, 1952.
7. See *Sport in the USSR*, no. 9 (1971), p. 2.
8. See "Täna paremini kui eile, homme paremini kui täna" [Better Today than Yesterday; Better Tomorrow than Today], *Kehakultuur*, no. 19 (October 10, 1962), p. 578.
9. See "Pidupäeva künnisel" [On the Threshold of Celebration Day], *Kehakultuur*, no. 15 (August 10, 1962), p. 451.
10. See "Vigor, Skill and Courage," *Sport in the USSR*, no. 3 (1972), p. 3.
11. See "Üleliiduliselt seitsmendad" [Seventh in the All-Union], *Kehakultuur*, no. 11 (June 10, 1973), p. 324.
12. See "Spordieetika rikkujad said karistada" [The Violators of the Sports Ethics Were Punished], *Spordileht*, no. 124 (October 17, 1973), p. 2.

References

Adamson, K.

   1973   "Rahvaspordist, selle funktsioonidest ja võimalikest arenguperspektiividest" [Mass Sport, Its Functions and Possibilities, in Developmental Perspective]. *Rahva Hääl*, April 11.

Alekors, H.

   1970   "Võrdleme rekorditabeleid" [Let Us Compare the Record Tables]. *Kehakultuur*, no. 9 (May 8), pp. 269-270.

Arusoo, K.

1973   "Tugevamaks spordi kasvatuslik môju" [Strengthening the Beneficial Effects of Sport]. *Rahva Hääl*, August 2.

Laas, J., ed.

1971   *Kehakultuurlase Aastaraamat 1970* [Yearbook of the Physical Culturist]. Tallinn: Eesti Raamat.

Laine, A.

1972   Personal interview with A. Laine, chief secretary of the Finnish Sports Federation. Helsinki, July 26, 1972.

Legostaev, F.

1951   *Fizicheskoe vospitanie i sport v SSSR*. Munich: n.p.

Mandre, J.

1965   *25 Spordiaastat* [Twenty-five Years of Sport]. Tallinn: Punane Täht.

Matvei, B.

1963   "Sport teaduse teenistuses" [Sport in the Service of Science]. *Kehakultuur*, no. 6 (March 25), p. 166.

Morton, H.

1963   *Soviet Sport*. New York: Collier.

Nurmberg, Reet

1972   "Sport and Physical Education in Estonia." Doctoral dissertation, University of California, Berkeley, Calif.

Okk, I.

1966   *Tootmisvôimlemine* [Industrial Exercising]. Tallinn: Eesti Raamat.

Pennar, J.
1968   "Nationalism in the Soviet Baltics," in *Ethnic Minorities in the Soviet Union*, ed. E. Goldhagen. New York: Praeger.

Rand, M.
1973   "Pilguga tulevikku" [A Look into the Future]. *Kehakultuur*, no. 2 (1973), pp. 51-52.

Salmre, V.
1973   "Water in the Blood." *Sport in the USSR*, no. 9, pp. 24-27.

Sisak, H.
1969   "Uutele rööbastele" [Unto New Rails]. *Kehakultuur*, no. 1 (January 10), pp. 3-4.

Tamjärv, K., ed.
1952   *Kehakultuuri-Liikumisest* [On the Physical Culture Movement]. Tallinn: Punane Täht.

Vardys, V. Stanley
1975   "The Role of the Baltic Republics in Soviet Society," in *The Influence of East Europe and the Soviet West on the USSR*, ed. Roman Szporluk. New York: Praeger.

Viirsalu, E.
1955   *Women and Youth in Soviet-Occupied Estonia*. East and West Series, no. 7. London: Boreas.

Viru, A.
1972   "Praktilisest ülesannetest teaduslikus töös" [On Practical Tasks in Scientific Work]. *Spordileht*, no. 79 (July 7), p. 3.

Part 3
Aspects of Culture

7

Estonian Literature

George Kurman

With the Soviet annexation of Estonia in 1940, private publishing houses were closed, socialist realism was decreed to be the only permissible method and style of imaginative writing and literary criticism, and the Estonian Writers' Union was reorganized along political lines. Many writers chose to remain silent (or were silenced), but others continued to publish. The predominant genre was poetry, with Juhan Sütiste and Jaan Kärner joining Johannes Vares-Barbarus in praising the new order. But the injustices of the first year of Soviet rule were so extreme that even writers who in theory might have preferred a dictatorship of the proletariat to prewar native authoritarianism were disillusioned by August 1941, when Estonia's first year as a Soviet republic was terminated by the arrival of Hitler's armies.

The Nazi occupation of Estonia resulted in the departure of those writers who had supported the Soviet order. Thus, Johannes Semper, J. Barbarus, A. Jakobson, J. Kärner, A. Hint, and others were in wartime exile in the Soviet rear. While their work was being censored or destroyed in German-occupied Estonia, by 1943 the Soviet Estonian Writers' Union

---

I would like to acknowledge the financial support granted by the International Research and Exchange Board during the preparation of this essay. It should be made clear, however, that neither the board nor Estonian writers at large necessarily concur with my judgments.

had reorganized and met in Moscow. The three years spent in the Soviet Union proper by more than twenty Soviet Estonian writers resulted in some publications, chiefly collections of verse and almanacs, and laid the groundwork for close ties with the literature of Soviet Russia. A contemporaneous development was the acquaintance made by several of these writers with Estonian "proletarian literature," a minor tributary of the mainstream of Estonian letters, which had been initiated in Estonia during the revolution of 1905, revived there between 1917 and 1920, and intermittently continued in Leningrad until the 1930s. Not belles lettres in the traditional sense of the term, this proletarian literature had political agitation as its main objective and, in the words of Endel Nirk (1970:194), "was characterized by high-flown glorification of the socialist revolution, [and] romantic and abstract visions of the building of a new world. . . ." Similarly, the Estonian literature written in the Soviet rear, because of its blatantly political direction, was almost always too topical, too propagandistic, and too hurriedly executed to be of any lasting value.

With the impending return of the Red Army in 1944, the majority of Estonian writers and critics, who had not cast their lot with the Communists, fled to the West. The result, in effect, was a split of Estonian literature into two branches—the emigré and the Soviet (or socialist realist). For more than a decade after the war, Estonian emigré literature clearly exceeded, both in quality and in quantity, the output of belles lettres in Soviet Estonia, in spite of the fact that the dispersed emigré community constituted only some 10 percent of the language group. Writers in Soviet Estonia, in the meantime, were confronted with the difficulties posed not only by a wartorn nation and a new political and social order but also by an entirely new concept of the creation and function of literature: namely, socialist realism.

Even after 1944, however, few Soviet Estonian writers were prepared to accept the notion of the total subservience of literature to the party. As Nirk phrased it, "The assimilation of the new literary concepts was not easy even for those who had taken a firm stand in support of socialism. Nearly all of them had to re-evaluate their former principles and activities, and adopt new methods of creation," in which "one of the prime tasks of literature was . . . to inculcate a Soviet outlook of life into the minds of the masses . . . [in order] to show the advantages of socialist ideology and collectivism . . . [and] to foster the feelings of Soviet patriotism" (1970:279, 285). In spite of the apparent prominence given to realism, it soon became clear that the writer was not permitted to see life as it actually was but rather must describe life as it should be seen in the opinion of the party theoreticians.

Poetry

Soviet Estonian poetry can be divided into four distinct periods: (1) the wartime and postwar period from 1940 to 1955; (2) the "thaw," beginning in 1956, which had all but ended by 1959; (3) the remarkable fluorescence of new, vital, and aesthetically satisfying verse during the 1960s; (4) the close of this last movement, marked by a period of consolidation which began around 1968 and is not yet final.

Critics generally agree that the first period of Soviet Estonian poetry left almost nothing of enduring artistic value. The poetry published in 1940 and 1941 during the first Soviet year in Estonia was preoccupied with political matters, while the Estonian poets in the Soviet rear were affected not only by the adversity of war and exile but also by a censorship that regarded poetic production exclusively in terms of its contribution to the war effort. As a result, "passive reflections and narrow personal lyrics are practically absent" from the poetry of this period (Kääri and Peep, 1965:17). Yet after the victory over Germany was assured, accusations began to be made about the overly nationalistic tenor of Soviet Estonian wartime verse and about its "formalistic, bourgeois" vestiges.

As a result, after 1945 the established poets, joined by the younger writers who had made their debuts during the war, continued to stress subjects related to war, often linking these with the theme of friendship among the Soviet peoples. Added to this theme were topics related to postwar reconstruction and the collectivization of agriculture, in addition to obligatory praise of the party and its Flawless Leader—all done in a style so conventional and flat as to invite comparison with the long-outdated poetry written in Estonia during the first years of the twentieth century.

Those poets who had neither emigrated nor cast their lots with the Soviets (among them Betti Alver, August Sang, Heiti

Talvik, Kersti Merilaas, and Uku Masing) were now silenced, either by choice or as a result of circumstances. It was an age in which Juhan Smuul enthusiastically described Comrade Stalin as "wise, beloved, and humane. . . . The conscience of the world." It was an age in which the poet Mart Raud publicly criticized Semper's poem "Two Urns" in the following words: "It is harmful to symbolize the Soviet regime by an unattractive yet useful pot while representing the past (and future) with a comely vase. These and other errors could not have been made by the poet if he had penetrated more deeply into ideological matters."

While Raud, Vaarandi, Smuul, Parve, and others were temporarily ascendant in the late 1940s, penning made-to-order didactic verse, their betters as poets were being either silenced or deported. While the former poets addressed their verse to such topics as industrialization, improving the yields of the collective farms, the bankruptcy of all bourgeois values, the cold war, and the peril posed by Estonian emigrés and their literature, the number of poets publishing decreased and the quality of Estonian verse declined even more sharply. From 1951 to 1955, for example, only ten new collections of poetry appeared (including only two debuts), compared to twenty-eight new collections (with nine debuts) during the period 1945-1950.

In the meantime, the poets Alver, Merilaas, Sang, Semper, Viiding, and others had been stricken from the membership of the Writers' Union and publicly denounced. The charges against them were, of course, fabrications. During the Third Estonian Writers' Congress in 1954, the party went on record as congratulating itself for "having waged a tireless struggle for the ideological purity of Soviet [Estonian] literature," which, the resolution continues, "has grown and become stronger in the struggle against bourgeois-nationalistic ideology, cosmo-politanism, and other hostile influences."

But Stalin was irrevocably dead; and, although some reacted to his passing with fear, too many others had been afraid for too long to allow a Stalinist regime to continue. Until 1954-1955 nature poetry and the love lyric had been far in the background of Soviet Estonian verse—even condemned outright by some critics and censors. As late as 1954 some poets still argued strongly for the necessity of approaching lyrical poetry dialectically and of distinguishing, for purposes of evaluation, between verse which portrayed the "world" and verse depicting the poet's "inner life." And even though some critics warned against "the siren-song of revisionism"—which had already begun, as Paul Kuusberg put it, "to seduce those whose faith was weaker toward the deceptive chimera of idealistic aesthetics"—most of the poets themselves, along with their public, had had enough. Conditions had to change and did. As Oskar Kruus observed, "After the hollow pathos and love of inflated rhetoric typical of the Stalinist years, in the shadow of which one tended to forget the realities of actual life as well as the poetry of the ordinary objects and circumstances which surround us, a pressing need arose to grow more mundane, to confront the simple things" (*Looming*, 1965:1408-1416). This trend was but one aspect of the reaction displayed in the poetry of the mid-1950s. In addition, the lyric now tended virtually to exclude the didactic narrative poem. Contemporary and topical themes yielded to the perennial charms of nature and love; the tone of poetry grew more intimate.

In 1955, most of the poets who earlier had been unjustly accused of ideological crimes and publicly denounced were readmitted into the Writers' Union. Also, many deported Estonian writers had returned by this time to their native soil. Whereas earlier only former Red Army soldiers and party members—such as Smuul, Kesamaa, Beekman, Suislepp, and Laht—had been free to publish collections of verse, the number of Estonian poets now increased rapidly. Compared to one new collection of verse in 1954, and three in 1955, 1957 saw five poets making their debuts with published works; nine collections of verse appeared in 1958.

Of all the verse debuts of the 1950s, that of Jaan Kross was artistically the most satisfying as well as the most influential in charting the future course of Estonian poetry. Indeed, Kross's *Söerikastaja* [The Coal Concentrator], published in 1958 but including pieces written as early as 1941, is one of the true landmarks of Estonian verse. Fresh, polemical, erudite, witty, and controversial, this volume, the publication of which had been delayed for years, opened new vistas in subject matter and technique. Amid the storm of controversy surrounding its publication, the seeds for the real renaissance of Estonian verse in the 1960s undoubtedly were sown. The fresh breezes loosed upon the literary landscape by Kross in the late 1950s made plain the damage inflicted on Estonian poetry during the preceding two decades. Even more important, they drew in their wake those who earlier had meekly submitted, those who had maintained silence, and those who were about to launch their first verses.

Thus, Ellen Niit (Jaan Kross's wife) was soon able to follow in 1960 with a distinguished and distinctive contribution to Estonian poetry, *Maa on täis leidmist* [The Earth Is Full of Discoveries]. And Uno Laht, who had earned his writer's spurs while a youthful Red Army soldier and who later sharpened them as an agent of the political police and as a journalist, could emerge by the late 1950s as an original lyrical talent as well as a satirical critic of contemporary social conditions. Although Laht had earlier, wittingly or unwittingly, served as a safety valve for the status quo by publicly "scourging" minor errors—without ever addressing himself to their real source—and thereby masquerading as a tolerated and free critic of the regime, he remains a unique voice from whom there is reason to hope for further achievement.

In the wake of the eased restrictions and greater tolerance that characterized literary life in the middle and late 1950s, a number of other poets who had been publishing since the war were able to change the tone and increase the quality of their literary production. Since that time Vaarandi, for example, in her later collections *Unistaja aknal* [The Dreamer at the Window], 1959, and *Rannalageda leib* [Bread of the Seaside Plain], 1965, has displayed a lyricism that is personal rather than programmatic and a breadth of feeling which was largely absent from her earlier production. Similarly, Paul Rummo's achievements in the longer narrative poem date from 1955, and only in 1958 did Vladimir Beekman show himself to be more than a preprogrammed poet; his collection published in that year, entitled *Tuul kanarbikus* [The Wind in the Heather], indicated that he, too, had become sensitive to the change in the wind. Even the versatile veteran Johannes Semper published a new collection of verse in 1958 which was largely free of the declarative, prepackaged rhetoric that had characterized much of his poetry from 1940 until that date.

Indeed, 1958 was the high-water mark for the literary thaw in Estonia, the year in which—to change the metaphor—the first valuable harvest of post-Stalinist Estonian poetry was gleaned. However, the following year marked the thaw's end—

the official retreat from permissiveness by an orthodoxy embattled by "revisionism." In 1959 only four collections of poetry were published. Smuul (1959:85-103), one of the poets whose work appeared that year, taking a cue from Khrushchev's May 1959 speech to the Third Writers' Congress of the Soviet Union, complained of "influences from bourgeois ideology breaking into poetry through the back door and manifesting themselves in [the Estonian poet's] shutting himself into his ivory tower of subjectivism, and in abstract humanism and pacifism in the style of the League of Nations of 1925." Smuul further railed at the "aestheticized atmosphere" surrounding the Young Writers' League and its "high praise of anything . . . narrowly personal" (see, for example, his 1959 essay in the literary monthly *Looming*, no. 1, pp. 85-103). Other critics, writing on the eve of the Twenty-first Party Congress in the summer of 1959, added similar, predictable sentiments. Lembit Remmelgas, in another 1959 *Looming* article, for example, scourged the revival of "art-for-art's-sake principles" among critics and attacked their concealed "nihilistic" attitude toward the "achievements" of eighteen years of Soviet Estonian literature. Paul Kuusberg, while looking back nostalgically to the verse of the 1940s, similarly predicted a second death for poetry reflecting "revisionist sentiments" and labeled critics supporting this trend as outdated, accusing them of "employing the tactics of the smuggler" (*Looming*, 1959:429-443).

Even though the thaw had run its course, however, the growth of Estonian poetry did not cease. Although from 1959 to 1961 the situation seemed uncertain, during the following six years (1962-1967) a series of striking debuts, along with the publication of new collections from older poets who had published little for decades, served permanently to change the face of Estonian poetry. As Peep (1967:29) observed, "A real sensation was created by twelve young poets who made their debut with collections of verse published in 1962-1964." Among younger poets whose debuts helped launch what can justly be termed a renascence of Estonian poetry—and whose subsequent verse has further enriched the language and broadened its realm—are Paul-Eerik Rummo, Jaan Kaplinski, Viivi Luik, Mats Traat, Hando Runnel, Enn Vetemaa, and Aleksander Suuman. Foremost among this group, perhaps, is Rummo, a poet whose first three collections of verse were sold

out by the time he was twenty-six years old. Arvo Mägi
(1968:73) sees Rummo's poetic consciousness as having shat-
tered and radically transformed the realistic view of the world.
In its place, Mägi observed, the poet has "created a new, many-
hued, and expressive world, and attained a strikingly original
intuitive association of ideas."

Kaplinski's *Tolmust ja värvidest* [From Dust and Colors]
treated the ubiquitous theme of man's oppression of nature
and of his fellow man in fresh and graceful verses. One critic
remarked, "In his poetry Kaplinski achieves a convincing
synthesis of the concrete and utopian realms and of radical and
conservative thought patterns" (Grabbi, 1973:660). In the same
article Grabbi translated Kaplinski's poem "Culture Is" into
English, from which the following excerpt is appropriate:

> honored judges I too confess that I have made very many
> mistakes but I am simply a black sheep you are a
> sarcoma
> you are a carcinoma which doesn't know better but to
> grow at the expense of the living tissue of nature free
> enterprise that doesn't know anything but to destroy life
> to destroy itself
> honored judges I am a witness to the indictment I am not
> the first one and I will not remain the last
> I speak what all speak I speak for those who are no more
> for the annihilated species and forgotten peoples I
> speak for the tongues which are not spoken any more
> I speak for the fire-islanders I speak for the whales I speak
> for those who were burned to ashes in Auschwitz for the
> dead whose throat was cut for those whose mouth is
> filled with frozen earth and cannot take the witness
> stand themselves
> I speak for the sea birds who perished in oil spills for the
> leopards elephants dolphins kangaroos globeflowers
> moccasin flowers barn swallows who have no place in
> your brave new world. . . .

Of equal importance with the debuts of these younger poets
was the concurrent reemergence of several established writers.
Foremost among the latter group was Betti Alver, who in 1962,
after nearly two decades of silence, published a group of six of
her earlier long poems, written between 1934 and 1942, *Mõ-
rane peegel* [The Cracked Looking Glass], 1962, and then in

1966 released a new collection of verse, *Tähetund* [The Astral Hour]—all 10,000 copies of which were sold out within hours, according to Aspel (1969:46). This was followed in 1971 by a third collection, *Elu helbed* [Life Petals], in which verse from 1932 to 1940 and from 1966 to 1970 appeared.

A second important Estonian poet who made his debut in the 1930s, endured the years of Stalinist terror in silence, and then reemerged in the 1960s, was August Sang. Sang's verses expressed, in a minor key, the conscience and aspirations of his nation, as the following excerpt demonstrates:

O my fatherland, my people!
What is there that could be done
so that everything would sooner,
sooner be just as it should?
(from "Laul Kärsitusest" [A Song of Impatience],
written in 1953 and published in 1962).

Sang's subdued, artistically mature but technically fresh voice was seldom wide of the mark, especially when it addressed—in the poet's veiled but firm manner—the crimes and criminals of the Stalinist years, as in the poem "Galilei":

Those who till then seemed to stand securely
suddenly grew fearful that they'd fall.
Trembling church-fathers felt that surely
this would wreck their good, old-fashioned world.

Like Alver, Sang was also active as a translator of poetry, specializing in German (Goethe's *Faust*, Heine, and Brecht), Russian (Nekrassov), and French (Molière). The career of Sang's widow, Kersti Merilaas, ran roughly parallel to those of both her husband and Alver insofar as Merilaas, too, saw her first collection of verse published in the 1930s, did not participate actively in literary life for decades, and emerged as a poet again in the 1960s. Merilaas painted a poetic picture of the Estonian literary scene of the early 1960s in "Ööbikute org" [The Valley of Nightingales], written in 1963:

On high, on the hilltops, a new renascence rustles.
But below
from between the green banks of the valley,
as slender as a buggy-whip there rises

a quiet
blue curl
   of smoke—
from your pipe, my beloved.

       .   .   .   .

It will be good for us then to serve our dear guests
my yellow curdcakes
and feel on our shoulders the weight of their feet.

In addition to Jaan Kross, the two most important poets
who could be viewed as situated between the separate generations portrayed in Merilaas's poem are Ain Kaalep and
Artur Alliksaar. Alliksaar's verse, an important factor—
along with his personal influence—in the development of many
younger poets of the 1960s, was known only through privately
circulated manuscripts until 1968, largely because he declined
to compromise with the authorities who supervised publication.

Alliksaar died of cancer in 1966. His first published work,
which appeared in 1968, was thus posthumous—a selection
made by the young poet Paul-Eerik Rummo entitled *Olematus
võiks ju ka olemata olla* [Nonbeing Might as Well Not Have
Been]. In a review of this work in *Books Abroad* (1968, no. 4,
pp. 621-622), Ivar Ivask notes that Alliksaar appears to have
been influenced by the exile Estonian poet Ilmar Laaban, and
indeed, that "after Laaban, Alliksaar is the second genuine
surrealist in modern Estonian poetry."

Similarly, although Kaalep published his first poem in 1949,
his first collection appeared thirteen years later. Kaalep's
Samarkandi vihik [Samarkand Notebook], 1962, appeared in
15,000 copies, reportedly the largest first printing ever recorded for any first collection of poetry in the world. The
manuscripts of *Samarkandi vihik* and *Aomaastikud* [Dawn
Landscapes], also issued in 1962, were not published until
years after they had been submitted, in spite of Kaalep's great
productivity in periodicals as a poet and translator of poetry
since the middle 1950s. (Kaalep is one of the most prolific and
versatile translators in the history of Estonian literature, and
some of his best work has been done in this capacity.) Two
additional Kaalep collections have appeared since then: *Järve-
maastikud* [Lake Landscapes], in 1968, and *Klaasmaastikud*

[Glass Landscapes], in 1971. Kaalep's *oeuvre* is distinguished by the author's mastery of form and his commitment to statement, the latter feature repeatedly having generated friction with the literary watchdogs. Minni Nurme, who is chiefly known for her elegiac verse about the soil of Estonia and the families it has nurtured and whose work has enriched Estonian poetry, might also be mentioned as part of this subgeneration.

By 1963, then, it was clear that a new generation of poets had emerged; a generation better educated and more accomplished poetically than all but a few of its predecessors; a generation disposed to decide more critically—and hence more freely— which styles of dress and thought and life and poetry it favored. Rather than apologizing for the past and cosmeticizing the present, the younger poets looked to the future in terms of themselves as individual artists, as in this excerpt from V. Villandi's "Mina ja masin" [The Machine and I] (*Looming*, 1964):

> . . . I am replete like a winepress
> with thoughts of my very own.
> They boil and ferment within me.
> Spuming, now and then I pop my cork
> and spill over,
> on the wrong side, perhaps.
>
> Orders are fine things
> and someone must obey them—
> otherwise there would be no order.
> But must it be *me*
> who piles the dead birchlogs
> into wooden stacks
> with their dry bark crackling?
>
> Why is it, then, that empty kegs
> do not forgive the full winepress?
> Why do stacks of cordwood hate
> the growing birchtrees?

The younger generation had demonstrated its undeniable talent and had won both popular support and critical acclaim. In 1966, at the peak of the postwar renascence of Estonian poetry, twenty books of verse were published in quantity—a figure which strongly suggests that Estonia produced more volumes of verse per capita than any other nation in the world. Yet no true revolution in the arts can be sustained for long without compromising its novelty, creative force, and aesthetic level: imitation and repetition of success soon leads to standardization; defense of unprecedented achievement ends in consolidation. By the late 1960s the renascence was clearly over, although its fruits are still being reaped.

The first years of the 1970s have suggested that a mood of reflection, experimentation with forms and formats, and occasional stridency will characterize Estonian poetry during this decade. As of this writing, Paul-Eerik Rummo has not yet revealed the new poetic course he undoubtedly is charting; Kaplinski's most recent collection suggests condensed, thoughtful stasis cut by the edge of despair (like Merilaas, he turned to writing drama and prose in the 1970s). Jüri Üdi's wit and amazing virtuosity with form and rhyme leave no doubt about his skill as a verbal conjurer, while not yet establishing him as a singer or seer quite on a level with his immediate predecessors. Nevertheless, Üdi's sensibility is so unusual and his gifts are so singular that he may well mold popular and critical taste in the wake of his literary production. And, just as Üdi has recently written award-winning prose, so Andres Ehin, among the most promising younger poets of the later 1960s, has penned a well-received drama. Mats Traat has published two short novels along with many stories; like Kaplinski and other poets, he has turned increasingly to writing verse in the South Estonian dialect. Johnny B. Isotamm, especially popular from public readings of his verse, has enriched the force, candor, and intimacy of the poetic idiom of his language.

The apparent stasis of Estonian poetry in the early 1970s may indicate that the genre has arrived, not at a dead end, but rather at the juncture of the realizations commonly termed existentialist and grotesque with the instinctual realities of sex and death. In order to progress, the medium will have to invest the erotic with an appropriate literary form—a form infused with a viscerally convincing content drawn from a penetrating awareness of death. The result will be the portrayal of the human condition as a mystery—an enigma for which neither the older Estonian poets nor dialectical materialism has furnished a satisfactory answer. Indeed, it may turn out that prose, rather than poetry, will offer this envisioned synthesis.

Prose

Since the history of the Soviet Estonian novel is patterned somewhat differently from that of poetry, it is too early even at this writing to consider the Estonian long-prose genre as having reached maturity. Indeed, future historians of Estonian prose may well concur that after more than one-third of a century of Soviet control of literature, the post-1940 Estonian novel has not yet regained the prewar level. Of course, the writing of aesthetically sound long-prose narratives to the prescription set by socialist realism was not by any means easy. The task was not made lighter by the virtual absence of a precedent: with the exception of several proletarian novels from the early 1920s, along with fragments published in the Soviet Union during the following decade, Estonian prose in the approved mode simply did not exist. Until 1955 only five Soviet Estonian authors managed to publish novels at all—for a grand total of eight books—and the majority of these works fared badly at the hands of party critics. For example, in 1951, volume 1 of the soundest of these novels, Aadu Hint's multi-volume *Tuuline rand* [The Windy Coast], a work dealing with the revolution of 1905 on the Estonian islands, was scored for (1) not treating the Russo-Japanese war in greater detail, (2) paying relatively little attention to the characters' attitude toward the czar, and (3) not stressing the leading role of the Russian proletariat during the abortive revolution. In brief, the historical novel was expected to be a dogmatic textbook. Furthermore, former "bourgeois writers" (for example, R. Roht, O. Luts, and E. Krusten) who tried to adjust to the new requirements during the 1940s and early 1950s were criticized on both ideological grounds, for not distinguishing between "essential" and "nonessential" facts, and aesthetic grounds, for trying to accommodate the new ideology by introducing extraneous characters whose sole function was to pronounce Communist verities.

During the war years and the ensuing decade, the short story fared somewhat better; at least that genre appeared more frequently and was less frequently subjected to adverse criticism. The narrower focus and correspondingly greater selectivity characteristic of the shorter prose form generated, first, a spate of "patriotic" tales connected with the war and, later, didactic, exhortative stories about industrialization, the cold war (including occasional references to the menace posed by emigré Estonians), and the collectivization of agriculture. Typical plots involved the crypto-*kulak* who systematically sabotaged a factory or collective farm until he was found out by an alert party member and the ideologically wavering intellectual who was set on the only true path by a Communist worker or collective farmer. Kääri and Peep considered the most important characteristic of Estonian prose of this period to be the fact that "literary characters were almost entirely determined by their social position. The plot, in its turn, was determined by the laws of class struggle. . ." (1965:29). On the whole, the literature of this period was characterized by rational constructivity and by the underestimation of the emotional power of belles lettres.

With the change in political climate that occurred during the mid-1950s, the Estonian novel began to chart a new course. The turning point in this regard may well have been Rudolf Sirge's *Maa ja rahvas* [The Land and the People], 1956, a novel set in rural Estonia during the pivotal year 1940. Sirge's work was the first Soviet Estonian novel to avoid—albeit only sporadically—the vulgar historical myths, pat ideological answers, and stereotyped cast of characters typical of earlier long-prose works. Thus, while the cryptofascist villain of Sirge's book has false teeth, speaks in an affected, foreign manner, and smokes opiated cigarettes, the author manages to view the villain's *kulak* father with some sympathy, even investing him with many traditional virtues, including religiosity. Prior to the publication of Sirge's work, the historical novel had established itself as the most acceptable type of prose narrative; earlier revolutionary periods, seen in terms of official historical myth, understandably were the safest epochs to portray.

In the early 1960s the themes treated in Soviet Estonian prose broadened, most outstandingly in novels by Raimond Kaugver, Villem Gross, and Aimée and Vladimir Beekman. Nevertheless, the authors' basic approach continued to be the same.

As was the case with poetry, however, the 1960s witnessed the debut of a younger generation of prose writers who were equipped—and were permitted—to depart significantly from the somewhat orthodox and dreary style, themes, and attitudes of their elders. It is significant that in most cases the younger generation chose forms briefer than the panoramic novel—

short novels, stories, and prose miniatures—as its favored modes of literary expression. (During this period the influx and influence on all of the arts, including literature, of such movements as Italian neo-Realism, the French *nouveau roman*, abstract expressionism from America, and the angry young man from Britain—with his American beatnik second cousin—began to be evident.)

One of the most original and provocative authors among the younger generation of prose writers who emerged in the 1960s was Arvo Valton, whose first collection of stories and miniatures revealed and probed the significance of apparently insignificant people and objects to the contemporary Estonian scene with a lightness of touch and undercurrent of melancholy that soon became the author's trademarks. During the second half of the decade, Valton's prose gained in allegorical resonances; during the 1970s his work has continued to expand, not only widening in temporal and spatial perspective but also evidencing a decided turn toward the problematical and grotesque. Valton's stories have already been translated into more than a dozen languages; should circumstances permit, he is sure to make a contribution as a novelist as well.

Even more typical of the mood of the middle 1960s was the writing of the precocious Mati Unt—who, gifted with the ability to write the kind of fluent, seemingly effortless prose which all too often was absent from earlier Soviet Estonian writing, published two short novels before the age of twenty. The second of these, *Võlg* [The Debt], published in 1964, ranks as one of the turning points of Estonian prose, a breakthrough as thematically and technically decisive as that achieved by the new poetry of the period. In addition to its insistence on the uniqueness of the individual, Unt's short novel was also regarded as "bold" by official literary standards in its treatment of sex and politics. The quintessence of communism was expressed by Unt's protagonist not in ideological terms but in the simple desire to "wish a stranger a good appetite and be answered with a smile." The rusty-zippered puritanism of earlier prose treatments of love provoked this reaction on the part of Unt's teen-aged hero: "Our books have a damnably small vocabulary for that kind of thing: 'He stayed for the night'; 'She spent the night with him'; 'He turned off the nightlamp.' Don't you sometimes have the feeling that the majority of Estonian writers are eunuchs?" After a period of activity as a playwright and of association with the Tartu theater, Unt returned in the early 1970s to the long story form, in which he appears to be gathering momentum for a creative effort of wider scope.

In 1968 Ivar Ivask stated, "Besides Mati Unit, [E.] Vetemaa is the most original young prose-writer in Estonia today" (*Books Abroad*, 1968:310-311). Vetemaa, who had made his debut as a poet in the early 1960s, addressed himself to the acute problem of personal conscience during the Stalinist years in two short novels set in the capital city of Tallinn: *Monument* [The Monument], 1965, and *Pillimees* [Musician], 1967. It remains to be seen how Vetemaa, who has recently been active as a playwright and satirist, will continue to deploy his undeniable gifts as a writer. In the meantime, his collected fiction has been published in a second edition of two volumes.

Perhaps the most significant development in recent Estonian prose has been the startlingly successful debut of Jaan Kross as a historical novelist. Kross, whose first published collection of poetry was virtually epochmaking, turned in 1970 to historical prose. Writing in an archaic style imitative of the language of an earlier age (as first essayed in Estonia by the Finnish writer Aino Kallas) and perceiving in former times analogies to the present (in a manner similar to that of the emigré novelist Karl Ristikivi), Kross has managed to bring the history of his beloved capital city to life through an artistic synthesis of accurate detail, verbal flourishes (including occasional Low German interpolations characteristic of the speech of Hanseatic Tallinn centuries ago), and contemporary relevance. In *Neli monoloogi Püha Jüri asjus* [Four Monologues concerning St. George], 1970, expressing an affirmation of the right to live reminiscent of the work of Bertolt Brecht, Kross has his hero, the native Estonian painter Michael Sittow, hesitate before deciding to meet the requirements set by the local, German-controlled artists' guild, but then accede. "But what of it?" Kross's Sittow reflects. "This form of self-defense must be allowed me—in the name of my sweetheart, this precious town, and all else that is dear to me." Thus the Estonian painter submits to the formal demands set by his artistic inferiors, secure in the knowledge that there will be time enough for the important things, "once the town has become mine, as it justly should."

L. Promet, A. Beekman, and M. Traat also deserve mention

among the writers of Soviet Estonian prose of the 1960s, as
does J. Smuul. Smuul, productive in many genres and chairman of the Writers' Union of the Estonian SSR from 1953 until
his death in 1969, made his prose debut in 1955 with *Kirjad
sôgedate külast* [Letters from the Village of the Blind], which,
in spite of its own blindness and boy scout–like didacticism,
was a cut above some of the other prose being published at the
time. Smuul also had the distinction of having authored the
Estonian work that has become the most popular (in terms of
number of editions, number of copies, and number of languages into which it has been translated) outside of Estonia's
borders, *Jäine raamat* [The Icy Book], 1959.

The major prose genre, the novel, has been hampered in its
development by the official requirements of political orthodoxy, by puritanical restrictions on the treatment of love and
death, and by the unspeakable bugbears of formalism and
aestheticism. Common examples of such obstacles were the
frustrating demands made by editors (who usually also served
as censors and publishers) on novelists for extensive, time-
consuming, almost always vitiating revisions of manuscripts
submitted for publication. This trend began as early as 1940,
during the first year of Soviet rule, when the veteran novelist
Mait Metsanurk repeatedly attempted to "improve" the manuscript of his "Suvine pööripaev" [The Summer Solstice]—
apparently never managing to satisfy the authorities, for the
novel has remained unpublished. Even authors who enjoyed
official favor, for example Jakobson and Sirge, were induced
to revise novels first published during the prewar years.
Without exception, in spite of the time and energy spent in
attempting to align new versions of works with the critical
perspectives that prevailed after 1940, such revisions have been
failures. Thus it comes as no surprise that during the 1970s,
when Estonian prose has been in a situation of dynamic flux
comparable to that of poetry a decade earlier, shorter forms,
rather than the exhaustive or panoramic novel, have held
center stage.

A second salient feature of recent Estonian prose is its search
(perhaps because of the restrictions placed on the long novel)
for new dimensions. As examples of such new dimensions,
consider the use of dialect (such as the South Estonian employed by Traat or the islanders' idiom recorded by Smuul);

the archaism of Kross, Valton, Peegel, and Vetemaa; the exploration of historical perspectives beyond the official Marxian versions of revolutionary periods; and the increasing attention devoted to allegory, especially to myth.

Translations and Literary Criticism

Between the years 1940 and 1968, translations accounted for 62 percent of the belles lettres published in Estonian. This statistic—which, of course, does not take into consideration the appreciable Estonian literature published in the West since the war—appears less startling if we consider, first, that all highly literate (and literary) small nations "import" a large quantity of foreign literature and, second, that the Soviet annexation of Estonia brought with it a Russian cultural imperialism. In 1940, the number of works translated from Russian into Estonian rose sharply. Not until after 1955 did Russian literature to some degree give way to other literatures of the world in furnishing reading matter for the Estonian public.

From 1940 to 1955, 611 volumes were translated from Russian into Estonian, while 153 volumes stemming originally from beyond the USSR—many of which originated in the people's republics—were translated into Estonian during the same period. (The number of Estonian originals published during these years was 676, while 92 volumes were translated into Estonian from other languages of the Soviet Union.) In the subsequent decade (1956-1965), the number of translations of Russian works dropped to 423, while non-Soviet translations—including those from the people's republics— rose to 525. (During this decade, 655 original Estonian works appeared, along with translations of 119 pieces from other languages of the USSR.)

Statistics cited in 1967 tend to support the view that the popular demand for translations of Soviet literature was not nearly so great as the official pressure for producing them: between 1940 and 1965 nearly 1,200 literary works by Soviet writers were translated into Estonian in some 14 million copies, while a circulation of more than 13.5 million was enjoyed by the fewer than 700 titles translated from non-Soviet sources.

Bare statistics do not, of course, tell the entire story. Thus, while by 1972 literature from sixty-eight languages, representing writing from eighty-five lands, was reported to be available to the Estonian reader, it should be remembered that until the mid-1950s, translations were regularly "improved" by means of blatant omissions and tendentious renderings. Even in the 1960s, Estonian translations of foreign literature were often introduced by lengthy prefaces (or followed by afterwords) designed to promote orthodox interpretations of the text in question; apparent heresies were neutralized by explanatory notes. Even under such conditions, however, there was ample room for the individual Estonian translator to achieve positive results and for staffs of translators to perform an important service for their native literature by judiciously selecting and ably translating foreign masterworks that were acceptable to the authorities. While as recently as 1960 it was not unheard of for an Estonian translation from some other language to be based on a Russian version of the foreign work, at present there exists an active cadre of translators—many of them original literary artists in their own right—competent to render masterpieces from the world's two dozen or so major literary languages (not to mention many lesser-known ones) directly into Estonian. As a result, most of the classics of world literature, from Homer to Hemingway, can be read in Estonian versions, and translated contemporary literature appears frequently (chiefly in the inexpensive and popular series *Loomingu raamatukogu* [The Library of *Looming*], which was initiated in 1957). In all, about 2,300 translations of foreign literature have been published in Soviet Estonia, totaling more than 35 million copies (Nirk, 1970:292).

It is interesting to note that many works which apparently have not been translated into Russian or Ukrainian have been published in Estonian. Kafka's *Trial*, for example, appeared in Estonian in 1966, prefaced by a translation of the chapter on Kafka from Roger Garaudy's controversial book *D'un realisme sans rivages*. More recently, works by such writers as Peter Weiss, Albert Camus, Harold Pinter, Isaak Babel, and Mihkail Bulgakov have appeared in Estonian versions. Moreover, masterful translations of such poems as Brecht's "An die Nachgeborenen" and Eluard's "Liberté" have served significantly to supplement original Estonian poetry.

Among foreign literatures, the one most in evidence has of course been Russian. Maxim Gorky's theories about socialist realism and his practice of writing *ocherki* (documentary sketches) are reflected in Estonian literature, even as the Estonian novels of the 1950s were clearly influenced by the Russian "epic" novel. Mayakovsky, Sholokhov, and Tvardovsky are among other contemporary Russian writers who, along with the nineteenth-century Russian classics, have left an imprint upon Soviet Estonian letters. (The relationships between these two literatures have been extensively studied and are beyond the province of this chapter.) Until the mid-1950s, however, almost anything "progressive" to found in all of Estonian literature was ascribed to the salutary influence of Russia. A more objective balance in the study of Russo-Estonian literary relations has been reached during the last fifteen years.

Among Western writers, those major figures whose political persuasion has been acceptable—e.g., Eluard, Neruda, Aragon, Brecht, and Sartre (although Sartre was branded "a tool of the Maoists" in 1973)—have been most often translated. Twain, Hemingway, and Salinger rank among the most popular American writers, and Heinrich Heine has fascinated Estonian poets and translators since the last century. It should be noted, however, that there is a world of difference between translation statistics and actual influence on Soviet Estonian literature: the former are based on empirical fact; the latter remains problematical and needs further study.

A second problematical area is the relationship between Estonian emigré literature and Soviet Estonian writing. By the mid-1960s, the works of a number of formerly ignored or even abused emigré writers began to be openly discussed and published. Well before that time, the influence of the emigré poets Ilmar Laaban and Kalju Lepik and of the novelist Karl Ristikivi, all residents of Sweden, could be discerned in Soviet Estonian letters. However, the trend toward dealing with emigré writers openly seems to have been retarded and even reversed since about 1970. Someday, pre-Soviet literature in Estonia (along with the literary depiction of pre-Soviet society) will no doubt be studied, as will the Soviet reaction to emigré literature and the Soviet fictional portrayal of emigré life. At present, however, these topics are too sensitive for investigation in Soviet Estonia.

A related area of study involves literary relations between the three Baltic republics—Estonia, Latvia, and Lithuania.

While scholarly inquiry in this field conducted in the West (for example, within the framework of the Association for the Advancement of Baltic Studies) is derided by Soviet commentators, efforts have been made within the USSR to explore this area. Thus, in 1968 writers and critics representing the three Baltic languages met in Tallinn, joined by their colleagues from Moscow, in order to discuss "new trends in the prose of the Baltic republics."

A final word remains to be said about the proliferation of Soviet Estonian literature outside the Estonian SSR. According to recent statistics cited by P. Rummo (*Looming*, 1972:1530-1551) and Mallene (1973), 930 works of Estonian belles lettres have been translated into forty-two languages. More than half of these works appeared in Russian. Of the total, 708 were rendered into twenty languages of the Soviet Union and 222 into other languages, chiefly those of the people's republics but also including Spanish, Dutch, English, Japanese, French, Swedish, and Finnish. (The majority of the translations into Western languages were prepared in Moscow.)

While many of the Estonian works translated into the lesser-known languages of the Soviet Union were first translated into Russian, these Russian translations have been executed by such capable artists as A. Akhmatova and V. Rozhdestvenski. Nevertheless, it should be noted that artistic merit is seldom the sole criterion for selecting Estonian writing for translation. Consider, for example, the fact that the Estonian poets Beekman, Parve, Raud, Smuul, and Vaarandi—all members of the Communist party—were represented in Russian translation by a total of twenty-six works, while the group of Alver, Kaplinski, Kross, P.-E. Rummo, and Sang—several levels above the former quintet in literary importance and quality—can show only three volumes translated into Russian among them. That a similar situation obtains for the translation of Estonian prose suggests that a second order of official censorship operates in selecting the Estonian material that is to be translated and still a third in choosing the languages into which these works are rendered.

During the war years there was little published of literary theory, criticism, or history. Those writers as well as critics who remained active were groping in an effort to master the new "method" of socialist realism in a manner that would promote their continued existence as living Estonian writers. What criticism was published in the immediate postwar years was not yet completely prescriptive or defensive, for it was written largely by the writers themselves. At the First Congress of the Soviet Estonian Writers' Union in 1946, for example, while "formalism" was perceived to be an enemy of the development of Soviet poetry, the term had not yet been insanely misconstrued, nor was emphasis on poetic form seen as necessarily harmful. Soon thereafter, however, all published criticism began to reflect the *proletkult* line; the "typical" hero now required of literature had in fact to be an active, faultless Communist, and the "theory" of the absence of social conflicts was advanced as a prescription to all writers. All reference to form in literature disappeared, inasmuch as form was interpreted as a vestige of "formalism." In short, literary scholarship was paralyzed. From 1948 to 1954, not a single critical or scholarly book appeared in Estonia, with the dubious exception of vulgar school texts (under the editorship of E. Sôgel) which made no mention whatsoever of the subsequently rehabilitated deans of Soviet Estonian literature, F. Tuglas and J. Semper, nor of the twentieth-century Estonian classics written by G. Suits, M. Under, and H. Visnapuu (the latter three had emigrated to the West). Meanwhile, judging from the agenda, the Second Congress of the Soviet Estonian Writers' Union, held in 1951, was devoted exclusively to the discussion of Stalin's brilliant work in linguistics and its application to the fields of Estonian literature, Soviet literature, and scholarly translation. Similarly, literary scholarship at the University of Tartu during this period consisted of little more than a skein of quotations from Marx, Lenin, and Stalin, interspersed with other slogans and an occasional textual reference.

After the Twentieth Party Congress and Khrushchev's official denunciation of the "cult of personality" in 1956, almost all of the literary arbiters—who apparently had experienced little difficulty of conscience in maintaining their positions during the previous decade—began to change their collective tune. They, too, now loaned their voices, virtually in chorus, to denouncing earlier "mistakes." However, the twin specters of rebellion abroad and revisionism within soon halted the thaw. In the Soviet literary sphere, the heresies of Lukács in Hungary and Vidmar in Yugoslavia were regarded as especially menacing, insofar as the former questioned the

Marxist premise that a writer's political views were of primary importance to his artistic creation and the latter outrageously suggested that if literature wished to retain its true function, it should continue to be critical—even, if need be, of Marxist society itself.

Moscow's negative reaction to revisionism was all the encouragement that certain crypto-Stalinist Estonian critics needed. After the Twenty-first Party Congress had officially branded impressionism, symbolism, futurism, expressionism, surrealism, and existentialism as decadent, these critics emerged once more, in full force and in good voice. P. Kuusberg's paranoid blustering against those writers who did not rush to place their talents in the service of a Stalinized Estonia and against those critics who dared harbor views different from his own is a matter of record. Yet, when no new Stalin-like regime developed after the thaw, such literary hacks as Ants Saar, E. Sôgel, and E. Päll found it convenient to subscribe to a pendulum "theory" of literary opinion, of course staking out for themselves the territory of the golden mean. What virtually amounted to an ill-disguised neo-Stalinism was now, according to Saar, to be the happy medium between the extremes of toadyism and slander. Meanwhile, the problem of responsibility was easily disposed of by this same clique, functioning as its own judge and jury. "We will take care of our own errors," Saar wrote. "We will not come asking for advice from the likes of you" (see *Looming*, 1962:923).

Saar was responding to the challenge posed by the younger Estonian literati and to the ever-convenient "bourgeois" element. The fact that this posture was sustained is revealed in Beekman's later judgment that writers whose works embodied "abstractionism, formalism, and decadence" were guilty of attempting "to erode Soviet society from within" (*Looming*, 1963) and in Sôgel's remarks to his colleagues at the Fifth Congress of Soviet Estonian Writers in 1966. "We already have artistic freedom," Sôgel declared, concluding that "any argument concerning this question is not necessary" (*Looming*, 1966:497).

The power of such a reactionary critical mentality was also exerted closer to the roots of imaginative literature; namely, upon the manuscripts of younger authors. Writers who had submitted their prose to nationwide competitions received ideological guidance from such reliable counselors as A. Hint, who in 1961 railed against interior monologues and in one case complained that a male character "thinks somehow in a feminine manner, like an affected old maid." In the same year, P. Kuusberg puzzled over the apparent lack of "social function" in submitted poetry and prose. Certain "authorities" on poetry in about the same period fastened on such features as lack of punctuation and "impurity" of rhyme in their criticisms. A catalogue of such guidance received by younger Estonian writers would make sad reading indeed, except for the happy fact that it was, whenever possible, blithely ignored—as both the poetic renascence of the 1960s and the advances in prose of recent years give witness.

Nevertheless, different conclusions—drawn, admittedly, from Marxist premises—continued to be expressed. The Russian critic V. Turbin's controversial book *Comrade Time, Comrade Art* (1961) made an impression on literary theory and criticism, as did R. Garaudy's *D'un realisme sans rivages* (1963). Although the Soviet worker was praised in Estonia in 1961 as "rising ever higher on the wall of the Communist edifice which he is building," in the following year readers of *Literaturnaya Gazeta* made the acquaintance of a forced-labor camp mason named Ivan Denisovich. Humanism, heretofore contemptuously prefixed by the term "abstract," became "militant humanism" in Marxist jargon when its existence could no longer be denied.

In 1968 B. Runin, a Moscow literary critic, addressing himself primarily to Estonian literature, praised both A. Solzhenitsyn and the Estonian prose writer M. Unt as "having begun to reclaim the eternal and absolute virtues of generosity, honesty, etc." Similarly, the formerly maligned *Bildungsroman* was accommodated into official critical schemes. In short, the dictatorially prescriptive function of the critic began to give way, in the mid-1960s, to a more interpretive, theoretical, and speculative role. It was indeed high time, for, as V. Lakshin observed, "Criticism does not yet have the required authority in the eyes of readers—chiefly because it has not managed entirely to free itself from the burden of dogmatic thinking which became rooted during the postwar years" (*Novy Mir*, 1965). Thus, by the late 1960s, problems of form and content and nationalism in literature were being discussed, and trailblazing studies were being made in semiotics at Tartu. However, critics still tended to avoid thorough treatment of stylistics—perhaps because of the old bugbear of "formalism"—and the study of the sociology of literature was largely avoided, probably because its findings might conflict too clearly with the ideological function assigned to belles lettres or tend to expose to public scrutiny the actual mechanics of censorship. Like the literary essay, the critical essay—because its inherent nature implied freedom and originality—remained in eclipse, and Estonian literary critics continued to be hampered by lack of access to the work of their Western colleagues. It is not surprising, therefore, that in the 1970s the book review has emerged as the primary critical genre, with the historical dimension evidenced in longer articles commemorating authors' birthdays. Open-ended theoretical discussions continue to appear infrequently, and only under special circumstances.

The absence of intellectual rigor in developing, defining, and defending socialist realism as a critical and creative method is well known. Indeed, debates about the nature and limits of socialist realism virtually amount to a new scholasticism, which, at the time of this writing, has not yet been crowned by a *summa* of any rigor that stands in close relation to the real world. Therefore, it is not surprising that Soviet Estonian critics whose purposes are served by adhering to the official doctrine have been no more successful—nor less obscure—than others in their treatment of socialist realism. It is, after all, a simple matter to express the opinion that literature should reflect actual life; it is an enterprise of a significantly higher order of difficulty to diagram the optics of this "reflection." As a result, since the mid-1950s the trend in Soviet Estonia has been to muddle through, permitting a broad-enough gamut—under existing circumstances—of literary styles and critical views. None of these views, however, is permitted to challenge directly the basic premises of the state or its doctrine of art—in short, to criticize the official mythology. Consequently, since about 1960 the tendency in Estonia has been for both writers and critics to remain within the prescribed boundaries, but to go about their business without paying much attention to specific restrictions. This is, of course, not to say that state control over literature has in any way ceased to make itself felt. Statistics from 1940 to 1965 strongly indicate that a writer whose views are in accord with those of the state will be published and translated far more widely, irrespective of artistic merit, than a writer who is viewed less favorably by the authorities. In the twenty-five-year period after 1950, the following authors, almost all of them party members, published the following numbers of editions: V. Beekman, nineteen; A. Hint, twenty-six; A. Jakobson, fifty-seven; M. Kesamaa, twenty-three; F. Kotta, twenty-two; E. Krusten, nineteen; R. Parve, thirty-nine; E. Rannet, nineteen; M. Raud, twenty-two; J. Smuul, twenty-eight. Contrast these statistics with the numbers of volumes published by B. Alver (one), A. Kaalep (two), J. Kross (three), and A. Sang (two) during the same period, in spite of the fact that the latter group of four, from the standpoint of the aesthetic excellence of their (however limited) production, clearly outweighs the former group of ten.

Statistics tend further to suggest that the disproportion in published volumes such as that cited above does not reflect the reading preferences of the public. In 1963, for example, only 1.2 readers per month borrowed V. Beekman's *Ida Euroopa valgus* [Light in Eastern Europe] from the M. Gorky Library in Tallinn, in spite of the fact that this collection of poems had received much official critical praise, while 4.4 readers per month checked out A. Kaalep's *Aomaastikud* [Dawn Landscapes] from the same lending library; the corresponding figure for A. Sang's *Vôileib suudlusega* [A Sandwich and a Kiss] was 8.0 (see *Looming*, 1964).

Thus, one can propose the thesis that almost every real advance, every enduring achievement—and there have been many—in Estonian literature under Soviet rule has occurred in spite of and counter to the spirit of prevailing dogma.

References

Aarna, A., et al., eds.

1975   *Nôukogude Eesti: entsüklopeediline teatmeteos* [Soviet Estonia: An Encyclopedic Reference Work]. Tallinn: Valgus.

Adson, Artur

1962   "Ob estonskoi proze." *Novii Zhurnal* 70: 114-125.

Aspel, Aleksander

1968   "Littérature Estonienne," in *Encyclopédie de la Pléi-
        ade*. Histoire des Littératures 2: Littératures Occi-
        dentales, second ed. Paris.
1969   "The Hour of Destiny: The Poetry of Betti Alver."
        Books Abroad 43 (Winter): 46-49.

Beekman, Vladimir

1971   "Eesti nõukogude kirjanduse arengujoontest ja prob-
        leemidest kahe kongressi vahel 1966-1971" [On De-
        velopments and Problems in Estonian Soviet Litera-
        ture between the Two Congresses, 1966-1971].
        Looming, no. 6.

Grabbi, Hellar

1973   "For a New Heaven and a New Earth: Comments on
        the Poetry of Jaan Kaplinski." *Books Abroad* 47
        (Autumn): 656-663.

Grünthal, Ivar

1970   "Får då en sanning vara enkel? Ny estnisk lyrik"
        [May a Truth Be Simple? New Estonian Poetry].
        Horisont (Organ för Svenska Österbottens Littera-
        turförening) 17.

Ivask, Ivar

1965   "The Main Traditions of Estonian Poetry," in *Esto-
        nian Language and Poetry*, ed. Viktor Kõressaar and
        Aleksis Rannit. New York: Estonian Learned Socie-
        ty in America.
1966   "Viron runouden elävä perinne: Heiti Talvik - Betti
        Alver" [The Living Tradition of Estonian Poetry:
        Heiti Talvik and Betti Alver]. *Suomalainen Soumi*
        34: 224-231.
1968   "Recent Trends in Estonian Poetry." *Books Abroad*
        42 (Autumn): 517-520.
1970   "Window-Comlex and Street-Labyrinth: The Prose
        of M. Unt and E. Vetemaa." *Lituanus* 16 (Summer):
        29-37.

1973a   "Baltic Literatures in Exile: Balance of a Quarter
         Century," in *Baltic Literature and Linguistics*, ed.
         Arvids Ziedonis et al. Columbus, Ohio: Association
         for the Advancement of Baltic Studies.
1973b   "Estonian Literature," in *World Literature since
         1945*, ed. Ivar Ivask and Gero von Wilpert. New
         York: Frederick Ungar.
1975   "The Dream Poetry of the Estonian Poet George
         Marrow." *Journal of Baltic Studies* 6 (Summer/
         Fall): 185-189.
1976   "Estonian Literature," in *Columbia Dictionary of
         Modern European Literature*, ed. Horatio Smith and
         Jean-Albert Bede. New York: Columbia University
         Press.

Jänes, Henno

1965   *Geschichte der estnischen Literatur*. Studies in His-
         tory of Literature no. 8, Acta Universitatis Stockhol-
         miensis. Stockholm: Almquist and Wiksell.

Jüriado, Andres

1973   "Nationalism vs. Socialism in Soviet Estonian Dra-
         ma." *Lituanus* 19 (Summer): 28-42.

Jürma, Mall

1959   "Literature in Soviet Occupied Estonia." *Baltic Re-
         view*, no. 16, pp. 54-61.
1966a   "Sowietisierung der Literatur in Estland." *Acta Bal-
         tica* 5 (1965): 200-216.
1966b   "Literature in Estonia." *Baltic Review*, no. 32, pp. 28-
         40.

Kääri, Kalju, comp.

1975   *Kirjandus kriitiku pilguga* [Literature from the View-
         point of the Critic]. Tallinn: Eesti Raamat.

Kääri, Kalju, and Harald Peep

1965   *A Glimpse into Soviet Estonian Literature*. Tallinn:
         Eesti Raamat.

Kangro, Bernard

1965 "Eesti kirjandus siin- ja sealpool piiri" [Estonian Literature on This and That Side of the Border]. Part 1, *Tulimuld* 16, no. 2: 112-118; part 2, ibid., no. 3: 175-182; part 3, ibid., no. 4: 231-239.

Kurman, George

1972 *Literatures in Contact: Finland and Estonia.* New York: Estonian Learned Society in America.
1974 "Vaino Vahing and Soviet Estonian Literature." *Journal of Baltic Studies* 5 (Winter): 385-395.

Kurrik, Maire

1973 "Juhan Smuul's Moral Propaganda." *Journal of Baltic Studies* 4 (Fall): 226-235.
1975 "Modernism in Estonia: the Prose of Mati Unt." *Journal of Baltic Studies* 6 (Summer/Fall): 170-179.

Kuusberg, Paul

1966 "Eesti nôukogude kirjanduse arengujoontest aastail 1959-1965" [On Developments in Estonian Soviet Literature during the Years 1959-1965]. *Looming*, no. 3.

Looming

Soviet Estonian literary and cultural monthly.

Mägi, Arvo

1965 *Viron kirjallisuuden historia* [A History of Estonian Literature], trans. M. Rauhala. Helsinki: Suomen Kirjallisuuden Seura.
1968 *Estonian Literature: An Outline.* Stockholm: Baltic Humanitarian Association.
1972 "Kodumaine kirjanduselu" [Literary Life in the Homeland], in *Eesti saatusaastad 1945-1960*, vol. 6, ed. Richard Maasing et al. Stockholm: Kirjastus EMP.
1973 "Uuemast kodumaisest eepikast" [On New Develop-

ments in the Epic in the Homeland]. *Tulimuld* 24, no. 2: 94-99.

1974   "Uuemast kodumaisest lüürikast" [On New Developments in Lyrics in the Homeland]. *Tulimuld* 25, no. 2: 81-85.

Mallene, Endel

1973   *Estonskaya Literatura v 1971 Godu.* Tallinn: Eesti Raamat.

Nirk, Endel

1970   *Estonian Literature: Historical Survey with Biobibliographical Appendix.* Tallinn: Eesti Raamat.

Nirk, Endel, and Endel Sögel, comps.

1975   *Eesti kirjanduse biograafiline leksikon* [Biographical Dictionary of Estonian Literature]. Tallinn: Eesti Raamat.

Oras, Ants, with E. Blese and A. Senn

1969   *Storia delle letterature Baltiche*, second ed. Milano.

Parming, Tönu

1977   "Developments in Nationalism in Soviet Estonia since 1964," in *Nationalism in the Soviet Union and Eastern Europe under Brezhnev and Kosygin*, ed. G. Simmonds. Detroit: University of Detroit Press.

Peep, Harald

1967   *Soviet Estonian Literature.* Ten Aspects of Estonian Life Series. Tallinn: Eesti Raamat.

Puhvel, Jaan

1969   "From Golden Hoop to Shifting Rainbow: The Seven Creative Decades of Friedebert Tuglas." *Books Abroad* 43: 365-367.

Rannit, Aleksis

1964 *The Current State of Baltic Literatures under Soviet Occupation.* Washington: U.S. Government Printing Office. (Testimony given before the Committee on Foreign Affairs, U.S. Congress.)

1975 "Heiti Talvik, an Estonian Poet (1904-1947?): From Decadent Dream to Martyrdom." *American PEN* 7 (Spring): 10-19.

Remmelgas, Lembit

1959 "Eesti kirjanduskriitika olukorrast ja ülesannetest" [On the State of Estonian Literary Criticism and Its Tasks]. *Looming,* no. 11, pp. 104-122.

Ristikivi, Karl

1955 "National Literature under the Soviets." *East and West* (London), no. 5, pp. 57-64.

Rummo, Paul, comp.

1967 *Eesti luule* [Estonian Poetry]. Tallinn: Eesti Raamat.

Saar, A.

1962 "Kônelus iseenda ja teistega" [Conversations with Others and Myself]. *Looming,* no. 6, pp. 923-934.

Salu, Herbert

1961 "Estonian Literature," in *Aspects of Estonian Culture,* ed. Evald Uustalu et al. London: Boreas.

Smuul, Juhan

1959 "Eesti nôukogude kirjandus aastail 1954-1958 ja kirjanduse ees seisvad ülesanded" [Estonian Soviet Literature during the Years 1954-1958, and Tasks Which Stand before It]. *Looming,* no. 1, pp. 85-103.

Taagepera, Rein

1975 "The Problem of Political Collaboration in Soviet Estonian Literature." *Journal of Baltic Studies* 6 (Spring): 30-40.

1976   "The Impact of the New Left on Estonia." *East European Quarterly* 10, no. 1: 43-51.

Talve, Ilmar

1965   "Viron kirjallisuus" [Estonian Literature], in *Otava Iso Tietosanakirja*, vol. 9. Helsinki: Otava.

Vaarandi, E., et al., comps. and eds.

1955   *Eesti luule antoloogia* [An Anthology of Estonian Poetry], vol. 2. Tallinn: Eesti Riiklik Kirjastus.

Valgemäe, Mardi

1973   "The Broken World of Arvo Valton's 'Eight Japanese Girls.'" *Books Abroad* 47 (Autumn): 653-657.

Translations of Soviet Estonian Literature

Krusten, Erni

1966   *Une gouette dans la mer (Dix chapitres de la vie d'Eduard Laul)*, trans. D. Sanadze. Moscow: Progress.

Leberecht, Hans

1950a   *Licht über Koordi*, trans. O. Braun. Second ed., 1952; third ed., 1955. Berlin: Neues Leben.
1950b   *La Lumière à Koordi*. Paris: Editeurs français réunis.
1951   *Light in Koordi*, trans. L. Stoklitsky. Moscow: Progress.
1960   *Unter einem Dach*, trans. H. Eschwege and W. Lange. Berlin: Neues Leben.
1961   *Soldatem aus Tallinn*, trans. W. Berger. Berlin: Deutsche Militärverlag.
1963   *Die Paläste des Wassars*, trans. L. Remané. Berlin: Kultur und Fortschritt.

Semper, Johannes

1960   *Rote Nelken*, trans. A. Baer. Rostock: Hinstorff.

Smuul, Juhan

1962   *Das Eisbuch: eine Reise in die Antarktis*, trans. F.
Loesch. Berlin: Kultur und Fortschritt.
1963   *Antarctica Ahoy!*, trans. D. Skvirsky. Moscow: Progress.
1967   *Der Wilde Kapitän*, trans. J. Elperin and K. Eiden.
Berlin: Lied der Zeit.

Special Issues and Bibliographies

Books Abroad 47, no. 4 (Autumn).
1973

Kabur, V., and O. Kivi, comps.

1958-   *Eesti kirjandus, kirjandusteadus ja kriitika: Biblio-*
1968   *graafia 1954-1958* [Estonian Literature, Literary
Scholarship, and Criticism: A Bibliography from
1954 to 1958], published in 1958; . . .*1959-1962*,
published in 1963; . . .*1963-1966*, published in 1968.
Tallinn.

Literary Review 8, no. 3 (Spring).
1965

*Oeuvres et opinions (Revue mensuelle éditée par l'Union des
écrivains de l'URSS,* no. 116 (August).
1968

Parming, Marju Rink, and Tönu Parming, comps.

1974   *A Bibliography of English-Language Sources on
Estonia.* New York: Estonian Learned Society in
America.

Soviet Literature (Moscow), no. 8.
1972

Articles about and reviews of Estonian literature may be
found in the following publications: *Books Abroad* (University
of Oklahoma, United States), *Keel ja Kirjandus* (Soviet Esto-

nian monthly), *Journal of Baltic Studies* (Association for the Advancement of Baltic Studies, United States), *Lituanus* (Lithuanian quarterly, United States), *Looming* (Soviet Estonian monthly), *Mana* (semiannual, United States), *Tulimuld* (quarterly, Sweden).

8

Drama and the Theater Arts

Mardi Valgemäe

In an extant fragment of a comedy by the second-century B.C. Roman author Titinius, there occurs a contemptuous reference to people who speak the Oscan dialect because of their ignorance of Latin. About 200 years later the Greek geographer Strabo, who had traveled widely through the Roman world, noted that the Oscan race had died out and that their language survived among the Romans chiefly in plays that were put on during a "certain native festival." If we were to substitute Estonian for Oscan and Russian for Roman, would it be possible to read in some literary handbook of the future: "The Estonian dialect probably once had its literature, and the language survived alongside of Russian until the twenty-second century"? Fifteen years ago the answer to this conjectural question could conceivably have been a reluctant "yes." In the 1960s, however, a new and refreshing aesthetic turbulence stirred the realm of Estonian socialist realism, leaving a pronounced impact especially on the drama. Thus, in the 1970s it may seem somewhat premature to link the Estonians with the lost tribe of the Oscans. On the contrary, insofar as the theater is concerned, the Estonians are alive, if not well, and trying hard to keep a step ahead of the Soviet avant-garde in their productions of such influential although officially discredited Western playwrights as Bertolt Brecht and Samuel Beckett as well as in their home-grown brand of Aesopian absurdist allegories.

The First Decade of Soviet Rule

The first decade of postwar Soviet rule in Estonia, from 1944 until the death of Stalin in 1953, produced no drama of artistic merit. The most widely published playwright of the period was August Jakobson (1904-1963), who in the late 1920s had distinguished himself as a writer of Zolaesque proletarian fiction. Jakobson's plays of the forties and fifties, however, are crude propaganda pieces that follow the tenets of what A. A. Zhdanov, in his famous "Speech to the First All-Union Congress of Soviet Writers, 1934," had labeled socialist realism (1950:15). Jakobson's most successful play, later made into a popular motion picture (indeed, the best-known dramatic work of Stalinist Estonia), is *Elu tsitatellis* [Life in a Citadel], staged in 1946. Modeling his work on Ibsen's dramas of the 1880s and 1890s—in fact, one of the characters in *Life in a Citadel*, a master builder by trade, is at one point referred to as Solness—Jakobson attempted to create psychological and symbolic tension. A retired classics professor has surrounded his house with a high wooden fence. While a battle rages outside (the time is September 1944 and the Soviets are invading Estonia for the second time in four years), the scholar, declaring himself to be above politics, turns to translating Homer. As the action (involving an incredibly noble Red Army officer and a pair of caricatured Nazis) invades the professor's citadel to the accompaniment of offstage storm sounds, the scholar comes to the realization that individualism must yield to communism, whereupon the wind topples a part of the fence.

Jakobson's *Life in a Citadel* could in certain respects be compared to Ibsen's *An Enemy of the People*. Both plays pit an individualist against social conformity. Yet, whereas Ibsen champions the truth-seeking nonconformist, Jakobson allows society to triumph over individualism. Jakobson's views coincide, of course, with the dictates of the Communist party, which were reiterated as late as 1967 at the Fourth Congress of Soviet Writers. According to A. Salynsky (1967), the three cornerstones of Soviet dramaturgy are "closeness to the masses [*narodnost*], revolutionary humanism and faith in the Party [*partiinost*]." To underscore the ideational gulf separating Jakobson from Ibsen, we need only recall Dr. Stockman's words in *An Enemy of the People*: "A [political] party is like a sausage machine; it mashes up all sorts of heads together into the same mincemeat." Not only does Jakobson's reliance on Ibsen turn out to be superficial, he dissipates much of the play's psychological realism by introducing techniques associated with melodrama and the Scribean *pièce bien faite*. His characters are shallow; the conflict is simplistic (all Communists are good, whereas the Germans and their collaborators are evil); the plot involves sensational secrets as well as a hackneyed misunderstanding; there is the cliché of violent gunplay; and the dénouement is predictable, given the playwright's political philosophy.

Jakobson carried his brand of playwriting into the late 1950s and early 1960s with a six-part work of epic proportions, *Tôrmisolmed* [Stormknots], 1962.[1] As noted even by Soviet Estonian critics, this play is sorely lacking in dramatic qualities. Nagelmaa (1965) pointed out that Jakobson had justly called his mammoth work a "dramatic chronicle" and went on to say that "not a single theatre has attempted to stage even a part of it." The dramas of Jakobson and his literary comrades of the Stalinist period, such as Johannes Semper (1892-1970), Aadu Hint (b. 1910), and Mart Raud (b. 1903), are crudely constructed didactic melodramas. Unhappily, these plays lack the quality of theatricality that makes, say, Bertolt Brecht's equally didactic Marxist *Lehrstücke* palatable even to a non-Communist audience.

The Post-Stalinist Period

After Stalin's death in 1953, greater flexibility in form as well as in subject matter became noticeable in Soviet Estonian drama, which was dominated from the mid-1950s to the mid-1960s by the work of three playwrights: Egon Rannet, Ardi Liives, and Juhan Smuul. Of these, Rannet (b. 1911) is the oldest and the most conservative. Adhering to the party line, he glorified collective farming and the Red Army and attacked such obvious targets as private enterprise, religion, and modernism in art. Nevertheless, he was at times able to create dramaturgically satisfactory scenes that fused plot, character, dialogue, setting, and symbolism into concrete stage action. In *Salakütid* [The Poachers], 1960, for example, Rannet employed illegal game hunting in a state forest as a theatrical metaphor for poaching in the thickets of love as well as in the jungles of the art world. Throughout his *oeuvre*, however—as in his latest and most sensational play, *"Kriminaaltango" ja väga korralikud inimesed* [Criminal Tango and Very Decent People], 1968, Rannet has remained faithful to the dictates of the party. Such adherence to orthodoxy has elevated him to the front rank of Soviet Estonian dramatists, a fact attested to by the popularity of his plays. According to Nirk (1970:358), Rannet's *Kadunud poeg* [The Prodigal Son], originally produced in 1958, has been staged in about 200 theaters in the Soviet Union and other socialist countries. Yet, from a broader perspective, hiring oneself out to a repressive political ideology carries with it the danger of becoming a party hack. Writers in the Soviet Union must steer a perilous course between the Scylla and Charybdis of official truth, with aesthetically disastrous consequences, and freedom of creation, with attendant political—and often literal—suicide. Rannet, like Jakobson, is one of those unfortunates who perished as artists while trying to navigate in such treacherous waters.

Liives (b. 1929), too, has written Stalinist propaganda pieces—for example, *Sinine rakett* [The Blue Flare], 1959, later recast as *Mürgi perenaine*. Yet occasionally, as in *Robert Suur* [Robert the Great], 1957, and *Uusaasta öö* [New Year's Eve], 1958, he has treated themes that are above political considerations. He even occasionally ventures to criticize the violent excesses of Soviet rule, though he is careful to do so in a "safe" context. Thus, in *Siinpool horisonti* [This Side of the Horizon], 1962, a politically unreliable character exclaims, "At every step of the way, I see people who have not even arrived at socialism yet. . . . What are we to do with them? String them up?" Elsewhere in the play, the same character points out that one would need more than the fingers of both hands to count the shortcomings of the socialist paradise. Liives expressed this idea most vividly in his *Viini postmark* [The Viennese Postage Stamp], 1964, in which Soviet construction methods are described in terms of walls that are crooked, showers that have no water, and toilets that lack sewage pipes. Liives' most noticeable departure from socialist realism occurs in *Neljas, lõpetamata portree* [The Fourth, Unfinished Portrait], which appeared in *Looming* in 1971. An attempt at capturing the public recollections as well as the private memories of an aging artist, the play juxtaposes brief dramatic scenes against the extended monologue of the protagonist, thus leading to a moderately interesting (though predictable) psychological portrait of the successful artist as a personal failure. Liives certainly has the ability to entertain audiences. It is just that he fails to illuminate the inner recesses of man's heart of darkness, and thus remains the Neil Simon of contemporary Soviet Estonian dramaturgy.

Extremely prolific, Liives is the author of about thirty stage plays, numerous librettos of musical comedies, and many radio plays. Smuul (1922-1971), on the other hand, has only six dramatic works to his credit, and one of these is a rather weak film scenario. Smuul was also a Lenin Prize winner (for nonfiction), and, like Semper and Jakobson before him, he was chairman of the Writers' Union of the Estonian SSR. Yet he is the least doctrinaire and most experimental of the establishment playwrights. As a character called Historic Truth puts it in Smuul's stageworthy *Kihnu Jõnn ehk Metskapten* [Jõnn of Kihnu, or The Wild Captain], 1965, the author is in flight from "certain basic tendencies in contemporary dramaturgy"—i.e., socialist realism. Having paid homage to Stalinism with *Lea* [Leah] in 1960, Smuul became an innovator with *Polkovniku lesk ehk Arstid ei tea midagi* [The Colonel's Widow, or The Doctors Don't Know What They Are Talking About], 1968, a satiric monodrama. Ostensibly a monomaniacal ranting against the stupidity of physicians, the tirade reveals the widow's own superficial, spurious, and parasitic character. A descendant of Molière's imaginary invalid, she is a hypochondriac, perennially dissatisfied with her physicians' diagnoses. At last she consents to be suffering from "Nihilissimus acutus" and "Logorrhoea gradus gravis," which—alas!—turn out to be a "big nothing" and a "severe case of verbal diarrhea."

With the exception of *Kaks viimast rida* [The Last Two Lines], 1973, a family drama with autobiographical overtones by Kersti Merilaas (b. 1913); Smuul's own later plays; and Enn Vetemaa's (b. 1936) *Õhtusöök viiele* [Supper for Five] (in Reiljan, 1974), which played a successful engagement in the Finnish theater in 1974, the charge of verbal diarrhea and a corresponding lack of genuine dramatic action can be brought against the work of the Soviet Estonian realists. The most consistent formal experimenter among the established playwrights is Ralf Parve (b. 1919), who borrows techniques from the expressionists, the Brechtian epic theater, and the tradition of documentary drama. At the same time, Parve's satiric allegories reveal a rigid ideological adherence to the party line. As a consequence—and as a result of his own limitations as a playwright—Parve's work lacks both psychological subtlety and the grotesque power of the expressionist's objectification of subjective reality, the penetrating intellectual analysis associated with the epic approach and the stylized theatricality that characterizes the best of the Living Newspapers and other forms of documentary drama. Even less can be said of Erni Krusten (b. 1900), whose two full-length plays of the 1950s preserve the pedestrian, verbose approach of Jakobson and Rannet. Recently Krusten published three dramatic miniatures that hint at a severing of his umbilical cord from socialist realism, but his impact as a serious playwright remains minimal. Equally inconsequential from the aesthetic point of view are the comedies of Mai Talvest (b. 1909) as well as the plays of about thirty other published dramatists. A typical example of such run-of-the-mill Soviet Estonian playwriting is Paul Kilgas' (b. 1920) *Ööbik laulis koidikul* [The Nightingale Sang at Dawn], 1961. This work, which pits wholesome Estonian Communists against degenerate home-grown Nazis, is subtitled "A Tragedy in Two Parts." Though Kilgas tries hard to establish an action resembling the Shakespearean Macbeth–Lady Macbeth relationship between the spineless protagonist and his depraved wife, who browbeats him into betraying an innocent friend, the play fails as tragedy because its central character lacks nobility of soul. Furthermore—as is more or less true of the entire Soviet Estonian dramatic output before the Aesopian absurdists—Kilgas' play lacks substance in terms of appropriate language, mythic action, adequate dramatic and moral turbulence, and what Jean Cocteau has called the visual *poésie de théâtre*.

Toward the Theater of the Absurd

The antirealistic revolution in European drama that began with the symbolists and included the expressionists as well as the surrealists produced the theater of the absurd in the 1940s and early 1950s. While Jakobson was laboring over his excessively verbal pseudo-Ibsenesque plays in Soviet Estonia, Samuel Beckett, Eugène Ionesco, Jean Genet, and others were

shaping in France a new drama that substituted visual meta-
phors for language. Instead of talking about man's frustrations
and the cosmic meaninglessness of the human condition, the
new playwrights actually showed it on stage by means of
absurdly grotesque and exaggerated images and actions.

East European writers who did not reside in the Soviet
Union proper but rather lived in the satellite countries of the
Soviet bloc, and who therefore experienced the post-Stalinist
thaw sooner than anyone else, quickly perceived in the absurdist mode an opportunity for confounding the censors and for
expressing the hitherto inexpressible. In Czechoslovakia, for
example, according to playwright Ivan Klíma (Klaidman,
1968:52), "Writers could speak out in allegorical and symbolic
ways and say things that ordinary people couldn't say in
ordinary ways." The structural device of absurdist allegory—
pioneered by another resident of Prague, Franz Kafka—has
therefore been used by a number of dramatists, including
Václav Havel, whose *The Memorandum* has emerged as the
best-known Czech play of the postwar period. Seemingly
about a grotesquely cumbersome artificial language, *The
Memorandum* is actually an allegorical satire of the de-
Stalinization campaign. Havel himself has called the work a
political metaphor, in which the synthetic language represents
"some kind of dictatorship" (Polster, 1968). When questioned
about the production of *The Memorandum* in Prague in 1965,
Havel replied, "The situation was such that things expressed
metaphorically were possible and far less critical ideas told in
straight terms could not be staged" (Funke, 1968:11).

The earliest and most widespread flowering of East European absurdist allegory occurred in Poland. Though the
impact of Beckett, Ionesco, and Alfred Jarry on the Polish
theater was electrifying, it must not be forgotten that Poland
boasts its own tradition of absurd expressionism in the works
of S. Wyspiański, S. I. Witkiewicz, and W. Gombrowicz.
Among the more recent dramatists who write in the new mode
are T. Różewicz and Slawomir Mrożek. The latter's *Tango*, a
skillfully constructed political allegory, is the most widely
performed East European play in the idiom of the absurd.

Mrożek's *Tango* and Havel's *The Memorandum* were first
performed in their respective countries in 1965. Two years
later, in 1967, *Tango* appeared in an Estonian translation
(three of Mrożek's short plays were shown on Estonian

television between December 1966 and June 1967); the Estonian version of *The Memorandum* was published in 1968. As the American scholar Deming Brown has noted, there is a tendency in the Soviet Union to translate ideologically or formally disreputable works only into certain minority languages (such as Ukrainian, Lithuanian, or Estonian) and to make them available to the readers of these languages long before they are published in Russian. "Everything else being equal, Estonian or Ukrainian writers," says Brown, "would seem much more likely to have been influenced by Polish, Czech or Slovak literary tendencies than would their Russian colleagues" (Brown, 1975:134).

*   *   *

The first Estonian play in the new mode, Artur Alliksaar's (1923-1966) *Nimetu saar* [The Nameless Island], appeared in print in 1966, the year of the Estonian translation of "A Large Wig" by the Slovak dramatist Peter Karvaš. Both works make use of Aesopian language to comment on the absurdity of power. Karvaš develops a conflict between the hairy and the hairless in the manner of Swift's Big-Endians and Little-Endians. Alliksaar's *The Nameless Island* seems at first to be an exciting tale of space adventure set in the interplanetary future. This facade of seemingly innocent fantasy nevertheless conceals bold allegorical satire directed against the political practices of the nameless island, which is ruled by a masked man wearing a field marshal's uniform—an obvious allusion to Stalin. Alliksaar, who died in 1966 at the age of forty-three and whose *The Nameless Island*, his only published play, was printed just a few months before his death, may some day be known as the Estonian Georg Büchner. Much of his work (mostly poetry) is still in manuscript, and *The Nameless Island*—which, in its intensity, is totally unlike anything that precedes it in Estonian drama (the only other political allegory that comes to mind is A.-H. Tammsaare's *Kuningal on külm* [The King Is Cold], 1936)—has not yet been given a stage production.

Characterized by a high level of linguistic competence, *The Nameless Island* functions on at least three planes. Superficially, it is science fiction. On a deeper level, it is a condemnation of totalitarianism. Alliksaar gives us enough hints to suggest that he is dealing specifically with Soviet tyranny. For example, in front of the island's parliament building waddles a symbolic Russian bear, accepting sweets from the repressed citizenry. Yet when the island's dictator dons a mask and makes a speech about destroying the world, he relies heavily on imagery derived from what is one of the strongest bastions of make-believe—the theater. Coupled with the visual device of the mask, Alliksaar's images suggest that, on a third level of action, *The Nameless Island* is an attempt to illuminate the border regions of illusion and reality.

The first moments of *The Nameless Island* establish the surrealistically absurd tone of the work. Marius lights a cigarette, setting fire to the newspaper that hides the Reader's face. When the flames burn his fingers, the Reader drops the paper, whereupon Marius speaks the first line of the play: "What? So it isn't you after all?" The Reader replies: "Of course it is I and no one else." We soon learn, however, that the Reader suffers from amnesia. Thus begins a Pirandellian game of finding the face behind the mask. What reinforces the essential theatricality of *The Nameless Island* is Alliksaar's skillful blending of the various planes of action in episodes that involve the spectator's sight as well as hearing, his emotions as well as intellect. To cite just a single instance, the incredibly lifelike statues that adorn the island turn out to be executed political prisoners who have been frozen, as it were, into a solid state. The compression into a single visual image of a fantastic method of judicial punishment and the metaphoric restriction of body freedom (with the overtone that all citizens of a totalitarian state are thus imprisoned), as well as the deceptive appearance of the statue, speak to us eloquently—and in the proper visual language of drama—of space-age adventure, political tyranny, and the difficulty of separating truth from illusion. Alliksaar was indeed a consummate artist. One hopes that it will not be necessary to wait seventy-seven years for a production of *The Nameless Island*, as was the case with Büchner's *Woyzeck*.

* * *

Just as *Woyzeck* anticipated both naturalism and expressionism, Alliksaar's seminal play has contributed to the development of two trends in contemporary Soviet Estonian drama. On the one hand, *The Nameless Island* provided a native model for Aesopian political allegories that are set in some mythical or otherwise faraway land or time. On the other, Alliksaar's home-grown example encouraged the utilization of techniques borrowed from the theater of the absurd. Though there is considerable overlapping, especially since the absurdism in these plays frequently reaches toward politics as much as toward metaphysics, it is nevertheless possible to distinguish between the two approaches.

In 1967, the year Ionesco's *Rhinoceros* and Mrożek's *Tango* were published in Estonia, Theater Vanemuine staged Ain Kaalep's (b. 1926) *Iidamast ja Aadamast ehk Antimantikulaator* [Of Idam and Adam, or The Antimanticulator]. Though Kaalep's play is in no way derivative of the former works, all three are thematically related. *Rhinoceros* pits an easygoing individualist against an ever-increasing herd of pachyderms; *Tango* confronts a romantic idealist with the brutal dictatorship of the proletariat; *Of Idam and Adam* opposes a trio of humanists against a totalitarian state of cybernetic apes. Kaalep's play contains echoes of Orwell, Huxley, Čapek, and Mayakovsky. Nevertheless, it is an original retelling of the story of Adam and Eve. Rebelling against a restrictive society that has set up free sex centers while outlawing love, two young apes decide to become human and hide in the dwelling of an old creature called Hamlet, whom the state regards as an idiot because he speaks in blank verse and is known for his intellectual skepticism. The lovers are tracked down by a wily official called Lucifer, who goes on to tempt Eve with a bottle of applejack. Just as the Supreme Computer is about to pass sentence on the young revolutionaries, a general uprising of the apes interrupts the dreaded proceedings. Lucifer regrets that he has been unable to save the apes from becoming human and vows to return at a later date.

Though Kaalep has amusingly rephrased Genesis as well as *The Origin of the Species* in creating an Aesopian allegory in the tradition of Ionesco, Mrożek, and Alliksaar, his formal handling of the subject matter is quite Brechtian. Others, notably Parve and Smuul, have borrowed elements of Brecht's epic dramaturgy, but Kaalep is the first Estonian playwright to do so extensively. *Of Idam and Adam* begins with a verse prologue that not only outlines the fable but also (and here Kaalep out-Brechts Brecht) informs us that this is precisely what is happening, thus divorcing the audience from the fluctuations of the plot and forcing them instead to think about the reasons underlying the action on the stage. As Kaalep himself, who has translated and written about Brecht, expressed it, "In Brecht's art 'what' and 'how' are inseparable" (1970:8). Among the other alienation effects in *Of Idam and Adam* are projected quotations and reproductions of art work, masks for the characters, and the use of film in act 3. The last is there to establish the epic historicity of the play's action. Though Kaalep's use of these techniques does not always achieve full Brechtian incisiveness, his attempt is praiseworthy, for the reception of Brecht's concepts in the Soviet Union has been slow and painful.

Notwithstanding the fact that Brecht was awarded the Stalin Peace Prize in 1954, he was constantly being reprimanded by the party for writing "historically wrong" and "politically harmful" plays, a charge which led to the banning, in East Berlin in 1951, of his *Trial of Lucullus*, though his *Threepenny Opera* had been staged in Moscow (as well as in Estonia) as early as 1930. Brecht's concept of epic theater, with its techniques of alienation and *gestus*, was too flamboyantly theatrical, too formal, for Zhdanov's socialist realism. Following Stalin's death, Brecht's works soon caught on in Poland, and the world-famous Berliner Ensemble was invited to give performances in Moscow in 1957. This led to local productions of two minor Brecht plays in 1958, though the initial staging of a major play did not occur in Moscow until 1960. The first postwar Brecht production in the Soviet Union was mounted in Tallinn, Estonia, where Voldemar Panso staged *Puntila and His Servant Matti* (on which Brecht had collaborated with the Estonian-born Finnish playwright Hella Wuolijoki) during the 1957-1958 season.[2]

In 1968 Panso staged Smuul's *Enne kui saabuvad rebased (Pingviinide elu)* [Before the Arrival of the Foxes, or Life of the Penguins]. Like Kaalep's *Of Idam and Adam*, Smuul's last play is an animal fable that makes use of masks as well as imaginative sets and costumes in the best tradition of "decadent bourgeois formalism." The story line of the play is blatantly allegorical, being based on the conflict between large and complacent emperor penguins, representing Russians, and much smaller Adélie penguins, symbolizing Estonians. The latter talk constantly about their own language, ethnic origin, and national pride. Smuul's political satire becomes pointed when we learn that the name of the leader of the emperor penguins is Daft. A nonsense syllable in Estonian, the word has of course a very specific meaning in English, a language quite popular in Soviet Estonia. It may also be pointed out that in the Tallinn production Daft was made up to look like Khrushchev (for a photograph, see Grabbi, 1968:108). There is a further contest between old conservatives and radical young Renaissance Boys, and the play ends with the arrival of arctic foxes. Before proceeding to devour the penguins, the foxes are identified as belonging to a (Western imperialist?) peace corps.

Another allegory of 1968, the first drama to be staged in the rebuilt Theater Vanemuine, Mati Unt's (b. 1944) *Phaethon, päikesepoeg* [Phaethon, Son of Helios], takes the ancient story of the mythic Greek youth who persuaded his celestial father to allow him to drive the sun chariot, with predictably disastrous results, and expands it into a struggle for freedom and self-realization in the face of indifference, corruption, brutality, tyranny, and death. Modeled partly on Anouilh's Antigone and Schiller's Don Carlos, Unt's Phaethon expresses sentiments of libertarian idealism. He is also something of an existentialist in that he refers to the world as the vomit of the gods and comments on being and nothingness. Another character refers to time as a spider web around her face, but then corrects herself: "No, like a reel of barbed wire." Unt ends the play (which incorporates into its text poems by Alliksaar) with a Brechtian device that forces the audience to intellectualize about the action they have just seen. The god who a moment ago had murdered the idealistic young protagonist now invents the textbook version of what ostensibly happened: Phaethon, he says, was unable to control the celestial horses and had to be destroyed in order to save the world from a fiery end. As someone puts it elsewhere in the play, "History is a prostitute."

The allegorization of history is the aim of Lilli Promet (b. 1922) in her *Los Caprichos* [Caprices], produced in 1973. The work purports to be an outright attack on the Spanish Inquisition but manages to comment on much more than the excesses of historical Christianity. The church censors everything and fights against liberal ideas that await transmission across its tightly sealed borders. Local poets, artists, and politicians manufacture lies in the name of higher truth. Upright citizens are forced to flee their native land. As a monk ravishes a lady and another cleric attempts to soothe her, a bystander remarks,

"That's what happens to women and countries; as they are raped, one always says, 'Shut up, you fool! We're only trying to help you.'" There are moments in the play when the author attempts parallels between Catholic Spain and Nazi Germany. Yet, what about the United States "coming to the aid" of the Vietnamese—or the Soviet Union "liberating" the Baltic states? No matter at whom or what Promet's satire is directed, her use of masks, masses of people, short, intense scenes, Brechtian ballads (written by Parve), and projections of etchings from Goya's famous "Los Caprichos" series (the source of the play's title) supply considerable theatricalism to enliven her Aesopian allegory.

* * *

If theatricalist political allegory, the legacy of Ionesco, Mrożek, Havel—and Alliksaar—constitutes a recognizable trend in contemporary Soviet Estonian drama, another discernible direction has been established by the assimilation of absurdist elements into native dramaturgy, a development first noticeable in Alliksaar's *The Nameless Island*. The most illustrious example of the Soviet Estonian theater of the absurd is Paul-Eerik Rummo's (b. 1942) *Tuhkatriinumäng* [Cinderellagame], which opened at Theater Vanemuine on February 19, 1969. Rummo's play has the further distinction of being the first Estonian play to be performed professionally in the American theater. On April 7, 1971, New York's famed La Mama experimental theater club presented the English-language première of *Cinderellagame*. Rummo's complex drama is unquestionably the best Soviet Estonian play. It may even be the best Estonian play this side of August Kitzberg's *Libahunt* [The Werewolf], 1912. Jaak Rähesoo, the most erudite commentator on this work, places it among the peaks of Estonian drama (1969:1093). Similarly, Karin Kask, the leading Soviet Estonian theater historian, said, "In the future one cannot speak of our native drama and its staging without taking into account *Cinderellagame*, which turns a new page in our dramaturgy" (1969). The Renaissance Boys, whom Smuul derided in *Before the Arrival of the Foxes*, have left a permanent imprint on the theatrical landscape of Estonia.

The fairy tale of Cinderella ends with a rebirth as its heroine moves literally from ashes to diamonds. Rummo's *Cinderella-game* begins where the fairy tale ends. The Prince, having married Cinderella nine years ago, leaves his entourage and journeys alone to the former home of his wife. There he encounters a new Cinderella, whose foot seems to fit the slipper, but the shoe turns out to be a fake. While trying to discuss matters with the Second Daughter, he is lured into the warm bed of the First Daughter. Both remind him of the girl in the kitchen. His problem is indeed complicated: with his wife, the court Cinderella, hard at his heels, which of the four is the real Cinderella? Though he has two probing talks with the Master of the House, the Prince fails to unravel life's motives for giving him the wrong girl—if, indeed, he did get the wrong girl—until he encounters the stepmother, here called the Mistress of the House, whereupon the annual visit draws quickly to a close.

The cyclical structure of Rummo's play, incorporating the journey metaphor, suggests some kind of archetypal seasonal pattern. According to the *Encyclopaedia Britannica* (1958), the almost universal fairy tale of the little cinder girl originated in a nature myth, in which Cinderella was the dawn, oppressed by night clouds (cruel relatives) until rescued by the sun (the prince). Thus we begin our examination of *Cinderellagame* with overtones that conjure up the ancient rituals of seasonal change, of fertility, of death and resurrection, which lead to Euripides' *The Bacchae* and eventually to the off-off-Broadway production of *Dionysus in 69*. For the best drama of all ages concerns itself not so much with social or political reform but instead reveals man's gradual—and painful—awareness of his human condition. Such movement toward tragic perception may be the legacy of ancient myths and rituals. As Claude Lévi-Strauss has argued, "Myths and rites are far from being, as has often been held, the product of man's 'myth-making faculty,' turning its back on reality" (1966:16). On the contrary, they constitute "the remains of methods of observation and reflection" and therefore "still remain at the basis of our own civilization." The major area in which these ancient forms flourish today is of course art; for art, according to Lévi-Strauss, has retained the element of "savage thought" (1966:219).

How then does Rummo extract the "savage thought" from a shopworn fairy tale? Among the many devices at his disposal are the use of a ritualized *poésie de théâtre* and the injection of absurdist images.[3] Rummo does indeed depict a universe that is devoid of the familiar and the comprehensible. Instead of a storybook Cinderella and her Prince Charming, there are several pretenders to these titles. Furthermore, the Prince not only has a double but is reputedly simply one of many princes who inhabit a multitude of castles that abound in the hostile countryside. Though he is the legitimate heir to the country's throne, the Prince is powerless, for the ruthless and cunning dictator in the play is the crippled Mistress of the House, who sits in a wheelchair. Is Rummo suggesting that usurped power not only corrupts but actually induces illness, that totalitarianism is a disease? Perhaps. But Rummo is clearly writing more than political allegory, for he creates another plane of meaning by equating the Mistress, who "choose[s] by chance," with capricious life. When she produces some sheets of paper that are supposed to reveal the "rules" of the game, no one is able to read the strange markings on the few pages that are not completely blank. Thus we are quickly transported from the realm of politics into that of metaphysics and, like Tertullian of old, cry out: *credo quia absurdum est.*

Rummo concretizes the idea of the absurdity of man's condition in a visually brilliant scene in which the Prince chases after the crazily wheeling Mistress, while obstacles drop from the flies to impede his movement. It is at this point in the play that the Prince realizes the meaninglessness of his quest to unmask the real Cinderella, who has come to represent truth and happiness. This tragic perception is dramatized by a shift from prose to blank verse and by the literal opening up of the stage, both in height and depth, for until that moment most of the action has taken place in a single, as it were, almost exclusively linear dimension. The Estonian production, directed by Evald Hermaküla, underscored the elements of ritual and absurdity in the text by introducing the techniques of Antonin Artaud's sexual theater of cruelty. In scene 3, during the Prince's seduction by the First Daughter, members of the Vanemuine audience are on record, according to Kään (1969), as having yelled in derision, "Shame on the Estonian theater!" In the scene in which the Prince beats Cinderella, the agonizing depiction of violence, reported Kään, brought gasps of "Oh my God!" and "Enough!" from the audience. Artaud spoke of "being like victims burnt at the stake, signaling through the flames" (1958:13). We all burn at the stake of life. The fire may stifle our cries, but our gestures reveal the pain. This is the "savage thought" that lies at the core of the theater of cruelty. The cosmic agony of the Prince in search of his elusive Cinderella ranges from casual sex to calculated sadism, but he cannot free himself from the flames. In the recognition scene, Hermaküla bared the stage to the extent of exposing the lighting system as well as all the visible stage machinery (see Stolovitš, 1969:48; Kään, 1969; Matjus, 1969:792; Unt, 1972:135), but even this did not bring forth the real Cinderella or reveal any carefully guarded secret: the ultimate truth may be that there is no ultimate truth.

Rummo's absurdist universe is indeed turbulent and savage. But the playwright's world view is not nihilistic. For it is the element of play in *Cinderellagame* that injects a significant note of meaning and order into an apparently meaningless and chaotic cosmos. As Johan Huizinga pointed out, "From the point of view of a world wholly determined by the operation of blind forces, play would be altogether superfluous. Play only becomes possible, thinkable and understandable when an influx of *mind* breaks down the absolute determinism of the cosmos" (1955:3). Thus one of the ways in which man could survive the absurdity of the universe would be to transform reality into play. This, of course, is precisely what happens in, say, Beckett's *Endgame*. The Cinderella game involves a ritualized quest for truth (and happiness), represented by the title figure. The rules of the game are made by the Mistress, and each of the puppet characters—except, of course, the Prince— receives orders from her. Cinderella plays unawakened innocence. The First Daughter flaunts her sensual charms. The Second Daughter poses as a bluestocking. Court Cinderella pretends to sophistication. The Master becomes the existential "foolosopher." The Mistress herself assumes the role of Mother Earth and points to the power of play: "I am not old, as long as I can play. / My strength is in the game." As the Prince says, "It seems that everyone is playing the part he was once given and puts up with that part." The Prince's own role is that of the seeker. Disillusioned with the life of the senses (First Daughter) as well as with the intellect (Second Daughter), not to mention phony sophistication (Court Cinderella), he eschews existentialism (the Master) and finds momentary release in the quest itself, for play has made it possible for his mind to conquer "the absolute determinism of the cosmos."

Hand in hand with play in the contemporary theater of the

absurd goes the awareness of multiple levels of time. The chief categories of performance time may be termed real time, play time, and symbolic time. The passage of real time during the production of *Cinderellagame* takes roughly two and a half hours. Play time, however, lasts an entire day. Symbolic time involves the better part of a lifetime, with the action of the play representing the journey of life, the archetypal quest, and man's final perception that he is doomed to failure. In the last scene the Prince and Cinderella, like Didi and Gogo in Beckett's *Waiting for Godot*, talk about the passing of time:

PRINCE: What did you do here all this time?
CINDERELLA: Waited.
PRINCE: Is waiting doing something?
CINDERELLA: Waiting is very much doing something. There's a lot to do while you're waiting.
PRINCE: And what else did you do while you waited?
CINDERELLA: Waited some more.
PRINCE: And then?
CINDERELLA: Some more. And I baked beans. Scorched them.
PRINCE: They'll do.
(The PRINCE *sits . . . and pitches beans into his mouth. . . .)*
CINDERELLA: But you?
PRINCE: What, me?
CINDERELLA: Prince.
PRINCE: Yes?
CINDERELLA: Yes. Prince. But what did you do all that time, Prince?
PRINCE: I? *(Chokes on a bean.* CINDERELLA *slaps his back.)* I didn't do a thing. Didn't bake, didn't wait.

A few moments later the fire dies in the hearth, lighted ceremonial candles create a funereal atmosphere, and the Prince steps out of the warm room into a snowstorm. The Cinderella game is over. Real time, play time, and symbolic time have all come to an end. But have they? The Prince is dead. Long live the Prince! As the final curtain falls, the Mistress, who has been equated with life, winds up the alarm clock and tells Cinderella about the ball to which she will go tomorrow. Having once more failed in his quest, man may die but life goes on, forever holding up the glittering promise of

tomorrow. Even though the performance has ended for to-
night, tomorrow night the actors will play again.

The beans Cinderella has been baking in the play are used by
her to decorate a cake with the number nine. According to
James George Frazer's *The Golden Bough* (1959:562-566), the
festival of the Twelfth Night (in January) featured a King of the
Bean and the baking of a great cake with a bean in it. Beans are
clearly a variant of wheat, corn, or rice as fertility images, just
as the eating of the vegetation gods frequently took place in the
form of cakes. Frazer notes, furthermore, that certain Finno-
Ugric tribes offered cakes in the shape of sacrificial animals to
their gods, and hints that the number nine may have been
sacred to these people (1959:461, 525). A more suggestive
political implication of the repeated references to the number
nine in *Cinderellagame* involves the realization that ancient
kings (like contemporary American presidents) held a maximum tenure of eight years, of which seven- and nine-year
periods are common corruptions.

As in the ancient myths of seasonal change, the winter of
Rummo's discontent must sooner or later yield to the eternally
recurring thaw of spring; and, as we recall in an earlier speech
by the Prince, the fear of (allegorical?) wolves will eventually be
replaced by a feeling of Dionysiac ecstasy:

> February, February! Wolves scent you; . . . you,
> hungry, scent the thaw. . . . The wolves stalk after
> you, and you stalk after hope. . . . The thaw, the
> thaw. Where can it be? It has to come. . . . soon all
> this will crack apart, . . . and the wolves' starved
> cadavers will crack on the roads and on the road-
> banks. The thaw! The thaw! You run around as if
> drunk. How everything drips with joy!

By endowing the action of *Cinderellagame* with what at first
appears to be an absurd cosmic happening which then develops
into an artful—and meaningful—game, Rummo seems to be
suggesting that, though Dionysus may have been caught in the
web of totalitarian *realpolitik*, he can be released within each of
us, if only for the space of two and a half hours, by means of
ritualized play.

* * *

While other Renaissance Boys, such as Kaalep and Unt, write Aesopian allegories in the manner of Ionesco and Mrożek, Rummo's affinities lie more with the metaphysics of Beckett. As was the case with Brecht, literary commissars have been doing their best to discourage Beckett's influence in the Soviet Union. That they have succeeded by and large is attested to by a recent *New York Times* report that "the USSR has never produced or published Samuel Beckett."[4] Though this may be true of Moscow and Leningrad, Beckett's *Happy Days*, *Krapp's Last Tape*, and *Act without Words I* were published in an Estonian translation in 1969, with *Waiting for Godot* and *Endgame* following in 1973. Even more significantly (for there is, in fact, a Russian translation of *Waiting for Godot*), *Krapp's Last Tape* was shown on Soviet Estonian television as early as 1967. It was staged in 1973, and in 1969 Rummo directed a semiprivate production of *Happy Days*. Again tiny Estonia finds herself in the unusual position of serving as a cultural bridge between the European West and East.

Estonia's role as mediator between Western avant-garde art and Soviet socialist realism is strengthened by the fact that, following the controversial production of *Cinderellagame*, other innovative dramatists have begun to incorporate absurdist elements into their Aesopian allegories. Thus Unt's recent *Viimnepäev* [Doomsday], published in *Looming* in 1972, fuses politics and metaphysics in a domestic setting of dynamic theatricality. The family as well as a few friends of a motor-pool driver in contemporary Soviet Estonia are celebrating the employee's sixtieth birthday and retirement. As the conversation drifts toward flying saucers and cosmic visitors, an armed German soldier and officer enter and terrorize the household. Though the visitors turn out to be local pranksters—or at least one of them is—the action and the dialogue suggest that they could represent Jesus Christ.

The allegory of *Doomsday* functions on a number of levels. The reappearance of the Germans in Soviet Estonia, like the second coming of Christ, would clearly be a doomsday event. The Germans, as did the historical Christians, convince everyone of their authenticity and lead the microcosmic roomful of people to "believe in them." Within the context of officially sanctioned Soviet atheism, religious faith is clearly negative. The harmful aspect of Christianity is reinforced by linking it to Nazism. In fact, the officer identifies himself as "Kanter," the very name Kilgas assigned to a fascist bigwig in *The Nightingale Sang at Dawn*. Though the local militiamen eventually arrest the pranksters, one of whom had menaced the eighteen-year-old daughter of the house, at the end of the play the friend of the family begins to speak in German and lures the girl away from her beau. Two explanations are possible: there are still Nazis in our midst, or the Germans here represent totalitarianism per se. Such a reading adds a whole new dimension to the play. Third, one of the Germans turns out to be a bit player from the local theater. The numerous references to play in the dialogue, including the friend's "my life is a *grosses Spiel*," and the actual games the characters engage in on stage, conjure up the conceit of life as a game and man as *homo ludens*. It is also significant that we are not told anything about the background of the bogus officer; and, even though he is shot six times, he is not harmed. There is of course one explanation for the latter—perhaps he is a cosmic visitor after all.

The allegorical substance of Unt's play is enhanced by specific absurdist techniques. People speak in clichés or burst into rhapsodic non sequiturs (the beginning of the piece, especially, is reminiscent of Ionesco); watches stop; the party is interrupted by a lively ball game that juxtaposes death and such concepts as earth, moon, sun, and wedding ring; there is strange dancing à la Mrożek's *Tango*; later everyone dances in place as (according to the stage directions) "Ecstasy mounts." Unt's *Doomsday* is one of the finest examples of the new theatricalism in Soviet Estonian drama. The fact that it, along with Alliksaar's *The Nameless Island*, is still unproduced, speaks volumes.

Vaino Vahing's *Suvekool* [Summer School], on the other hand, received a production in 1972. Like Arthur in *Tango*, the Son in Vahing's play exhibits peculiar ideas in endeavoring to teach his parents how to live. Like Havel's characters in *The Memorandum* who carry personal fire extinguishers, he sports a large red and black whistle for summoning everyone to fire drills. A psychiatrist by profession, Vahing (b. 1940) has proclaimed that his protagonist is perfectly sane and that the play deals with truth while depicting falsehoods (Aller, 1972).

Hence, observes Vahing, an individual intolerant of even the tiniest of lies may appear as insane to the "normal" people around him. Such words sound ominous in a totalitarian state that rewards its most gifted writers by incarcerating them in insane asylums. As in *Tango*, the big lie in Vahing's play (Mrożek called it "the joke") seems to be political: the price of truth is death. And if Havel's personal fire extinguishers implied a society that no longer protects the individual, the following speech by Vahing's thirty-four-year-old protagonist should be read with the production date of *Summer School* in mind: "Fire drills: these were the nicest experiences of my youth. . . . I grew up in the midst of such drills and competitions; it is just that I was too young then and was not allowed to participate. Now that I wish to be an instigator myself, I'm labeled queer."

Lest such a reading of Vahing's play sound too topical, it should be kept in mind that the action of *Summer School* is consistently absurdist. Among the more unusual scenes is one in which the Son gropes in the mouth of his aunt, bringing to mind the relationship between Goldberg and McCann in Harold Pinter's *The Birthday Party* (which appeared in an Estonian translation in 1970). Underlying such incidents is the Son's cosmic despair. Vahing's hysterical protagonist, preoccupied with suspicions of everyone and everything, confesses to his wife that he is afraid of something happening very soon: "What is needed is a single crystal so that the emptiness surrounding it would quickly grow, only to collapse with a roar." While Rummo's Master of the House represented a satiric treatment of existentialism, Vahing has endowed his Son with the capacity to feel genuine existential despair. Yet a Rummoesque dimension of play pervades Vahing's work when the Wife pleads with the Son's parents, "Can't you understand that this is his game, exaggeration . . . simply *Spiel*; understand? . . . *SPIEL, igra, play*, game. . . ." Furthermore, the ideational content of *Summer School* embraces the archetypal conflict between conformity and nonconformity: it is as if Vahing was attempting to make amends for Jakobson's profanation of Ibsen in *Life in a Citadel*.

Elements of the absurd are to be found also in Rein Saluri's *Külalised* [Visitors], which received a controversial production by Kaarin Raid in 1974. Saluri's play, a probing of the painful past of the war years, a quest for the truth as well as for one's

roots, fuses psychological realism with considerable ambigui-
ty, not the least of which is the hallucinating shifting and
multiplication of roles. Much lighter in tone is Enn Vetemaa's
Püha Susanna ehk meistrite kool [St. Susan, or The School for
Masters], 1974, an allegory of miracles that perpetuates the
concept of play. Unt, Vahing, Saluri, and Vetemaa all rely on
grotesque stage images that place their work in the tradition of
the theater of the absurd.

Soviet Estonian Theaters

Not only have the more imaginative Soviet Estonian dramatists successfully transcended the limitations of socialist realism by creating absurdist allegories, some segments of the
theater, specifically the production styles of certain young
directors, have shifted considerably in the direction of Western
avant-garde developments. There are nine professional theaters in Soviet Estonia, of which one presents plays only in
Russian. Of the eight Estonian-language theaters, one is a
children's puppet theater and another, Tallinn's RAT Estonia,
limits its repertoire to opera and ballet. Of the remaining
six professional houses, RAT Vanemuine, Estonia's oldest
(founded in 1870), is located in the university city of Tartu. V.
Kingisepa Nimeline Tallinna Riiklik Akadeemiline Draamateater (henceforth Draamateater) and Eesti NSV Riiklik
Noorsooteater (Noorsooteater), the youngest, are situated in
the capital city of Tallinn. The remaining three are in Pärnu,
Viljandi, and Rakvere. There are also ten (not counting puppet
theaters) semiprofessional "people's theaters" (*rahvateatrid*),
as well as numerous amateur theater clubs. Though the
number of professional theaters may appear to be small, it
must be remembered that the population of Estonia is a mere
1.4 million (1970 census). Thus it comes as a mild shock to
discover (see "Täna algab. . .") that during the 1965-1966
season, for example, attendance at Estonia's legitimate theaters exceeded 1.3 million.

Insofar as it is possible to monitor Soviet Estonian theatrical
activity from the West, the work of several directors stands out:
Voldemar Panso's at the Draamateater, Mikk Mikiver's at the
Noorsooteater, Kaarin Raid's in Pärnu, and, above all, Kaarel
Ird's at Theater Vanemuine, which is noted for its experimental

productions. Though both the Draamateater and the Vanemuine have gained attention outside the Soviet Union (the
former by touring Finland in 1965 and the latter by performing
in Hungary in 1972 and in Finland in 1974), restrictions placed
on the creative imagination of a director by state censorship
undoubtedly have an effect on the selection of the repertoire as
well as on the aesthetic shaping of a production. (For an
analysis of the repertoire of Soviet Estonian theaters, see
Siimisker, 1969.) A case in point involves Jonas Jurašas of the
Kaunas State Theater. An innovative and highly regarded
Soviet Lithuanian director, Jurašas protested publicly against
"endless disputes with security-minded types" in 1972. He was
immediately fired and demoted to a stonecutter. Jurašas'
"Open Letter" (1974:89), which has of course not been published in the USSR, charges that many of his productions,
including those of *Tango* and *The Mammoth Hunt* (by the
Lithuanian absurdist Kazys Saja), were either closed or tam-
pered with, robbing them "of their artistic suggestiveness."
Notwithstanding the threat of harassment (for conditions in
Estonia are not markedly different from those in Lithuania),
the young directors Evald Hermaküla and Jaan Tooming have
managed to pioneer a new directorial approach.[5]

Hermaküla made his debut as a director in 1966 with a
dramatization (by Rummo) of Arvo Valton's short stories
(*Lugusid argielust ehk valtoniana*) at the Vanemuine. In 1969
he directed Rummo's *Cinderellagame*—which was subsequently removed from the boards for ideological plastic
surgery—and staged, with Jaan Tooming, a dramatization of
Gustav Suits' poetry (*Ühte laulu tahaks laulda*). Like certain
scenes of *Cinderellagame*, this production employed techniques associated with the work of the Polish director Jerzy
Grotowski and derived from Artaud's theater of cruelty. The
Estonian theatrical establishment was outraged, and a public
debate ensued between Panso (1969) and Unt (1969d), who had
propagated the new approach, citing, in addition to Grotowski
and Artaud (selections of whose essays appeared in an Estonian translation in 1975), such models as Peter Brook and the
Living Theatre. Hermaküla followed this experiment with a
controversial television production of Irene Haak's *Armastus,
armastus* [Love, Love], while Tooming staged, also in 1969,
Laseb käele suud anda [Permits Her Hand To Be Kissed] at
Vanemuine.

A reworking of a minor play (*Enne kukke ja koitu*) by Kitzberg, Tooming's production of *Permits Her Hand To Be Kissed* shifted the emphasis from the text to grotesque visual images and ritualistic enactment of the relationship between feudal Estonian serfs and German overlords. On a stage cleared of everything but four large chains suspended from the flies, Tooming depicted the serfs as a pack of growling, whimpering dogs (Luik, 1970), a device reminiscent of the 1968 Living Theatre production of Brecht's *Antigone*, where Creon was accompanied by a chorus of sycophants who moved about on all fours, rubbed their heads against the king's thighs, licked his hands, and nuzzled his crotch. Predictably, many considered Tooming's approach to be a desecration of the work of Estonia's classic dramatist, but, according to Taavas (1970), Tooming's use of "elements of the Estonian ritual theatre, folk songs and games" was most effective. Siimisker, too, confessed that she could not remember "as dynamic a production on the stage of Vanemuine" (1970:1261), while Allik declared, "The director has clearly been guided by certain theatrical principles of Jerzy Grotowski" (1970:69). Of the subsequent productions of this controversial pair, Hermaküla's 1971 staging of Leonid Andreyev's *He Who Gets Slapped* appears to have been in many ways similar to Richard Schechner's celebrated *Dionysus in 69* and has been singled out as being especially indebted to the Polish directorial avant-garde (Baum, 1972) and as being a mixture of the methods of Grotowski and the theater of the absurd (Tobro, 1971). Such evaluations are undoubtedly correct; in a 1970 interview (Unt, 1970:15), Hermaküla lists among his influences Grotowski and Brook (whose *Empty Space* appeared in an Estonian translation in 1972). Moreover, in 1971 he visited Poland, where he spent some time with Grotowski's troupe, and a private communication stresses Hermaküla's self-confessed affinity with the theoretical writings of Schechner.

Conclusion

In any attempt at the periodization of thirty years of Soviet Estonian drama and theater from 1944 to 1974, two dates, 1953 and 1966, stand out as pivotal. The first decade was dominated by the crudely fashioned didactic pieces of Jakobson and could be characterized as the period of melodrama. Stalin's death in 1953 somewhat relaxed the ideological grip on the arts, and the second half of the 1950s and the first half of the 1960s represented the heyday of uninspired socialist realism. The leading dramatists of this period were Rannet, Liives, and the early Smuul. The publication in 1966 of Alliksaar's *The Nameless Island* and the directorial debut, also in 1966, of Hermaküla ashered in a period of increasing theatricalism. Supplementing the impact of Ionesco, Mrożek, Havel, and Brecht, Alliksaar's play paved the way for the Aesopian allegories of Kaalep, Smuul, Unt, and Promet. The absurdist overtones of Alliksaar, reinforced by the influence of the French theater of the absurd, most notably of Beckett, anticipated the plays of Rummo, Unt, Vahing, and Saluri. Rummo's *Cinderellagame*, especially, brought considerable Dionysiac turbulence to the Estonian drama, which had been rather colorless since Kitzberg. Hand in hand with the tensions and ambiguities in the work of the Renaissance Boys go the directorial methods of Hermaküla and Tooming, who draw inspiration from Brook, Grotowski, Schechner, and Artaud's ritualistic theater of cruelty. After almost a quarter-century of politically motivated melodrama and dull socialist realism, the new theatricalism of Soviet Estonian absurdist allegories has at last touched the quivering soul of contemporary dramaturgy.

As is usually the case with successful but widely resisted aesthetic developments, the new movement in Soviet Estonian drama has given rise to considerable satire, ranging from dramatic feuilletons through subdued satiric allusions to parodies that seem to end up, in a beautifully absurd fashion, supporting the object of ridicule. In the first category belong Jaan Kruusvall's *Rändurid* [Wanderers], a burlesque of a key scene in Ionesco's *The Bald Soprano*, and Riho Mesilane's *Amor ja Psyche* [Amor and Psyche], which makes good clean fun of the Grotowski method. More subtle are the allusions in Lembit Vahak's (a pseudonym of Andres Ehin?) *Karske õhtupoolik* [Sober Afternoon], 1972. Vahak's science-fiction drama, which sandwiches an ecstatic and ritualistic scene in ancient Burma between two satiric acts of parvenu life in contemporary Soviet Estonia, involves a time machine. Along with a pointed reference to simians, this device is a clear allusion to Kaalep's *Of Idam and Adam*, with its "antimanticulator" and humanistic apes. Similarly, the blank verse dénouement of Vahak's work brings to mind the recognition scene of *Cinderellagame*, for the speaker in *Sober Afternoon* sounds very much like Rummo's Mistress of the House. The most ambitious—as well as the most "absurd"—case of parody is also the earliest. In Enn Vetemaa's television drama *Illuminatsioonid keravälgule ja üheksale näitlejale (pauguga lõpus)* [Illuminations for Ball Lightning and Nine Actors (With an Explosion at the End)], published in *Looming* in 1968 and televised the following year, caricatured allegorical figures on Mount Parnassus are menaced by an ever-increasing red sphere of ball lightning. We learn, however, that there is no danger, for the building is protected by lightning rods, and the electrical display itself is being monitored by a safety engineer. In other words, the battle against lightning is meaningless. Having come to a similar realization, a character in this intensely comic play tears the lightning rods from the building—thus triumphing, as he claims, over inevitability by once more making man the master of his own fate—whereupon a gigantic ball of electricity invades the room, concluding the play with the promised explosion.

At the same time, the parodic tone of Vetemaa's *Illuminations* and the mock absurdity of the play's concluding scene are tempered by a number of serious lines. For example: "There is lightning at our windows; perhaps it will soon be at yours." The comic allegory that began with a parody of existentialism and Beckett's *Krapp's Last Tape* (shown on Soviet Estonian television the previous year) assumes even more serious proportions when we recall a still earlier speech that has by now acquired a tragically ironic meaning. "Dear fellow humans," it began, "we all live in the twentieth century. Don't you really understand that this tiny ball of fire does not represent anything serious? If it were truly dangerous, then . . . the entire human race would unite with us. All men of good will would join us in rolling it into the trash bin of history." Instead of doing anything of the sort, the firemen of our world, as the absurdists—and Vetemaa—so well know, are all arsonists.

Illuminations is significant, finally, because an oft-recurring image in Vetemaa's allegory is that of a dead sea gull, which immediately brings to mind a seminal work of the Russian theater. Chekhov's sea gull, once the proud emblem of the Moscow Art Theatre, and hence symbolic not only of the wide-ranging influence of Stanislavsky's realism but of Russian imperialism as well, now lies dead and rotting, polluting the very atmosphere.[6]

Notes

1. Many of the plays referred to in this study were initially published in the literary magazine *Looming* and only later were issued in book form. Quite a few have been reprinted in volumes containing the collected or selected works of individual authors. Whenever such a collection exists, it will be cited in the references to this chapter. Unless otherwise indicated, all translations are mine, and each date given in the text is that of the initial publication in book form, as this study is limited to published plays.

2. See Karin Kask, "Poolsajand Draamateatrit (1916-1966)" [Half a Century of the Draamateater, 1916-1966], in *Teatrimärkmik 1965-1967*:465; cf. 427 (see References entry for "Eesti NSV Teatriühing"). For Brecht in Soviet Russia, see Henry Glade, "The Death of Mother Courage," in *Drama Review* 12 (Fall 1967):137-142. See also part 3 of Martin Esslin's *Brecht: The Man and His Work*, revised ed., Garden City, N.Y.: Doubleday, 1971, especially p. 229.

3. In a twenty-nine-page letter dated July 1969, in which Rummo commented on the commentators on *Cinderellagame*, he claimed, on the one hand, that while writing the play he tried to go beyond—or around—absurdism (p. 24); on the other hand, he admitted that *Cinderellagame* is absurdist (p. 27). Rummo denied, furthermore, the existence of ritual in his play, but he discussed ritual in terms of Christianity. This context suggests that his apologia may have been motivated by extra-aesthetic considerations. All quotations from *Cinderellagame* are from the translation by A. Männik and M. Valgemäe, which served as the text for the La Mama production.

4. Margaret Croyden, "New Trends in Russia?," in the *New York Times*, July 29, 1973, sec. 2, pp. 1, 4. See also the Drama

Mailbag of the *Times* for letters by A. Schneider (September 2) and M. Valgemäe (August 12) concerning Beckett in the Soviet Union.

5. Since the writing of this chapter, Jurašas has been allowed to leave the Soviet Union.

6. Portions of this study have appeared in *Books Abroad*, the *Bulletin of the Institute for the Study of the USSR*, *Comparative Drama*, and *Lituanus* (see References for details).

References

Aller, R.

1972   "Väikestest valedest suure valeni" [From Little Lies to a Big One]. *Pärnu Kommunist*, October 14.

Allik, Jaak

1970   "Mis see jumal meid on loonud" [Wherefore God Hath Us Created]. *Noorus* 25, no. 3 (March): 65-70.

Alliksaar, Artur

1966   *Nimetu saar* [The Nameless Island]. Tallinn: Perioodika.

Artaud, Antonin

1958   *The Theatre and Its Double*. New York: Grove Press.

Baum, Silvia

1972   " 'Vanemuine' nii ja teisiti" [*Vanemuine* Thus and So]. *Tartu Riiklik Ülikool*, March 31.

Brown, Deming

1975   "Czechoslovak and Polish Influences on Soviet Literature," in *The Influence of East Europe and the Soviet West on the USSR*, ed. Roman Szporluk. New York: Praeger.

Eesti NSV Teatriühing [Theater Association of the Estonian SSR]

1963- *Teatrimärkmik* [Theater Notebook], 9 vols. to date.
1974 Tallinn: Kirjastus Eesti Raamat. The first volume was called *Teatrimärkmeid* [Theater Notes] and the first three were published by Eesti NSV Teatriühing. The volumes cover the following years (publication dates in parentheses): 1961-1962 (1963); 1962-1963 (1964); 1963-1964 (1966); 1964-1965 (1967); 1965-1967 (1969); 1967-1968 (1970); 1968-1969 (1972); 1969-1970 (1972); 1970-1971 (1974).

Encyclopaedia Britannica

1958 "Cinderella," in vol. 5: 712. Chicago: Encyclopaedia Britannica, Inc.

Frazer, James George, and Theodore H. Gaster

1959 *The New Golden Bough*. New York: Criterion.

Funke, Lewis

1968 "Czech Metaphor." *New York Times*, April 28.

Grabbi, Hellar

1968 "Jooni Eesti palges: Sügis 1968" [Features in the Visage of Estonia: Fall 1968]. *Mana* 11, no. 2: 101-120.

Hint, Aadu

1949 *Kuhu lähed, seltsimees direktor?* [Where Are You Going, Comrade Director?]. Tallinn: Ilukirjandus ja Kunst.

Huizinga, Johan

1955 *Homo Ludens*. Boston: Beacon Press.

Ird, Kaarel

1970 *Semper idem*. Tallinn: Eesti Raamat.

Jakobson, August

1954   *Näidendeid 1* [Plays 1]. Tallinn: Eesti Riiklik Kirjastus.
1955   *Näidendeid 2* [Plays 2]. Tallinn: Eesti Riiklik Kirjastus.
1962   *Tormisôlmed* [Stormknots], 2 vols. Tallinn: Eesti Riiklik Kirjastus.

Järv, A., and A. Nagelmaa

1971   "Pilk eesti näitekirjandusele" [A Glance at Estonian Drama], in *Eesti Näidendeid* [Estonian Plays], ed. Järv and Nagelmaa. Tallinn: Eesti Raamat.

Jurašas, Jonas

1974   "An Open Letter to Soviet Authorities." *Index* 3 (Spring): 89-90.

Jüriado, Andres

1973   "Nationalism vs. Socialism: The Case of Soviet Estonian Drama," in *Baltic Literature and Linguistics*, ed. Arvids Ziedonis et al. Columbus: Association for the Advancement of Baltic Studies.

Kaalep, Ain

1968   "Fantaasia killapeod" [Clan Parties of Fantasy]. *Looming*, no. 10 (October), pp. 1592-1595.
1969   *Iidamast ja Aadamast ehk Antimantikulaator* [Of Idam and Adam, or The Antimanticulator]. *Mana* 12, no. 2: 17-39.
1970   "Bertolt Brechtist ja bukulobitsipitaaliast" [Of Bertolt Brecht and Bucolobiceptalism], in *Mees on mees. Galilei elu. Arturo Ui* [Estonian trans. of *Mann ist Mann, Das Leben des Galilei, Der aufhaltsame Aufstieg des Arturo Ui*], by Bertolt Brecht.
1973   "Helikindlate seinte vahel" [Between Soundproof Walls]. *Looming*, no. 1 (January), pp. 170-171.

Kään, H.

1969   "Mäng" [Play]. *Edasi*, April 13.

Kask, Karin

1969   "Juurdeütlemisi ja edasimõtlemisi" [Additional Comments and Further Thoughts]. *Sirp ja Vasar*, July 25.

1972   "Kas teater on noor?" [Is the Theater Young?]. *Noorus* 27, no. 7 (July): 41-45.

Kavolis, Vytautas

1973   "Literature and the Dialectics of Modernism," in *Literary Criticism and Sociology*, ed. Joseph P. Strelka. University Park, Pa.: Pennsylvania State University Press.

Kilgas, Paul

1961   *Ööbik laulis koidikul* [The Nightingale Sang at Dawn]. Tallinn: Eesti Riiklik Kirjastus.

Klaidman, Stephen

1968   "Czech Writer Probes Art of Allegory." *New York Times*, December 3.

Krusten, Erni

1956   *Mina elan* [I Live]. Tallinn: Eesti Riiklik Kirjastus.
1959   *Ameeriklased tulid* [The Americans Have Come]. Tallinn: Eesti Riiklik Kirjastus.
1970   *Ühemunakaksikud* [Identical Twins]. *Looming*, no. 2 (February), pp. 231-237.
1971   *Seal Üleval* [Up There]. *Looming*, no. 11 (November), pp. 1608-1615.
1972   *Veritas. Looming*, no. 5 (May); pp. 746-752.

Kruusvall, Jaan

1972   "Rändurid" [Wanderers]. *Sirp ja Vasar*, June 16.

Kurrik, Maire J.

1973   "Juhan Smuul's Moral Propaganda." *Journal of Baltic Studies* 4 (Fall): 226-235.

Lévi-Strauss, Claude

1966   *The Savage Mind.* Chicago: University of Chicago Press.

Liives, Ardi

1957   *Robert Suur* [Robert the Great]. Tallinn: Eesti Riiklik Kirjastus.
1958   *Uusaasta öö* [New Year's Eve]. Tallinn: Eesti Riiklik Kirjastus.
1959   *Sinine rakett* [The Blue Flare]. Tallinn: Eesti Riiklik Kirjastus.
1962   *Siinpool horisonti* [This Side of the Horizon]. Tallinn: Eesti Riiklik Kirjastus.
1964   *Viini postmark* [Viennese Postage Stamp]. Tallinn: Eesti Riiklik Kirjastus.
1971   *Neljas, lôpetamata portree* [The Fourth, Unfinished, Portrait]. *Looming,* no. 9 (September), pp. 1339-1367.

Luik, Hans

1970   "Julgus on ainult pool vôitu" [Courage Is Only Half the Victory]. *Rahva Hääl,* February 7.

Matjus, Ü.

1969   "Maskita näod" [Maskless Faces]. *Looming,* no. 5 (May), pp. 789-792.

Merilaas, Kersti

1973   *Kaks viimast rida* [The Last Two Lines]. Tallinn: Perioodika.

Mesilane, Riho

1972   "Amor ja Psyche" [Amor and Psyche]. *Sirp ja Vasar,* April 14.

Nagelmaa, Abel

1965   "Muretsemisi dramatismi pärast meie draamakirjanduses" [Concern over the Dramatic in Our Dramatic Literature]. *Sirp ja Vasar,* December 10.

1969   "Teatrikuul vôiks rääkida ka näitekirjandusest" [One Could Talk about Drama during the Theater Month]. *Sirp ja Vasar*, March 21, March 28.

Niinivaara, Eeva

1972   "Lydia Koidulasta Paul-Erik Rummoon: Virolainen näytelmä on elänyt sata vuotta" [From Lydia Koidula to Paul-Eerik Rummo: Estonian Drama Has Lived One Hundred Years]. *Helsingin Sanomat*, February 13.

Nirk, Endel

1970   *Estonian Literature*. Tallinn: Eesti Raamat.

Panso, Voldemar

1969   "Dramaturgia, teater, kriitika" [Dramaturgy, Theater, Criticism]. *Sirp ja Vasar*, April 25, May 2, May 9. Reprinted in *Teatrimárkmik 1968-1969*, pp. 20-32 (see Eesti NSV Teatriuhing).

Parv, Ralf

1959   *Ôndsuse labürint* [The Labyrinth of Beatitude]. Tallinn: Eesti Riiklik Kirjastus.
1964   *Seitsmemagaja-päeval* [On the Feast of the Seven Sleepers]. Tallinn: Eesti Riiklik Kirjastus.
1971   *Pimedus tähendab ööd* [Darkness Means Night]. Tallinn: Eesti Raamat.

Polster, Sandor M.

1968   "After the Thaw." *New York Post*, May 15.

Promet, Lilli

1973   *Los Caprichos* [Caprices]. *Looming*, no. 9 (September), pp. 1414-1454.

Rähesoo, Jaak

1969   "See maailm ja teised" [This World and Others]. *Looming*, no. 7 (July), pp. 1073-1093.

Rannet, Egon

1971   *Näidendid* [Plays]. Tallinn: Eesti Raamat.

Raud, Mart

1967   *Lavavalgelt* [From the Illumined Stage]. Tallinn: Eesti Raamat.

Reiljan, R., ed.

1973   *Valik näidendeid* [Selected Plays]. Tallinn: Eesti Raamat.
1974   *Eesti näidendeid 1972* [Estonian Plays 1972]. Tallinn: Eesti Raamat.

Rummo, Paul-Eerik

1969   *Tuhkatriinumäng* [Cinderellagame]. Tallinn: Perioodika. For the Lithuanian translation of scene 1 see *Metmenys*, no. 23, 1972, pp. 50-64.
1972   Sissejuhatuseks [Introduction], in *Thespis*, ed. Mati Unt. Tartu: Privately published.

Runnel, Hando

1973   "Vaino Vahingu üksildus" [The Loneliness of Vaino Vahing]. *Looming*, no. 2 (February), pp. 338-343.

Salynsky, Afansy [Salônski, Afanassi]

1967   "Nôukogude dramaturgia traditsioonide praegune areng" [Current Development of the Traditions of Soviet Dramaturgy]. Excerpts from speech at the Fourth Congress of Soviet Writers. *Sirp ja Vasar*, June 2.

Saluri, Rein

1974   *Külalised* [Visitors]. Tallinn: Perioodika.

Semper, Johannes

1961   *Näidendid* [Plays]. Tallinn: Eesti Riiklik Kirjastus.

Siimisker, Leenu

1969   "Kaasaegne repertuaar teatrilaval ja raamaturiiulil" [Contemporary Repertoire on Stage and the Bookshelf]. *Sirp ja Vasar*, April 11, April 18.

1970 "Kaks retsensiooni alustepanijate loomingu kohta" [Two Reviews concerning the Work of Seminal Artists]. *Looming*, no. 8 (August), pp. 1253-1262.

Smuul, Juhan

1972 *Valus valgus* [Painful Luminescence]. Tallinn: Eesti Raamat.

Stolovitš, L.

1969 "Dialoog Paul-Eerik Rummo *Tuhkatriinu* puhul" [Dialogue concerning Paul-Eerik Rummo's *Cinderella*]. *Noorus* 24, no. 4 (April): 46-51.

Taavas, Ü.

1970 "August Kitzberg ja Jaan Tooming." *Edasi*, February 1.

Talvest, Mai

1969 *Näidendeid* [Plays]. Tallinn: Eesti Raamat.

"Täna algab teatrikuu: 1321000."

1967 [The Theater Month Begins Today: 1321000]. *Noorte Hääl*, March 1.

Tobro, Valdeko

1971 "Õigus eksperimendile võrdub kohustusega kontrollida tulemust" [The Right To Experiment Equals the Obligation To Check the Results]. *Sirp ja Vasar*, December 10.

Tonts, Ülo

1969 "Sügise ja suve vahel" [Between Fall and Summer]. *Sirp ja Vasar*, June 27, July 4, July 11.

1972 "Juhan Smuuli värsi- ja draamaloomingust" [Concerning the Poetry and Drama of Juhan Smuul]. *Keel ja Kirjandus* 15, no. 10 (October): 577-589.

1973 "Algupärasest näitekirjandusest—kirjandus- ja teatripildis" [Concerning Original Plays in the Context of Literature and Drama]. *Keel ja Kirjandus* 16, no. 2 (February): 112-113.

Tormis, Lea

1969   "Juurdeütlemisi teatrihooaja lôpetuseks" [Addition-
        al Comments To End the Theater Season]. *Sirp ja
        Vasar*, July 18.

Unt, Mati

1968   "Kiri teatri kohta" [Letter concerning the Theater].
        Noorus 23, no. 11 (November): 61-62.
1969a   *Môrv hotellis. Phaethon, päikese poeg* [Hotel
        Murder. Phaethon, Son of Helios]. Tallinn: Perioo-
        dika.
1969b   "Intervjuu Evald Hermakülaga" [Interview with
        Evald Hermaküla]. *Edasi*, February 16.
1969c   "Gustav Suitsu ôhtu järel" [After the Evening Devot-
        ed to Gustav Suits]. *Looming*, no. 4 (April), pp. 633-
        636.
1969d   "Šokiteatrist" [Concerning the Theater of Shock].
        Sirp ja Vasar, July 18.
1970   "'Vanemuine' 100." *Noorus* 25, no. 9 (September):
        13-17.
1972   "Theater: Siin ja praegu" [Theater: Here and Now].
        Teatrimärkmik 1968-1969, pp. 128-139 (see Eesti
        NSV Teatriühing).
1973   "Mitmesuguse teatri poole" [Toward Diverse The-
        ater]. *Kultuur ja Elu* 16, no. 2 (February): 23-25.
1974   *Viimnepäev* [Doomsday], in *Mattias ja Kristiina*
        [Matthias and Christina], by Mati Unt. Tallinn: Eesti
        Raamat.

Vahak, Lemit

1972   *Karske ôhtupoolik* [Sober Afternoon]. Tallinn: Pe-
        rioodika.

Vahing, Vaino

1972   *Suvekool* [Summer School]. *Looming*, no. 8 (Au-
        gust), pp. 1305-1330.

Valgemäe, Mardi

1966 "Pilk Nôukogude eesti näitekirjandusele" [A Glance at Soviet Estonian Drama]. *Mana* 9, no. 4: 9-14 (Mana 31).

1969a "Tartu fööniks ehk Uuestisünni poisid Vanemuise teatris" [The Phoenix of Tartu, or The Renaissance Boys at Theater Vanemuine]. *Mana* 12: 32-43 (Mana 35).

1969b "Recent Developments in Soviet Estonian Drama." *Bulletin of the Institute for the Study of the USSR* 16 (September): 16-24. Translated into Swedish as "Utvecklingslinjer i det sovjetestniska dramat." *Horisont* 17, no. 3 (1970): 114-121.

1970 "The Ritual of the Absurd in P.-E. Rummo's *The Cinderella Game.*" *Lituanus* 16 (Spring): 52-60.

1971 "Socialist Allegory of the Absurd: An Examination of Four East European Plays." *Comparative Drama* 5 (Spring): 44-52.

1972 "Death of a Sea Gull: The Absurd in Finno-Baltic Drama." *Books Abroad* 46 (Summer): 374-379. Translated into Finnish as "Absurdismi Suomessa ja Baltiassa." *Uusi Suomi*, December 27, 1973.

Vetemaa, Enn

1968 *Illuminatsioonid keravälgule ja üheksale näitlejale (Pauguga lôpus)* [Illuminations for Ball Lightning and Nine Actors (With an Explosion at the End)]. *Looming*, no. 9 (September), pp. 1294-1313.

1974 *Püha Susanna ehk meistrite kool* [St. Susan, or The School for Masters]. Tallinn: Perioodika.

Zhdanov, A. A.

1950 *On Literature, Music and Philosophy*. London: Lawrence and Wishart.

9

Ethnographic Studies

Gustav Ränk

Soviet Estonian scholarship in ethnography can be best understood by viewing it within a historical context. In Estonia, as elsewhere in the world, this is a fairly recent branch of scholarly endeavor. In Estonia it received full recognition as a specialized discipline only in 1922, when it was incorporated into the program of the Faculty of Philosophy at the University of Tartu as an area of instruction. In accordance with traditions then existing in Eastern Europe, the field was named ethnography (*etnograafia*), although in Estonia it was also known as *rahvateadus*, which may be taken as equivalent to the German term *Volkskunde*. However, the Estonian *rahvateadus* differs from the German *Volkskunde* tradition in that it delimits subject interest to material culture and associated norms and customs. Folklore, folk beliefs, and folk religion, as well as the norms and customs related to these, became subjects of a separate discipline at the University of Tartu. The study of social organization and social structure in all their aspects remained peripheral.

In a practical sense, Estonian ethnography may be historically adjudged to be an outgrowth of the interest shown in folk culture by Estonian learned circles beginning in the second half of the nineteenth century. At that time, the country's rural population still lived to a very large degree in a traditional economic setting, as reflected in the prevalence of handmade tools and implements, folk clothing, folk art, and so forth. The prolific use and concomitant availability of such materials

319

stimulated among the Estonian learned organizations of the
period the idea of forming a native folk museum. The collection
efforts were undertaken, with this in mind, by such organizations as the Estonian Literary Society (Eesti Kirjanduse Selts),
the Estonian Learned Society (Õpetatud Eesti Selts), and the
Estonian Farmers Society (Eesti Põllumeeste Selts). By 1909
the holdings were sufficiently extensive to found an Estonian
National Museum (Eesti Rahva Muuseum) in the university
city of Tartu.[1] This event did not, however, lead to an abate-
ment in the collection effort; rather, it signaled an intensification of it. By 1920, and during the early years of the Republic of
Estonia, the collection approached 20,000 items. The role of
the museum in the emergence of Estonian ethnography has
been covered byRänk (1928).

In 1922 the museum employed its first director with a
specialized ethnographic education, the Finnish scholar Dr.
Ilmari Manninen, who was simultaneously appointed docent
of ethnography at the University of Tartu. The joint appointment held by Manninen in itself was extremely beneficial for
the future development of Estonian ethnography. Thus, the
man who provided theoretical instruction at the University of
Tartu also directed field-work seminars at the museum and
additionally employed his students in practical research exercises among the rural population. Manninen was a scholar of
very wide perspectives who incorporated into both instruction
and research activity all aspects of folk culture. For example,
he focused on such areas as folk-based food and cooking
economics, a subbranch of ethnography which even up to the
most recent times has often been ignored elsewhere in the
world. In undertaking the expansion of the museum's holdings, Manninen introduced the systematic interviewing of the
peasantry through his students. The result was a steady growth
of the museum's archival materials, which were continually
expanded through the network of rural correspondents which
Manninen had established. Without such an intensive and
systematic collection of materials, the museum's holdings
would have never attained the importance they did. The overall
effort allowed the preparation of a large number of ethnographic maps depicting the geographical patterns of occur-
rence of specific aspects of Estonian folk culture. The museum's holdings also served as a basis for the preparation of the
monographic research reports which were beginning to be

published by the institution. Additionally, from 1925 onward the museum published an annual *Yearbook* [Aastaraamat] which featured brief research reports. These publications in turn served as a basis for the exchange of scholarly materials with ethnographic museums and institutions all over the world (see Manninen, 1929; Ränk, 1956).

Ties between the museum and the University of Tartu were continually strengthened. In 1939 the chair of ethnography at the latter was elevated from docent to professorial level, with a provision for the subsequent addition of junior faculty. The new professorial chair was filled by this writer, the first native Estonian to head ethnographic instruction in the country. Primarily as a result of the early creation of a chair of ethnography at the University of Tartu, Estonian scholarship in this area has had from the beginning a strong methodological and theoretical base. Thus Estonia's scholarly activity in ethnography even today continues to outrank that found in the two southern Baltic countries, Latvia and Lithuania. In the former, university-based specialized training in the field was introduced very late during the interwar period; in the latter, there is no specialized training at all.

Reorganization of Scientific Activity during the Soviet Period

The Soviet entrance into the Baltic states in the summer of 1940 resulted not only in major changes in political life but also in the full reorganization of scientific life. The year of Soviet rule during 1940-1941, which preceded the outbreak of German-Soviet hostilities and the subsequent German occupation of the Baltic states, provided an early insight into the types of changes which would be forthcoming under a permanent Soviet regime. In a general sense, it may be asserted that during that year the whole organizational base of scientific, educational, and cultural life, as it had been built up during the period of the Estonian Republic and even in the decades before it, was destroyed.

The changes were especially pronounced in the area of ethnography. The large organizations which in one way or another had been involved in the study of folk culture were abolished. Among the organizations banned were the Estonian Learned Society, founded in 1838, and the Estonian Literary

Society, founded in 1907. Simultaneously, the Estonian National Museum was redesignated the State Museum of Ethnography of the Estonian SSR. Its activities were fully restructured (see Ränk, 1955). A large part of its archival holdings were transferred to a newly created separate facility, the Friedrich R. Kreutzwald Museum of Literature. Part of the art collection was transferred to the Tartu Museum of Art. Although additional personnel were added to the museum's staff in 1940, their energies were devoted not to scholarly activity but to the bureaucratic and administrative work resulting from the reorganization. Moreover, the new regime abolished the professorial-level chair of ethnography at the University of Tartu. The new position of docent of ethnography was placed under the chair of archaeology. However, both of these latter positions were subsequently abolished after the Soviet reentry into Estonia in late 1944. The new and temporary programs of instruction introduced at the university in 1940 were overladen with such subject areas as the history of the Communist party, the history of the Soviet Union, historical materialism, and other aspects of Marxist-Leninist teaching and doctrine.

In the introductory article in a volume dealing with Soviet Estonian ethnography edited by Moora and Viires (1964), one finds the following statement:

> During the years of the bourgeois Republic of Estonia, 1918-1940, ethnography became even more an "academic" discipline, which in many respects idealistically placed itself in the service of the ruling bourgeoisie.

No examples are given as to how Estonia's ethnographers of the republican period served the bourgeoisie, and one can only conjecture whether the aforenoted judgment is to be taken as a justification for or an excuse for the elimination of the chair of ethnography at the University of Tartu and other organizational changes. The elimination of the chair of ethnography has left Soviet Estonian ethnography without a directing theoretical authority—the presence of which is a prerequisite for the advance of any scientific discipline. This fact, incidentally, is also lamented by the Soviet Estonian ethnographer Peterson (1966:10).

The German occupation from 1941 to 1944 and the war in general resulted in more extensive changes to ethnography as a discipline. For example, cultural collections, archives, and libraries containing a large share of the ethnographic museum's holdings had been evacuated from the cities and sheltered in a multitude of locations. As it was, the museum's physical facilities were destroyed through war activity. Its director died in 1942 in Siberia, a victim of the Soviet deportations of 1940-1941. The remainder of the museum's scientific staff fled to the West before the Soviet reentry into Estonia late in 1944. It should be noted that many members of the faculty of the University of Tartu also fled at that time, preferring exile in Western European countries to Soviet rule in Estonia. Upon the Soviet reentry, a directive of the Council of Ministers of the Estonian SSR restored to the museum its former name, the Estonian National Museum, and reestablished a professorial chair of ethnography at the University of Tartu. When the Communists' political position had become firmer, these directives were annulled. Both the professorial position and that of docent, established during the initial Soviet occupation, were now abolished, along with the chairs of archaeology and folklore. Thus there was an abrupt decline in the level of academic activity in the three areas—ethnography, archaeology, and folklore—which dealt with the Estonian past and which served indirectly as mechanisms facilitating the development of a national consciousness or identity. The position of docent of folklore was, however, subsequently reestablished.

Since the immediate postwar years, Soviet Estonian ethnography has undergone further changes. The core institution in the area is again the Museum of Ethnography, as was the case prior to the establishment of the Estonian Republic. However, in many respects the museum has begun to play a much more significant role than was the case earlier. Since there is no chair of ethnography at the University of Tartu, it has become customary for ethnographic instruction there to be given by a member of the museum's scientific staff. (In regard to the museum's activities, see Linnus, 1966, 1967, 1968a, and 1969.) The museum in Tartu has itself been supplemented by the establishment in 1964 of an ethnographically oriented Outdoor Museum (*Vabaõhumuuseum*) near the capital, Tallinn (see Korzjukov, 1961). This museum displays buildings and relics of the old peasant culture. A third institution dealing

with ethnography is also to be found in Tallinn at the Soviet
Estonian Academy of Sciences, where a section on ethnography and archaeology was founded in 1952 as a subdivision of
the Institute of History.

The scientific staff which fled the country in 1944 was
replaced during the postwar years with a new generation, the
training of which was the work foremost of a now deceased
professor, Harri Moora. Having been a professor of archaeology during the prewar period and possessing some cross-
training in history and ethnography, Moora was the only
scholar in Estonia upon the Soviet return in 1944 who was
competent to organize the discipline anew and to train new ethnographers. An overview of Moora's contributions in this area
is to be found in Linnus (1968b) and Viires (1970).

Because of Professor Moora's efforts, the Museum of
Ethnography was able to continue operations on the basis of
the principles and objectives which had evolved during its
earlier history. The museum has continually expanded its
holdings, which by 1963 had exceeded the 65,000-item level
and which had reached 73,000 by 1973. This expansion was
necessitated by two specific factors: first, there was an urgent
requirement to replace items destroyed or lost as a result of the
war; second, it became necessary to collect quickly and preserve the relics of the rapidly disappearing peasant culture,
which was the inevitable victim both of the agricultural
collectivization undertaken in 1949 and of general industrialization. The second factor undoubtedly contributed to the
initiation of an intensive effort to inventory peasant dwelling-
construction techniques, an effort that included taking photo-
graphs and preparing detailed schematic plans. This project
was executed mostly by personnel from the Museum of
Ethnography. Because this area of folk culture had been
thoroughly studied during the prewar period, as a consequence
of the vigorous postwar effort it can be now stated confidently
that there is hardly any culture or country in the world where
folk construction has been studied so systematically. The
expeditious establishment of an outdoor ethnographic museum, an idea predating the war, may be similarly taken as
reflecting the desire to preserve aspects of traditional peasant
culture before modernization destroyed that culture fully.

Another pattern suggesting the continuation of the ethnographic traditions of the period of the republic is related to the

nature of the Museum of Ethnography's archival holdings and the methods of its collection. A renewed effort to collect data and artifacts in rural areas was undertaken after the war. As before, some of the work was done by individual field workers and some by a network of correspondents, a topic covered in greater detail in Eisler and Luts (1967). Complementing this method was an innovation worthy of note: namely, interdisciplinary expeditions to rural areas, with the aim of intensively investigating all aspects of a given locality. These expeditions, which were especially prominent during the decade of the 1950s, were often multinational in composition and were operated under the direction of a representative of the Soviet Academy of Sciences. However, in recent years little has been heard about such activities, which earlier covered various parts of the Baltic states.

The Soviet Academy of Sciences vigorously involved itself in Baltic ethnography during the postwar decades—primarily, it seems, in order to establish and secure Russian theoretical and methodological approaches. Its representative and instructor in Estonia from 1952 onward was A. Tšeboksarov. Even today, an "expert" from Russia is present in ethnographic explorations, presumably with the responsibility of ensuring that ethnography in the provinces moves along the same ideological and theoretical lines as it does in the Soviet research centers in Moscow and Leningrad (see Ränk, 1956).

According to the traditions of the earlier Estonian National Museum, the Museum of Ethnography continues to publish a yearbook in addition to, when possible and appropriate, special monographs. The first yearbook to be published during the Soviet era did not appear until 1947. It was titled *Yearbook of the Estonian National Museum*, as such annuals had been called during the republic, and its series number, 15, similarly implied a continuity. However, the next issue did not appear until 1959, at which time the new title was *Yearbook of the Museum of Ethnography*. Since then the publication has appeared annually, with a series enumeration dating to the founding of the republic. Articles of ethnographic substance have appeared also in the Soviet Estonian Academy of Sciences' *Toimetised* [Transactions] series and in specially issued volumes.

The number of people working in the area of ethnography is presently at a satisfactory level: fourteen at the Museum of

Ethnography and four or five in the section of ethnography
and archaeology at the Academy of Sciences (1965 data). What
is astounding, however, is that the central institution in this
area, the museum, continues to operate in an old building in
Tartu which was not constructed for this purpose. A new
physical plant would allow the museum to achieve both a
major expansion and a realization of its potential.

Circumstances of Scientific Work in Soviet Estonia

In a general sense, one may conclude that ethnographic
scholarship in Soviet Estonia has remained more or less
faithful to the traditions developed earlier, both in subject
matter pursued and in methods utilized. As noted previously,
Estonian ethnography from its beginnings dealt primarily with
material aspects of folk culture, and this focus has remained
preeminent to the present. The subject areas are, then, so
concrete and well defined that no theoretical-ideological controversy could ensue from them or from the methods used to
study them. The old typological-evolutionary approach, which
tended to dominate the ethnography of the Scandinavian-
Baltic region, was a carryover from archaeological traditions;
it never played a significant role in Estonia. While a researcher
of relics can of course never escape the use of typologies, in
Estonia these were viewed primarily as aids in the classification
of items rather than as research principles or as ends in
themselves. Rather, Estonian ethnographic research was characterized by historical realism, with its concomitant requirements of objectivity—a result of the influence of the Austrian-
German school of cultural history. The influence of this latter
tradition is noticeable in Estonian ethnography even at the
present time, even though it has been strongly criticized and
condemned as representing "objectivism." We shall return to
research done in this spirit subsequently. In the meantime,
attention should be drawn to some new trends which have been
officially encouraged, trends which have a tendency to shift the
subject discipline toward greater harmony with existing political ideology.

In the Soviet Union, ethnography in general is viewed
primarily as a branch of history—specifically, as that subdisci-
pline dealing with human culture, especially its material

aspects. (See, for example, the comments of Persits and
Tšeboksarov, 1968:9.) It is not unfair to state that Soviet
ethnography has remained largely untouched by the newer
currents in the study of human culture and society which began
to manifest themselves in the West after World War I. Concepts of cultural and social anthropology, as well as the
theoretical and methodological currents of structuralism and
functionalism, have remained alien. The theoretical base for
the story of culture in many respects remains even today the
classical evolutionism of Morgan and Engels, even though
actual research does not build major conclusions on this base.
Rather, what is closer to research efforts is historical materialism in its Marxist-Leninist variation, which purports to view
cultural development in the context of class conflicts and
dynamics (see, for example, the writing of Persits and Tšeboksarov, 1968:8-9). It appears that those who do not heed the
official line may be accused of "objectivism."

The annexation of the Baltic states by the USSR introduced
a new theme into scholarship: that of the "friendship of
peoples." This development has had practical consequences.
For example, it is demanded that scientists prove that the
renewed affiliation of the Baltic states with Russia has meant
the concomitant renewal of an assumed primeval friendship
between the peoples involved. In conjunction with this as-
sumption, it is expected that ethnographers will demonstrate
that this friendship and the Communist order within which it
has been implemented have brought sharp improvements in
the lives of the inhabitants in the Baltic. A Soviet Estonian
ethnographer, Peterson (1966:22), has explicitly stated that the
study of the relationships between the Western Finnish peoples
(Estonians, Karelians, Finns, and Livs) and the Slavs is one of
the two major thematic areas in Soviet Estonian ethnography.
The other theme is related to Estonian folklore, culture, and
other related ethnographic topics. A general overview of the
"great friendship theme" is offered by Tillett (1969).

The themes of class causality and the benefits of Russian
friendship are clearly present in the 1947 *Yearbook of the
Estonian National Museum* in two articles dealing with programs of research and study (Moora, 1947; Vassar, 1947). The
same line has been further enunciated by the Soviet ethnographer Tšeboksarov (1950) in the Russian-language periodical
Kratkije Soobscenija. Throughout the Stalinist period, these

ideas were repeated frequently—in Estonia as well as elsewhere. During this era a special emphasis was placed on the
demonstration of the progressive influence of Russian culture
and friendship on the culture of the Baltic people. Within the
framework of this campaign, references were made not only to
a Russian neighbor but to one who was always praised by such
adjectives as "great," "powerful," and "friendly." There was,
simultaneously, great caution exercised in the treatment of the
Russians' smaller neighboring nations. In 1949 the well-known
Russian authority on Finno-Ugric languages, D. Bubrich, was
admonished by the "Estonian expert" Tšeboksarov (1949) for
having observed in a presentation at a Leningrad scholarly
conference that there had been an ancient Finno-Ugric cultural
unity, even though only on a linguistic basis.

One of the specialized branches of Soviet ethnography is
ethnogenesis, which is defined as the study of ethnic history. In
this branch, research departs from a restricted path in order to
take into account all cultural factors as a single complex entity
(see, for example, Persits and Tšeboksarov, 1968:11-15). The
application of this approach has facilitated the demonstration
of how smaller nations in the Baltic area belonged primevally
to a Russian culture zone. Here we may see, in fact, the
revitalization of the old Austrian-German *Kulturkreislehre*,
which otherwise does not enjoy great favor among Soviet
scholars.

Nevertheless, the encompassing ethnic-history approach has
led to the publication of two noteworthy scholarly volumes in
postwar Estonia: one edited by Harri Moora (1956), dealing
with the country as a whole; the other a monograph by his wife,
Aliise Moora (1964), dealing with the area near Lake Peipsi.
Both are substantial and important studies by "older" Estonian
scholars who have attempted to avoid points of view not in
accordance with their personal convictions. However, several
concessions to Soviet doctrine have seemingly been made. For
example, one may note the radical shift in one aspect of Harri
Moora's thinking. In his doctoral dissertation, completed in
1938, he had emphasized the primacy of cultural relationships
between ancient Estonia and the Germanic tribes inhabiting
the area of the mouth of the Vistula River during the iron age.
During the first years of Soviet rule, Moora was forced to
publicly admit his "error" in this regard; a revised interpreta-
tion appeared in his later work (H. Moora, 1956:85).

The doctrine of the class nature of folk culture has in actuality remained an empty declaration. While on one or another occasion it is invoked, it has seldom been applied to research dealing with material culture. Soon after the collectivization of Baltic agriculture in the late 1940s, a new research direction was introduced: the study of all aspects of the newly created socialist society. As late as 1968 this approach was emphasized in an article by Persits and Tšeboksarov:

> One of the principal tasks of Soviet ethnography during the present time is the study of the progress of ethnic and material processes which are intensively bound to the practices of building communism in the Soviet Union . . . (1968:9).

A sample product of this effort in Estonia is volume 21 of the museum's yearbook (1966), which dealt with the southern Estonian region of Vôru, adjudged to be a typical Estonian area.

Behind this new trend was an obvious desire to demonstrate how the socialist order had fundamentally altered people's lives and, specifically, improved them in relation to the past. Activity of this type lasted but a few years and then subsided. The political leaders accused the scholars of being responsible for the scheme's failure. The latter were admonished by the former for their lack of requisite academic skills. Yet the responsibility for the failure obviously lay with the political planners themselves, who were unfamiliar with the realities of scientific inquiry. Such an effort required researchers to compile irrelevant descriptive statistics about the present— which, lacking the perspective of time, could not be compared to situations as they were in the past. Consequently, it was not startling that this pragmatically motivated experiment culminated in a fiasco. In itself, the tendency to expand ethnographic horizons to the present cannot be condemned. What is, however, condemnable about the scheme described above is its "vulgar-sociological" application.

The shifting of the Soviet Estonian ethnographic research focus to the contemporary period has meant that the subject matter pursued is no longer related solely to peasant culture; it must account additionally for the urban bourgeois culture as well as for that of the workers. These latter segments of society

have in fact come into Soviet Estonian ethnography as research subjects, although more in pronounced programs than
in field research; in regard to this matter, see Viires (1965:348-
349).

Research Results to Date

If ethnographers in postwar Estonia continued exclusively
to pursue research subjects and apply research methods developed during the prewar years, such a conservative attitude
might be adjudged a shortcoming. Indeed, social aspects of
culture—for example, social organization, social structure,
and values and norms related to these—still are almost fully
ignored. Yet a scrutiny of the situation reveals that the exploration of material cultural topics through the history-of-culture
approach, which strains toward objectivity, has provided a
protective cover—perhaps the only one possible—under which
the study of folk culture is feasible under the sharp eye of
Soviet ideology. Although, as noted, there have been attempts
to direct ideologically the study of Estonian folk culture,
reality has progressed calmly along its own path. Evidence of
this assertion is provided by an analysis of the museum's
yearbooks since the first volume in 1947: for every three articles
of ideological bent, which place new contemporary requirements on research, there simultaneously appear, say, six
scholarly pieces which do not appear in the least influenced by
such ideological declarations. The continued utilization of
methods already tested is, of course, of great advantage in the
study of folk culture in a confined space. Methods providing
new possibilities for appraising human culture in a global sense
tend to lose their meaning in such a narrow space as Estonia or
even in the whole area of the Baltic states.

The work done by Estonian ethnographers during the last
three decades may be characterized as an intense inventory of
various aspects of folk culture. This effort has produced not
monumental monographs but, rather, brief research reports, in
which scholars have attempted to define the smallest possible
details. Such efforts do not bring the authors great personal
fame; such is better attained through proposing new general
theories. In the long run, however, this mode of research will

provide a foundation on which future scholars can build with confidence.

The favorite topics of Soviet Estonian ethnography, as was the case during the period of the republic, are those which deal with building design and structure, folk costumes, and textile arts. The topics least covered are those related to means of livelihood; for example, fishing, hunting, animal husbandry, and herding. The focus of studies dealing with folk construction techniques has always been on the unique Estonian peasant dwelling, which grew out of a wheat drying and threshing facility (*rehi*). Although many authors have attempted to ascertain the age, spatial development, and geographical distribution of these unique living quarters, a consensus has yet to be achieved. Further clarification may be expected from materials which have recently been collected but which have yet to be completely analyzed. Extensive coverage of these subjects may be found in Tihase (1974), a recently published monograph.

Folk dress had been thoroughly studied and analyzed during the prewar years; as a consequence, present researchers have been able only to add details or suggest reevaluations. A major monograph on this topic was published in 1957, the result of a collective effort by the ethnographic museum's staff (Moora et al., 1957). In addition to color prints of excellent quality, this work includes many maps depicting geographical-occurrence patterns of specific designs. Monographic treatment has also been accorded to such textile products as mittens, hosiery, rugs, and embroidery (for examples, see Linnus, 1955; Hallik, 1957). Specialized treatment has also been accorded to folk costume jewelry and other folk jewelry made from silver. A scholar of Estonian art history, Helmi Üprus (1947; 1969), has made references in her studies of peasant jewelry and clothing items to prototypes which were outside the traditional peasant culture. These prototypes were found to have their origin in urban bourgeois culture or in general medieval art forms. Such appraisals, presented from the perspective of art history, open wider horizons for interpreting the development of one part of peasant culture.

New materials have also been brought forth by scholars dealing with folk handicraft techniques, traffic and transportation means, and food economics. In this regard, a person worthy of special recognition is Ants Viires, a researcher in the ethnographic and archaeological section of the Academy of Sciences, who published in 1960 a thorough monograph on woodworking techniques which has been translated into English (Viires, 1969). Viires' work is an important complement to Manninen's (1931-1933) two-volume work on the subject, which was not completed because of his death. Viires has also concentrated his efforts on traffic and transportation methods. To date he has published works on horseback riding, techniques of bridling and harnessing, sleighs, wagons, and one type of carrying frame. Another researcher, Jüri Linnus, presently the scientific secretary of the Museum of Ethnography, has made exhaustive studies of peasant artisans, especially smiths and smithery, primarily using historical archives as sources (see his recent monograph, 1975). Folk food economics, the most ignored aspect of folk culture everywhere, has found enthusiastic students in contemporary Estonia. Monographic studies devoted to archaic drinks and foods—for example, products made from hemp seeds—have been published. Aliise Moora has almost completed a major study on foods and drinks prepared from cereals. See Ränk (1971) for an overview of Estonian ethnographic work on folk food economics.

An interesting recent trend has been the study of the Estonian folk calendar (for an example, see Lätt, 1970). Similarly, although social structure and organization have been beyond the traditional scope of Estonian ethnography, a recent brief book on Estonian folk wedding customs by Tedre (1973) might represent a welcome harbinger of changing trends.

This chapter has taken into account all of the major activity in the realm of ethnography in Soviet Estonia. A brief review of the same subject is offered by Peterson (1966). A more thorough, although dated, coverage of problems, themes, and methods is to be found in the German-language work *Arbiss der Estnischen Volkskunde*, edited by Moora and Viires (1964). Excepting certain propagandistic phrases in the conclusions of the contributors to the latter compendium, its coverage of the subject matter is generally objective. A systematic overview of published ethnographic works is given by specialized bibliographies compiled by Viires and Linnus (1967) and Karu (1974).

Notes

1. The Estonian institutional name *Eesti Rahva Muuseum* can be translated in three different ways: Estonian People's Museum, Estonian Folk Museum, or Estonian National Museum. The last of these was the official English-language translation of the name of the institution. Its obvious nationalistic connotation might be one reason why the name of the museum has been changed several times during the Soviet period.

References

Belicer, V. N.
  1949   "Iz istorii estonskogo žilišča," in *Kratkije Soobščeni-ja*, vol. 11

Dunn, Stephen P., and Ethel Dunn, eds.
  1974   *Introduction to Soviet Ethnography*, 2 vols. Berkeley, Calif.: Highgate Road Social Science Research Station.

Eisler, Hele, and Arved Luts
  1967   "Eesti NSV Riikliku Etnograafiamuuseumi korrespondentide vôrgu tööst" [On the Work of the Network of Correspondents of the State Museum of Ethnography of the Estonian SSR], in *Etnograafiamuuseumi Aastaraamat* [Yearbook of the Museum of Ethnography], vol. 22.

Hagar, Helmut
  1965   *A Bibliography of Works Published by Estonian Ethnologists in Exile, 1945-1965*. Stockholm: Institutum Litterarum Estonicum. (See also Ränk, A., 1975.)

Hallik, C.

1957   *Silmuskudumine* [Knitting]. Tallinn: Eesti Riiklik
        Kirjastus.

Karu, Ellen

1974   *Eesti Nõukogude etnograafia. Bibliograafia 2* [Esto-
        nian Soviet Bibliography, vol. 2]. Tallinn. (Comple-
        ments 1967 bibliography by Viires and Linnus.)

Korzjukov, O.

1961   "Eesti Riiklik Vabaõhumuuseum" [The Estonian
        State Outdoor Museum], in *Eesti NSV Muuseumid*
        [The Museums of the Estonian SSR], comp. I.
        Rosenberg. Tallinn: Eesti Raamat.

Lätt, S., comp.

1970   *Eesti rahvakalender 1* [The Estonian Folk Calendar,
        vol. 1]. Tallinn: Eesti Raamat.

Linnus, H.

1955   *Tikand Eesti rahvakunstis I. Põhja-Eesti ja saared*
        [Embroidery in Estonian Folk Art. Vol. 1: Northern
        Estonia and the Islands]. Tallinn: Eesti Riiklik Kir-
        jastus.

Linnus, Jüri

1966   "Eesti NSV Riikliku Etnograafiamuuseumi tegevus-
        est 1964. ja 1965. aastal" [On the Activities of the
        State Ethnographic Museum of the Estonian SSR in
        1964 and 1965], in *Etnograafiamuuseumi Aastaraa-
        mat*, vol. 21.
1967   "Eesti NSV Riikliku Etnograafiamuuseumi tegevus-
        est 1966. aastal" [On the Activities of the State
        Ethnographic Museum of the Estonian SSR in
        1966], in *Etnograafiamuuseumi Aastaraamat*, vol.
        22.
1968a   "Eesti NSV Riikliku Etnograafiamuuseumi tegevus-
        est 1967. aastal" [On the Activities of the State
        Ethnographic Museum of the Estonian SSR in

1967], in *Etnograafiamuuseumi Aastaraamat*, vol. 23.

1968b "Harri Moora ja Etnograafiamuuseum" [Harri Moora and the Museum of Ethnography], in *Etnograafiamuuseumi Aastaraamat*, vol. 23

1969 "Eesti NSV Riikliku Etnograafiamuuseumi tegevusest 1968. aastal" [On the Activities of the State Ethnographic Museum of the Estonian SSR in 1968], in *Etnograafiamuuseumi Aastaraamat*, vol. 24.

1975 *Maakäsitöölised Eestis 18. sajandil ja 19. sajandi algul* [Rural Handicraftsmen in Estonia during the Eighteenth and Early Nineteenth Centuries]. Tallinn: Valgus.

Manninen, Ilmari

1929 *Übersicht der ethnographischen Sammelarbeit in Eesti in den Jahren 1923-1926*. Tartu: Verhandlung der Estnischen Gelehrten Gesellschaft.

1931- *Die Sachkultur Estlands*, 2 vols. Tartu: Verhandlung
1933 der Estnischen Gelehrten Gesellschaft.

Moora, Aliise

1956 "Ajaloolis-etnograafilistest valdkondadest Eestis" [On the Subject Realms of Ethnography and History in Estonia], in *Eesti rahva etnilisest ajaloost* [On the Ethnic History of the Estonian People], ed. Harri Moora. Tallinn: Eesti Riiklik Kirjastus.

1964 *Peipsimaa etnilisest ajaloost. Ajaloolis-etnograafiline uurimus eesti-vene suhetest* [On the Ethnic History of the Area Northwest of Lake Peipsi: A Historical-Ethnographic Study of Estonian-Russian Contacts]. Tallinn: Eesti Riiklik Kirjastus.

Moora, Harri

1938 *Die Eisenzeit in Lettland. 2.* Tartu: Der Gelehrten Estnischen Gesellschaft (Verhandlungen no. 29).

1947 "Eesti etnograafia nôukogulikul ülesehitamisel" [The Soviet Building-up of Estonian Ethnography], in *Eesti Rahva Muuseumi Aastaraamat*, vol. 1 [15].

1956   "Eesti rahva ja naaberrahvaste kujunemisest arheo-
        loogia andmeil" [On the Development of the Estoni-
        an Nation and Neighboring Nations on the Basis of
        Archaeology], in *Eesti rahva etnilisest ajaloost* [On
        the Ethnic History of the Estonian People], ed. Harri
        Moora. Tallinn: Eesti Riiklik Kirjastus.

Moora, Harri, ed.

1956   *Eesti rahva etnilisest ajaloost. Artiklite kogumik* [On
        the Ethnic History of the Estonian People: A Collec-
        tion of Articles]. Tallinn: Eesti Riiklik Kirjastus.

Moora, Harri, and A. Viires, eds.

1964   *Abriss der Estnischen Volkskunde*. Tallinn: Est-
        nischer Staatsverlag.

Moora, Harri, et al., eds.

1957   *Eesti rahvarôivad 19 sajandist ja 20 sajandi algult*
        [Estonian Folk Costumes from the Nineteenth and
        Early Twentieth Centuries]. Tallinn: Eesti Riiklik
        Kirjastus.

Persits, A. I., and N. N. Tšeboksarov

1968   "Pool sajandit nôukogude etnograafiat" [Half a
        Century of Soviet Ethnography], in *Etnograafia-
        muuseumi Aastaraamat*, vol. 23.

Peterson, Aleksei

1961   "Eesti NSV Teaduste Akadeemia Etnograafia Muu-
        seum" [The Ethnographic Museum of the Academy
        of Sciences of the Estonian SSR], in *Eesti NSV
        Muuseumid* [The Museums of the Estonian SSR],
        comp. I. Rosenberg. Tallinn: Eesti Raamat.

1966   "Eesti nôukogude etnograafia aastail 1940-1965"
        [Estonian Soviet Ethnography during the Years
        1940-1965], in *Etnograafiamuuseumi Aastaraamat*,
        vol. 21.

Ränk, Aino

1975   *Ethnology 1945-1975: A Bibliography of Works Published by Estonian Scholars in Exile.* Folia Bibliographica, no. 5. Stockholm: Institutum Litterarum Estonicum.

Ränk, Gustav

1928   "Das Estnische Nationalmuseum und die ethnographische Arbeit in Eesti 1922-1927," in *Eurasia Septentrionalis Antiqua*, vol. 3.
1955   *The Small Nations under Soviet Rule.* East and West Series, no. 4. London: Boreas.
1956   "Die estnische Volkskundeforschung in der Jahren 1945 bis 1955." *Zeitschrift für Ostforschung* 5, no. 2.
1971   "Ethnologische Nahrungsforschung in den Baltischen Staaten," in *Ethnologia Europaea*, vol. 5.

Rosenberg, I.

1961   "Eesti muuseumide arenemisteest" [On the Development of Estonian Museums], in *Eesti NSV Muuseumid* [The Museums of the Estonian SSR], comp. I. Rosenberg. Tallinn: Eesti Raamat.

Slygina, N. V.

1956   "Estonskoe krestijanskoe žilišče v. 19 -nacale 20 v." *Baltijskij Etnografičeskij Sbornik.* Trudy Instituta Etnografii, vol. 32. Moscow.

Tedre, Ü.

1973   *Eesti pulmad. Lühi ülevaade muistsetest kosja- ja pulmakommetest* [The Estonian Wedding: A Brief Overview of Ancient Wooing and Wedding Customs]. Tallinn: Eesti Raamat.

Tihase, Karl

1974   *Eesti talurahva arhitektuur* [The Architecture of Estonian Peasants]. Tallinn: Kirjastus Kunst.

Tillett, Lowell

1969   *The Great Friendship: Soviet Historians on the Non-Russian Nationalities.* Chapel Hill, N.C.: University of North Carolina Press.

Tšeboksarov, N. N.

1949   "Etnograficeskaja rabota v Sovetskoj Pribaltike," in *Sovetskaja Etnografija 1949.* Moscow.
1950   "Etnograficaskaja rabota v Estonskoj SSR." *Kratkije Soobscenija* 12.

Üprus, Helmi

1947   "Hôbehelmeid ja eesti soost ehtemeistrid" [Silver Ornaments and Ornamental Smiths of Estonian Descent], in *Eesti Rahva Muuseumi Aastaraamat*, vol. 1 [15].
1969   "Eesti rahvakunst kunstiajaloo aspektist" [Estonian Folk Art from the Perspective of Art History], in *Etnograafiamuuseumi Aastaraamat*, vol. 24: 7-40.

Vassar, Artur

1947   "Etnograafilise korjamistöö ülesanded Nôukogude Eestis" [The Tasks of Ethnographic Field Work in Soviet Estonia], in *Eesti Rahva Muuseumi Aastaraamat*, vol. 1 [15].

Viires, Ants

1965   "Über die etnographische Forschungsarbeit in Sowjetestland." *Finnisch-ugrische Forschungen* 35.
1969   *Woodworking in Estonia: A Historical Survey.* Translated from Estonian by J. Levitan, Israel Program for Scientific Translations, Jerusalem. Published for the Smithsonian Institution, Washington, D.C., by the Israel Program for Scientific Translations, Jerusalem. (Originally published in Tallinn in Estonian in 1960.)

1970   "Harri Moora ja eesti etnograafia" [Harri Moora and Estonian Ethnography], in *Studia Archeologica in memoriam Harri Moora*, ed. M. Schmiedehelm et al. Tallinn: Valgus.

Viires, Ants, and Jüri Linnus

1967   *Eesti nõukogude etnograafia bibliograafia* [A Bibliography of Estonian Soviet Ethnography]. Tallinn. (Complemented by Karu, 1974.)

Part 4
Higher Education, Research, and Science

10

The Structure of
Higher Education and Research

Teodor Künnapas and Elmar Järvesoo

On the one hand, Soviet Estonian institutions of higher learning and research have a continuity from prewar times. On the other hand, the structure of higher education has undergone appreciable change under Soviet rule. At present the Estonian SSR has six institutions of higher learning. Of these, the University of Tartu (Tartu Riiklik Ülikool) and the Estonian Agricultural Academy (Eesti Põllumajanduse Akadeemia) are in Tartu, while the Tallinn Polytechnic Institute (Tallinna Polütehniline Instituut), the Tallinn Pedagogical Institute (Tallinna Pedagoogiline Instituut), the Art Institute (Eesti NSV Riiklik Kunstiinstituut), and the Tallinn Conservatory (Tallinna Riiklik Konservatoorium) are located in Tallinn. The primary research facility, the Estonian Academy of Sciences (Eesti NSV Teaduste Akadeemia), is also headquartered in Tallinn, although many of its subordinate institutes and laboratories are located elsewhere. All of these institutions have pre-Soviet roots.

Major changes during the Soviet period include the following: massive administrative reorganization; introduction of new areas of teaching, scholarship, and research reflecting modern world scientific trends; expansion of the overall educational and research plant; and appreciably greater funding of education and research. However, probably the most radical change from prewar times is the integration of the educational and research process with political ideology. The Communist party has dictated new goals and methods for academic and scholarly life, and it has a direct and integral administrative role within educational and scientific organizations and structures. New chairs have been created for purposes of political indoctrination, integration, and mobilization. In the latter respects, the situation in Soviet Estonia merely reflects general Soviet patterns.

After the implementation of Soviet rule in Estonia, the institutions of higher education and research were at first subordinated directly to the Ministry of Higher and Secondary Specialized Education of the USSR in Moscow. In 1941 the Committee for Higher and Secondary Specialized Education was established by the Council of Ministers of the Estonian SSR, and responsibility for running the local institutions was delegated to this body. Subsequently, these responsibilities were transferred to the newly created Ministry of Higher and Specialized Education of the Estonian SSR. The only present exception to local administrative control is the Estonian Agricultural Academy, which is under the jurisdiction of the Ministry of Agriculture of the USSR in Moscow.

The highest academic rank in the teaching staff is that of professor (or acting professor), followed by docent (assistant professor in the United States), then senior and junior instructors and assistants. Appointment to a professorship presupposes a doctoral degree; since such degrees are relatively rare in the Soviet Union, only 9 percent of the teaching staff of the University of Tartu, for example, had professorial rank in 1971 (only 4 percent at the Estonian Agricultural Academy). Docents account for about one-fourth to one-third of the total teaching staff, while the rest is made up of junior and senior instructors and assistants.

The undergraduate course of study typically lasts five years except in the medical faculty, where it is six years. In the Faculty of Physical Education at the University of Tartu, the course of study is an exception in that it lasts only four years. Typically, universities and other higher schools have three categories of students: resident students, who are full-time day students, nonresident evening students, and nonresident correspondence students. The second and third categories of students make up a very significant proportion of the total enrollment—in Soviet Estonia, nearly one-half in recent years.

Admission to higher educational establishments is normally achieved through competitive entrance examinations, since the number of applicants usually far exceeds the available places. There are minor exceptions to this rule: "gold medal graduates" of secondary schools (comparable to summa cum laude or cum laude graduates) are excused from the examinations. Also, applicants who pass the first subjects of the entrance examinations with the highest marks are not required to take the rest of the exams. The entrance examination includes the Estonian and Russian languages, mathematics, and some additional subjects from the proposed field of study. A Komsomol recommendation is weighted heavily in the selection of candidates.

In the past, one or two years of work experience after secondary school was required. This requirement has been dropped, but work experience is still encouraged and is viewed very favorably. Institutions arrange special short refresher courses in entrance examination subjects in an effort to help applicants with work experience, so that they can compete with recent secondary-school graduates on a more equitable basis. The procedures just described apply only to full-time resident students. Evening students and correspondence students are normally enrolled without entrance examinations, so long as their chosen fields of study are related to their current employment. However, examinations may be required if their proposed fields of study are unrelated to their occupations, if laboratory or work space is limited, or in such special fields of study as music and graphic arts.

About 70 percent of the full-time students in Estonia receive fellowships based solely on academic achievement. A regular fellowship provides about 40 rubles a month, a stipend that normally covers about half of a student's total expenses. Consequently, family support, or part-time employment for students from low-income families, is usually necessary. A few fellowships are available for especially talented students which approximately meet all study-related expenses. The highest paying are the Lenin fellowships: 100 rubles per month for undergraduate students. Besides scholastic achievement, active participation in Komsomol or party organizations is expected of candidates for special fellowships.

It is noteworthy that female students in Estonia constitute 51-52 percent of all students enrolled in higher education.

Table 1

Number of students and freshmen enrolled
in Soviet Estonia, 1950 - 1974

	1950	1960	1970	1971	1972	1974
Total students enrolled	8,813	13,507	22,078	21,980	21,790	22,212
Full-time resident students	6,791	7,578	12,215	12,491	12,812	13,432
Evening students	207	551	2,621	2,626	2,504	2,493
Correspondence students	1,815	5,378	7,242	6,863	6,473	6,287
Total freshmen enrolled	2,284	3,226	4,911	5,023	4,794	5,110
Full-time students	1,652	1,688	3,050	3,078	3,109	3,210
Part-time students (employed)	632	1,538	1,861	1,945	1,685	1,900

Source: Eesti NSV rahvamajandus, 1976:327.

Among full-time resident students and correspondence students, women accounted for 53 percent in 1971; and among evening students, 42 percent. About 60 percent, or 7,600, of the nearly 12,500 full-time students now reside in dormitories—an innovation in Estonia, where students traditionally had to find accommodations in private homes (*ERM*, 1972:323; *ERM*, 1974:308). Summary data on enrollment and specialization patterns are presented in tables 1–3.

Attrition among undergraduate students is relatively high, considering the favorable conditions. Since 1960, the number of graduates has varied from 55 percent to 63 percent of the number of freshmen enrolled five years earlier (*ERM*, 1972:321; *ERM*, 1974:305). Table 2 presents an overview of graduates of higher education from 1945 through 1974 by specialties. In recent years, about 3,000 students have graduated annually.

Although postgraduate studies toward advanced degrees in the Soviet system involve relatively little formal course work, they require more individual research and independent studies under the guidance of a major adviser than is the case in America. Also, the selection of degree candidates (aspirants) is probably more stringent academically and politically in Estonia than in the United States. Consequently, there are proportionately fewer aspirants relative to the number of undergraduate students. Since it is not necessary for an aspirant to be

Table 2

Graduates of higher education by specialties
in Soviet Estonia, 1945 - 1974

	1945– 1955	1956– 1960	1961– 1965	1966– 1970	1970	1972	1974	Total 1945– 1974
Geology	92	221	90	89	20	16	15	543
Energetics	246	257	243	351	92	59	69	1,355
Machine construction	213	586	793	1,483	385	398	360	4,536
Electronics	–	–	3	124	36	25	36	242
Chemical technology	317	332	200	373	85	69	51	1,449
Lumber, paper, and pulp technology	73	51	–	–	–	–	–	124
Food technology	–	63	88	351	86	64	53	773
Civil engineering	507	433	504	653	151	101	167	2,633
Hydrology and meteorology	–	7	5	–	–	–	–	12
Agriculture and forestry	1,236	1,714	1,514	1,452	412	435	390	7,532
Transportation	–	61	75	106	33	30	30	357
Economics and law	1,017	728	1,033	1,857	463	592	608	7,052
Health and physical education	1,437	1,004	1,148	1,101	211	252	243	5,668
Education	4,465	3,862	2,824	3,570	795	832	872	17,992
Arts	475	258	300	494	119	123	123	1,982
Other	–	–	16	–	–	–	–	16
Totals	10,078	9,577	8,835	12,004	2,888	2,996	3,023	52,266

Source: Eesti NSV rahvamajandus, 1976:380.

enrolled as a regular student at an institution of higher education, candidates are frequently found at research institutes, usually within the Academy of Sciences, or at agricultural experiment stations and research institutions under the jurisdiction of the Ministry of Agriculture. Once admitted, all aspirants draw fellowships, the amounts of which vary. If a full-time aspirant was previously employed, his fellowship will match the salary he earned up to a maximum of 100 rubles per month. Like part-time correspondence undergraduate students, part-time aspirants can pursue advanced studies without interrupting their employment.

In 1971 the total number of aspirants in Estonia was 536. In 1972 the number was 494, and in 1974 it declined to 453. The number of full-time aspirants dropped from 330 in 1971 to 287 in 1972 and 202 in 1974, while others pursued part-time studies. It is not unusual to find *sovkhoz* directors, *kolkhoz* chairmen, or leading personnel of other socialist establishments among part-time nonresident aspirants. In all, twenty-one educational and research establishments in Estonia have been approved for admitting and training aspirants. In 1974, 238 (58 percent) of all aspirants were associated with the six educational institutions; of these, 129 were studying full time and 109 part time. Of the remaining 215 aspirants, 93 were full-time and 122 were part-time students (*ERM*, 1974:309). Between 1948 and 1974 a total of 2,286 aspirants completed their studies, averaging 85 completions per year (*ERM*, 1974:310). In recent years this figure has been between 130 and 150.

Engineering sciences represented nearly 26 percent of the 453 Estonian aspirants in 1974, a proportion that reflects the Soviet emphasis on industrialization and corresponding manpower-training programs. Economics ranked second, with 61 aspirants (13 percent of the total), followed by physics-mathematics with 58 aspirants (13 percent). Medical sciences, chemistry, biology, agriculture, and philology trailed, with 25 to 31 aspirants in each field.

The University of Tartu

The oldest among the six Estonian institutions of higher education is the University of Tartu, the founding of which dates to 1632 (Inno, 1972; Kangro, 1970). With the implementation of Soviet rule the university has undergone many radical changes in organization and still more in its academic curricula, a process described in greater detail by Oras (1948). First, the Faculty of Theology was closed on the ground that it was incompatible with Communist doctrine. Many courses were abolished, while new all-university Marxist indoctrination teaching chairs were established and new courses initiated. In 1951, the faculties of agriculture, forestry, and veterinary science were separated from the university to become the foundation for a new, independent institute of higher education—the Estonian Agricultural Academy. Subsequent reorganizations have split some of the other faculties of the university.

Currently, the university has nine faculties: history, linguistics, medicine, biology-geography, physics-chemistry, mathematics, physical education, economics and business, and law. There are also special general faculties for professional improvement. In 1974, two such faculties were in operation: one for physicians, dentists, and pharmacists; the other for physical education.

The number of teaching chairs has changed over the years, showing in general a tendency of growth. In 1961 the university had sixty-five teaching chairs, a number which had increased to seventy-six by 1974. Six all-university chairs are outside of the faculties, reporting directly to the president (rector). Four of these are sociopolitical chairs: Communist philosophy, history of the Communist party of the Soviet Union, Marxism, and political economy and scientific communism. In addition, pedagogy and methodology and military science are also all-university chairs whose courses are compulsory for all students.

Within the faculties, the Faculty of History has four chairs and Linguistics has eight teaching chairs: Estonian language, Estonian literature and folklore, Finno-Ugric languages, Russian language, Russian literature, Russian history, history of the Soviet Union, and general history. However, there is no chair for Estonian history.

The Medical Faculty is the largest one at the university, comprising twenty-three chairs, including one of dentistry. The Faculty of Biology and Geography has seven teaching chairs: genetics and Darwinism, zoology, plant physiology and plant biochemistry, geology, physical geography, economic geography, and geobotany. The Faculty of Physics and Chemistry has six chairs, the Faculty of Mathematics also has six, and the Faculty of Physical Education has seven, including one for sports medicine (the latter is the only such chair in the Soviet Union).

The Faculty of Economics and Business has five teaching chairs: organization of trade, methods of commodity testing, accounting, money and credit, and national economy. The Faculty of Law has only four teaching chairs: criminal law and proceedings, constitutional and administrative law, history of constitutional law and jurisprudence, and common law and civil proceedings. In comparison, it might be noted that in prewar Estonia, the University of Tartu in 1938 had 127 professorial chairs.

The former Faculty of Humanities has experienced the most profound change through its reorganization into the Faculties of History and Linguistics. In this reorganization Estonian studies suffered most, giving way to greatly expanded Russian studies. In the prewar university, ethnic-related disciplines were represented by nine professorships: Estonian language, Baltic-Finnish languages, Uralic linguistics, Estonian and world literature, Estonian and comparative folklore, Estonian and comparative ethnography, Estonian and regional archaeology, and Estonian and regional history (the last with two professorial positions). Presently, there are only three teaching chairs for Estonian ethnic disciplines: Estonian language, Estonian literature and folklore, and Finno-Ugric linguistics. In addition, Estonian history is being taught only to a limited degree within the chair for the history of the Soviet Union. Research into Estonian history has been removed from the university altogether as a result of the transfer of responsibilities to the Institute of History of the Academy of Sciences in Tallinn. Research in archaeology was also moved to Tallinn.

The university's teaching staff currently numbers a little more than 640. In 1974 it included 64 professors and acting professors, 200 docents and acting docents, some 230 senior instructors (lecturers) and instructors, 115 assistants, and 36 military science instructors. Only 95 of these had doctoral degrees, 380 had candidate of sciences degrees, and the remaining 169 faculty members and 36 military instructors had no advanced academic degree. Nearly 24 percent of the university teaching staff is in the Medical Faculty, 17 percent is in the Faculty of Linguistics, and 12 percent are associated with the all-university teaching chairs. The remaining 47 percent are divided among six faculties, of which physics and chemistry and physical education are the largest and law and economics is the smallest. There are also many teaching aides and other technical personnel who are partly supported by contract research conducted for various institutions and firms.

Since 1965 the number of enrolled students has been rather stable, fluctuating between 6,100 and 6,300. However, of these, only about 3,500 are resident students. Of the residents, about 1,300 are in the Medical Faculty, including those in dentistry and pharmacy. In this faculty, virtually all students are resident students. Nonresident and part-time students are more typically found in the faculties of history and linguistics, pedagogy, and economics and law, where their number is double or triple that of resident students. Physical education and biology-geography also have large proportions of nonresident and

Table 3

Total number of students enrolled and freshmen admitted
in institutions of higher education in Estonia, 1960 - 1974

Establishment	1960	1965	1970	1974
Total number of students enrolled (including part-time students)	13,507	21,363	22,078	22,212
Tallinn Polytechnic Institute	3,978	9,594	9,162	9,168
Tartu State University	5,534	6,122	6,273	6,262
Tallinn Pedagogical Institute	1,302	1,836	2,109	2,115
Tallinn State Conservatory	201	324	337	435
State Institute of Art	219	323	471	486
Estonian Agricultural Academy	2,273	3,164	3,726	3,746
Freshmen admitted	3,226	4,959	4,911	5,110
Tallinn Polytechnic Institute	1,134	2,385	2,159	2,181
Tartu State University	891	1,335	1,342	1,390
Tallinn Pedagogical Institute	576	401	529	555
Tallinn State Conservatory	51	73	89	122
State Institute of Art	49	57	91	87
Estonian Agricultural Academy	525	708	701	775
Number of graduates (in calendar year)	2,002	2,043	2,888	3,023
Tallinn Polytechnic Institute	352	570	1,093	1,070
Tartu State University	708	740	799	920
Tallinn Pedagogical Institute	539	287	372	404
Tallinn State Conservatory	25	49	72	59
State Institute of Art	20	62	60	89
Estonian Agricultural Academy	358	335	492	481

Source: Eesti NSV rahvamajandus, 1976:328-329.

part-time students, approximately one-half of the total number. Between 1965 and 1974 the University of Tartu graduated from 680 to 930 students annually. Freshman enrollments during the same period ranged between 1,292 and 1,394, of whom 800 to 900 were resident students (see table 3).

The University of Tartu is also a significant research center. Research is conducted partly within the teaching chairs and partly within the university research institutes and laboratories. Much of the research is funded from outside the university on a contract basis. In 1974 there were twelve budget-supported research institutes and "problem laboratories." The largest and best known among these are the Central Medical Laboratory (which has several sectors), the Computer Center, the Electroluminescense and Transistor Laboratory, the Aeroinisation and Electroaerosol Laboratory, the Biophysics and Electrophysiology Laboratory, and the Electrochemistry Laboratory. Among the laboratories financed mainly by outside industrial funds is the recently established Industrial Psychology Laboratory. There are also laboratories for Communist education and sociological research. Research laboratories are fairly well supplied with supporting personnel—research workers, engineers, and technicians. The Computer Center, for example, had in 1974 a total of fifty regular staff members in addition to twenty-two people working on contract research and assignments.

Nonacademic organizations with considerable influence at the university include the Communist party, the Komsomol, and the trade union. The party organization is operated by a full-fledged committee and a full-time secretary, supported by twelve party bureaus: one in each faculty, one in the chair for military sciences, and some in larger departments. It is the primary function of the party to ensure that the academic work of the university is firmly and unswervingly based on Marxist-Leninist foundations. The Komsomol organization has the mission of organizing and conducting Communist indoctrination among the students. About 60-70 percent of the student body belongs to the Komsomol, a proportion that perhaps reflects the fact that it is difficult to be admitted otherwise. The university trade union includes the entire teaching staff, students, and nonprofessional employees, and it runs, among other things, all dormitories, dining halls, and various recreational facilities. The Student Scientific Association at the university and at other institutions encourages scientific investigation among undergraduates through sponsoring competitions and symposia.

The dominant language of education is still Estonian, although parallel courses are conducted in Russian in several fields and in the Medical Faculty a complete program is offered in Russian. In military science the majority of instructors do not speak Estonian at all. During the last two decades the top executives of the university, the rectors, have been ethnic Estonians, but Russian-born and educated. Fiodor Klement, a physicist from Leningrad, wore the mantle of the rector from 1951 to 1970; since then the post has been held by Arnold Koop, a candidate of history and a former *apparatchik*, a graduate of the party academy in 1960. Born in 1922 near

Leningrad, he moved to Estonia after World War II and after 1952 was associated with the Tallinn Pedagogic Institute as a teacher, dean, and rector (1960-1968).

The Tallinn Polytechnic Institute

In comparison with the University of Tartu, the Tallinn Polytechnic Institute is a relatively young institution. In its present form it dates to 1936, at which time a former technical college in Tallinn and the Faculty of Technology of the University of Tartu were merged to form a new institution. The present name dates to 1941. The institute, with its enrollment of more than 9,000 students, is now the largest institution of higher education in Estonia. In 1967 the institute moved to a newly built campus in Tallinn's Mustamäe area, about three miles northeast of the city center. Its function is to provide higher technological education and to conduct research in a wide variety of fields.

The institute has six faculties: energetics, electrical engineering, civil engineering, technical engineering, chemical engineering, and economics and business. In addition, there are separate departments for night students and nonresident students. Each faculty is headed by a dean and a vice-dean. There is also an academic council that acts in an advisory capacity, whose function it is to discuss and advise the dean on important academic matters.

Teaching chairs number thirty-eight: six in energetics, six in electrical engineering, seven in civil engineering, five in mechanical engineering, four in chemical engineering, and four in economics and business. In addition, there are six all-university teaching chairs for the history of the Communist party of the Soviet Union, philosophy, scientific communism, political economy, Russian language, foreign languages, and physical education and sports. Seven specialized laboratories are primarily designed for applied industrial research. They include an industrial heat-power engineering laboratory, an industrial processes automation laboratory, a building-materials laboratory, a sanitary engineering laboratory, a machine-building technology laboratory, an oil-shale synthesis laboratory, and a mineral fertilizer and feeds laboratory. The teaching staff numbers about 500. Very few of the faculty have doctoral degrees, but nearly one-third have candidate of sciences degrees.

The structure of the student body and the smaller number of research institutes at the Polytechnic Institute explain why it has a smaller teaching staff than that of the University of Tartu. While the total number of students has been consistently more than 9,000 since 1965, less than 4,000 are resident students. About 1,800 are enrolled on a part-time basis in night school and 3,500–3,700 are nonresident students. Thus, nearly 60 percent of the students are not at the institute on a full-time basis. The numbers of students enrolled and the sizes of freshman and graduating classes are given for the 1960-1974 period in table 3.

The aspirants at the institute number about 100, in twenty-seven major fields. In some narrowly specialized fields the aspirants are dispatched to other institutes of the Soviet Union. More courses at the Polytechnic Institute are taught in Russian than at the University of Tartu. Nearly all evening courses are taught in both Estonian and Russian. From 1960 to 1976 the rector's post at the institute was held by an Estonian-born and Estonian-trained chemistry professor, Agu Aarna. He was succeeded by Estonian-born (1930) Boris Tamm, a computer scientist.

Research is being conducted on a broad spectrum of technological problems. Main research themes are nevertheless focused on a limited number of problem areas directly related to the utilization of republic-level raw materials and resources. Research topics include utilization of Estonia's most important natural resource—oil shale—as fuel in giant thermoelectric power plants; improvement of the mining methods for local mineral resources; development of rational methods in the technical servicing of automobiles; design of electromagnetic pumps for melted metals (an area in which the institute is among the leaders in the Soviet Union); problems relating to powder metallurgy, metal fatigue, optimal processing conditions, and abrasive wear; development of transistors manufactured with cadmium-sulfide compounds; construction physics of dwellings, public buildings, and livestock shelters; and pollution of lakes, rivers, and certain sounds of the Baltic contaminated by industrial effluents. The special research staff, which includes research scientists, engineers, and supporting personnel, numbers about 150 persons.

The Estonian Agricultural Academy

As noted earlier, the Estonian Agricultural Academy was organized in 1951 by removing faculties from the University of Tartu in agriculture, forestry, and veterinary science. The newly created academy inherited from the university 95 faculty members and 850 students. In the following year, 53 agricultural engineering students were transferred to the academy from the Tallinn Polytechnic Institute. The academy is located in Tartu, and many of its institutes still use their old buildings, particularly veterinary science laboratories and clinics. However, the activities of the academy have been considerably expanded, a fact that reflects both the importance the Soviet Union places on agriculture and the need for an independent institution of higher education. A new and larger campus is under construction in a suburb. The academy is administratively under the jurisdiction of the Ministry of Agriculture of the USSR in Moscow.

The original three faculties inherited from the university were reorganized into six faculties: agronomy, animal science (zootechnics), veterinary science, agricultural engineering, forestry and land amelioration, and economics (Tammeorg, 1973). There are thirty-seven teaching chairs in the academy. In addition, special interdisciplinary departments operate for nonresident study programs, professional improvement, and certain other specialties. In some faculties teaching chairs have been combined into departments. Although Estonian is the primary teaching language, classes are conducted in Russian in agricultural engineering, animal science, and veterinary medicine. The predecessor of the Faculty of Veterinary Science, the Tartu Veterinary School (established in 1848), was the first veterinary school in czarist Russia.

In 1974, more than 3,750 students were enrolled at the academy, some 70 persons attended professional-improvement courses, and 73 persons took remedial courses. (Other information regarding students and graduates can be found in table 3.) The faculty included 13 professors, 109 docents, 68 senior instructors, 44 assistants, 15 instructors, and 183 laboratory assistants and other supporting personnel. The administrative and service staff included 221 people. The academy's library had more than 350,000 volumes of native- and foreign-language books and journals.

The teaching and experimental farm of the academy, Üle-nurme, near Tartu, comprises about 7,500 hectares (18,750 acres) of land and is being equipped with modern operating facilities suitable for teaching and research. The Faculty of Forestry and Land Amelioration operates an 11,400-hectare (28,500-acre) teaching and experimental forest, Järvselja, which includes nearly 6,000 hectares (15,000 acres) of managed woodland. This facility is used as a teaching laboratory for students and as a research base for the faculty.

In 1964 a special research sector was established within the academy, funded by monies from the republic's budget. Currently, about twenty research workers and eleven laboratory assistants are supported by these funds, which are divided among different teaching chairs in eight research groups. Contract research had been started as early as 1959. In 1964, when the research sector was established, contract research funds totaled 164,000 rubles. In 1970, 110 contract research projects were active, supported by more than 500,000 rubles of research funds.

Research problems with which the academy is currently involved include detailed soil mapping, characteristics of local soils and enhancement of their productivity, influence of the seed germination environment on the development of cultivated crops, control of plant diseases and insect pests, establishment and utilization of improved pastures with optimal proportions of leguminous plants and grasses, application of mathematical methods to production planning and management, systems mechanization and the rational repair and maintenance of mechanisms, land drainage and irrigation, increase in livestock production and improvement of the quality of dairy and meat products, minerals and vitamins in animal feeds and their assimilation, nutritional value of local feeds, prevention and control of common animal diseases, and improvement of productivity of forests and forest stands. Research findings are published primarily in the series *Proceedings of the Estonian Agricultural Academy*, of which more than 100 volumes have appeared to date.

During its years of existence, the Estonian Agricultural Academy has graduated more than 8,000 specialists in such diverse fields as agronomy, grassland cultivation, livestock production, veterinary medicine, meat and meat-product technology, milk and dairy-product technology, forestry, land amelioration, land utilization, agricultural engineering, farm accounting, economics, and organization of agriculture. In recent years some 500 students have graduated annually (see table 3). Resident students number about 2,000, or a little more than half of the total (3,800) enrolled. Only a few (about 150) study in the evening department, while the rest are nonresident part-time students.

During 1954-1969 the academy operated under the rectorship of Minna Klement (she is not related to Fiodor Klement, former rector of University of Tartu). An agricultural engineer trained in Leningrad, she has no advanced degree. She is a graduate of the Communist Party Academy of the USSR. Since 1969 the rector's post has been held by Arnold Rüütel (b. 1928), who was born and educated in Estonia and is a member of the Party Central Committee in the Estonian SSR.

Other Institutes

The Eduard Vilde Tallinn Pedagogical Institute is the successor to the former Tallinn Teachers' Seminary and Pedagogium, which in 1947 had been organized into the Tallinn Teachers' Institute, primarily to train teachers for the junior high schools. In 1952 the institute was further reorganized into a full-fledged institution of higher education and was renamed the Tallinn Pedagogical Institute; its mission was to prepare teachers for both junior and senior high schools. Since 1955 the institute has borne the name of the noted Estonian novelist and playwright Eduard Vilde.

The teaching staff in the 1971-1972 academic year numbered nearly 200, of whom 63 had advanced (but not doctoral) degrees. In addition, more than 100 persons taught courses part time. Nearly 1,200 resident and 930 nonresident students were enrolled that year (see table 3). Since its establishment in 1952, well over 5,000 students have been graduated with diplomas, of whom more than 2,800 were resident students and more than 2,400 were nonresident students. In recent years the institute has graduated about 400 students annually.

From 1968 to 1974 the rector of the Tallinn Pedagogical Institute was Johannes Jakobson, a docent and candidate of history who formerly headed the University of Tartu teaching chair for the history of the Communist party of the Soviet

Union. K. Koger became the new rector in 1974.

The Institute of Art, located in Tallinn, was established in 1951 through a merger of the former Tallinn Applied Art Institute and the Tartu Art Institute, both of which dated to prewar times. In comparison with the four institutions described thus far, the Art Institute (like the Tallinn Conservatory) is a relatively small school, with only 300–450 students (see table 3).

The Art Institute has two faculties: graphic and applied arts and architecture. There are eleven teaching chairs, among them those of Marxism-Leninism and art history, textile arts and costumes, artistic ceramics and decorative glass, decorative metalwork, decorative leatherwork, decorative woodwork, and architecture. The teaching staff numbers about 90 persons, including 15 professors and 33 docents. The number of students has ranged between 400 and 430, divided nearly equally between the two faculties. Graduates have numbered nearly 100 per year in recent years. During the 1951-1968 period 718 students were graduated, of whom 558 were in graphic and applied arts and 160 in architecture.

The institute is presently under the leadership of Jaan Vares, an Estonian born in Estonia and educated in the Soviet Union. The Institue of Art enjoys a good reputation within the Soviet Union and attracts many students from outside the Estonian SSR.

The Tallinn Conservatory, established in 1919, is presently under the directorship of docent Victor Gurjev, a well-known concert singer. The conservatory provides higher education in music and the dramatic arts. Its structure includes nine teaching chairs, covering major instrument classifications, voice, composition, musicology, conducting, and dramatic arts. The teaching staff has numbered nearly 70 in recent years and the student body more than 400. In 1974, 59 students graduated: 40 in music and 19 in dramatic art. Several graduates have won prizes in all-union and international competitions of young musicians.

The Academy of Sciences of the Estonian SSR

When the Soviet Union annexed Estonian in 1940 it liquidated the Estonian Academy of Sciences, which had been founded in 1938. Initially, there were no indications that it would be revived. Nevertheless, after the war, a new and reorganized Academy of Sciences of the Estonian SSR was founded in 1946. There were at first fourteen active members (academicians) and ten corresponding members; not surprisingly, about half of them were "imports" from the Soviet Union. The new Academy of Sciences was modeled after the academies of the other constituent Soviet republics and the Academy of Sciences of the Soviet Union. The Presidium of the union academy in Moscow must approve its basic research programs and all significant research projects.

The Academy of Sciences, according to its bylaws, is the central and supreme scientific establishment in the Estonian SSR, uniting leading scientists. Most of the important research institutes operate within its framework, and scientific associations are affiliated with it. The only major exceptions to this organizational pattern are research projects in medicine, agriculture, and engineering. Although these were originally included in the structure of the academy, they were later transferred to the direct jurisdiction of each respective ministry.

The Estonian Academy of Sciences is financed by and operates directly under the jurisdiction of the Estonian Council of Ministers (that is, the government of the Estonian SSR). The supreme administrative and policymaking organ of the academy is its General Assembly, which includes all active and honorary members. Current business is conducted by the academy's Presidium, elected for a four-year term by the General Assembly. In 1975, there were twenty-two active members and twenty-three corresponding members. The Presidium offices, the large scientific library, and most of the research institutes are located in Tallinn, although a number of research institutes and affiliated scientific associations are elsewhere—primarily in Tartu, where they cooperate closely with the University of Tartu. Since 1973 the president of the academy has been the Estonian-born (1926) physicist Dr. Karl Rebane, and the post of scientific secretary in the Presidium has been held by Estonian-born (1926) Dr. Arno Köörna.

The academy has three departments or sections, each headed by its own academician-secretary, who coordinates the activities in that particular field. The departments are (1) physics, mathematics, and technology, which has sixteen active and corresponding members and of which Dr. Ilmar Öpik is the secretary; (2) chemistry, geology, and biological sciences, with eleven members, headed by Dr. Erast Parmasto; and (3) social sciences, with thirteen members, of which Dr. Juhan Kahk is the secretary. A special council at the Academy of Sciences of the USSR in Moscow coordinates the scientific activities of the republic-level academies. All academies of science are also under the jurisdiction of the State Science and Technology Committee at the USSR Council of Ministers.

Actual research work at the Estonian academy is carried out in ten research institutes and eight other establishments and organizations. The personnel of these, as of January 1, 1975, comprised a total of 3,698 employees, of whom 909 were professional research workers and the rest supporting research technicians and clerical and administrative personnel. Of the professional staff, 56 (6 percent) had doctoral degrees and 486 (53 percent) had candidate-of-sciences degrees. The following discussion deals with the general research structure and activities of the departments. (The subsequent chapter focuses on specific areas of research in greater detail.)

The Department of Physics, Mathematics, and Technological Sciences has three research institutes. The Institute of Physics and Astronomy has been headed since 1950 by a well-known astronomer, Dr. Aksel Kipper, and is located in Tartu. In addition to the Tartu establishment, the institute has newly established observatory facilities in Tôravere, near Tartu. Six of the ten sectors of the institute work in Tartu, four sectors in Tôravere. Its total personnel in 1969 numbered 313, of whom 107 were professional research workers.

The Institute of Cybernetics was established in 1960 in Tallinn. The director of the institute from 1969 to 1976 was Dr. Boris Tamm, who then became rector of the Tallinn Polytechnic Institute. The staff numbers about 156 people, including 55 professional research workers.

The Institute of Thermodynamics and Electrophysics counts as its predecessor the Estonian Central Industrial Research Institute, established in 1944 in Moscow. The institute is now headquartered in Tallinn, and its director since 1960 has been L. Vaik. The staff exceeds 140, of whom 40 are professional research workers.

The Department of Chemistry, Geology, and Biological Sciences has four research institutes; also affiliated with it are the Tallinn Botanical Gardens, the Technological Experimentation Base, and the Naturalists' Society.

The Institute of Chemistry, established in 1947 in Tallinn, deals primarily with research in oil-shale chemistry and employs in its six sectors well over 200 people, of whom more than 90 are professional research personnel. Since 1960 the director of the institute has been Dr. Oskar Kirret.

The Institute of Experimental Biology, established in 1957, is located in Harku, near Tallinn. Its research activities are focused on the genetics and biological processes of plants, animals, and microorganisms; the photosynthesis and nutrition of plants; and the biochemistry and biophysics of plant viruses, including control of plant virus diseases. This institute has five sectors and a staff of more than 130 people, including about 50 professional researchers. Since its establishment, the institute's director has been Dr. Oskar Priilinn.

The Geology Institute, established in 1947 in Tallinn, concentrates its research on the geological structure of Estonia, specifically on bedrock structure, quaternary deposits of the Paleozoic era, lithostratigraphy, geomorphology and its genesis, and hydrogeology and mineral resources, including oil shale, phosphorites, and natural building stones. The institute is organized into five sectors with a total staff numbering more than 90, of whom at least 40 are professional workers. Dr. Karl Orviku served as the director from 1954 to 1968; since 1969 the position has been held by D. Kaljo.

The Institute of Zoology and Botany was also established in 1947 but is headquartered in Tartu. Its primary fields of investigation include the development of Estonian fauna, microevolution of mammals, waterfowl numbers, ecological physiology and migration of birds, entomofauna and biological control of plant pests, composition of local fauna, geobotany and mycology, ichthyology and fisheries, and nature conservation. The institute has five sectors, one of which is located at the Vôrtsjärve Limnological Station and another at the Marine Ichthyological Laboratory in Tallinn. The staff numbers about 150 people, including more than 60 professional researchers, and is headed by Dr. Harald Haberman.

The Technological Experimentation Base was established in 1957 in Tallinn, primarily to develop and test methods in chemical technology.

The Naturalists' Society, established in 1853 by professors

and researchers at the University of Tartu, was closely associated with the university until 1946, at which time it became an affiliate of the Academy of Sciences. The society furthers nature research, has initiated many research projects, popularizes natural sciences, and activates and coordinates phenological observations and birdwatching among its more than 750 members and 629 correspondents and local nature observers. It also publishes a yearbook, instructions for nature observation, and other reports. The president of the society is Dr. Hans V. Trass, a professor of botany at the University of Tartu.

The Tallinn Botanical Gardens, established in 1961, is located about five or six miles east of the city center in a rural setting, on about 150 acres of land (the farm of the former president of the Republic of Estonia, K. Päts). Its research objectives include the formation of economical and rational methods in landscape architecture and planning, the design of city and rural open spaces and parks, and the introduction and acclimatization of foreign plant materials, trees, shrubs, and other decorative plants. Since its establishment, the director of the Botanical Gardens has been A. Pukk.

The Department of Social Sciences includes three research institutes (in economics, history, and language and literature) and the Kreutzwald Literary Museum. Also affiliated with the department are the Mother Tongue Society and the Estonian Geographical Society.

The Institute of Economics was established in 1946 in Tallinn. Its research objectives include long-range planning of the Estonian economy and analysis of underlying scientific principles, allocation of productive forces, application of mathematical methods in planning industrial development, attainment of economic efficiency in intensive agriculture, and solutions to theoretical problems in constitutional law and jurisprudence. The institute has nine sectors, including one for law. The staff numbers about 150 people, of which about 70 are professional research workers. The director of the institute from 1966 to 1973 was Dr. Arno Köörna. He was succeeded in 1974 by Dr. Vello Tarmisto, formerly head of the Estonian Geographical Society.

The Institute of History, established in 1947 in Tartu but moved to Tallinn in 1951, has as its primary objective conducting investigations related to the history of the Estonian territory and people from ancient times to the present. Specific fields include Estonian archaeology, ethnography, anthropology, numismatics, the working class and peasantry, art, and the theater. Recently, studies in contemporary sociology have been added. In five sectors, the staff numbers about 100, with more than 60 professional researchers. The director of the institute since 1974 has been Dr. K. Siilivask. The institute recently completed a Marxist version of the history of Estonia which was published in three volumes between 1955 and 1971.

The Institute of Language and Literature was established in 1947 in Tartu but transferred to Tallinn in 1952. Research activities include linguistic studies of Estonian and related languages, the history of Estonian literature and its contact with other literatures, and Estonian folklore. Three volumes of its five-volume history of Estonian literature have been published to date, and a four-volume annotated anthology of Estonian folk songs was recently issued. The institute is divided into six sectors and employs about 120 people, including nearly 70 professional research workers. The director of the institute since 1968 has been Dr. Endel Sõgel.

Closely related to the Institute of Language and Literature is the work of the Mother Tongue Society, which was established in 1920 at the University of Tartu for the study and development of the Estonian language. The society has been affiliated with the Estonian Academy of Sciences since 1946. Since its inception, the society has been involved with publications; a major publishing outlet since 1955 has been its yearbook. Special attention has been accorded to the study of Estonian dialects. The society in 1974 had about 300 members. A special commission makes recommendations for preferred usage and orthography of contemporary Estonian. The president of the society since 1968 has been Dr. Arnold Kask, professor of Estonian linguistics at the University of Tartu.

The Estonian Geographical Society, established in 1955, is a branch organization of the Geographical Society of the Soviet Union. Affiliated with the Estonian academy since its inception, the society includes among its objectives the comprehensive investigation of Estonian geography and the dissemination of geographical knowledge. Its main publication is a yearbook. It also issues other nonperiodical publications, in particular, popular tourist travel guides. The society numbers more than 300 members.

Research outside the Academy of Sciences

Other institutes, formerly part of the structure of the Estonian Academy of Sciences but later transferred to the jurisdiction of republic-level ministries, include research establishments in agriculture, medicine, and construction, the Historical Museum, and the Ethnographic Museum.

Agricultural research is organized under two institutes: the Research Institute of Agronomy and Land Improvement, for crop production; and the Animal and Veterinary Science Research Institute, for livestock production and management.

The Agronomy Institute, with headquarters in Saku, about ten miles south of Tallinn, was established in 1956 as an agency of the Ministry of Agriculture by combining a number of existing research institutes and experiment stations within and without the Academy of Sciences. Research is concerned with cultural practices having to do with farm crops and soil fertility, plant breeding, plant protection, land improvement, mechanization of field work, and economics of crop production. The institute includes twelve departments, the Jõgeva Plant Breeding Station, several laboratories, and fourteen experimental farms. Professional research workers number more than 160, headed by Dr. Ilmar Jürisson. The institute publishes a series of collections of research reports, of which more than forty volumes have been issued to date.

The Animal and Veterinary Science Research Institute was organized in 1947 as an agency of the Academy of Sciences and was transferred to the Estonian Ministry of Agriculture in 1956. It is headquartered in Tartu, and its activities include livestock and poultry breeding; research into the nutritional value of local feeds, dairy production, and cure and control of animal diseases; and improving labor productivity, mechanization, and automation in livestock production. The institute has eight departments, three experimental stations—in Kehtna (hogs), Kurtna (poultry), and Vändra (dairy cattle)—and eight experimental farms, which include six bull stations for artificial insemination and six performance-testing stations. The research staff numbers nearly 90 professional people and is headed by Dr. E. Valdmann. Almost forty periodic collections of research reports have been published thus far.

The Institute of Experimental and Clinical Medicine was

organized initially as an agency of the Academy of Sciences in 1947. In 1963 it was transferred to the Medical Academy of the Soviet Union, and in 1966 it was moved to the Estonian Ministry of Public Health. Among other research problems, much attention is devoted to the prophylaxis and therapy of occupational diseases related to oil-shale mining and processing, particularly those associated with carcinogenic substances, and to the toxicity of oil-shale derivatives and industrial residues (pollutants). The institute has nine sectors and three laboratories which employ more than 70 professional researchers. The director of the institute since 1968 has been Dr. V. Küng.

The Institute of Building Research was established in 1947 in Tallinn as part of the Academy of Sciences. In 1963 it came under the jurisdiction of the Building Committee of the Estonian Council of Ministers, where it has remained. Main directions of research include technology, development, and utilization of construction materials derived from the cement of oil-shale cinder; reconstruction of rural settlement patterns within the republic; and utilization of mathematical methods in construction activities. The institute has seven sectors with more than 160 people, including about 50 professional research workers. Since 1950 V. Polonski has been the director. The institute issues a Russian-language publication series, *Izsledovaniia po stroitelstvu.*

Interrelationships and Comparisons with Other Republics

The Soviet Union had during the 1974-1975 academic year 842 establishments of higher education with 4.8 million students, of whom 2.5 million were full-time students (*Narodnoe . . .*, 1974:711). Universities numbered only 40; the majority of college-level schools were specialized institutes or academies, among them 169 engineering and construction schools, 96 agricultural academies or institutes, 241 schools of education (accommodating 30 percent of all college-level students), and 98 medical and physical-education schools. The Latvian SSR had ten and the Lithuanian SSR twelve schools of higher education, while the Moldavian SSR had eight and the Tadjik SSR nine; the Turkmen and Estonian SSRs had only six college-level schools. The Soviet Union averaged 3.4 such schools per million residents; Estonia had 4.6, Latvia 4.3, and Lithuania 3.9.

There is some interchange of Estonian students with those of other republics—particularly with the universities and other institutes of the Russian SFSR, which has more than half of all college-level educational institutions in the Soviet Union, including many narrowly specialized ones. In 1960-1961, more than 1,800 Estonian students attended schools outside the Estonian SSR. About 1,680 of these were studying in the Russian SFSR, primarily in nearby Leningrad, which has many first-rate schools. In 1967, Estonian students outside Estonia numbered 2,300. At the same time, more than 2,400 students from other ethnic groups of the Soviet Union attended higher schools in Estonia, including 1,930 Russians, about 150 Ukrainians, and 126 Jews. In the fall of 1974, the University of Tartu had 663 students (15 percent of the total enrollment) who were non-Estonian. These students included nearly 450 Russians; Ukrainians, Jews, Finns, Latvians, Georgians, Hungarians, Lithuanians, and Germans were represented in smaller numbers.

References

Eesti nôukogude entsüklopeedia

1968-   [The Estonian Soviet Encyclopedia]. Eight volumes.
1976   Tallinn: Valgus.

Eesti NSV Riiklik Kunstiinstituut: 50 aastat kunstialast haridust

1964   [The State Art Institute of the Estonian SSR].
         Tallinn: Eesti NSV Kunst.

Eesti NSV Teaduste Akadeemia aastail, 1965-1972

1973   [History of the Academy of Sciences of the Estonian
         SSR, 1965-1972]. Tallinn: Eesti NSV Teaduste Aka-
         deemia.

Eesti NSV Teaduste Akadeemia: Tagasivaated, uurimissuunad, liikmeskond, 1946-1971

1971 [Academy of Sciences of the Estonian SSR: A Look Back, Research Directions, Membership, 1946-1971]. Tallinn: Eesti NSV Teaduste Akadeemia.

Eesti Põllumajanduse Akadeemia 20

1971 [Yearbook of the Estonian Agricultural Academy, vol. 20]. Tallinn: Valgus.

ERM (Eesti NSV rahvamajandus) 1971

1972 [The National Economy of the Estonian SSR in 1971]. Tallinn: Statistika.

ERM (Eesti NSV rahvamajandus) 1972

1974 [The National Economy of the Estonian SSR in 1972]. Tallinn: Statistika.

ERM (Eesti NSV rahvamajandus) 1975

1976 [The National Economy of the Estonian SSR in 1975]. Tallinn: Eesti Raamat.

Inno, K.

1972 *Tartu University in Estonia during the Swedish Rule, 1632-1710.* Stockholm: Vaba Eesti.

Kangro, Bernard

1970 *Universitas Tartuensis.* Lund: Eesti Kirjanike Kooperatiiv.

Kivik, M.

1974 "Kõik kokku on kodumaa" [All Combined Is the Homeland]. *Nõukogude Naine* 30 (August): 4-5.

Kotsar, K., ed.

1972 *E. Vilde nimeline Tallinna Pedagoogiline Instituut.* Tallinn: Eesti NSV Kõrgema ja Keskhariduse Ministeerium.

Narodnoe khoziaistov SSSR v 1973 godu

1974 Moscow: Statistika.

Nirk, E.

1970   *Estonian Literature.* Tallinn: Eesti Raamat.

Oras, A.

1948   *Baltic Eclipse.* London: Victor Gollancz.

Sbornik zakonov SSSR 1938-1961

1961   Moskva: Izvestiia Sovetov Deputatov Trudiash-chikhsia SSSR.

Schmidt, E.

1971   *Kôrgema hariduse areng Nôukogude Eestis* [Development of Higher Education in Soviet Estonia]. Tallinn: Valgus.

Science in Soviet Estonia

1965   Tallinn: Eesti Raamat.

Tallinna Polütehniline Instituut

1967   [The Tallinn Polytechnic Institute]. Tallinn: Valgus.

Tallinna Riiklik Konservatoorium 1919-1969

1965   [Tallinn State Conservatory 1919-1969]. Tallinn: Eesti Raamat.

Tammeorg, J.

1973   "Üle 200 teadusliku sideme" [Over 200 Scientific Connections]. *Kodumaa*, January 24, pp. 3, 7.

Tartu Riikliku Ulikooli struktuur ja isikuline koosseis

1973   [Structure and Personnel of the Tartu State University]. Tartu.

Tehver, J., and J. Parre, eds.

1973   *Kôrgema veterinaarhariduse ajaloost Tartus 1848-1973* [On the History of Higher Education in Veterinary Medicine at Tartu, 1848-1973]. Tallinn: Valgus.

11

Selected Aspects of Scientific Research

Heino Susi

If scholarship and scientific research in Estonia have a long tradition, credit is primarily due to the University of Tartu, founded in 1632. As early as 1803 A. Scherer organized a modern chemistry department which paid particular attention to the then-revolutionary principles of Lavoisier (Palm, 1971). From 1872 to 1881 Wilhelm Ostwald investigated the principles of chemical equilibria which formed the basis for chemical thermodynamics, later advanced by Helmholtz and Gibbs. Ostwald's student, G. Tammann, made major contributions to physical chemistry; for example, in the study of phase equilibria, later pursued by Gibbs (Biltz, 1931). Tammann's work won the highest possible praise from Mendeleyev, who compared the former's achievements with Van der Waal's pioneering work on intermolecular interactions (*Items*, 1971). Economist and statistician E. Laspeyres published his aggregate index theory during his Tartu years in the 1870s. Outstanding contributions in astronomy were made by Struve, who began his scientific work at Tartu in 1813 and was among the first to determine the distance of a fixed star and compile a catalog of double stars. Outstanding work in astronomy was continued by Ernst Öpik during the interwar years. The mathematician Adolf Kneser was one of the first to explore the variation method, which later became important in quantum mechanics (Kneser, 1901). The biologist Karl Ernest von Baer (1792-

1876), also with roots at Tartu, was a founder of modern embryology. August Rauber's textbook on human anatomy was still widely used during the interwar period. The plant breeder Mihkel Pill was a leading exponent of the rediscovered laws of Mendel. His first detailed exposition on heredity in an Estonian student publication in 1908 heralded the beginning of Estonian national pride in scientific achievement. A student of the Russian academician Behterev, L. Puusepp became an early and leading expert in neurosurgery (Puusepp, 1932). He lived and worked in Tartu, published in German and French, and maintained close ties with Russian colleagues in the Soviet Union. In chemistry, P. Kogerman pioneered oil-shale analysis. O. Maddison worked on problems of applied mechanics a few decades before the subject of his special research, thin shells, became a matter of extraordinary interest and importance.

The postwar University of Tartu has built on its earlier scientific traditions. The Estonian Academy of Sciences had been established in 1938 as a central body for scientific planning, coordination, and interchange. With the advent of Soviet rule in 1940, the academy was closed, but it was reopened in 1946 along Soviet lines. Accordingly, the postwar academy has become not only a planning and evaluative body but also an institution with major research activities in its own right.

Oil-Shale Research

The oil-shale industry is an important component of Estonia's economy. Consequently, it should not be surprising that scientific research pertinent to the mining, processing, and utilization of oil shale also plays an important role. Part of the research is theoretical and is done at various institutes of the Estonian Academy of Sciences. However, applied research is often carried out outside the academy. Thus, the separate Oil-Shale Research Institute has existed since 1958 at Kohtla-Järve. This institute, which initially employed about 250 people (of whom 53 were professional researchers), is not part of the republican research system but rather operates under the jurisdiction of all-union agencies, as does the entire oil-shale industry.

Oil shale has attracted attention as a possible alternative energy source in various parts of the world; however, it has often been abandoned for technological as well as economic reasons. In general, oil shale contains 45–90 percent inorganic material and 10–55 percent organic material. Obviously, only the latter is useful as fuel. In Estonian deposits the average organic content is relatively high, around 50 percent (H. Martinson, 1973; Marksoo, 1961). The heat of combustion of the unrefined mineral is 2–3.5 kilocalories per gram; comparative figures are 5-8 kcal/g for coal and about 10 kcal/g for petroleum. If burned as such, the inorganic constituents leave very large amounts of ashes which have to be utilized or disposed of. The organic material, largely high-molecular-weight ("heavy") hydrocarbons and heterocyclics, is in itself not the most suitable fuel compared to coal or petroleum; less than half of it can be manufactured into good motor fuel. Some of its constituents, however, can serve as raw materials for a variety of products of the chemical industry (plastics and plasticizers, detergents, wood preservatives, and adhesives, among other things).

It is estimated (*ENE*, 6:305) that total reserves of about 10 billion metric tons of oil shale exist in the northeastern part of the Estonian SSR in an area of about 2,500 square kilometers (about 900 square miles). Eighty-one percent of the total oil-shale production of the Soviet Union in 1973 was in Estonia. About 75 percent of the oil shale is being used in its raw form as a rather inefficient industrial fuel, primarily in two thermo-electric plants; the rest is refined.

A few facts should be kept in mind in discussing the social and economic implications of the Estonian oil-shale deposits: First, if the estimate of total reserves (10 billion metric tons) is correct, at an annual exploitation of 30 million tons (3 million tons more than the 1974 figure), the reserves would last for 330 years. Second, the extraction and refinement of oil shale for liquid fuel is a cumbersome procedure at best, compared to processes for refining coal, petroleum, or natural gas. Nor is oil shale a unique source for any essential chemical or raw material. But because the industry is a "heavy industry," and because it supplies Leningrad with gas, both the region and the industry are operated under much tighter control by Moscow than is the rest of the economy. Finally, the exploitation of oil shale has resulted in severe pollution and in the defacement of an originally peaceful forest region of great natural beauty. The stench alone is horrifying. Sulfur-containing chemicals are deposited into the atmosphere. Rivers and the Gulf of Finland are polluted with by-products. Huge mountains of ashes are piled up.

But there are other more positive aspects as well. Oil shale served as a local fuel supply before the war and still is an important local source of industrial fuel. In addition, its extraction provides a focal point and a justification for a great deal of research and technological activity. The fact that these activities are centered around a local raw material has served to develop specific skills on a broad front. In this context, another important factor must be taken into consideration: Although the Estonian oil-shale reserves are relatively small, vast amounts are found in other parts of the world, including the United States. Given limited petroleum reserves, huge untapped oil-shale reserves might well attract considerable attention in the near future. New technology must be developed; problems of economical refinement, utilization of by-products, and handling of pollution must be faced. In this area, technology developed in Estonia might well prove to be of considerable global importance.

At present, activities related to oil-shale utilization keep a considerable part of the Estonian technological and scientific community going. The lion's share of approved research projects at the Institute of Chemistry of the Estonian Academy of Sciences is related in some way to oil-shale utilization. In the course of these investigations, new techniques and procedures have been developed (for example, specialized techniques and instruments of analytical chemistry) which have broad significance and which have enhanced the standing of Estonian scientists within and without the Soviet Union. Research institutes and laboratories of the Tallinn Polytechnic Institute are kept busy with problems related to by-product utilization. Even the Institute of Medicine is involved, conducting pioneering research in industrial hygiene and occupational hazards associated with oil-shale technology.

Chemistry

The Estonian tradition of chemical research has two main

facets: research geared to the advancement of the science of chemistry, as practiced in the University of Tartu in the nineteenth century by Ostwald, Tammann, and others; and research in applied chemistry, with the emphasis on oil-shale utilization. The two are certainly intertwined, but some division along administrative lines persists. Until recently, the Institute of Chemistry of the Estonian Academy of Sciences was almost exclusively devoted to oil-shale research (or at least it had to justify its activities in these terms). Other research was pursued at the University of Tartu, the Institute of Cybernetics, and elsewhere. It is nevertheless true that many activities of the Institute of Chemistry have developed into areas of research which have broad significance far beyond the specific original goals.

The organic matter of oil shale is a highly complex mixture of high-molecular-weight materials called kerogen. Volatile distillation products contain well over 500 components. A thorough analysis of such a product presents formidable difficulties. Until World War II the main tools were chemical modification, identification of characteristic reaction products, and fractional distillation. In the late 1940s and early 1950s, new analytical instrumental techniques were developed, primarily in the English-speaking countries. Among the most important techniques were molecular spectroscopy and gas chromatography. Scientists at the Estonian Institute of Chemistry were among the first (and appear to have been the most successful) in the Soviet domain to pick up and develop the new "miracle technique" of gas chromatography. Soon they could claim to have shortened the time necessary for analyzing a sample of shale-oil gasoline from about three years to twenty-four hours (H. Martinson, 1973:20). The Estonian chemists obviously recognized a good thing when they saw one. The analytical instrument can be constructed without unduly elaborate facilities and has a very wide application in biochemistry, refined organic syntheses, and general analytical chemistry. New models constructed and produced in the Special Instrument Construction Bureau of the academy were sold all over the Soviet Union under the names PGK-3 and Vôrukom (H. Martinson, 1973; Rebane, 1971; *Eesti*, 1965). This development was not strictly chemical, nor was it original in a true sense, but it involved much original developmental work and was recognized as a major achievement in the Soviet Union. It is to be noted that such work in Estonia started in the early 1950s, when gas chromatography was still in its infancy everywhere in the world. Much credit for revitalizing chemical research after the war belongs to the chemists Kogerman and Kirret, who were trained in prewar Estonia, and to the man at the center of gas chromatography studies, O. Eisen.

The other major branch of instrumental analysis—molecular spectroscopy—was not so easy to develop, primarily because spectroscopic instrumentation requires very complex production facilities. Instruments imported from Germany, the United States, and the Soviet Union were used whenever available. A major breakthrough was accomplished, nonetheless, in one of the most complex branches of molecular spectroscopy: nuclear magnetic resonance. (This subject will be discussed subsequently in conjunction with the Institute of Cybernetics.)

Along the lines of synthetic and industrial chemistry, much effort is devoted to the production of aliphatic dicarboxylic acids from oil-shale kerogen. These acids are important constituents of high polymers, synthetic fibers, and plastic materials (nylon is an example). A process has been developed to convert up to 50 percent of kerogen into a mixture of dicarboxylic acids which could provide raw materials for foam plastics, low-temperature plasticizers, and other synthetic products. It appears that the separation of the obtained mixture into individual acids presents difficulties, and research is under way to use the obtained mixture as such for polyamide plastics. Large-scale conversion of oil-shale by-products to synthetic polymer production is, of course, an economic problem that has republic-level as well as union-level ramifications.

Other endeavors in applied chemistry involve the production of nerosiin, a specialized heavy oil for stopping land erosion in various parts of the Soviet Union. This material is also useful as an antidust agent for unpaved roads. Other research involves biodegradable detergents, utilization of phenols as preservatives and adhesives, and direct problem-solving activity in conjunction with oil-shale utilization as an energy source. In fact, the Institute of Chemistry is deeply involved with chemical-engineering problems associated with the last activity. In cooperation with the former Institute of Energetics (now affiliated with the Soviet Academy of Sciences), detailed procedures have been worked out and pilot plants have been constructed for a so-called energy-technological method of utilization. Solid heat exchangers in the form of ashes are used in the process; the oil obtained is used for producing electrical energy, and other products are used as raw materials for the chemical industry. As of 1973, the process was on the verge of leaving the pilot plant on the way to large-scale operations. To provide an idea of the hoped-for utilization, available data indicate that 1,000 kilograms of oil shale containing 335 kilograms of organic matter yields 172 kilograms of fuel oil, 15 kilograms of gasoline, and 50 kilograms of gas. In other words, 23.7 percent is utilized in the form of fuel, based on total weight; 70 percent based on organic content (H. Martinson, 1973).

However, it is being gradually realized that oil shale, with its complex composition, is no match for petroleum as a source of raw materials for the chemical industry, not to speak of fuel. On the other hand, even a short time ago such sophisticated substances as laboratory reagents, photochemicals, biological chemicals, special surfactants, and the like were "still extremely expensive and defective" in the USSR, and were imported in large quantities (H. Martinson, 1973). The Institute of Chemistry has a considerable background in isolation, physico-chemical characterization, and analyses and custom syntheses of very pure chemicals. Work has been done on unsaturated hydrocarbons, terpenes (vitamins and cosmetics), surfactants, dicarboxylic acids, and other organic chemicals not necessarily tied to shale oil.

The establishment of production facilities for fine chemicals requires little capital, little manpower, and little raw material—but a high level of skill. More than 70 percent of the research employees of the institute are already involved in "fancy organic synthesis." Oil shale would provide large quantities of raw materials, but raw materials in such quantities are not essential for producing relatively small quantities of high-grade products. Although the industry is estimated to be profitable, skill, not raw materials, is of the essence.

All these factors are being recognized and discussed (H. Martinson, 1973). The basic question is quite rational: Why devote excessive energy to the production problems of a heavy industry which is under all-union control, if a highly specialized and technologically challenging line of work is possible using local skills, while satisfying both local and union needs?

Estonia could produce fine chemicals the way Switzerland produces fine watches. Such a development would be gradual, of course. However, it would allow Estonian chemists to attain leadership in still another field otherwise neglected in the Soviet Union.

The tradition of theoretical and academic research in organic chemistry has been continued at the University of Tartu. Like many other disciplines, organic chemistry has drastically changed since World War II. The basic principles of classical organic chemistry had been worked out by the beginning of this century. What followed was the development of skills in the art of organic synthesis, leading to synthetic dyes, drugs, plastics, fibers, rubber, and even gasoline. During the postwar era, attention in academic institutions again turned toward more theoretical approaches: general rules and regularities of reactions, electronic structure and molecular orbits, true molecular structure, reaction mechanisms, reaction kinetics, and thermodynamics. The result was a new discipline generally referred to as physical organic chemistry. It is in this field that chemists at Tartu have made a distinguished contribution. Chemical thermodynamics, the science that predicts the direction and energetics of chemical reactions on the basis of general principles of physics and probability (as developed by Gibbs, Helmholtz, and Lewis), was for a long time mostly applied to such simple systems as ideal gases and ionic crystals. Now the discipline has been extended to cover complex organic reactions. At Tartu, free energy relationships of complex molecules are studied in detail; reaction kinetics and mechanisms are explored. The results of this research are usually published in a remarkable journal called *Organic Reactivity* (edited by V. Palm), which appears in Tartu in Russian with English summaries. The journal—which is, to a large degree, the result of local initiative—contains contributions from leading research laboratories from all over the Soviet Union as well as some from abroad. Its publication testifies both to the prominent role of the University of Tartu within the Soviet Union and to Estonia's scientific contact with the rest of the world.

Another aspect of the broad field of physical organic chemistry, the determination of molecular structure, is pursued at the Institute of Cybernetics. Molecular structure studies require familiarity with modern physics, quantum mechanics, and advanced mathematics, as well as very complex and usually expensive hardware (electronics, optics, magnetism) and computing facilities. The more rigorous aspects are usually called chemical physics. Although theoretical aspects of molecular structure have been studied in the Soviet Union for many years (cf. Eliashevich, 1940), hardware has consistently presented problems. The development in the Estonian Academy of Sciences of nuclear magnetic resonance spectroscopy, one of the most sophisticated techniques for molecular structure investigation, must be viewed in this light. The basic resonance effect was discovered in 1945 by Bloch at Stanford University and Purcell at Harvard University. In 1952 they jointly received the Nobel Prize in physics for this discovery. Application of the new methodology to the investigation of organic structures was developed, mainly in the United States, in the 1950s. In the early 1960s several Estonian scientists, notably E. Lippmaa and his coworkers, started construction of elaborate and highly complex instrumentation from scratch. A few years later they were pioneers on a world scale in developing an entirely new approach which could distinguish between carbon atoms of an organic molecular network, depending on their specific location. This work involved theoretical physics, sophisticated instrumentation, and computer technology in about equal proportions, and required familiarity with worldwide developments in each of these fields. Today, Estonian scientists are leading experts in this discipline in the Soviet Union. Professor Lippmaa is one of the five regional editors of the international journal *Organic Magnetic Resonance*, published in London.

On of the most challenging areas of modern chemistry is the structure and functioning of biological macromolecules—a field basic to biology, medicine, and nutrition, among others. The exact structure (or conformation) of these huge molecules cannot be studied by classical techniques, yet it provides the key to a real understanding of biological functions. The functioning of enzymes, one of the most important problems in this context, has been studied in Tallinn with considerable ingenuity (Lippmaa and Arro, 1967). The application of physical techniques to such problems, a discipline frequently called biophysics, is continuing, and advanced nuclear magnetic resonance methods such as those being developed in Tallinn are among the most promising tools.

The Institute of Cybernetics

The term "cybernetics," coined in the 1940s by Norbert Wiener, a Massachusetts Institute of Technology mathematics professor, is defined by Webster's New International Dictionary (1971 edition) as follows: "The comparative study of the automatic control system formed by the nervous system and brain and by mechano-electrical communications systems and devices (as computing machines, thermostats, photoelectric sorters)." Wiener himself offered a more concise definition in the title of his 1948 book, *Cybernetics, or Control and Communication in the Man and the Machine.* (Wiener's *The Human Use of Human Beings. Cybernetics and Society* was translated into Estonian in 1969.)

In Estonia, if judged by the organization and activities of the Institute of Cybernetics, the term could mean the latter and some other things as well. To avoid confusion, it should be pointed out that the emphasis is on machines and technology, not on control of the human brain. The institute has developed into a broad-based research laboratory encompassing diverse fields of activity, with digital computers at its center. The availability of computing facilities and the caliber of associated personnel have elevated the research performed at this institute to a remarkably high level of performance and accomplishment, despite the fact that the computing hardware itself has not always been the most sophisticated. The same is true of software, which has had to be developed as work progressed.

The origin of the Institue of Cybernetics illustrates some facets of science and research in present-day Estonia in general. In the late 1950s, physicists and mathematicians working on the theory of thin shells decided that no further progress was possible without computers, and that Estonia "could not afford to stay away from computer technology, which by then had engulfed the whole world" (*Eesti*, 1970). Because no computers could be purchased in the Soviet Union at that time, the construction of one in Tallinn was undertaken. It was also decided to identify lines of research which could be pursued under the heading "cybernetics." In 1960 the Institute of Cybernetics—the first of its kind in the Soviet Union—was established by a joint decision of the government of the Estonian SSR and the Soviet Academy of Sciences.

To start with, research groups concerned with applied

mechanics, applied mathematics, and automation were transferred from the Institute of Energetics. In order to permit the application of improved computing procedures, a computer center was established and staffed with mathematicians. A computing laboratory was set up with an M-3 digital computer (slow, and with severely limited storage, even for 1960). A year later, physicists and chemists joined the effort and initiated research in molecular structure and instrumental analysis, specifically nuclear magnetic resonance spectroscopy and gas chromatography. Both of these specialties had played an almost revolutionary role in physical chemistry abroad, but had developed at a slow pace in the Soviet Union because of technological problems.

The nucleus of the institute was thus formed by a group of dedicated engineers, mathematicians, physicists, and chemists gathered around a small, slow computer. Much of the equipment initially available to the physicists and chemists was, technologically, on a barely adequate level. In 1966 a sector, or research group, for operations analysis was added; in 1968 a sector for scientific information storage and retrieval; and in 1969 a semiindependent bureau for programming. Although relations with Soviet science in general were close, the institute retained its unique character. A fair number of awards were soon received from Estonian as well as all-union authorities, among them the Award of the Estonian SSR and the Federal Script of Honor of the Anniversary of Lenin.

In the past few years, more powerful solid-state computers (the M-3 employs electron tubes) have been acquired; namely, the Minsk-22 and Minsk-32. While still small and slow compared to the high-speed computers necessary for large-scale data processing and elaborate computations, these machines represent a considerable improvement over the equipment initially available. A Special Instrument Construction Bureau has been established, and close cooperation exists with the Computer Language Department of the all-union Institute of Electronic Computers. The nature of the work is such that close contact with the outside world is continuously required. The scientific staff of the institute is almost exclusively of native Estonian origin.

In 1970, the general areas of activity at the Institute of Cybernetics could be summarized as follows (*Eesti*, 1970): applied mathematics (methodology, statistics), operations analysis (economic planning, transportation, city planning), algorithms and programming (problem-oriented algorithms, special versions of ALGOL), optimization of industrial processes (chemical engineering, oil-shale technology), voice and sound analysis (oral communication with computers and related subjects), hardware improvement and service to other institutions, applied mechanics (with emphasis on shell theory), and chemical physics (nuclear magnetic resonance, gas chromatography, biophysics).

Applied mechanics had a very basic and special place in the development of the institute. In Estonia, interest in this field probably originated with the late Professor Ottomar Maddison. Despite its modest title, applied mechanics today involves extremely complex mathematics, physics, and computing procedures. It is a discipline of significant importance to a broad range of engineering problems, including those related to aviation and space technology. This is true in particular for the complex subject of shell theory, which receives particular attention at the Institute of Cybernetics (Nigul, 1969).

Many aspects of physical chemistry also belong in the category of research activities in which no progress is possible without computers. The previously mentioned technique of nuclear magnetic resonance spectroscopy definitely belongs in this category, although it presents formidable instrumentation problems as well. Its measuring instrument, the spectrometer, yields data on the differences between quantized energy levels; these data must then be interpreted, with the help of a computer, in terms of molecular structure: for example, which atom is next to which in a molecule? Is the molecule planar? If not, which way is it bent? Until a few years ago, most such information was obtained through investigation of the hydrogen atoms of a molecule of unknown structure. Now, carbon atoms can be directly observed by using a method called Fourier transform spectroscopy. In this approach, no molecular information can be obtained without a computer. In many countries, commercial instruments of this type are sold as a package with a computer. In the Estonian Institute of Cybernetics, however, the technique was developed and the art advanced with whatever means was available. This was done at an early stage and with a thoroughness that elevated the Tallinn group to prominence and leadership both within and without the Soviet Union (Lippmaa and Radman, 1969;

Sinivee, 1965, 1969; Stothers, 1972).

In addition to magnetic resonance, other areas of physical chemistry pursued intensively at the Institute of Cybernetics include biophysics and theoretical gas chromatography, both of which were discussed in the section in this chapter on chemistry. These examples illustrate not only what can be and has been done but also how little one can learn about progress in science by studying only statistics, organization charts, and formal names of institutes or even research groups.

Physics

In physics it is even more difficult to distinguish between fundamental and applied research than it is in chemistry, biology, or almost any other branch of natural science. Studies in physics and astronomy enjoy a broader latitude in the Estonian Academy of Sciences than do most other disciplines (*Eesti*, 1965:8). Advances in physics are made primarily in the world of the very large (astrophysics, relativity) and the world of the very small (atomic, molecular, and nuclear structure, quantum mechanics, solid-state quantum physics, detailed crystal structure).

A swing toward a more basic approach in teaching and research in the realm of physics occurred in Estonia during the postwar years with the introduction of theoretical physics at the University of Tartu. The subject was initially taught by the prewar Estonian scientists Keres and Kipper. Both are devoted to astrophysics and have made substantial contributions to the theory of relativity and the treatment of magnetic and gravitational fields of stars.

Studies in solid-state physics were initiated in the early 1950s by a Soviet physicist of Estonian descent, F. Klement. Many theoretical aspects of the solid state were treated thoroughly in the Soviet Union at an early date. In 1962 Davydov's fundamental work, *Theory of Molecular Excitons*, appeared in English translation and had a marked effect on the thinking and even the terminology of American investigators dealing with solid-state spectroscopy.

Solid-state work in Estonia was focused largely on ionic crystals and their luminescent properties, under the direction of Tš. Luštšik (*Eesti*, 1964; *Nôukogude*, 1968). Among other crystals, potassium bromide received early attention. It was the first crystal to be later used in the United States for the construction of an ultraviolet laser. The study of solid-state luminescence is still a field in which much empirical knowledge is required and in which, according to one authority, technical application involves plenty of "cookbook" skill. Systematic studies have been carried out on absorption and emission bands of alkali halides containing different impurities. Much of the necessary instrumentation had to be constructed on the spot, including such instruments as vacuum ultraviolet monochromators. Such research is considerably broader than these few lines would indicate and involves a multitude of approaches, ramifications, and possible applications.

The lattice dynamics of crystals, with and without impurities, studied by K. Rebane and his coworkers is a relatively recent field of activity for physicists (and occasionally physical chemists) which requires sophisticated instrumentation, deep theoretical knowledge, and computational skill, as well as elaborate facilities. This field involves both classical and quantum physics. Instrumentation requires far-infrared monochromators, light-scattering techniques, lasers, Raman techniques (called combinational scattering spectra in the Soviet Union), Fourier transform optical spectrometers, and computers. Ultrasensitive electronic detection systems based on a principle called photon counting are frequently needed to measure the extremely weak signals produced by scattered radiation. The hardware problems encountered in such a line of research are significant, as can be imagined. Even in the United States, the development of stable lasers for molecular and crystal spectroscopy and suitable monochromators for measuring the intensity and frequency of scattered radiation is quite recent.

Theoretical investigations have involved the theory of resonance scattering, the secondary emission of crystal impurities, "hot luminescence," lattice vibrations, special aspects of quantum mechanics, relativity, and Einstein's theory of transition probabilities (Rebane, 1971, 1972). Although the actual list is much longer, these few examples provide an indication of the width and depth of the studies. Much of this research is pure science on a high level. The nature of the work is such that it is not easy or even possible to give a just qualitative description. Matter-of-fact communications are written in technical language from one expert to another. Such spectacular achievements as transistor electronics and space travel represent the cumulative results of long and patient studies by many scientists in many parts of the world.

Along lines closer to obvious immediate applications, physicists at the University of Tartu have worked with gas-phase ionization and the production of charged aerosols, studies which led to the construction of specialized industrial and medicinal equipment. The studies of thin shells carried out at the Institute of Cybernetics under the direction of N. Alumäe represent another branch of physics. Even though the latter field is called applied mechanics, the complexity of the problem is substantial, even if compared to theoretical physics. The nuclear magnetic resonance studies carried out at the Institute of Cybernetics constitute still another branch of physics, in the most rigorous sense of the term.

Investigations carried out at the Institute of Thermophysics and Electrophysics are of a somewhat different nature. Here, emphasis has been on applied technology and on the economic factors involved in energy supply. Oil-shale technology has received a high priority, along with rural electrification. Cost calculations, efficiency factors, and problems related to chemical and electrical engineering have been attacked. Until 1963 this institute was affiliated with an all-union institution under the umbrella title Institute of Energetics. The work of the institute has resulted in pilot plant studies and complete blueprints for large-scale oil-shale utilization that permits electrical energy to be produced on the spot with maximum efficiency.

Life Sciences and Geology

Biology, in a broad sense, is pursued in two institutes of the Academy of Science: zoology and botany, and experimental biology. The bulk of the work in the Institute of Zoology and Botany is descriptive and concentrated on the flora and fauna of Estonia. Estonia is, in fact, one of the most thoroughly studied countries in the world insofar as its vegetation is concerned. The completion of an eleven-volume reference work, *The Flora of the Estonian SSR*, is well under way (seven volumes had appeared in print by 1971).

Along more popular lines, an interesting volume entitled *Eesti järved* [Estonian Lakes] has been compiled by this institute. The book describes in some detail 150 small lakes (the two largest ones, Peipsi and Vôrtsjärv, are excluded). Plants, fish, birds, chemistry (water composition), and other aspects are covered. This work is geared to describing the homeland to its natives. It is noteworthy that funds and other resources are available for such work. Its significance in international science cannot and need not be evaluated. The recently published *Eesti metsad* [Estonian Forests] is in the same vein.

The Institute of Geology is to a large degree concerned with problems associated with oil-shale reserves and oil-shale production. Such deposits have been classified, and recommendations have been made for more effective long-range utilization. The studies involve both the territory formally under the control of the Estonian SSR and the western part of the Leningrad Oblast, a part of the Russian SFSR. In addition, studies are carried out on underground water supplies and their possible utilization. Geophysical investigations are concerned with deep crystalline layers. Descriptive studies are conducted on the geology of Estonia and its prehistoric origin.

The Institute of Experimental Biology is concerned with laboratory research in the life sciences. It is equipped with such instrumentation as ultracentrifuges, electron microscopes, electrophoresis equipment, various kinds of chromatography instruments and spectrophotometers, and equipment for classical physical chemistry. In some ways, this institute functions as an advanced laboratory for special problems in agricultural research. Potato viruses receive major attention; so do problems of soil microbiology and nitrogen availability. Photosynthesis and the mechanism of carbon-dioxide assimilation are studied by methods of physical chemistry. Genetics—in particular, the influence of chemicals and radiation on mutations—is investigated in connection with the development of better crops. Even though such studies are carried out with pragmatic justification, they nevertheless illustrate the lapse of time since the days of Lysenko.

Problems related to conservation and the reforestation of defaced strip-mining areas, along with antipollution measures, have recently acquired a new urgency. An entire session of the Estonian Academy of Sciences was devoted to these problems in 1970. It is recognized, in the words of the president of the academy, that "the protection of nature is not limited to the protection of specific species or the establishment of protected areas (parks). The protection of nature is, above all, the protection of the environment of life, the protection of life itself" (Rebane, 1971).

Conclusion

The overview presented in this chapter, though necessarily incomplete, nevertheless indicates that a very high level of basic scientific research and supportive technological-developmental research exists in the Estonian SSR. Clearly, a great many of these activities reflect changes instituted during the Soviet period: the expansion of the Academy of Sciences, capital investments, the expanded educational base, contact with Russian scientific life per se. Yet, although the postwar administrative setup is new, many characteristics of the present scene cannot be divorced from their historical background. Estonia has a clear tradition of research into problems of fundamental significance, passed on from master to student. The University of Tartu has remained, and the Academy of Sciences has become a major meeting place for the scientific life of the East and the West—present ties with Russian science and research are indeed strong, but scientific communication with the West is also considerable. There exist both the old tradition of national pride in science and scholarship and the new concept of the universality of science and scholarship. Many scientists trained during the prewar years achieved eminence and recognition during the postwar years and have trained a new generation of scientists. Finally, there is the old drive of a small nation to achieve recognition through accomplishment. All of these factors—the prewar heritage as well as the postwar reality—have contributed to the truly astounding breadth and quality of present scientific life in Estonia.

References

Biltz, W.

1931   "Gustav Tammann zum siebzigsten Geburtstag."
        Zeitschrift für anorganische und allgemeine Chemie
        198:3.

Clark, G. L., and G. G. Hawley

1966   *The Encyclopedia of Chemistry*. New York: Rein-
        hold.

Davydov, A. S.

1962   *Theory of Molecular Excitons*. New York: McGraw-
        Hill.

Eesti NSV Teaduste Akadeemia Aastail 1956-1964

1965   [The Academy of Sciences of the Estonian SSR from
        1956 to 1964]. Tallinn: Eesti NSV Teaduste Akadee-
        mia Kirjastus.

Eesti NSV Teaduste Akadeemia Küberneetika Instituut

1970   [The Institute of Cybernetics of the Estonian Acade-
        my of Sciences]. Tallinn: Eesti NSV Teaduste Aka-
        deemia Kirjastus.

Eesti Panga Aastaraamat

1939   [Yearbook of the Bank of Estonia]. Tallinn: Eesti
        Pank.

Ehituse Teadusliku Uurimise Instituudi tegevusest

1972   [Activities of the Institute for the Scientific Study of
        Construction]. Tallinn: Valgus.

Eliashevich, M.

1940   *Comptes rendus de l'académie des sciences de
        l'URSS* 28: 605.

ENE (Eesti Nôukogude Entsüklopeedia)
1973   [The Estonian Soviet Encyclopedia], vol. 6. Tallinn: Valgus.

Greenish, H. G.
1931   "Some Recollections of Dorpat." *Eesti Rohuteadlane* 6:87.

Items from the History of Science in the Estonian SSR
1971   Tartu: Academy of Sciences of the Estonian SSR.

Kneser, A.
1901   "Beiträge zur Theorie und Anwendung der Variatsions-rechnung." *Mathematische Annalen* 55: 86.

Korol, Alexander
1965   *Soviet Research and Development: Its Organization, Personnel, and Funds.* Cambridge, Mass.: Massachusetts Institute of Technology Press.

Kümme Aastat Eesti NSV Teaduste Akadeemiat
1956   [Ten Years of the Academy of Sciences of the Estonian SSR]. Tallinn: Eesti NSV Teaduste Akadeemia Kirjastus.

Lippmaa, E., and I. Arro
1967   "The Active Site and Active Fragments of Enzymes." *Seventh International Congress of Biochemistry Abstracts 4, F272.* Tokyo.

Lippmaa, E., and P. Luiga
1971   "Concentration of Organic Air Contaminants by Sorbents." *Proceedings of the Second International Clean Air Congress,* p. 562.

Lippmaa, E., and S. Radman

1969 "Line Splittings and Splitting Thresholds in Spin-Tickling NMR Spectra." *Journal of Chemical Physics* 50: 2766.

Lippmaa, E., T. Pelik, and T. Saluvee

1971 "Chemical Polarization of Carbon 13 and Nitrogen 15 Nuclei in Thermal Decomposition Reactions." *Industrie Chimique Belge* 36: 1070.

Lippmaa, E., T. Saluvee, and S. Laisaar

1971 "Spin-Lattice Relaxation of Nitrogen-15 Nuclei in Organic Compounds." *Chemical Physics Letters* 11: 120.

Marksoo, Ann

1961 *Eesti Pôlevkivi Tarbimise Geograafiast* [The Geography of Consumption of Estonian Oil Shale]. Tallinn: Eesti NSV Teaduste Akadeemia Kirjastus.

Martinson, H.

1973 *Keemia Instituudi Tänapäev* [The Institute of Chemistry Today]. Tallinn: Eesti NSV Teaduste Akadeemia Kirjastus.

Martinson, Karl

1973 *Teadlane ja teaduslik pulikatsioon Eesti NSV-s* [The Scientist and Scientific Publications in the Estonian SSR]. Tallinn: Eesti NSV Teaduste Akadeemia Kirjastus.

Nigul, U.

1969 "Regions of Effective Application of the Methods of Three-Dimensional Analysis of Transient Stress Waves in Shells and Plates." *International Journal of Solids and Structures* 5: 607.

Nôukogude Eesti Füüsikute Töömailt
1968   [The Work of Soviet Estonian Physicists]. Tallinn: Valgus.

Nôukogude Eesti Teadus
1965   [Soviet Estonian Science]. Tallinn: Eesti Raamat.

Palm, U. V.
1971   "Tartu University as an Important Center of Chemistry in the Baltic Countries in the Last Century," in *Items from History of Science in the Estonian SSR*, ed. J. Eilart. Tallinn: Eesti NSV Teaduste Akadeemia Kirjastus.

Pill, M.
1908   "Päätükk loodusteadusest" [A Chapter about Natural Science]. *Sirvilauad*, no. 12.

Puusepp, L.
1932   *Chirurgische Neuropathologie*. Tartu.

Rebane, K.
1971   *Teadlase Töömailt* [Scientists at Work]. Tallinn: Eesti Raamat.

Rebane, K., T. Mauring, and R. Vanem
1972   "Hot Luminescence from Vibrational Transitions of the OH Molecular Ion in KBr and KCl Crystals." *Eesti NSV Teaduste Akadeemia Toimetised: Füüsika-Matemaatika* 21: 215.

Sinivee, V.
1969   "On Spin Tickling Line Shapes." *Molecular Physics* 17: 41.

Sinivee, V., and E. Lippmaa

  1965   "Weak Perturbing Radio Frequency Field Effects in Nuclear Magnetic Double Resonance." *Eesti NSV Teaduste Akadeemia Toimetised: Füüsika-Matemaatika* 16: 258.

Stothers, J. B.

  1972   "^{13}C NMR Spectroscopy: A Brief Review." *Applied Spectroscopy* 26: 1.

Von Baer, K. E.

  1835   *Development of the Fistus*. Dorpat.

Wiener, Norbert

  1948   *Cybernetics, or Control and Communication in the Man and the Machine*. New York: Wiley.

12

Computers, Computer Sciences, and Computer Applications

Rein Türn

Before we can examine computers, computer sciences, and computer applications in Soviet Estonia, it is necessary to give an overview of the general development of the field. Furthermore, we must briefly examine the development of computers and related fields within the Soviet Union as a whole.

Computer science is a young, rapidly advancing discipline that found its modern beginning in the late 1940s in the United States. The first stored-program electronic digital computer, EDVAC, was completed at the Moore School of Engineering at the University of Pennsylvania in Philadelphia in 1950. Prior to EDVAC, several electromechanical calculators were constructed at Harvard University and at the Bell Telephone Laboratories, and the experimental, externally programmable electronic digital computers ENIAC and EDSAC had been built.

The early history of digital computers began with the French mathematician Blaise Pascal (1623-1662), and continued with the work of Leibnitz (1646-1716), Babbage (1791-1871), Hollerith (1860-1929), Turing (1912-1954), and von Neumann (1903-1957). They established the basic principles of computation and computer design. Background information on the early history of digital computers may be obtained from the books by Goldstine (1972) and Rosenberg (1969).

The field of computer science has evolved from applied and

numerical mathematics, formal logic, and electrical engineering. The earlier activity in computer science was in the design and construction of computer "hardware" and in writing programs for performing the desired computations—the computer "software." More recently, however, computer science has expanded into such other mathematical fields as recursive function theory, automata theory, and computability theory. The design of programming languages and of programming systems for controlling computer operations has acquired an increasingly important and dominating role in computer science.

Computer hardware consists of five major subsystems: the arithmetic unit, primary high-speed memory, secondary memories and mass memories, the control unit, and input-output devices. Modern mass memories include removable magnetic tapes and magnetic disc packs. The principal input-output devices are cardreaders and punches, line printers, optical character readers, graphic plotters, and keyboards or graphic terminals for man-computer interaction. Since space does not permit detailed description of modern computer systems, readers are referred to textbooks on computer systems by Richards (1966) and Davis (1971).

It is also useful to distinguish between different component technologies and levels of sophistication in computer design; these are used to define the so-called computer generations. Joseph (1973) has distinguished between three aspects of computer generations: one describes the nature of the predominant computing activity; the second, the hardware technology (components and subsystems) that is used; and the third, the computer's software and structural architecture (the computational flexibility and sophistication available to the users). The principal computer generations are defined in table 1. Further discussions of expected developments in computer design can be found in Türn (1974a).

Computer applications have evolved from the scientific and engineering calculations prevalent in the early days of computer history to general information-processing applications which involve automated record keeping, information storage and retrieval, control of processes and systems, and planning of economic activities. Advances in telecommunication systems and data-transmission techniques have resulted in the

Table 1

Generations of computer technology

Generation	Year of introduction	Uses	Hardware technology	Software and architecture
1	1951 – 1952	Scientific, business	Vacuum tubes; modularity on individual component level.	Machine language programming, symbolic assemblers, subroutines, program libraries. Special-purpose architectures.
2	1958 – 1960	General data processing	Transistors; modularity on logic gate level.	Higher-level languages (FORTRAN, COBOL, ALGOL), monitors macro-assemblers, executive programs. General-purpose computer architectures.
3	1963 – 1965	Information processing	Integrated semiconductor logic circuits. Modularity on multiple logic circuit level.	Operating systems, many programming and simulation languages, modular programs. Centralized, multiple-processor architectures; families of systems.
4	1970 – 1972	On-line remotely accessible information processing	Medium and large-scale integration. Modularity on subsystem function level.	Extendible languages, metacompilers, subprograms in hardware, conversational systems. Networks of computer systems.

Table 2

Number of installed computers

Country	1962	1967	1972	1974
United States	7,300	29,500	88,000	165,000
Great Britain	312	2,250	7,600	14,400
France	285	2,000	6,700	16,100
West Germany	548	2,960	8,500	18,800
Japan	500	3,200	13,000	26,100
Soviet Union	700	3,200–4,300	5,700–8,000	13–15,000
Estonian SSR	3–4	8–9	25–30	40–50

establishment of the first networks of computers (e.g., the ARPANET).

To illustrate the explosive growth in computer use, table 2 presents data on the number of computers in operation in the United States and other countries during the last ten to twelve years. Unfortunately, at the time this chapter was prepared, the number of installed computers in the Soviet Union had never been announced officially; hence the numbers given in table 2 for the Soviet Union are estimates that have appeared in the literature. This also applies to the estimate of the number of computers in the Estonian SSR.

Computer Technology in the Soviet Union

The first electronic digital computer in the Soviet Union, the MESM, was completed in 1951 at the Ukrainian Academy of Sciences in Kiev under the direction of the academician S. A. Lebedev. However, since MESM was primarily an experimental prototype, the history of computer science in the Soviet Union did not really begin until 1953. In that year, three events occurred which provided incentives for the Soviet development of computers: (1) Joseph Stalin died, (2) the second computer designed by Lebedev, the BESM-1, was completed in Moscow, and (3) an article was published in the

influential journal *Voprosy filosofii* attacking cybernetics—
the new science of communication and control in biological as
well as inanimate systems which had been established in the
West by Norbert Wiener (see Wiener, 1948). This article
labeled cybernetics a "misanthropic pseudoscience" in the
service of the "imperialist war gods," and predicted that
cybernetics was doomed to failure even before Western imperialism itself (*Materialist*, 1953).

These three events, however, actually served to strengthen
the development of cybernetics and led to advances in computer construction and applications. But eight more years passed
before cybernetics was accepted in Communist ideology. In
1961 a collection of articles, "Cybernetics in Communism's
Service," was published under the editorship of the prominent
academician A. I. Berg, and the Twenty-second Congress of
the Communist Party of the Soviet Union pointed out that in
the course of the next twenty years cybernetics, electronic
computers, and automated control systems would be widely
applied in Soviet industry, transportation, scientific research,
and management (Levien and Maron, 1964).

By 1962, the design and manufacture of electronic computers was being pursued by several Soviet ministries and institutes. Thus, Lebedev's Institute of Precise Mechanics and
Computer Engineering in Moscow developed the BESM-2 and
M-20 machines; the Institute of Electronic Control Computers
in Moscow developed the M-1, M-2, and M-3 computers; the
Institute of Mechanics and Instrument Design of the Ministry
of Radio Industry designed and built the URAL-1 and URAL-
4 machines; the Institute of Physics and Mathematics of the
Byelorussian Academy of Sciences and the Minsk Ordzhoni-
kidze Plant manufactured the MINSK series computers
(MINSK-1 and MINSK-2); and other, less well-known com-
puters were developed in the Ukraine (KIEV, DNEPR-1),
Armenia (RAZDAN-1, EREVAN), and at other institutes.
Details of the history of Soviet computers may be found in
Rudin (1970).

The above-mentioned computer models accounted for nearly all installed computers in the Soviet Union in 1962. Several
one-of-a-kind computers were also built. By 1962, a total of 26
different computer models had been developed in the Soviet
Union. By the same year, however, more than 200 computer
types had been developed in the United States (Harman, 1971).

The Soviet computers were still first-generation machines, while the American computers were almost through the second generation and on the verge of entering the third generation. The delays in the acceptance of cybernetics and computers in the Soviet Union had taken their toll, resulting in a five- to ten-year lag in Soviet computer technology which still persists. This technology lag is especially severe in the area of input-output devices and mass-memory devices and in the overall reliability of Soviet computers.

In subsequent years Soviet computer technology moved into the second generation with the BESM-6 computer and the new additions to the URAL and MINSK series (URAL-11, -14, and -16; MINSK-22 and -32), which, to date, are still the principal computers in the Soviet Union. At the same time— that is, about 1965—the United States moved into the third computer generation with the IBM System 360 series computers. The Soviet Union was only in 1973-1974 beginning to manufacture its RYAD series computers (the ES-1020 and ES-1040 models), which are close copies of the IBM 360 series (Holland, 1973). The RYAD computer development has been under way since 1967 and has involved most of the Soviet bloc countries. However, the RYAD computers have lagged until recently because of design, quality-control, and management problems (Holland, 1972). Table 3 compares computer development in the Soviet Union with that in the United States, as well as the processing capabilities of the computers of the two countries.

In other areas of computer science, such as computer design theory, theories of algorithms and programming, and theoretical cybernetics, Soviet researchers are producing high-level work. Participating in this research as such prominent scientists as A. A. Lyapunov, A. I. Berg, A. N. Kolmogorov, L. I. Gutenmakher, and M. A. Ayzerman, and computer scientists A. A. Lebedev, V. M. Glushkov, and A. P. Ershov. Their work has concentrated on automatic control theory, programming and automata theory, and switching theory. Indeed, as pointed out by Brezhnev at the Twenty-third Congress of the Communist Party of the Soviet Union (Brezhnev, 1966), the gap between theoretical research in computer sciences in the Soviet Union and the practical application of research results in the

Table 3

Comparison of United States and Soviet computers

	USA		USSR	
Year	Model	Speed	Model	Speed
1952	IBM 701	.018	BESM-1	.015
1953	UNIVAC 1103	.02		
1954	IBM 650	.0001		
1955	IBM 704	.042		
1956	IBM 705	.01	URAL-1	.0001
1958	IBM 709	.042		
1959			URAL-2	.002
			M-20	.02
1960	CDC-1604A	.16	BESM-2	.001
	IBM 7090	.23	MINSK-1	.003
1962	IBM 7094-I	.25	URAL-4	.005
			MINSK-2	.005
1963	CDC 3600	.48	BESM-4	.02
	PHILCO 212	.67		
1964	IBM 7094-II	.71	M-220	.02
1965	IBM 360/20	.02	URAL-11	.003
	UNIVAC 1108	1.33	URAL-14	.01
			MINSK-22	.003
1966	IBM 360/65	.77	BESM-6	1.0
	CDC 6400	1.0	MINSK-23	.003
	CDC 6500	2.0		
1967	IBM 360/91	7.8	URAL-16	.07
	DEC PDP-10	.5		
1968	IBM 360/95	9.7	MINSK-32	.04
1969	CDC-7600	15.0	M-1000	.02
	B-6500	2.5	M-2000	.03
	IBM 360/85	4.4	M-3000	.06
1973	CDC STAR	50.0	ES-1020	.02
	ILLIAC-IV	128.0	ES-1040	.3
1974			ES-1060	1.5

Note: Speed estimated in MIPS (millions of instructions per second).

design and production of computers is rapidly increasing (see Kautz, 1966; Kassel, 1971; and DiPaola, 1967, for additional information on Soviet research).

In general, the application of digital computers in the Soviet Union has followed the same pattern as such application in the United States and other countries: first in scientific research and engineering design and later in accounting, inventory control, and other business data-processing activities. But the Soviet economists have also recognized that cybernetics and computers may provide the solution to their problems in planning and operating a centrally controlled economy. For example, academician Berg stated in his analysis of the uses of cybernetics in a Communist society:

> As distinct from the capitalist countries, where the various firms create, each for itself, separate auto-mated systems of control, under socialism it is per-fectly possible to organize a single, complex, auto-mated system of control of the country's national economy. Obviously, the effect of such automation will be much greater than that of automating control of individual enterprises (Levien and Maron, 1964).

The Twenty-second Party Congress in 1961 recognized the value of cybernetics and computers in the centralized control of the Soviet economy. This was reinforced at the Twenty-third Party Congress in 1966 (Brezhnev, 1966); subsequently, the development of the RYAD computer systems was ordered. The Twenty-fourth Party Congress in 1971 ordered an acceler-ated development of computer technology and, in particular, of the RYAD series computers. The party directives specifical-ly called for work to begin ". . . on the establishment and introduction of automated planning and management systems for branches of the economy, territorial organizations, produc-tion associations, and enterprises for the purpose of creating a state-wide automated information collection and processing system for accounting, planning, and management of the national economy based on a state network of computer centers and a unified automated communications network for the country." The associated five-year plan (1971-1975) called for the production of 12,000 to 15,000 third-generation com-puters (of the RYAD vintage), representing a planned 2.6-fold increase in the number of computers presently installed. Also planned were some 1,600 automated control systems (ASUs) for the largest enterprises and associations in the Soviet Union (Kozlov, 1971).

However, by 1974, three years through the five-year plan, it was clear that these goals in computer production could not be met. Indeed, the first RYAD computers were only then entering production. Still to be done was the gargantuan job of converting the existing second-generation computer programs to third-generation RYAD computers, which were incompatible with all existing Soviet computers.

Computer Technology in the Estonian SSR

The use of computers in the Estonian SSR and the participation of Estonian engineers and scientists in furthering computer technology can be examined within the context of developments in computer sciences in the United States and, more important, in the Soviet Union.

The role of the instrument and electronics industry in the Estonian economy is rather small, less than 10 percent of the industrial output in 1968. The major products are electrical appliances, electric motors, wires and cables, industrial control regulators, radio receivers and parts, and some semiconductor devices. It is not surprising, therefore, that no electronic computers are manufactured in Estonia. Indeed, nearly 95 percent of the output of the instrument and electronics industry is exported—mainly to the Soviet Union, but also to many countries in Europe, Africa, South America, and Asia (Tulp et al., 1972). However, the high educational level in Estonia is reflected in substantial contributions to theoretical development and research in computer science. For example, the Cybernetics Institute of the Estonian Academy of Sciences in Tallinn, founded in 1960, was the first institute in the Soviet Union devoted entirely to cybernetics research.

The first electronic digital computer in the Estonian SSR was a URAL-1 installed in 1959 at the University of Tartu. Subsequently, others were obtained, and by 1967 there were five computing centers in operation (Môand, 1966):

• The computing center at the University of Tartu, with a URAL-4 and a URAL-1 computer, was used for teaching, research in mathematics and management science, and providing computing services to local industrial establishments.

• The computing center at the Cybernetics Institute of the Estonian Academy of Sciences in Tallinn had a relatively modern MINSK-22 computer in addition to the M-3 and MINSK-2 computers which had been acquired in 1963 and 1964, respectively. These machines were used mainly for supporting the academy's research activities.

• A computer center at the Estonian Union of Consumers' Cooperatives was equipped with a MINSK-22 computer for introducing automated inventory control, shipping, and billing methods in the central warehouses. The center also supported the Eesti Kaabel cable and wire factory and the excavator plant in Tallinn.

• A URAL-11 at the Estonian Affiliate of the Central Economics-Mathematics Institute of the Soviet Academy of Sciences was used for developing automated control systems for industrial enterprises, especially for the experimental installation of such a system at the Tallinn Excavator Plant. In addition, the center was active in disseminating automated inventory control systems for other factories in Tallinn.

• A computer center at the Central Statistical Administration of the Estonian SSR had a MINSK-22 computer. This center was created in 1966 as the first link of the state computer network planned for the Estonian SSR, which, subsequently, was to be connected to the Soviet computer network.

During subsequent years, the Cybernetics Institute also obtained a MINSK-32 computer; in 1967 the Tallinn Polytechnic Institute acquired a MINSK-22; the University of Tartu received a URAL-14 and a MINSK-32; and several other computers were installed at various enterprises in Tallinn and Tartu. At present, there are approximately twenty computer centers in Estonia (Vendelin, 1972), mostly equipped with MINSK-22, MINSK-32, and URAL-11 computers. The older computers are also still in operation. For example, the URAL-1 computer from University of Tartu (the first computer in Estonia) is now at the Nôo secondary school, where it is used for programming instruction. The total number of computers in Estonia in 1974 has not been given in literature, but it can be estimated to be in the 25–30 range.

In general, from the point of view of computing capability, the computers installed in the Estonian SSR are not intended for processing large amounts of data, nor are their peripheral input-output devices anywhere close to those in the Western world or even to the newest Soviet computers. None of the computers is equipped with a large memory or a direct-access disc memory. Hence they cannot support time-sharing, multi-processing, interactive computing through remote terminals, or any other of the many innovations now common in Western computing centers.

The Estonian computer engineers are well aware of these limitations in their computers and have tried to improvise solutions. For example, the MINSK-22 and MINSK-32 computers of the Cybernetics Institute were connected into a cooperating system, and an important technical improvement to the MINSK-32 was made in the process (Järve, 1972).

In addition to applications already noted, Estonia is also involved in the Soviet effort to develop a statewide computer network of automated management systems. For this purpose, a special council was organized in 1971, headed by A. Vendel-in, deputy chairman of the Council of Ministers of the Estoni-an SSR (Gerasimova, 1971). The technical base for this effort is currently being set up. Existing computer centers are being redesigned, and new computer centers are being established in Tartu, Pärnu, Viljandi, and Kohtla-Järve.

In agriculture, work is being done on the development of an experimental automated management system for the planning, accounting, reporting, and economic management of experi-ments conducted in the Harju region. Also, the Ministry of Agriculture has established a data bank that contains a set of the economic indicators provided in the annual reports of the Estonian *kolkhoz*es and *sovkhoz*es. Such information is used for generating optimal plans for livestock feeding (Vendelin, 1972).

Applications of more conventional data-processing tech-niques in agriculture are also advancing. For example, a calculating station employing punched-card equipment has been established in the Kingisepp region on the island of Saaremaa. Among other miscellaneous computer applications in the Estonian SSR are the following:
- Since 1969, a special-purpose computer, SOKOL, has been controlling the manufacture of coke in an oil-shale processing plant in Kohtla-Järve.
- An automated management system (ASU) has been

installed in the Kalinin truck-parts manufacturing plant in Tallinn.

• A MINSK-22 computer is used by the Estonian Ministry of Automotive Transport and Highways to determine optimal trucking and delivery routes.

One of the more innovative applications of computers is in the scheduling of radio and TV programs at the Estonian broadcasting studios in Tallinn. This was the first such application in the Soviet Union and even among the Eastern-bloc countries. Subsequently, in August 1972, the East European International Organization of Radio and Television held a symposium in Tallinn on the applications of computers and automation.

A special accomplishment was the design and construction by the engineers at the Tallinn Polytechnic Institute of a special-purpose computer, the STEM, for controlling metal-working machines. STEM has been installed in the Kirov plant in Leningrad and in several other metalworking factories in the Soviet Union. The designers of the STEM, directed by A. Ariste, received an Estonian SSR state prize.

The principal institutions involved in computer research in the Estonian SSR are the Institute of Cybernetics of the Estonian Academy of Sciences, the University of Tartu, and the Tallinn Polytechnic Institute. Each has made substantial contributions to one or more areas of computer science and cybernetics and has received recognition both in the Soviet Union and in the international computer-science community.

In the area of experimental adoption of computerized methods to economic management, Estonia is one of the leading Soviet republics. The accomplishments of Estonian computer scientists in this area are particularly noteworthy because they have not been supplied with advanced computers. Increasingly, ministries of the Soviet Union are turning to Estonia and to the other two Baltic republics for relatively small-scale implementation of computer applications that will eventually be expanded to embrace the entire country. In this respect, the Baltic republics of the Soviet Union are becoming laboratories for the development of national economic-management systems.

We will now examine in more detail the research in computer sciences and cybernetics performed at the three research institutes of the Estonian SSR.

The Cybernetics Institute

In 1971, the Academy of Sciences of the Estonian SSR had nearly 800 scientific workers and researchers. Among these were 40 doctors of sciences and 400 candidates of sciences. The Cybernetics Institute is the youngest of the academy's eleven institutes. Its director since 1969 has been Dr. Boris Tamm. Others in leadership positions at the Cybernetics Institute are Dr. Hillar Aben, vice-director for science; Dr. Ivar Petersen, vice-director for science and director of the section on mathematical methods; and Kalju Leppik, director of the operations analysis section and of the programming bureau.

Dr. Tamm is Estonia's foremost cyberneticist and computer scientist. His specialties are the development of problem-oriented languages for the automatic programming of special-purpose systems and the development of general principles of automatic programming. He has participated in numerous international meetings; in 1967 he headed the Soviet delegation to the Fifth International Congress on Cybernetics in Belgium. One of his major accomplishments was the development of the first automatic programming system for numerically controlled metalworking machines in the Soviet Union. For this he was awarded an Estonian SSR state prize.

Work at the Cybernetics Institute involves applied mechanics and physical chemistry as well as technical cybernetics and computer sciences. The last include mathematical modeling of controlled processes and systems, optimal control theory, computer technology, and programming languages and systems.

Following are the major developments and accomplishments in computer sciences at the institute (Rebane, 1971):

Research has been performed on statistical methods in optimal control and in developing algorithms for controlling technological processes. Algorithms were written for adaptive control of continuous nonstationary technological processes in the production of the chemical formalin. Subsequently, a centralized control system was developed for formaldehyde production for the MINSK-22 and MINSK-32 computers. By the end of 1970, ten production steps had been automated, and the system was in use at several factories in the Soviet Union. This effort was initiated by I. Petersen and R. Tavast. For the development of the formaldehyde production-control system,

R. Tavast and others were awarded an Estonian SSR state prize for science.

Research was conducted on mathematical modeling of controlled systems and processes and on optimization techniques. New techniques were developed for evaluation and optimization of functions on the basis of experimentally obtained data. This research was directed by I. Petersen. His more recent activities in this area include the application of mathematical methods to the optimization of very large systems by decomposition and suboptimization techniques. In the same area, E. Raik has been working on the qualitative relationships between various versions of the stochastic programming problems.

Applications of the research in mathematical modeling and optimization theory include the mathematical modeling of urban development and the optimization of route planning and scheduling in transportation systems. In the former area, H. Aben, J. Kajari, and I. Adamson developed mathematical models for the optimal scheduling of construction in residential areas and the optimal layout of apartment-house floor plans. For the optimal solution of transport problems, K. Leppik, B. Tamm, M. Reigo, and K. Marge developed a set of computer programs for Tallinna Autoveod (Tallinn's Autotransport).

Research in computational mathematics has involved work in the numerical solution of systems of nonlinear equations as they arise in optimal control problems. In this area, Dr. Sulev Ulm developed a general theory of differential relationships in Banach spaces and a number of algorithms. More recently he has worked on studies of the optimization of very large systems by decomposition and suboptimization.

Automatic recognition of human speech for man-computer interaction has also been investigated. E. Künnap and M. Rohtla studied the power spectra of vowels and worked on the modeling of the human speech tract as a control system. They produced a number of computer programs for speech-recognition research and built special-purpose equipment for speech signal analysis.

Work has also been done on studies of computer components and switching elements. For example, M. Sinisoo and E. Germ derived a general theory of magnetic circuits and have used their results to improve the operational parameters of special-purpose magnetic memory units. They hope that this work may lead to the establishment of a micromagnetics industry in the Estonian SSR.

In the area of algorithmic languages and programming systems for computers, the research focus has been on the development of problem-oriented languages for modeling and controlling technical and engineering processes and on the computer solution of problems in economics. Among the achievements in these areas are (Tamm, 1967):

• MALGOL, a precise subset of the ALGOL programming language for solving a wide range of problems on the MINSK and URAL computers, was completed in 1965 by M. Kotli, P. Hanko, and others. It has generated considerable interest in other computer centers in the Soviet Union and in Eastern-bloc countries.

• SAP-1 and SAP-2, automatic programming systems for special-purpose applications (especially for programming numerically controlled metal-cutting machinery), were developed by B. Tamm and others in 1962 and 1964, respectively.

• APROKS, a system for the automatic preparation of control information for machines used for cutting metal plates for ships' hulls and for layout and precision design of these parts, uses a language that permits technologists to write language models of the cutting processes. It was developed by B. Tamm and J. Pruuden for MINSK-22 computers and has been put into use in the Soviet shipbuilding industry. For this development, Tamm and Pruuden were awarded the Estonian SSR state prize for science (see Pruuden, 1968).

• VELGOL, a programming system for the solution of problems in economics, was developed by V. Kuusik, E. Sarv, and L. Heinla and is now in use in numerous computing centers throughout the Soviet Union. The VELGOL-1 language was completed in 1966. Subsequently the VELGOL-2 system was developed, and work is continuing on more advanced versions (Kuusik, 1968). The VELGOL language is similar to the well-known list-processing languages LISP and IPL but also contains elements of ALGOL.

• TSIMOD, a language developed by H. Salum, is used for recording block diagrams of digital subsystems for the purpose of computer simulation of their operation and interactions (Salum, 1965).

Other efforts in this area include the development of a

modular programming system for the MINSK-22 computer (Tinn et al., 1970), a questionnaire-based system for gathering and processing economics data (Sarv and Heinla, 1970), and work on the general principles of problem-oriented automatic programming languages (Tamm, 1968, 1969).

Recent research directions at the Cybernetics Institute are related to the establishment of a statewide network of computer centers and automated control systems. The institute is contributing toward the development of a scientific and theoretical basis for such networks, and will participate in the experimental interconnection of the first computers. Work will continue on modeling the economic processes to be controlled and on generating the necessary programming languages and systems.

University of Tartu

At the University of Tartu, computer-sciences research is performed by the university's computing center and the chair of computational mathematics. Both are directed by candidate of physics and mathematics Ülo Kaasik. He may be credited with pioneering the work in computer applications in the Estonian SSR and advancing both research and education in computer sciences. His major interest is the application of mathematical and numerical techniques (e.g., linear programming) to the solution of problems in management sciences.

The research in computer applications in management sciences has focused on the economic behavior of enterprises and organizations and on the application of research results to the planning and development of automated management systems. Researchers in this area include I. Kull, E. Tiit, E. Tamme, and A. Vôhandu.

Among other activities in computer sciences and their applications are the development of the ALGOL-60 programming language translator for the URAL-4 computer, work on pattern recognition, and applications of computational techniques in sociology and other sciences. The educational activities in computer sciences are, of course, of major importance at the University of Tartu. These will be discussed in another section of this chapter.

The university has hosted a number of all-union and international (Eastern-bloc) conferences and symposia at its Kääriku conference facility. Among these were the all-union conference on management sciences in 1966, a meeting of URAL-type computer users, also in 1966, and the all-union seminar on pattern recognition in 1970.

Tallinn Polytechnic Institute

In the 1969-1970 academic year, there were 543 faculty members and 6,068 students at the Tallinn Polytechnic Institute. The Faculty of Electrical Engineering, headed by Professor Jaan Tomson, had 67 members. Although no detailed information on its curriculum is available, it is certain that courses in computer design were offered and that research on computer components, subsystems, and technical applications was conducted. Indeed, Gerasimova (1971) stated that the Tallinn Polytechnic Institute was training engineers who were specializing in the processing of economic information and in computer technology.

A major achievement of the institute was the design and construction of the STEM special-purpose computer mentioned previously (Tinn and Tôugu, 1969). This machine uses second-generation componentry (transistors and printed circuits) and is equipped with a keyboard terminal for data input and output and controlling computations. A special-purpose control unit and associated programs permit direct input of operants in the decimal representation. As noted, the developers of STEM—A. Ariste, Ü. Kess, H. Tani, K. Tinn, E. Tôugu, and A. Vaus—were awarded an Estonian SSR state prize for science in recognition of this work.

Education in Computer Science in the Estonian SSR

The planned large-scale utilization of computers in the Estonian economy requires large numbers of qualified specialists: computer-applications analysts, programmers, and operators. To meet the demand, principles of programming are introduced in some secondary schools in a special curriculum that leads to qualification as a computer programmer upon graduation from high school. The curriculum involves courses in programming theory and practice as well as the "hands-on" programming of computers at the University of Tartu and the

URAL-1 at the Nôo secondary school. In 1967 three secondary schools offered the computer-programmer specialty; they graduated 60 students in this curriculum. In 1970 the number of graduates rose to 100. Approximately 360 have graduated since 1964.

Higher education in computer science is offered at the Mathematics Faculty of the University of Tartu. Between 1963 and 1972 the Mathematics Faculty graduated approximately 200 (40) mathematicians and 35 (15) candidates in mathematical sciences. (The numbers in parentheses represent those whose candidate theses or undergraduate-degree theses indicated a specialization in computer sciences, management sciences, or cybernetics.)

Among Estonian scientists with computer-science interests who received their doctoral degrees during the 1965-1970 period are U. Nigul, H. Aben, L. Ainola, B. Tamm, G. Vainikko, I. Petersen, and S. Ulm. In general, the candidate and doctoral dissertations are written in Russian, and nearly all candidate and doctoral committees include professors from Soviet universities and institutes. For example, the preparation of B. Tamm's doctoral dissertation, "Elements of a Theory of Modeling Engineering Processes with Specialized Programming Systems," was guided by a committee consisting of Professors S. S. Lavrov and B. N. Naumov from Moscow and Dr. G. A. Spônu from Kiev.

The principal journals in Estonia for publishing papers in computer science are *Eesti NSV Teaduste Akadeemia Toimetised. Matemaatika. Füüsika* (Transactions of the Academy of Sciences of the Estonian SSR in Mathematics and Physics) and *Tartu Riikliku Ülikooli Toimetised. Matemaatika- ja mehhaanika-alseid töid* (Transactions of the University of Tartu: Works in Mathematics and Mechanics). Articles in both journals are in Russian, but summaries in Estonian, English, and German are provided.

Two Estonian-language journals, *Tehnika ja Tootmine* (Technology and Production) and *Loodus ja Matemaatika* (Nature and Mathematics) also publish somewhat popularized articles on computer technology, mathematics, and computer applications. Since 1963, an irregularly published compendium of articles and news, *Matemaatika ja Kaasaeg* (Mathematics and the Present Times) has contained articles on computer programming, cybernetics, and management sciences (see Türn, 1967, for a review of this compendium).

Textbooks in computer science are mostly written in Russian, but a number of Estonian-language paperbacks have been published. The authors are from the University of Tartu and the various institutes in Tallinn.

The Future of Computer Sciences in the Estonian SSR

It is certain that the Estonian SSR will not become a center for the manufacture of computers or computer equipment. The trend in the Soviet Union is toward standardization and unification of design; thus, any attempts to establish in any of the Soviet republics a "native" computer industry based on native computer designs will be suppressed. However, the design and assembly of special-purpose computers, such as STEM, is likely to continue in the Estonian SSR.

In other areas of computer science—for example, programming languages and systems, establishing computer networks, and the application of computers to economic problems— computer scientists in Estonia, as well as those in the Latvian SSR and Lithuanian SSR, will continue their contributions. Whether or not the Soviets are successful in establishing a national system of automated management-control centers, basic computer science will be advanced. Thus, we can expect the Estonian contributions to be concentrated on establishing programming languages and systems for multiprocessing, time sharing, interactive problem solving, and computer graphics. The prerequisites for further developments in these areas at the Estonian institutes already exist. And there is no doubt that everyone in the computer field in Estonia is enthusiastic about electronic digital computers and their applications.

Also arriving is a new area of application—the use of computers for storing and processing personal information about individuals. For example, the law sector at the Institute of Economics of the Academy of Sciences of the Estonian SSR is using computers to analyze the work performed by the city and regional commissions on juvenile affairs (Randalu, 1973). This work entails compiling and processing in computers data on juveniles for whom records have been established—data characterizing the personalities of the juvenile and his parents, his conduct, family status, marital status, and the crime or misdemeanor involved. In Western countries, the establishment of computerized personal-information data banks has caused grave concern about potential violations of the data subjects' rights and freedoms (see, for example, Türn, 1974b). Whether or not this factor will be regarded as a "nonproblem" in the Soviet society remains to be seen. The potential for computers to accumulate personal information and correlate such information with other data is tremendous; hence they can be used to establish total "information surveillance" of the citizens of a country. Whether such systems and capabilities will be established and how they will be controlled are decisions that depend entirely on the philosophies of those in power. One can only hope that information surveillance will not be a major computer application field in the Estonian SSR during the 1980s.

References

Brezhnev, L. I.

1966 "Report of the CPSU Central Committee of the Twenty-third Congress of the Communist Party of the Soviet Union," translated from *Pravda*, March 30, 1966. *Current Digest of the Soviet Press* 13, no. 12: 23.

Davis, Gordon B.

1971 *Introduction to Electronic Computers*. New York: McGraw-Hill.

DiPaola, Robert A.

1967 *A Survey of the Soviet Work in the Theory of Computer Programming*, Santa Monica, Calif.: The Rand Corporation (RM-5424-PR).

Doncov, Boris

1971 *Soviet Cybernetics Technology 12: Time-Sharing in the Soviet Union.* Santa Monica, Calif.: The Rand Corporation (P-522-PR).

Gerasimova, T.

1971 "EVM: Planirovanie, kontrol, upravlenie" [Estonia Acts To Computerize Economy]. *Izvestiya*, January 23, 1971. Translation in *Soviet Cybernetics Review* 1, no. 4 (July 1967): 67-68.

Goldstine, Herman H.

1972 *The Computer from Pascal to Von Neumann.* Princeton, N.J.: Princeton University Press.

Harman, Alvin J.

1971 *The International Computer Industry.* Cambridge, Mass.: Harvard University Press.

Holland, Wade B.

1972 "Ryad Arrives—and So Does the Party." *Soviet Cybernetics Review* 2, no. 3: 7-12.
1973 "ES-1040 Missing from Ryad Line-Up." *Soviet Cybernetics Review* 3, no. 3: 7-10.

Järve, Linda

1972 "Millest rääkisid küberneetikud?" [What Were Cyberneticists Talking About?]. *Noorte Hääl*, November 16, p. 2.

Joseph, Earl C.

1972 "Future Computer Architecture—Polymorphic Systems," in *Procedings, COMPCON '72.* New York: Institute of Electrical and Electro-Engineers.

Kaasik, Ü., R. Mullari, and E. Saareste

1964 "Majandusmatemaatika-alaseid töid Tartu Riikliku

Ülikooli arvutuskeskuses" [Work on Applications of Mathematics in Economics at the Computer Center of the Tartu State University], in *Matemaatika ja kaasaeg* [Mathematics and the Present Times]. Tartu.

Kassel, Simon

1971   *Soviet Cybernetics Research: A Preliminary Study of Organizations and Personalities.* Santa Monica, Calif.: The Rand Corporation (R-909-ARPA).

Kautz, William H.

1966   "A Survey and Assessment of Progress in Switching Theory and Logical Design in the Soviet Union." *IEEE Transactions on Electronic Computers* 15, no. 2: 164-204.

Kotli, M., and P. Hanko

1966   "Rukovodstvo po algoritmicheskomy yazyky MAL-GOL," in the collection *Programmy dlya ETsVM Minsk-2*, no. 4. Tallinn.

Kozlov, S.

1971   "Avtomatizirovannye sistemy v novoj pytiletke" [Summary of the Five-Year Automation Goals]. *Ekonomic-geskaya gazeta*, no. 25 (June). Translation in *Soviet Cybernetics Review* 2, no. 1 (January 1973): 7-8.

Kuusik, Vello

1968   "A Description of the VELGOL-3 Programming Language." Paper presented at the First All-Union Conference on Programming, Kiev.

Levien, Roger, and M. E. Maron

1964   *Cybernetics and Its Development in the Soviet Union.* Santa Monica, Calif.: The Rand Corporation (RM-4156-PR).

Materialist

1953 "Komy sluzhit kibernetika" [Whom Does Cybernetics Serve?]. *Voprosy filosofii* [Questions of Philosophy], no. 5. Translation in *Soviet Cybernetics: Recent News Items*, no. 7. Santa Monica, Calif.: The Rand Corporation, 1967.

Môand, H.

1966 "Electronic Computers in the Enterprises of Estonia." Translation of article in *Kommunist estonii* [Estonian Communist], no. 12 (December), in *USSR Economy and Industry, General Information*, pp. 33-41. Washington: Joint Publications Research Service, U.S. Department of Commerce, March 10, 1967.

Pruuden, J.

1968 "A Specialized Problem-Oriented Language for the APROKS System." Paper presented at the First All-Union Conference on Programming, Kiev.

Randalu, H.

1973 "The Use of Electronic Computers in the Work of Commissions on Juvenile Affairs." Translation of article in *Sovetskoye Gosudarstvo i Pravo*, no. 11, pp. 75-80, in *Translations on USSR Political and Sociological Affairs*, no. 505, pp. 36-43. Arlington, Va.: Joint Publications Research Service, March 5, 1974.

Rebane, K.

1971 *Teadlaste Töömailt Nôukogude Eestis Kaheksandal Viis-Aastakul* [Scientific Achievements in the Estonian SSR in the Eighth Five-Year Plan]. Tallinn: Eesti Raamat.

Richards, R. K.

1971 *Electronic Digital Systems*. New York: Wiley.

Rosenberg, Jerry M.

1969   *The Computer Prophets.* New York: Macmillan.

Rudins, George

1970   "Soviet Computers: A Historical Survey." *Soviet Cybernetics Review* 4, no. 1: 6-44.

Salum, H.

1965   *Eesti NSV Teaduste Akadeemia Toimetised. Füüsika. Matemaatika* [Transactions of the Academy of Sciences of the Estonian SSR in Physics and Mathematics] 14, no. 3: 464-472.

Sarv, E., and L. Heinla

1970   "A Questionnaire System for Processing Economics Data." Paper presented at the Second All-Union Conference on Programming, Novosibirsk, February 3-6.

Tamm, Boris

1967   "Problemy avtomatizatsii programmirovaniya v Estonskoj SSR" [Problems of Programming Automation in the Estonian SSR]. *Eesti NSV Teaduse Akadeemia Toimetised. Füüsika. Matemaatika* [Transactions of the Academy of Sciences of the Estonian SSR in Physics and Mathematics] 16, no. 3: 267-284. Translation in *Soviet Cybernetics: Recent News Items*, no. 15, pp. 21-28. Santa Monica, Calif.: The Rand Corporation, March 1968.

1968   "On the Principles of Universality and Simplicity in Automatic Programming Systems." Paper presented at the First All-Union Conference on Programming, Kiev.

1969   "Problem-Oriented Computer Languages as Tools for Simulating Engineering Processes," in *Proceedings of the IFIP Congress 68.* North-Holland.

Tinn, K. A., and E. H. Tôugu

1969   "The STEM Special-Purpose Computer." *Soviet Cybernetics Review*, January 1970, p. 55. Translation of excerpts of chapter 4 of *Tekhnologicheskie raschety na TsVM* [Technological Calculations on Digital Computers]. Leningrad: Mashinostoenie.

Tinn, K. A., E. H. Tôugu, and M. I. Unt

1970 "A Modular Programming System for the Minsk-22 Computer." Paper presented at the Second All-Union Conference on Programming, Novosibirsk, February 3-6.

Tulp, L., M. Vabar, and D. Rajango

1972 *Economic Ties of the Estonian SSR.* Tallinn: Eesti Raamat.

Türn, Rein

1968 "Matemaatika ja kaasaeg Tartus" [Mathematics and the Present Times in Tartu]. *Mana*, no. 33, pp. 111-115.

1974a *Computers in the 1980s.* New York: Columbia University Press.

1974b *Privacy and Security in Personal Information Databank Systems.* Santa Monica, Calif.: The Rand Corporation (R-1044-NSF).

Vendelin, A. G.

1972 "Scientific Methods in the Management of the Economy of Soviet Estonia." *Ekonomika i Matematicheshkie Metody*, no. 6, pp. 824-826. Translation in *Translations on USSR Economic Affairs*, no. 444. Arlington, Va.: Joint Publications Research Service, January 23, 1973.

Wiener, Norbert

1948 *Cybernetics: On Control and Communication in the Animal and the Machine.* New York: Wiley.

13
Astronomical Research

Valdar Oinas

The period of the Estonian Republic saw a rapid rise in the stature of the historic Tartu Observatory from the relative dormancy that had prevailed since the middle of the nineteenth century, following the departure of Wilhelm Struve to the Pulkovo Observatory. In large measure, this resurgence was due to the work of Ernst Öpik, an astronomer of unusually wide research interests, whose fundamental contributions spanned the spectrum from meteor studies to external galaxies. Of the 106 papers published by the observatory staff during this time, 65 were by Öpik. The general research trends of the observatory were continued during the post–World War II years. Stellar astronomy and galactic structure remained the main traditional fields of research, but work has continued on minor members of the solar system and, in recent years, stellar atmospheres and stellar structure. By tradition, the fields of geophysics and meteorology have been closely allied with the astronomical studies at the Tartu Observatory, an affiliation that has continued at the new observatory at Tôravere.

The first task following the end of the war in 1945 was the reconstruction of the heavily damaged main building of the observatory, which housed the eight-inch Zeiss refractor. Although only minimal repairs could be undertaken during the first years after the war, a thorough reconstruction was completed in the fall of 1950, adhering to the precept that the outside of the historic structure should remain unchanged. In 1947 the Zeiss refractor was refurbished, and the six-inch

Petzval camera was once again available for photographic observations.

In 1948 the observatory, which had been affiliated with the University of Tartu, was placed under the jurisdiction of the Academy of Sciences of the Estonian SSR as a part of the Institute of Physics and Mathematics (and Mechanics, until 1952). The former director of the observatory, Taavet Rootsmäe, remained a member of the university in the Faculty of Astronomy and Geophysics, while Vladimir Riives became the new director. Öpik had fled the country in 1944, as had several other physicists, geophysicists, and astronomers, producing some severe gaps in the staff of the institute. A thorough reorganization was undertaken in 1950, with Aksel Kipper named as the director of the institute and Harald Keres succeeding to the directorship of the observatory. Keres and two newly appointed research associates, Grigori Kusmin and Vladimir Riives, had obtained their degrees during the war years but were required to defend their theses a second time, since degrees granted during the German occupation were not recognized. By 1952 the observatory staff had been increased twofold from its five-member component of the prewar and immediate postwar days. Research topics during those early years included galactic structure (Kusmin and Einasto), variable stars (Albo), comets and asteroids (Riives and Raudsaar), gaseous nebulae (Kipper), and geodetic and gravimetric studies (Želnin, Keres, and Maasik). The *Publications of the Tartu Observatory* began appearing once again in 1952 after a hiatus of more than a decade.

Contacts between the Tartu Observatory and the observatories of other Soviet republics became gradually more frequent during this period. In 1947, Kusmin took part in a conference on cosmology in Moscow and was a member of a commission on variable stars in Kiev. In 1950 a four-member delegation from Tartu attended the general session of the meeting of the mathematics and physics section of the Academy of Sciences of the USSR in Riga; and in the spring of the same year, Keres and Kusmin undertook a wide-ranging tour of several major observatories of the Soviet Union for the purpose of promoting closer contacts and greater scientific collaboration with astronomers elsewhere in the Soviet Union. In 1952 the Academy of Sciences of the USSR suggested that a conference on astronomy be held in Tartu, with the main topic being the

structure and dynamics of the galaxy. A total of fifty participants from eleven institutions took part in that meeting, which
was held in May of 1953. Among those attending were such
distinguished astronomers as Shklovsky and Parenago from
Moscow, Mustel from the Crimea, and Mihhailov from
Pulkovo. In addition to the papers that were read and discussed (seven papers were presented by members of the host
institution), a critical evaluation was compiled of the work
being done in Tartu. It was noted that, although excellent
results were being obtained in stellar dynamics as well as in
other areas, much of the research was of a purely theoretical
nature and was limited by insufficient comparison with observational data—the reasons given being the lack of modern
observational equipment and a complete astronomical library
at Tartu. The evaluation committee recommended that the
observatory be equipped with fully modern instrumentation
and that theoretical research be continued and expanded.

It had been recognized many years before that a new
observatory, removed from the steadily increasing lights of
Tartu and equipped with new instruments, would be highly
desirable. In fact, a detailed plan had been drawn up by
Rootsmäe before the war, calling for construction at a site near
Elva in southern Estonia. In 1947 Riives, who was at that time
the director of the observatory, recommended that an observing station be set up outside Tartu which would house the Zeiss
and Petzval telescopes as well as a small Schmidt-Maksutov
camera. This rather modest plan was based on the fact that sky
conditions in northern latitudes are generally not so favorable
for astronomical observations as they are in more southerly
and arid regions. Another important factor was, of course, the
severely limited financial support available during the early
postwar years. Nonetheless, several members of the institute,
particularly Kipper and Keres, pushed for a more ambitious
undertaking, and in 1952 a detailed proposal calling for the
construction of an observatory complex at a suitable location
was submitted to the Academy of Sciences of the USSR. As
noted above, the concept of a modernized observing facility
had the support of the other astronomical centers of the Soviet
Union, and the project was approved by the academy.

Several preliminary site surveys were conducted during the
following years, and by the summer of 1956 the field had been
narrowed down to a location in the hilly country near Tôravere

in southern Estonia. The structure and layout for the new observatory were designed by the Leningrad branch of the Soviet Academy of Sciences, and the project was approved in January 1958 by the Soviet Estonian Council of Ministers. Construction was begun on May 26, 1958, precisely 150 years after the laying of the cornerstone of the old observatory building in Tartu.

It is perhaps worth noting that the philosophy behind the staffing and maintenance of an observing facility is somewhat different in the Soviet Union than it is in the United States. In the United States the observatory headquarters and support installations are all situated in cities or on university campuses, and an astronomer only goes to the actual observatory site when he has a scheduled observing run; whereas in the Soviet Union the astronomers actually live at the observatory, necessitating such facilities as permanent living quarters, medical-care centers, and food stores. By the early 1960s several of the buildings at Tôravere had been completed and the staff began moving in. Personnel at the site included not only astronomers but also geophysicists, meteorologists, theoretical physicists, and some mathematicians—i.e., most of the staff of the Institute of Physics and Mathematics. Up to this time the offices and laboratories of the institute had been in the old observatory building in Tartu, but now all that remained there was a laboratory for solid-state physics and luminescence.

The new instruments which were acquired at this time included a 47-centimeter reflecting telescope and a 20-centimeter refractor as well as various spectrographs and electronics equipment. Initially, the observatory was intended for the exclusive use of astronomers in Estonia, but in 1961 during long-range planning sessions the suggestion was made that work should be more closely coordinated with the various other observatories of the Soviet Union. In 1962 astronomers from the three Baltic states held several meetings which resulted in the consensus that Tôravere should become the center for optical observations in the Baltic countries, while the new observatory planned for Latvia should specialize in radio astronomy. It was further suggested that Tartu and Vilnius become the centers for the education of new astronomers. These proposals were accepted by the ruling bodies of the Academy of Sciences in the three Baltic countries, in which connection the feasibility of expanding the observational equipment at Tôravere soon arose. It was decided that a large multipurpose reflecting telescope would be needed if the facility were to live up to its expectations as a major regional observatory, and a proposal was submitted for the construction of a 1.5-meter reflecting telescope with a focal ratio of 3.5. The design called for both Cassegrain and coudée focuses and a battery of spectrograph-grating combinations allowing twenty different dispersions. The major use of the telescope would be for spectroscopy, since the light skies frequently encountered in the northern latitudes are not suited for direct photography of extended objects. Although the telescope was initially scheduled for completion in 1966, the timetable has been pushed back repeatedly and the instrument is still not finished. A second 47-centimeter telescope was, however, completed in 1965, to be used in tandem with the existing instrument—the idea being that, while one of the telescopes is recording observations of a specific star, the other can be used to monitor the changing sky background by observing a standard star. The telescopes have been employed primarily for variable star photometry, and their simultaneous use allows work to be done on nights when the background is too variable to allow meaningful results to be obtained with only one instrument. A slightly larger telescope, with a 70-centimeter mirror, was also installed; its major use was intended to be in the areas of moderate- and low-dispersion spectroscopy. The dedication of the observatory, which carries the official name Wilhelm Struve Tartu Astrophysical Observatory, took place in September 1964 in conjunction with a special two-day scientific conference attended by representatives of the major observatories of the Soviet Union.

Contacts between Tartu Observatory and the other observatories of the Soviet Union have become extremely close during the past decade, with astronomers from Estonia taking part in scientific conferences and colloquia at all the major observatories and universities in the other Soviet republics. This wide range of contacts has, of course, had an influence on the research trends of the observatory. For example, the study of variable and unstable stars, which has been vigorously pursued for many years in the Soviet Union, has become one of the major research areas at Tartu in both observational and theoretical aspects. One of the benefits of the close ties with the other research centers is the consequent availability of large telescopes for projects requiring greater apertures than are presently available at Tôravere. The Crimean Astrophysical Observatory, in particular, has been used by astronomers from Estonia for obtaining high-dispersion spectrograms for studies of stellar atmospheres. Close ties with other research centers have been maintained on an academic level as well as on a research level; i.e., several students from other observatories or universities have done their thesis work under the supervision of the astronomers at Tartu, and vice versa.

Contact with astronomers in the West, on the other hand, has been rather limited, although the situation has improved in recent years. Ten members of the observatory staff have been elected to membership in the International Astronomical Union (IAU), although only a few have attended the meetings or colloquia held outside the Soviet Union. One of the first trips to the West was made by Kipper and Keres, who attended the IAU meeting in Berkeley in 1961, after which they toured the major observatories in California for the purpose of gathering information and ideas that might be useful in the planning of the new observatory at Tôravere. More recently, J. Einasto and L. Luud have taken part in meetings and colloquia of the IAU held in Great Britain, H. Eelsalu has visited observatories in Sweden, and V. Unt, the interim director of the Institute of Physics and Mathematics since 1970, has spent several months at universities in England and the United States.

Mention should also be made of the work of the Astronomical and Geodetical Society, an organization of amateurs and professional scientists whose purpose is to promote interest in astronomy and geodesy among the general public. Among the activities of the society has been the establishment of an amateur-oriented observatory in Tallinn, equipped with an astrograph and a refracting telescope, which has been used for variable star observations. The society has also organized special courses and demonstrations for secondary schools and set up programs for the observation of noctilucent clouds and meteors. The society has branches in the other Soviet republics, and annual meetings are held for the discussion of common programs and policies.

Research Trends in Stellar Astronomy

Stellar astronomy—that is, that branch of astronomy dealing with the dynamics and kinematics of stellar systems, particularly of the galaxy—has been one of the traditional fields of study at Tartu ever since the days of Wilhelm Struve. Most of the important work in this area during the early postwar years was done by Kusmin and reported in a series of papers appearing in the *Publications of the Tartu Observatory*. In these investigations, the galaxy was assumed to be in a steady state and possessing axial symmetry. By analyzing the motions of certain well-defined groups of stars and using published values for their density distribution, Kusmin (1952) derived a value for the gravitational acceleration perpendicular to the galactic plane and thereby the density of matter in the solar neighborhood. The results are in fair agreement with the numbers derived by the Dutch somewhat earlier, using a slightly different method. A more important contribution was the analysis of the so-called third integral of stellar motion; i.e., a quantity depending on position and velocity coordinates that is conserved along the orbit of a star—the other two integrals being the energy and the angular momentum. The theory of the third integral was treated in several investigations, with a summary appearing in a paper presented at a meeting of the stellar astronomy section of the Soviet Academy of Sciences held in Moscow in 1955 (Kusmin, 1956). Theory and observations were combined to provide a model of the mass distribution of the galaxy, in which the surfaces of constant density are ellipsoids. A deficiency in the models is the insufficiently rapid decrease of the density at large distances from the galactic center—a situation that can be remedied, as noted by Kusmin, by an appropriate modification of the density law at large distances without doing undue violence to the applicability of the third integral.

In another important series of investigations, Kusmin (1957) analyzed some time-dependent phenomena in stellar systems, particularly the effect of inhomogeneities in the gravitational field (e.g., those caused by close stellar encounters) and slow changes in the strength of the field. The primary results were determinations of the rate of escape of stars from the system and of the change in the stellar velocity dispersion. This work was summarized in a paper presented at a meeting of the stellar astronomy section held in Moscow in 1957. In a paper read at a seminar of the working group of the Commission on Stellar Kinematics and Dynamics in Leningrad in 1962 (Kusmin, 1963), the theory was applied specifically to the galaxy, which was assumed to be in a quasi-steady state. Comparison with observations was not entirely satisfactory, however (i.e., the predicted vertex deviation was too small), because of the incompletely accounted-for irregularities in the gravitational field.

Not all the work in stellar astronomy done at the Tartu Observatory has dealt with questions related directly to the structure of the galaxy. For example, U. I. Veltmann (1961) has analyzed the dynamics of spherically symmetric systems, with an eye toward their application to elliptical galaxies and globular clusters. He has taken the approach of determining the velocity distribution of stars from a presupposed knowledge of their space distribution, subject to certain assumptions regarding the nature of the cluster. This approach is useful in that the space distribution of stars in a system can be determined by photometric methods, provided that some information can be obtained regarding the mass-to-light ratio. Although very little observational work has been done at Tartu in the field of stellar astronomy, Veltmann has begun a program of observing the spatial light distribution in globular clusters by means of a long, narrow slit that is scanned across the system, in order to compare his theoretical models with observations.

More recently, excellent work on the structure of external galaxies has been done by Einasto and his associates (Einasto and Rümmel, 1970). One interesting result is that the nucleus of the Andromeda galaxy appears to be much more massive than previously believed, while the total mass of the galaxy seems somewhat diminished. (Previous workers had included too massive a halo.) Other areas of research by various investigators have included statistical studies of the motion and brightness of stars of certain well-defined spectral types, utilizing data available in the literature.

Research Trends in Physics of the Solar System

The solar system has been an important area of research at the Tartu Observatory ever since the last century, when observations were made of eclipses and astrometric data were obtained for comets and asteroids. At the present time much of the work is centered around the so-called minor members of the solar system (comets and asteroids) and in an area more properly classified under geophysics, involving studies of noctilucent clouds and actinometry (the study of the absorption and reemission of solar radiation at the earth's surface).

The minor members of the solar system represent an area of astronomy in which large telescopes are not required, and much useful observational data have therefore been accumulated in this field by workers at Tartu. Extensive work on the positions of asteroids and comets has been done by H. Raudsaar. Although this type of activity lacks the glamour of some other branches of astronomy, it is nonetheless necessary for understanding the past and future of the solar system. Much of the data is sent to Leningrad, where a center exists for the calculation of orbits from astrometric measurements.

Some good results in asteroid photometry have been obtained by Riives, who studied variability in brightness as a means of determining shape. Most of Riives' research efforts, however, have been directed toward the photometry of comets, on which subject he has published a large number of papers. One of his most useful contributions was the development of a method for comet photometry by means of extrafocal images. In addition, Riives has done work on the forces acting on comet envelopes and tails as well as on the composition and structure of cometary nuclei (Riives, 1960).

The first postwar Soviet conference on comets was held in Tartu in July 1960 under the auspices of the Soviet Academy of Sciences, with a total of thirty-five participants from the major observatories of the USSR. Papers were read by Raudsaar on cometary orbits and by Riives on the forces acting on comet tails and their composition. During the discussions at the closing session of the two-day meeting, the work being done at the host institution was given high marks by the visiting participants.

The physics of noctilucent clouds represents another area of geophysics where important work was accomplished in the last century—this by Hartwig, an astronomer-observer at Tartu. New impetus was given to the research being done in this rather specialized area by the decision of the institute to participate in the activities of the International Geophysical Year in 1957-1958; as a result, Estonia became one of the chief centers for noctilucent cloud observations. Various symposia have since been held in Estonia on this subject, the largest being an international symposium in Tallinn in March 1966 which attracted many participants from Western Europe and the United States.

By far the most active worker in this field has been Ch. Villmann, who has conducted polarimetric observations of noctilucent clouds for the purpose of determining individual particle sizes and attempted to explain the formation of the clouds as being the consequence of a shock effect due to the solar wind. He has also studied the interrelationships between noctilucent clouds and global climatology (Villmann, 1966). In 1968 Villmann was elected chairman of an international working group for the study of these extremely high cloud formations, and under his leadership the Tartu Observatory has become an international center for noctilucent cloud research.

Research Trends in Astrophysics

The traditional fields of astrophysics—stellar atmospheres, stellar interiors, interstellar matter, etc.—remained somewhat in the background in comparison with stellar astronomy and solar-system physics until approximately the middle 1960s, at which time the new observing facility at Tôravere was completed. This new development undoubtedly had an important influence in channeling renewed interest toward problems related to astrophysics of the stars, particularly in its observational aspects. The number of astronomers working on astrophysical problems has increased markedly in recent years, with a corresponding increase in the output of published papers.

During the early postwar years Kipper worked on the development of magnetic fields in stars and on the physical processes in gaseous nebulae, in particular the two-photon emission mechanism as a means of producing the observed weak continuous energy distribution in nebulae (Kipper and Tiit, 1958). The major emphasis, however has been placed on observational and theoretical work related to variable and unstable stars, a field which has also been vigorously pursued at other observatories in the Soviet Union. On the observational side, work has been done by H. Albo for many years on the light curves of eclipsing binaries (Algol, epsilon Aurigae, etc.) and on the photometry of novae. In recent years L. Luud has been very active in following the irregular variability of the star CH Cygni and in analyzing the spectrum of the peculiar supergiant star P Cygni. He and his coworkers have studied the atmospheric structure and chemical abundances in several normal supergiants for the purpose of comparing them with the peculiar stars. The work on the spectrum of P Cygni was summarized in a paper presented at the IAU Colloquium on Variable Stars in Budapest (Luud, 1969). More recently Luud and M. Ilmas (1971) have calculated emission-line strengths in expanding atmospheres, using the theory of Sobolev, and compared the results with observations of P Cygni and other peculiar stars.

Theoretical work on radiative transfer has been done by T. Viik (1971), who has studied various methods of accounting for the radiation field in spherical atmospheres—a much more difficult problem than the usual case of plane-parallel stratification. He has also dealt with the solution of the equation of transfer in expanding atmospheres (Viik, 1970), subject to certain assumptions regarding the velocity distribution of the gas. These types of studies are of great importance in understanding the nature of the extremely extended atmospheres of cool supergiants as well as in forming a basis for analyzing the physical processes taking place in nova envelopes. Radiative transfer and reflection effects in rapidly rotating stars have been studied by Pustolnik (1971), with an eye toward application to the light curves of Algol-type close binary systems.

Work on the atmospheric parameters of normal stars (particularly of spectral type F) has been carried out by T. Kipper (1968), based on high-dispersion spectrograms he obtained as a guest observer at the Crimean Astrophysical Observatory. Some of the work done recently—e.g., on approximate model atmospheres and mean absorption coefficients (Kruusmaa, 1971)—appears slightly anachronistic, a consequence of the fact that in the Soviet Union the availability of high-speed and large-memory computers is still somewhat limited, thus forcing greater reliance on analytical as opposed to numerical methods of solution.

The field of stellar interiors was largely ignored at the Tartu Observatory until very recently, again possibly as a consequence of the severe demands that the calculation of interior models places on the availability of high-speed computer time. In the past few years, however, good work has been done by U. Uus on the interior structure of highly evolved stars, specifically on the growth of the carbon core and the thermal balance in nuclear-burning shells (Uus, 1970).

Some work in physics with a direct application to astronomy has been done by T. Feklistova (1971), who has calculated transition probabilities of a number of atoms and ions of astrophysical interest. The general theory of relativity as it applies to cosmology has been treated by a number of investigators, most recently by E. Saar (1971) in a series of articles dealing with cosmological models, including the effects of pressure. Most of the research being carried out in physics, however, has only a marginal connection with astrophysical problems. For example, excellent work is being done in the field of solid-state physics, particularly as it is related to the optical properties of crystals and the design of lasers. Good results have also been obtained in the study of aerosols and charged particles in the atmosphere; the primary application of such research, however, is to medicine.

Conclusions

In summary, astronomical research in Estonia is being carried out on a high level, with a great diversity in the types of problems that have been attacked. Stellar astronomy and solar-system astrophysics, which represented the backbone of the research efforts during the early postwar years, have recently been rivaled by the work being done on the astrophysics of the stars. Although a good start has been made in the direction of observational astronomy with the new observatory at Tôravere, the major emphasis is still on the theoretical side. The rather modest aperture telescopes presently available at Tôravere, while allowing good patrol-type work to be done (e.g., on variable stars), do not permit work on the present-day frontiers of observational astronomy (peculiar galaxies, quasars, etc.). Although the telescopes would be suitable for spectral-classification projects, this area has been largely ignored in Estonia—and in the Soviet Union as a whole. Of course, even the 1.5-meter telescope, when completed, will not rival the large reflectors in operation today, particularly in direct photography of faint objects, because of the unfavorable sky conditions in Estonia. The observing program planned for the telescope therefore mainly involves high-dispersion stellar spectroscopy, an activity that can be pursued even during the bright nights of midsummer.

Astronomers in Estonia are well versed in the new developments occurring in the West as well as in the progress being made at the observatories of the other Soviet republics. While articles by astronomers at Tartu have been published in the important Soviet journals, the majority appear in the *Publications of the Tartu Observatory*, generally in Russian. Unfortunately, knowledge of Russian in the scientific community in the West is rather limited, particularly in the United States, a fact which severely restricts the accessibility to the scientific literature being produced in the Soviet Union. Only a few journals are translated cover to cover by the United States government. It is for this reason that the astronomical research being carried out in Estonia is not as well publicized in the West as it deserves to be.

References

Eelsalu, H., ed.

1964 *Tähetorni Kalender* [The Observatory Calendar], vol. 40. Tallinn: Eesti Riiklik Kirjastus.

1965 *Tähetorni Kalender* [The Observatory Calendar], vol. 41. Tallinn: Eesti Raamat.

1966- *Tähetorni Kalender* [The Observatory Calendar],
1968 vols. 42-44. Tallinn: Valgus.

Einasto, J., and U. Rümmel

1970 "The Rotation Curve, Mass, Light, and Velocity Distribution of M31," in *The Spiral Structure of the Galaxy* (IAU Symposium no. 38), pp. 51-60. Dordrecht: D. Reidel.

Feklistova, T.

1971   "Calculation of C-3 Line Strengths in the Vacuum
        Ultraviolet Spectral Region of B Stars." *Eesti NSV
        Teaduste Akadeemia Toimetised* 20, no. 3.

Kahk, J.

1967   *Soviet Estonian Science.* Tallinn: Eesti Raamat.

Kipper, A.

1968   "Relative Abundances of the Elements in the Atmo-
        spheres of 41 Cyg, ν Her, and σ Boo." *Eesti NSV
        Teaduste Akadeemia Toimetised* 18: 65-72.
1971   "Evolutsiooniidee suunanäitajana astronoomilisele
        uurimistööle Eestis" [Astronomical Research in Es-
        tonia as Guided by Evolutionary Concepts], in *Eesti
        NSV Teaduste Akadeemia. Tagasivaated, Uurimis-
        suunad, Liikmeskond, 1946-1971.* Tallinn: Eesti
        Riiklik Kirjastus.

Kipper, A., and V. Tiit

1958   "The Role of Photon Distribution Mechanisms in
        the Physics of Nebulae." *Voprosy Kosmogonii* 6: 98-
        111.

Kruusmaa, A.

1971   "Mean Absorption Coefficients in Stellar Atmo-
        spheres." *Tartu Astronoomia Observatoriumi Pub-
        likatsioonid* 39: 273-281.

Kusmin, G.

1952   "Proper Motions of Galacto-Equatorial A and K
        Stars Perpendicular to the Galactic Plane, and the
        Dynamical Density of the Galaxy," in *Summaries of
        Works from the Tartu Observatory*, ed. H. Eelsalu,
        pp. 3-15. Tartu: Tartu Riikliku Ülikooli rotaprint.
1956   "Some Questions Relating to Dynamics of the Gal-
        axy." *Eesti NSV Teaduste Akadeemia Toimetised* 5,
        no. 2: 91-107.
1957   "Stellar Encounters and the Evolution of Clusters."
        *Tartu Astronoomia Observatoriumi Publikatsioo-
        nid* 33, no. 2: 75-102.

1963   "Dynamics of Stellar Systems, including Stellar Encounters." *Tartu Astronoomia Observatooriumi Teated*, no. 6, pp. 1-9.

Kusmin, G., ed.

1961-   *Tähetorni Kalender* [The Observatory Calendar],
1963   vols. 37-39. Tallinn: Eesti Riiklik Kirjastus.

Luud, L.

1969   "Some Remarks on the Spectral and Light Variability in P Cygni," in *Nonperiodic Phenomena in Variable Stars* (IAU Colloquium no. 4), pp. 197-201. Dordrecht: D. Reidel.

Luud, L., and M. Ilmas

1971   "Emission Lines in Stellar Spectra 4. Comparison with Observations." *Tartu Teated*, no. 36, pp. 111-124.

Pustolnik, I.

1971   "Radiative Transfer in Atmospheres of Algol-type Binaries." *Tartu Teated*, no. 35, pp. 3-49.

Raudsaar, H., ed.

1969-   *Tähetorni Kalender* [The Observatory Calendar],
1973   vols. 45-49. Tallinn: Valgus.

Riives, V.

1960   "Extra-Focal Photometry of Comets Arend-Roland and Mrkos." *Tartu Astronoomia Observatooriumi Publikatsioonid* 33, no. 4: 289-295.

Rootsmäe, T., ed.

1952-   *Tähetorni Kalender* [The Observatory Calendar],
1960   vols. 28-36. Tallinn: Eesti Riiklik Kirjastus.

Saar, E.

  1971   "Inhomogeneous World Models and the High Frequency Approximation." *Eesti NSV Teaduste Akadeemia Toimetised* 20: 420-425.

Uus, U.

  1970   "The Thermal Equilibrium of Thin Nuclear Burning Shells in Stars." *Nauchnyye Informatsii Astronomicheskogo Soveta Akademii Nauk USSR*, no. 17, pp. 48-59.

Veltmann, Ü. I.

  1961   "The Construction of Spherically Symmetric Stellar Cluster Models from an Assumed Density Distribution." *Tartu Astronoomia Observatooriumi Publikatsioonid* 33, no. 5-6: 387-415.

Viik, T.

  1970   "Radiative Transfer in Moving Spherical Atmospheres." *Tartu Astronoomia Observatooriumi Publikatsioonid* 38: 46-56.

  1971   "Method of Regional Averaging in Radiative Transfer." *Eesti NSV Teaduste Akadeemia Toimetised* 20: 285-288.

Villmann, Ch.

  1966   "Some Problems in Noctilucent Cloud Climatology," in *Noctilucent Clouds International Symposium*. Tallinn: Eesti Riiklik Kirjastus.